GREAT SOURCE

WriteTraits

Teacher's Guide

Vicki Spandel and Jeff Hicks

GREAT SOURCE

HOUGHTON MIFFLIN HARCOURT

www.greatsource.com
800-289-4490

With Thanks

For their insights and inspiration, the authors gratefully acknowledge the following sources:

Anderson, Jeff. 2005. *Mechanically Inclined.* Portland, ME: Stenhouse Publishers.

Codell, Esme Raji. 2003. *How to Get Your Child to Love Reading.* New York, NY: Algonquin Books of Chapel Hill.

Fletcher, Ralph. 1992. *What a Writer Needs.* Portsmouth, NH: Heinemann.

Fox, Mem. 1993. *Radical Reflections.* Orlando, FL: Houghton Mifflin Harcourt Publishing Company.

Janeczko, Paul B. 2005. *A Poke in the I.* London, UK: Walker Books Ltd.

King, Stephen. 2000. *On Writing.* New York, NY: Simon and Schuster.

Murray, Donald M. 2003. *A Writer Teaches Writing.* Florence, KY: Wadsworth Publishing.

Murray, Donald M. 1990. *Shoptalk.* Portsmouth, NH: Heinemann.

O'Conner, Patricia T. 2003. *Woe Is I.* New York, NY: G.P. Putnam's Sons.

O'Conner, Patricia T. 2000. *Words Fail Me.* Orlando, FL: Houghton Mifflin Harcourt Publishing Company.

Romano, Tom. 2004. *Crafting Authentic Voice.* Portsmouth, NH: Heinemann.

Walsh, Bill. 2004. *The Elephants of Style.* New York, NY: McGraw-Hill Books.

Zinsser, William. 1976. *On Writing Well.* New York, NY: HarperCollins Publishers.

Copyright © 2010 by Houghton Mifflin Harcourt Publishing Company

All rights reserved. No part of this work may be reproduced or transmitted in any form or by any means, electronic or mechanical, including photocopying or recording, or by any information storage and retrieval system, without the prior written permission of the copyright owner unless such copying is expressly permitted by federal copyright law. Requests for permission to make copies of any part of the work should be addressed to Houghton Mifflin Harcourt Publishing Company, Attn: Paralegal, 9400 South Park Center Loop, Orlando, Florida 32819.

Printed in the U.S.A.

ISBN-13 978-0-669-01555-3

ISBN-10 0-669-01555-5

1 2 3 4 5 6 7 8 9 10   0868   18 17 16 15 14 13 12 11 10

4500244506

If you have received these materials as examination copies free of charge, Houghton Mifflin Harcourt Publishing Company retains title to the materials and they may not be resold. Resale of examination copies is strictly prohibited.

Possession of this publication in print format does not entitle users to convert this publication, or any portion of it, into electronic format.

About the Authors

Jeff Hicks

Jeff taught for 18 years in the Beaverton School District (home of the 6-traits) where he enjoyed working with students to help them find their voices as writers. He is the co-author of *Write Traits Classroom Kits*, *Write Traits Advanced*, and *Write Traits Kindergarten*. Though his heart is still in the classroom, he is now a full-time writer, presenter, and professional development consultant. He lives in Beaverton with his wife and son, and he currently serves on the Beaverton School Board.

Vicki Spandel

Vicki is a founding coordinator of the 17-member teacher team that developed the original, nationally recognized 6-trait model for writing assessment and instruction. A specialist in teaching writing and revision to students of all ages, she is the author of *Write Traits Classroom Kits*, *Write Traits Advanced*, and *Write Traits Kindergarten*, as well as *The 9 Rights of Every Writer*, *Creating Writers*, and *Creating Young Writers*. She makes her home in the town of Sisters, Oregon, bordering the beautiful Three Sisters Wilderness.

Contents

UNIT 1: IDEAS
Introduce Trait 4
   Discussing Sample Papers 6
   Making the Literature Connection 12
   Writing a Personal Draft 15

Practice Trait 18
   Focus Trait Lessons 20
   Conventions & Presentation Lessons 50

Apply Trait 62
   Assessing and Revising Sample Papers 64
   Revising and Editing a Personal Draft 69

UNIT 2: ORGANIZATION
Introduce Trait 74
   Discussing Sample Papers 76
   Making the Literature Connection 82
   Writing a Personal Draft 85

Practice Trait 88
   Focus Trait Lessons 90
   Conventions & Presentation Lessons 116

Apply Trait 126
   Assessing and Revising Sample Papers 128
   Revising and Editing a Personal Draft 133

UNIT 3: VOICE
Introduce Trait 138
   Discussing Sample Papers 140
   Making the Literature Connection 146
   Writing a Personal Draft 149

Practice Trait **152**
   Focus Trait Lessons.. 154
   Conventions & Presentation Lessons.......... 180

Apply Trait **190**
   Assessing and Revising Sample Papers 192
   Revising and Editing a Personal Draft 197

UNIT 4: WORD CHOICE

Introduce Trait................................... **202**
   Discussing Sample Papers 204
   Making the Literature Connection 210
   Writing a Personal Draft................................ 213

Practice Trait **216**
   Focus Trait Lessons.. 218
   Conventions & Presentation Lessons.......... 243

Apply Trait **254**
   Assessing and Revising Sample Papers 256
   Revising and Editing a Personal Draft 261

UNIT 5: SENTENCE FLUENCY

Introduce Trait................................... **266**
   Discussing Sample Papers 268
   Making the Literature Connection 274
   Writing a Personal Draft................................ 277

Practice Trait **280**
   Focus Trait Lessons.. 282
   Conventions & Presentation Lessons.......... 308

Apply Trait **322**
   Assessing and Revising Sample Papers 324
   Revising and Editing a Personal Draft 329

Designed to turn students into successful writers, *Write Traits* includes everything you need to...

- **Build** a solid foundation in the traits of effective writing
- **Support** writing independence
- **Deliver** flexible, effective instruction

Build a solid foundation in the traits of effective writing

Write Traits delivers comprehensive, cumulative instruction that builds from one unit to the next while integrating lessons on Conventions and Presentation each step of the way.

VOICE

Unit 3 helps students find their unique voice so readers can connect to the person behind the words.

ORGANIZATION

Unit 2 delivers instruction in how to organize, shape, and support ideas in the most effective way.

IDEAS

Unit 1 begins with ideas, the heart and soul of good writing.

CONVENTIONS AND PRESENTATION

WORD CHOICE

Unit 4 focuses instruction on employing the most powerful language for the topic, purpose, and audience.

SENTENCE FLUENCY

Unit 5 emphasizes the importance of rhythm and flow in keeping readers moving smoothly from one idea to the next.

A Sequential, Integrated Approach

Traits are the interrelated qualities that define good writing. When students understand the six traits inside and out, they can revise their writing with incredible confidence and skill.

All writing begins with a message: a point to make, a story to tell . . . so, we begin with Ideas. This foundational trait affects all the others because the ultimate key to writing lies in knowing a topic well and having something to say. Next, we show students how to make the message easy to follow through effective Organization, how to reach readers with compelling Voice, how to fine tune the message with precise Word Choice, and how to make writing rhythmic and readable through Sentence Fluency.

Instead of tucking Conventions and Presentation into a little corner by itself, we bring it right up onstage from Day 1, showing how this vital trait supports, empowers, and connects to every other trait, eliminating distractions and making the writer's message clear and accessible for readers.

All units address the trait of Conventions and Presentation as it applies to the target trait—a feature that gives purpose to instruction that is often delivered in isolation.

Support writing independence

A student-centered approach to instruction empowers students with the skills and confidence to grow as writers.

The *Write Traits* approach engages students in their own learning and promotes independence with a strategic focus on . . .

- Building a critical understanding of weak versus strong writing through the analysis of mentor texts
- Supporting writing development through self-assessment, peer coaching, and discussion
- Connecting reading and writing so that students *write* like readers and *read* like writers
- Equipping students with effective strategies for taking their writing to the next level
- Providing opportunities for students to cement understanding of instruction in the context of personally important topics

The Importance of Independence

In traditional instruction, a teacher explains, assigns, and assesses writing. Our vision is different.

We see students as independent, active members of a writing community, who identify personally important writing topics and control their own writing processes. From the first, we seek their opinions, asking them to share their insights about writing—not just student work, but any writing you can think of. Using writers' language, students describe specific features that make a piece of writing work—a good lead, strong verbs, imagery, voice, and so on. They also learn to recognize problems such as lack of detail or vague language—then work in teams to solve those problems. Students who are insightful "readers" of writing and fearless troubleshooters are ready to revise independently—and to coach others. They know whether their writing is working, and what to do if it isn't!

Deliver flexible, effective instruction

A predictable three-step instructional routine promotes engagement, authenticity, and deep understanding.

1 INTRODUCE Trait

- Analyze two sample papers—one weak and one strong.
- Make the reading-writing connection.
- Begin a personal draft on a topic of choice.

② PRACTICE Trait

- Provide deep, guided practice across four lessons.
- Reinforce the reading-writing connection.
- Meaningfully connect Conventions and Presentation to the target trait.

③ APPLY Trait

- Analyze two more sample papers—and revise the weaker one, focusing on the target trait.
- Combine all strategies learned thus far to assess, revise, and edit the personal draft begun earlier.
- Publish writing.

How to Bring It All Together

The traits only work in coordination with writing process, so that's how we present them—surrounded by strategies for prewriting, drafting, revising, and editing. In each of the five units, students begin by exploring writing to see what makes it tick—both sample writing and good literature—then they create an original draft on a topic of their choice. That draft goes into personal folders (to be revised later) while writers work on focused lessons designed to make them strong revisers. That's when the real journey begins.

Focused lessons for each trait help writers think like readers, giving them a wealth of strategies for revising and editing. By presenting traits one at a time, we let students expand their repertoire of revision strategies at a steady, comfortable pace. At the close of each unit, students rehearse revision on a writing sample we provide, then apply new skills to their own drafts, making their writing clear and reader-friendly. Comparing rough drafts to final efforts gives teachers a visual snapshot of just how far their writers have come!

Program Overview T13

A Closer Look: Student Traitbook

Each unit of the Student Traitbook provides all the instruction, practice, and resources young writers need to succeed.

Mentor texts from **authentic literature titles** support trait instruction and provide concrete examples of strong writing.

Sharing an Example: *Escape! The Story of The Great Houdini*

Following is an example from the book *Escape! The Story of The Great Houdini* by Sid Fleischman. Read the passage carefully, pencil in hand, underlining words you find striking. These could be words that

- you know and like.
- just sound interesting, whether you know them or not.
- you would like to use in your own writing.

What exactly did he do that so excited the world's imagination? What razzle-dazzle fixed the name Houdini in the public memory so firmly that it is still remembered today, more than eighty years after his final disappearing act?
Watch him.
Tightly strapped and buckled into a canvas straitjacket designed to restrain the violently insane, he is being raised by his

Voice

Name _____ Date _____

Sample Paper 12
____ Checks for Voice
Behind the Scenes

Ask ten people, "What's your favorite movie?" and you are likely to get ten different answers. Some will start reciting lines, describing their favorite scenes, or imitating their favorite actors. But ask those same ten people, "Who is your favorite movie producer?" and you will probably get ten confused faces and a lot of silence. Most people couldn't even *name* three producers—much less pick out a favorite. A few dedicated fans know names of directors, but it takes a real movie *nut* to follow movie producers. I happen to be one of those nuts.

Here's the proof. Do you stay in your seat at the movie theater to read the credits? I do. I read all the credits at home, too—including the names of executive, associate, and assistant producers. I always wondered what all these people actually *did*, though, and since I couldn't find a single person who knew (surprise), I did a little research.

Sample papers include both strong and weak models for guided discussion and analysis of key concepts.

T14 Teacher's Guide

Writing to Remember

Nothing builds your knowledge of words like using them in your own writing. Try that now. Imagine that you are either

- Houdini, the famous magician himself;
- one of the police officers who puts Houdini into a straitjacket or handcuffs; OR

Designing your Writing

Use your own paper for this. Remember to take time to plan (prewrite). Think about your organizational design and, if it helps, create a list or graphic that helps you picture that design. You might

- draw a sketch.
- make a web.
- make

Charting Your Own Waters

This time, begin with a BIG topic of your own. Here are a few ideas—but, by all means, choose any topic you like:
- Politics
- Food
- Technology
- Entertainment

Remember, ask as many questions as you need in order to narrow your topic and feel *ready* to write. (That feeling of readiness is how you know your topic is small enough.)
Hint: It may only take two or three questions to narrow some topics and five or six questions to narrow others.

Step-by-step lessons include targeted practice that supports students in using the traits in their own writing.

Revising Checklist for Voice
- [ ] I feel strongly about this topic, so it was EASY to show that. OR . . .
- [ ] I plan to change my topic to
- [ ] I know a LOT about this topic, so I sound confident. OR . . .
- [ ] I plan to get more information from
- [ ] I read this aloud to myself, and it sounds *just like* ME.

Student Rubric for Ideas

6
- My main message or story is clear and will hold your attention.
- I know this topic inside and out and take readers on a journey of discovery.
- I included intriguing details a reader will notice and remember.
- My writing makes a point—or focuses on a clearly defined message or issue.

5
- My main message or story is interesting and easy to understand.
- I share important information—and tell enough to give readers a "full" picture.
- My paper contains many interesting details.
- I narrowed my topic enough to give readers an in-depth look at my subject.

4
- A reader can identify my main idea or make sense of my story.
- I have enough information for a first draft—more would help.
- My writing includes a few interesting details. Readers might want more.
- I think I need to narrow my topic a little. I'm trying to cover too much.

3
- A reader can guess what my main idea is—or tell what my story is about.
- I knew enough to start writing—then I had to guess or make some things up.
- My details are general—things many readers already know.

Student rubrics and **revising checklists** provide explicit criteria for evaluating a piece of writing. This reinforces instruction, promotes independence, and supports writer conferences.

Conventions & Presentation
Editing Level 1: Conventions
Workhorse Words

Conventions & Presentation
Editing Level 2: Presentation
Reaching the Audience

What if your writing were going to be
- displayed on a hallway bulletin board for students or guests to read?
- included in a school newspaper?
- sent home to parents in an informational flier?

When your writing is going to be published in some way, you need to think carefully about how it is *presented* to your audience. Presentation (Level 2 editing) ensures that your work is
- a good blend of text and art (photos, drawings, graphics).
- eye-catching enough to grab someone's attention.
- easy to scan for needed information.

Editing and Presentation work together to make sure that readers can breeze right through your writing with no errors to distract them—and that they will notice, understand, and remember your message.

Lessons for **Conventions and Presentation** are seamlessly integrated into each unit, highlighting the role this trait plays in supporting the other five.

Program Overview T15

A Closer Look: Teacher's Guide

Each unit of the Teacher's Guide features comprehensive, best-practice instructional support—from start to finish.

Authors Vicki Spandel and Jeff Hicks provide unique insight into the traits as they lead you through each unit in an informative and entertaining cartoon strip.

A consistent, easy-to-navigate **instructional routine**—complete with pacing suggestions—simplifies planning and makes it easy to integrate lessons into your existing program.

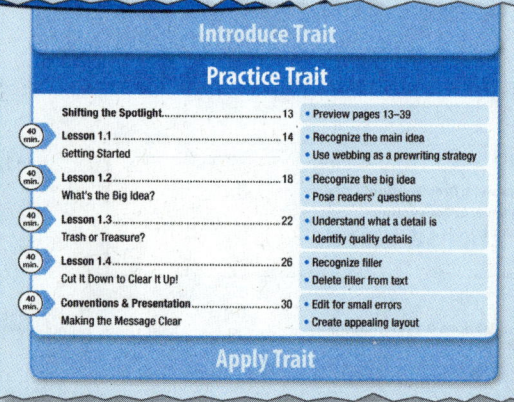

Coach's Corners provide advice, practical tips, and professional development pointers designed to help you deliver instruction that works.

T16 Teacher's Guide

Differentiated instruction embedded in every lesson helps you tailor instruction to the needs of each student—whether struggling, on level, or advanced.

> **Bringing everyone in... Differentiated Instruction**
>
> For some students, going back and forth between a list of questions and text will be difficult. Try this: Ask one question at a time and let students search the text to see if it is answered. If it is, check it off.

Extending the Lesson

- Choose a topic and then model writing a short paragraph on that topic. Read your sentences aloud as you go. Don't try to write things out of order, but don't try to be too orderly, either. Just write as things occur to you. You need about six to eight sentences to make this activity work. When you finish, ask students for help ordering your details. If *everything* is fine as is—well, either you're a very logical thinker or you got lucky with this writing! (Don't forget to ask if your lead could be improved.)
- Have students look at any piece of writing on which they are currently working and make sure all of the sentences are arranged in logical order.
- Have a pair of students write a set of directions for any simple

Extending the Lesson features provide suggestions for taking instruction to the next level through engaging activities, focused discussions, and technology.

> **Creating a Baseline Assessment**
>
> Ask students to revise *A Special Moment* (the weaker of the two introductory papers) working individually. Assess the *revised* drafts (using the Teacher Rubric for Ideas) to provide baseline scores in students' revision for this trait. Record those scores. At the close of the unit, following direct instruction in Ideas, you can compare these early revisions to the later revisions your students will do on their own writing and on Paper 4: *Is Pluto a Planet*? This comparison will tell you how much they have grown as revisers with respect to Ideas. (See Other Books You'll Love, page 11, for some suggestions on setting up the revision of *A Special Moment*.)

Targeted assessments provide a skills baseline and help you plan future instruction according to each student's strengths and areas of need.

Teacher Rubric for Ideas

6
- Main message or story is clear and compelling. It holds a reader's attention.
- Writer seems to have an in-depth understanding of the topic.
- Details are selectively chosen, making the writing memorable.
- Topic is narrowed to make the message focused and manageable.

5
- Paper makes sense from beginning to end. It is clear, never confusing.
- Writer knows enough about the topic to write expansively and convincingly.
- Writing contains many interesting details.
- Topic is narrowed so the main message stands out clearly.

4
- Reader can identify the main idea—even if it isn't stated directly.
- Writer has *some* knowledge of the topic: more would enrich the discussion or story.
- Enough unusual or intriguing details grab the reader's attention.
- Topic may be too broad: the writing loses focus now and then.

Teacher rubrics provide a shared language for discussing each trait and a set of shared expectations for performance.

Program Overview T17

A Closer Look: Additional Resources

Additional resources provide flexible tools to support instruction, review, and assessment.

The **Teacher Resource CD** provides electronic versions of the Student Traitbook and other handy resources.

- PDFs of all student pages are included for easy printing and copying.
- Student sample papers—designed for interactive white boards—support whole-class scoring, discussion, and guided revision.

A **full color poster set**, one for each trait plus a copyeditor's poster, provides continuous visual support.

- Trait posters reinforce the link between reading and writing, showing how the writer's actions impact the reader.
- The Copyeditor's Poster provides handy reminders of editor symbols used to mark text.

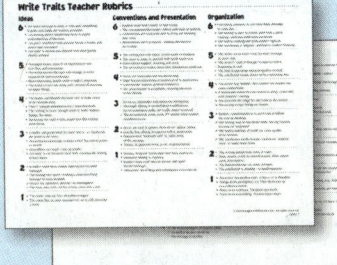

A convenient and sturdy **trait rubric chart** provides at-a-glance reference and convenient scoring for each of the traits.

Consumable packs of **trait sticky notes** aid in discussing assessment of student writing and revision skills.

- Removable notes allow you to post messages directly onto student writing.
- Tell students at a glance which traits are being assessed.

Using Write Traits

Flexible materials and instruction make it easy to integrate *Write Traits* into your existing reading or literature program.

How does trait-based instruction fit with writing process?

Writing process is the heart and soul of all good writing instruction, but process alone does not unlock the door to success. The six-trait approach enriches writing process by giving students a language for thinking like writers, teaching them specific revision strategies. Often students do not revise their writing thoroughly (or at all) because they simply have no idea what to do. Students who learn trait-based writing build a vast revision repertoire. They can look at a sample of weak writing and know precisely how to make it stronger.

How can I make this program work for my students?

- Use trait-based instruction to teach thinking skills. Let students come up with their own ideas about what makes writing work, which pieces are strong and why, and how they would revise.

- Encourage students to be assessors and to verbalize their responses to many pieces of writing, including other students' work, professional writing, and your writing.

- Be a writer yourself, modeling steps within the writing process and encouraging students to use their increasing knowledge of the traits to coach you.

- Give students their own copies of the writing rubrics as you introduce each trait. Use the rubrics to assess writing and to help students see those rubrics as guides to revision.

How do I use *Write Traits* with my existing literature program?

- Provide students with frequent, scaffolded opportunities to write the same kinds of texts that they are reading, such as personal narratives, essays, and reports.
- Point to fine literature—for example, stories with compelling ideas, essays with strong organization, and poetry with rhythmic sentence fluency—as mentor texts to build a deeper understanding of writing *and* reading.
- Use the rubrics, checklists, and other tools found in *Write Traits* to support skills in critical thinking and literary response.

Do I have to teach the traits in order?

We strongly recommend that you teach both traits and lessons in the order presented because we use a sequential approach in which skills build on one another. Ideas and Organization are foundational traits and need to be taught first. In addition, original writing tasks within each unit ask students to apply skills they have acquired in studying a previous trait. This way, nothing is "lost." Finally, the recommended assessment approach is cumulative, so that students are assessed first on Ideas alone, then on Ideas and Organization, and so on.

UNIT 1
Ideas

Overview

Ideas are sometimes called the foundational trait. All writing, from stories and poems to reports and PowerPoint presentations, begins with a message—with something to say. That's why this trait provides such a good place to begin writing instruction. And as we'll see in the units that follow, the writer's ideas influence every other trait in the spectrum.

In this unit, you will be helping students to

- clearly **define a writing topic.**
- **"defog" writing** to make meaning clear.
- **cut unnecessary details,** or filler, that detracts from the message.
- use details to **create a vivid character sketch.**
- understand how strong **conventions and presentation** work to make Ideas clear.

TRAIT DEFINITION

Ideas are all about information. They include the writer's central message and all the details that expand or clarify that message. Strong ideas depend on in-depth knowledge of a topic—knowledge that comes from reading, firsthand experience, or research. The details so vital to strong ideas also come from the writer's capacity for noticing what others might miss, in order to write with a confidence that inspires readers' trust. They offer information that goes beyond general knowledge. Details strengthen Ideas, but they also add to the trait of Voice. This is one of many ways in which traits are interconnected.

Vicki & Jeff

Unit at a Glance

Introduce Trait

Discussing Sample Papers...6
Making the Literature Connection.................................12
Writing a Personal Draft...15

Practice Trait

Lesson 1.1: Defining Your Topic....................................20
Lesson 1.2: Cutting Through the Fog............................27
Lesson 1.3: From Sketch to Portrait..............................34
Lesson 1.4: Packing Only What You Need....................40
Conventions and Presentation..48

Apply Trait

Assessing and Revising Sample Papers.........................64
Revising and Editing a Personal Draft..........................69

Unit 1   3

UNIT 1
Ideas

Introduce Trait

The Opening Act 5	• Preview pages 5–16
Discussing Sample Papers 6	• Introduce trait language and rubric
15 min. Sample Paper 1: *My Most Scary Experience* Score and Rationale	• Analyze weak and strong writing
15 min. Sample Paper 2: *How to Leave a Phone Message* Score and Rationale	
50 min. **Making the Literature Connection** 12	• Model the trait of Ideas in literature: *When Zachary Beaver Came to Town*
	• Connect reading and writing
50 min. **Writing a Personal Draft** 15	• Coach students in creating a piece of personal writing
	• Assess students' drafts to create benchmark scores

Practice Trait

Apply Trait

4   Unit 1

The Opening Act

Introduce the trait of Ideas by talking about the concept. Ideas are the writer's message—a clear main idea (or more than one) and all the details that support that main idea. Expand this definition by having students review the Student Rubric for Ideas and letting them see and hear Ideas in action, first in the writing of others, and then in a piece of literature. Once you've discussed the literature *(When Zachary Beaver Came to Town)*, students will create an original piece of writing on a topic of their choice. Later, they will revise and edit this piece for Ideas and for Conventions and Presentation. Here's the Opening Act in more detail.

1. **Discuss and assess the sample papers.** You will introduce the trait of Ideas with two sample papers: *My Most Scary Experience* (in which the writer wanders from the main message and gives insufficient attention to the most important idea) and *How to Leave a Phone Message* (in which the writer treats readers to numerous funny details).

   It is important for your student writers to talk, to mark up sample papers by making notes or highlighting features, and to refer often to their student rubrics. Help them understand that

   - **strong samples** give writers ideas for strategies *they* can try, while
   - **weaker samples** show problems to avoid and offer opportunities to practice revision strategies on someone else's copy.

2. **Connect the trait to literature.** Continue your conversation about the trait of Ideas by letting students hear how this trait sounds in the hands of a professional writer. The featured text for this unit is *When Zachary Beaver Came to Town* by Kimberly Willis Holt; it's the award-winning coming of age story about a 13-year-old boy whose life and thinking are transformed by an unexpected friendship. Use this or any text strong in the trait of Ideas. Allow a full class period (or more) for the literature lesson.

3. **Complete a personal draft.** Following the literature connection, have students write a personal draft on any topic of their choice. The writing may be inspired by *When Zachary Beaver Came to Town,* but it does not have to be. Have students put rough drafts into folders for a time. They will revise and edit them later, using skills they gain through the lessons that follow.

Coach's Corner

We recommend presenting the weaker paper first. Critics, including students, tend to see problems before seeing strengths. Let them discuss any problems they see with Sample Paper 1 first. They are then likely to appreciate Sample Paper 2 even more!

Coach's Corner

Share additional writing examples of your own writing as well as examples from newspapers or any publications. Go for contrast whenever possible—a strong one paired with a weak one.

Coach's Corner

Provide students with plastic sleeves and dry erase markers so they can mark up papers without writing on the originals.

Coach's Corner

Throughout this and other units, we will have students work with partners or in writing circles to expand their discussion. Discuss the importance of taking turns, keeping track of total time allowed for discussion, listening well, and even taking notes based on what others have to say.

Ideas

Introduce Trait
Discussing Sample Papers
Making the Literature Connection
Writing a Personal Draft

Practice Trait

Apply Trait

Coach's Corner
For any lessons where you want students to be the readers (we encourage this), give them some rehearsal time. This will make it easier for them to read with confidence and inflection that brings out both meaning and voice. Reading aloud goes a long way toward helping writers develop voice and fluency in their own writing.

Coach's Corner
Encourage students to think of the rubric as a writing guide. No rubric can tell all about any piece of writing. It simply gives us language to initiate a discussion about strengths and problems, and suggests how much revision remains.

Coach's Corner
Because many students (and teachers) equate rubric scores with grades, there is a tendency to see a score of 1 as failure. Actually, a 1 is a beginning point. The writer may still be "thinking on paper" or deciding among several ideas. This score tells the writer that he or she has additional drafting and revising to do.

Discussing Sample Papers

Student Traitbook pages 3–4; 215

Student Rubric for Ideas

Prior to presenting the introductory papers to students, read each one to become familiar with it. Plan to read both papers aloud to students (or have student volunteers do so) so that they can assess with their ears as well as their eyes. Review our suggested questions in advance, and please feel free to add your own questions and your students' questions to our list.

1. Have students turn to the Student Rubric for Ideas. Explain that it is a tool to help rate performance—the way people rate restaurants or movies. Explain that
   - 6 is the **strongest level** of performance.
   - 1 is a **beginning level** of performance.
   - the river marks the difference between performance in which problems outweigh strengths (scores of 1, 2, or 3) and performance in which strengths outweigh problems (scores of 4, 5, or 6).

   Student Traitbook p. 215

2. Give students time to read and discuss the rubric. Answer any questions about differences in levels or language used.

3. Explain that they will rate two pieces of writing: *My Most Scary Experience* and *How to Leave a Phone Message*. They will work in pairs, scoring each paper and giving reasons for that score.

Bringing everyone in . . . **Differentiated Instruction**

As a first step in scoring, ask your writers whether a piece leaps the river or not. This narrows the range of scores: It's in the 1, 2, or 3 range, OR it's in the 4, 5, or 6 range. Have them vote on scores by moving to a specific corner of the room. Such voting creates a strong visual representation of the class vote, encourages students to talk with others, and gets writers up and moving!

Coach's Corner

A score of 6 is given to a piece so strong in a trait that it could be used as a model when teaching or illustrating that trait. It is a paper that you might hold up and say, "This is what I mean by strong Ideas."

Sample Paper 1: *My Most Scary Experience*

Read *My Most Scary Experience* aloud. As you read, tell students to think about these

❓ Key Questions . . .

- *Does the paper have a clear main message?*
- *Does the writer focus on that message—or jump from topic to topic?*
- *Is the writer's main message too big to handle?*
- *Does the writer share helpful, unusual, or interesting details?*
- *Do those details create a clear picture in your mind?*
- *Does the writer include irrelevant details (filler) that only clutter up the writing?*
- *If appropriate, are there sensory details?*
- *As a reader, do you feel as if your most important questions are answered?*

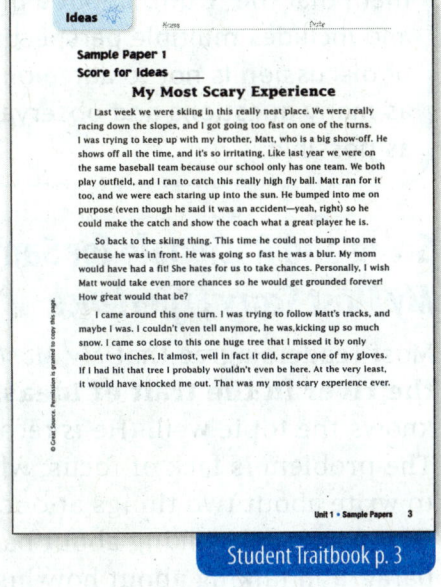

Student Traitbook p. 3

2. When you finish, have students score the paper with a partner. Remind them to refer to the Student Rubric for Ideas. Ask whether they think this paper leaps the river in the trait of Ideas (strengths outweigh problems) or not. They should take time to discuss the paper. Remind them to write on the paper, underlining strong moments, making notes, drawing arrows to show parts that need revision, and so on.

Coach's Corner

Remind students to ask first whether the paper leaps the river (strengths outweigh problems) before assigning a specific score.

Unit 1 7

Ideas

Introduce Trait
Discussing Sample Papers

3. When they finish, tally scores and tell students to defend their scores, using the Student Rubric for Ideas. Return to the key questions listed under Step 1 as part of your discussion.

> **Bringing everyone in . . .** **Differentiated Instruction**
>
> Students may look to you to explain the correct score. Explain that while there are NO correct scores, there definitely are defensible scores, which means that the rater can point to something in the paper that matches a description in the rubric. Feel free to share your own personal score, as well as our score for the paper (which may or may not match yours). Also remind them that the "truth" about a given piece of writing is very big and includes multiple perspectives and opinions. The purpose of discussion is not to agree on the right score, but rather to bring as many questions and observations about writing into the light as possible.

Coach's Corner
My Most Scary Experience is a personal narrative, writing that tells a story based on something that happened to the writer. A good narrative sets up the story, moves to a high point in the action, and winds down by telling how things have changed or explaining something the writer (or another character) has learned. Does this piece do those things?

Score and Rationale for Sample Paper 1: *My Most Scary Experience*

Most readers agree that *My Most Scary Experience* **does NOT leap the river in the trait of Ideas.** On the positive side, the writer knows the topic well. (He *is* recalling a personal experience.) The problem is lack of focus, which comes mostly from trying to write about two things at once. He spends a lot of time in the first paragraph talking about baseball, and most of the second paragraph talking about how his mom worries and how he wishes his pesky brother would take more chances and be grounded. We learn quite a lot about brother Matt's personality, but the title and first three lines of the paper suggest that the focus should be on the near-miss experience. He finally returns to this topic in Paragraph 3, which starts out very strong. But he ends abruptly without answering many remaining questions. Did he get hurt? How did he feel at the moment of the near miss? Did Mom find out? Answering these or similar questions (while eliminating filler) could provide a solid basis for revision. This paper would receive **a score of 3 in the trait of Ideas.**

Sample Paper 2: *How to Leave a Phone Message*

1. Refer students to the Student Rubric for Ideas. Answer any new questions they may have.

2. Continue to have students work in pairs, but switch partners, if you wish.

3. Read *How to Leave a Phone Message* aloud. As you read, tell students to think about these

   ### ❓ Key Questions . . .
   - *Does the paper have a clear main message?*
   - *Does the writer focus on that message?*
   - *Is the writer's main message too big to handle?*
   - *Does the writer share helpful, unusual, or interesting details?*
   - *Do those details create a clear picture in your mind?*
   - *Does the writer include irrelevant details (filler) that only clutter up the writing?*
   - *If appropriate, are there sensory details?*
   - *As a reader, do you feel as if your most important questions are answered?*

4. When you finish, have students score the paper with a partner. Remind them to use their Student Rubrics for Ideas. They should take time to discuss the paper. Encourage them to write on the paper, highlighting strong moments, and raising questions.

5. When they finish, tally scores and have students defend their scores, using the Student Rubric for Ideas. Return to the key questions listed under Step 3 above as part of your discussion.

Student Traitbook p. 4

Coach's Corner

Here are two tips for making the scoring of Ideas simpler. First, tell students to underline the sentence(s) that comes closest to expressing the writer's MAIN idea. If there is no such sentence, the main idea may be implied, or the writer may not have one yet. Second, tell them to highlight details that expand this main idea. If they find many such details, chances are the piece is strong in the trait of Ideas. If they don't find any, there's a problem.

Unit 1   9

Ideas

Introduce Trait
Discussing Sample Papers

Coach's Corner

Your scores do not have to agree with our suggestions. You may decide that *How to Leave a Phone Message* should receive a 5 or that *My Most Scary Experience* should receive a 2. That's fine, as long as you can defend the scores you assign. What matters most is students' skill in recognizing a strong or weak piece of writing and being able to articulate specific strengths or problems calling for revision.

Coach's Corner

How to Leave a Phone Message is a personal essay, an exploration of a topic/situation based on observation and personal experience. Such an essay needs a strong, clear main idea and details/examples that bring that idea to life. Does this piece have those qualities?

Score and Rationale for Sample Paper 2: *How to Leave a Phone Message*

Most students should see this paper as **strong in the trait of Ideas.** The writer has a clear main point and sticks with it throughout the piece: There are right and wrong ways to leave a phone message, and if you want your call returned, you need to follow some guidelines. The essay is filled with vivid and humorous details, such as how to spell your name, speak slowly, listen carefully, and so on. And of course, we also get the underlying hint to Mom and Dad: get some cell phones (or at least an answering machine). The humor of this piece comes from the writer recognizing the ridiculous nature of his situation, and sharing well-chosen details to help us recognize it, too. Humor also comes from the fact that as readers, we tend to identify either with the writer (victim of his parents' obsession with responsibility) or with the parents (trying to instill responsibility in a son who is clearly fond of them, but wishes they'd take a new approach). The piece is strong in both the traits of Ideas and Voice, and would receive **a score of 6 in the trait of Ideas.**

Creating a Baseline Assessment

Have students revise *My Most Scary Experience* (the weaker of the two introductory papers), working individually (it is fine for them to plan their revision with a partner or in a writing circle, however). Assess the revised drafts using the Teacher Rubric for Ideas to provide baseline scores in students' revision for this trait. Record those scores. At the close of the unit, following direct instruction in the trait of Ideas, you can compare these early revisions to the revisions your students will later do on their own writing and on Sample Paper 4: *Stop Smoking Now!* This comparison will tell you how much they have grown as revisers with respect to the trait of Ideas. (See **Extending the Lesson** for some suggestions on setting up the revision of *My Most Scary Experience*.)

Extending the Lesson

- Take one more look at *How to Leave a Phone Message*. Does this writer use any strategies your writers think they could imitate?

- Have each student slip any rough draft of his or her own into a plastic sleeve and star strong details or underline passages that are vague and need additional detail. What's the balance? Does their writing leap the river in the trait of Ideas? If not, what specific revisions would help?

- Have students identify passages from literature that have a strong, focused main idea, or vivid details that bring that idea to life. Create a collection or have students share passages aloud, either with the class or in writing circles.

- To prepare for revising *My Most Scary Experience*, give students time to talk with partners or in writing circles. Have them first consider which would make a better main topic: the near miss while skiing or the annoying personality of brother Matt. Then suggest that they make a list of details that would go with the topic they have chosen.

Bringing everyone in . . .   Differentiated Instruction

Revision of the whole piece may seem like a lot for some writers. Have them focus on Paragraph 3. After all, that's where the heart of the story lies! Here's another tip: Have them brainstorm three or four questions they have as readers, then simply answer them speaking as the writer. One more thing: Good stories always span a particular length of time, sometimes seconds, sometimes centuries. Because this story is focused on one small moment, it may span only two or three minutes. Writing it that way helps writers focus.

- Remind students that as they revise *My Most Scary Experience*, they are free to delete words or sentences (even whole paragraphs), expand details, or add new ones. It is just fine to invent! They may also change the title, especially if they decide to shift the focus to brother Matt. They should revise as if the writing were theirs.

- If students have computer access, have them revise on the computer. Electronic revision makes it far easier and faster to add or delete details, or to try multiple versions of a paragraph. Students probably won't print out a new draft each time they make a change. But what if they did? Tell them to guess how many drafts they actually created.

Coach's Corner

Planning prior to revision can be helpful to most writers, but it is vital for them to realize that they are not bound by partners' suggestions. Each writer should take his or her own approach to revision, creating a personal, individual draft.

Ideas

Introduce Trait
Discussing Sample Papers
Making the Literature Connection
Writing a Personal Draft

Practice Trait

Apply Trait

Coach's Corner

To teach the trait of Ideas, look for any book with a focused message and sharp, descriptive details that make the message understandable and memorable. Share the whole book or any passage that illustrates clear expression, insight, vivid imagery, creative use of sensory detail, or a helpful explanation of a complex concept.

Making the Literature Connection

 *When Zachary Beaver Came to Town* by Kimberly Willis Holt

Thinking like a reader and reading like a writer are essential in learning to revise with power and purpose. In this and the units that follow, we want students to expand their understanding of a trait—in this case Ideas—by seeing how it looks and sounds in the hands of a skilled professional writer. Our emphasis in Unit 1 is on providing a clear, detailed message. For this lesson, we have chosen Kimberly Willis Holt's book *When Zachary Beaver Came to Town*, a National Book Award winner from 1999. Toby Wilson is thirteen years old and struggling to handle the challenges most boys of his age face: girls, friends, parents, and figuring himself out. Into his life and small town comes Zachary Beaver, the "world's fattest boy." With starkly vivid, precise details, Holt creates real characters, places, and problems. And as in real life, only some of these problems have solutions.

Sharing the Text

1. Show students the book and share the title and author. Let them know it was published in 1999 and won the National Book Award for Young People's Literature for that year. You may want to familiarize your students with the National Book Award. Ask if any of your students are familiar with the book or with Holt's other books, including *My Louisiana Sky, Keeper of the Night, Loser, Dancing in Cadillac Light,* and *Part of Me: Stories of a Louisiana Family*.

2. Preview the book's main idea: Toby Wilson's Texas small town life is turned upside down by the arrival of Zachary Beaver, the world's heaviest boy. At first, Zachary is basically a touring roadside attraction, where paying customers get to file through his trailer for a peek. However, Toby and his friends end up reaching out to Zachary, first out of curiosity, then later out of true friendship and compassion.

Bringing everyone in . . .   **Differentiated Instruction**

This book deals with a sensitive subject in a forthright way. You may wish to lay some groundwork for this by talking about what a sensitive topic weight can be, and how important it is to treat the issue with understanding and compassion. If you have students who are severely overweight, you might confer with them personally to gauge their comfort with your sharing of the book. Please note that Zachary is referred to in the book as the "world's fattest boy." Many people consider the word *fat* insensitive, and you may wish to discuss this right up front. In the book Zachary suffers ridicule, but he also plays a heroic role, offering much needed friendship to Toby. You may also prefer to use an alternative text.

3. Tell students you are going to read an excerpt from this novel, Chapter Two and Chapter Three. In these chapters, readers first meet the main character Toby and his friends. They also get their first glimpse of Zachary. Take a moment to focus on just the opening two sentences of the book. They capture how many young people feel about their town, school, or home life.

4. Read the suggested excerpt. If you are familiar with the book, feel free to set up and share a favorite passage of your own.

5. With your students' help, recount Toby, Cal, and Tara's experience inside Zachary's trailer. Balance these with a discussion of sensitive reactions to people different from themselves. Turn the tables on this passage. Discuss Zachary's first impressions of the other characters as they file through his trailer. What are your students' experiences with first impressions? Are they always correct?

6. Have students identify moments in which they feel the ideas (especially details) are particularly strong. How does the author describe parts of the town, the trailer, or Zachary?

Coach's Corner

We have chosen an excerpt that is rich with detail—in this case, detail that creates characters, and even more important, it establishes a clear sense of place. In this book, the small Texas panhandle town of Antler is as much a character as any of the people who live there. Clearly, if the book engages your students, you may wish to read the whole novel aloud, or tell them to continue reading on their own (as you facilitate ongoing discussions).

Coach's Corner

When Zachary Beaver Came to Town is also available on CD, narrated by Will Patton. You may wish to check whether it is available in your media center or local library.

Unit 1

Ideas

Introduce Trait
Making the Literature Connection

Other Books You'll Love

Throughout this program, we rotate recommendations by genre.
- **Classic**—both traditional and contemporary
- **Poetry**—an individual poem or collection
- **Nonfiction**—picture book or longer text
- **Fiction**—picture book or longer text

Your own favorite books are almost certain to include clear central messages and vivid details that make them ideal for teaching the trait of Ideas. The more literature you share, the stronger your students' understanding of this trait will be. Following are other books to explore.

1. **Poetry:** *Hoops* by Robert Burleigh
   This picture book offers a poetic inside look at basketball that could be used to inspire student writing and poetry about the sports they love. The sensory-loaded language lives right inside the art by Stephen T. Johnson, giving the book energy and a sense of movement. Have students read it aloud to appreciate the incredible rhythm that mimics the game itself.

2. **Nonfiction:** *People* by Peter Spier
   Part picture book, part sociology book focusing on honoring and appreciating diversity, the book is a visual feast of details about the people of the world. It provides multiple messages for writers, including the value of expertise when describing people or events. Various pages show the world's variety of noses, eyes, lips, hair, clothing, language, work, religion, and history. Most students will find something of themselves within these pages.

3. **Classic:** *The Outsiders* by S.E. Hinton
   The Outsiders is read and discussed by middle school students and teachers around the country. Written when the author was still a teenager herself, the story is timeless: social divisions pitting one group of kids against another, friendship and love attempting to break down the barriers, teens struggling emotionally as they find their places in life. The writing has been both praised and criticized, but the characters and world of the Socs and the Greasers are vivid and memorable. This may become a gateway book for some reluctant readers.

Ideas

Writing a Personal Draft

Introduce Trait
Discussing Sample Papers
Making the Literature Connection
Writing a Personal Draft
Practice Trait
Apply Trait

1. Tell students that they are now going to have a chance to create their own piece of writing on a topic of their choice. Give them about 3–5 minutes to meet and confer with partners about writing ideas that jump out at them after hearing *When Zachary Beaver Came to Town*. Examples might include the following.
   - An original story based on difficulties people face growing up (narrative fiction)
   - Experiencing struggles as a family (poetry, expository, narrative)
   - Small town versus city living (narrative, expository, poetry, informational)
   - The meaning of home (narrative, expository, poetry)
   - Coping with differences that lead to isolation, teasing, bullying (informational, persuasive, narrative, expository)
   - An experience with a relative or close friend who has gone to war (narrative, expository, poetry)
   - Report on the real geography of *When Zachary Beaver Came to Town*—Texas, the Texas panhandle (informational, expository, poetry)
   - Biography of Kimberly Willis Holt (informational)
   - Review of the book *When Zachary Beaver Came to Town* (persuasive, response to literature)

2. Give students 5–8 minutes to discuss topics. This conversation is a vital component of prewriting, and one strategy that can help many writers begin with a strong focus on their message and genre.

3. To help further with topic selection, record some writing ideas for whole-class reference, and offer individual coaching as needed. Remind them that they may choose any topic that suits them, whether inspired by the book *When Zachary Beaver Came to Town* or not.

Coach's Corner
Zachary is baptized in one of the book's most important scenes. Writers who feel comfortable with the topic might choose to write about a religious belief or milestone that holds significance for their own life. If this is an acceptable and comfortable topic within your classroom, it can open the door to interesting discussions of diversity.

Coach's Corner
Some writers may wish to incorporate technology into their writing. Audio or video—even PowerPoint—can greatly enrich any presentation, and is another genre to consider.

Ideas

Introduce Trait
Writing a Personal Draft

I'm not a very good writer, but I'm an excellent rewriter.

—James A. Michener

Coach's Corner

If many students are still writing after thirty minutes, allow additional time during another class period. Also give students a two-minute warning so they have time to collect thoughts before they finish up for the day. Have students write a brief note at the end of the draft, reminding them what to do next when they return.

Coach's Corner

Good revision takes some mental distance. When writers put their work away for a time, they become more detached, seeing it more as they would see someone else's work. That not only makes revision much easier, but also makes the writer more ruthless!

Bringing everyone in . . . **Differentiated Instruction**

Topic choice is difficult for some students, especially those who are used to assigned topics and suddenly feel adrift. You can help by modeling your own topic selection. Do this routinely, changing topics, of course. Students will find it interesting as well as helpful. Focus on topics suggested by literature you share, or alternatively, on anything that's on your mind right now: planning for travel to a new place, getting used to a new pet, researching a kind of music, and so on. Help students understand that everyday experience can be the stuff of good writing IF the writer notices and recalls the right details. But part of the secret to strong ideas lies in knowing which topics just require good recall and a word web or list of questions, and which demand serious research.

4. Encourage prewriting in addition to the opening conversation. Students should spend about five minutes sketching, making a web, writing a list of questions or details, and so on.

5. Provide students with time to write a draft. We recommend 20–30 minutes (in addition to prewriting time), but please use your own judgment.

6. Remind students to double or triple space (even if they are composing on the computer) and to allow wide margins so there will be ample room for revision later. Model this!

7. When students feel they have a finished draft, have them confer with partners, reading their writing aloud so they listen for clarity and detail. It is fine to make any changes that occur to them at this time, but there will be time for more comprehensive revisions later, following direct instruction in the trait of Ideas.

8. This writing should now be placed in their writing folders. At the close of the unit, they will have time to look at this piece again and to revise it before it is assessed.

Bringing everyone in . . . **Differentiated Instruction**

Not all writers will finish their drafts during one class period, especially if their writing requires research. Let them know that by the end of the period they should have either a very rough draft or the beginning of a draft with a plan for next steps. You can then provide additional in-class time if possible, or ask for some writing to occur outside of class. We recommend setting a deadline and devoting one class period to sharing with partners or in writing circles. Otherwise, incomplete drafts may be forgotten.

Notes

UNIT 1
Ideas

Introduce Trait

Practice Trait

	Shifting the Spotlight..................19	• Preview pages 19–61
50 min.	**Lesson 1.1**..................20 Defining Your Topic	• Narrow a broad topic so it's manageable • Write a strong thesis statement
50 min.	**Lesson 1.2**..................27 Cutting Through the Fog	• Identify vivid details in a strong piece • Revise a vague piece by adding details
50 min.	**Lesson 1.3**..................34 From Sketch to Portrait	• Find details that bring a character to life • Create an original, vivid portrait
50 min.	**Lesson 1.4**..................40 Packing Only What You Need	• Separate important details from filler • Revise to eliminate filler
50 min.	**Conventions and Presentation**..................48 Making Editing Manageable Getting to Know You (in a Nutshell)	• Edit step by step • Create a bio for a book jacket

Apply Trait

Shifting the Spotlight

Your students have now assessed two papers, *My Most Scary Experience* and *How to Leave a Phone Message,* offering you baseline data on their initial understanding of the trait of Ideas. They have also seen and heard the trait in action through your sharing of the passage from the book *When Zachary Beaver Came to Town.*

It's time to shift the spotlight, helping students develop additional skills they can use in revising writing for the trait of Ideas. Once students have completed all focused lessons in this unit, they will apply what they have learned by (1) revising *someone else's* writing and (2) revising and editing their own writing. Follow these two steps:

1. **Complete Lessons 1.1 through 1.4.** Allow one or two days for each. Through these lessons, students will learn strategies for
   - narrowing topics and writing thesis statements.
   - revising to make vague, foggy writing clear.
   - using vivid details to create a clear character sketch.
   - cutting unnecessary details (filler).

2. **Link Ideas to Conventions and Presentation.** Allow two days for this lesson. On the first day (Editing Level 1: Conventions), students will learn to make a large editing job more manageable by taking it step by step. On the second day (Editing Level 2: Presentation), students will create a short bio for a book jacket.

Link reading and writing. Tell students to look at the Ideas Poster in the Student Traitbook. Various things the writer does appear on the left. Ask students how each decision the writer makes affects the reader, and have them fill in the blanks on the right: So the READER… Once you have discussed all four elements, put the actual poster on the wall so students can refer to it often, and if students think of additional elements, be sure to add them (using sentence strips).

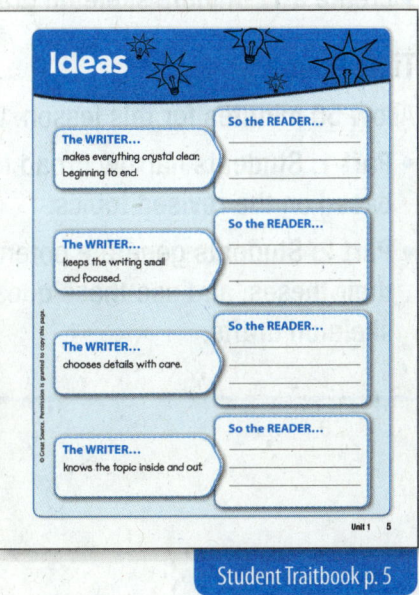

Student Traitbook p. 5

Unit 1   19

Ideas

Introduce Trait

Practice Trait
- Lesson 1.1
- Lesson 1.2
- Lesson 1.3
- Lesson 1.4
- Conventions & Presentation

Apply Trait

LESSON **1.1**

Defining Your Topic

Student Traitbook pages 6–11

Choosing a good topic to write about is an important first step. But it's not enough to get a writer ready to write. In this lesson, writers explore three more defining steps that actually put them in a good position to begin a rough draft: (1) narrowing the topic to make it manageable, (2) writing a thesis statement to give the writing focus, and (3) posing three writers' questions that help determine the scope of what the writing will cover.

Objectives

Students will
- recognize the importance of planning in getting ready to write a draft.
- practice strategies for taking a broad topic down to manageable size.
- distinguish between a topic and thesis, and practice writing thesis statements.
- learn to pose readers' questions that provide a framework for writing.
- create a 12-minute skeleton draft.

 ## Time Frame

Allow 50 minutes for this lesson. We suggest dividing it into two parts.
- **Part 1:** Students narrow broad topics and write thesis statements based on the revised topics.
- **Part 2:** Students generate potential readers' questions based on their theses, and use those questions as the basis for 12-minute skeleton drafts.

Setting Up the Lesson

Read the trait introduction and the Lesson 1.1 introduction from the Student Traitbook aloud. Tell students that when you take a trip, your first decision is usually about where you will go. But choosing a destination isn't enough. What other decisions do you need to make? Brainstorm a few.

Tell them choosing a topic isn't enough to get you ready to write. What other decisions are important? Make a list. We hope students will mention all the things we covered in the introduction, but if not, you can add those to the list. Their list may include any of the following (we've put an asterisk by those covered in this lesson).

- Narrowing a big topic to bring it down to manageable size*
- Doing research to learn more
- Writing a thesis to give the writing direction—think of your thesis as an arrow*
- Writing questions that reflect what readers most want to know*
- Choosing the best details to answer readers' questions
- Writing a quick first draft (skeleton draft) to get a sense of the whole piece*

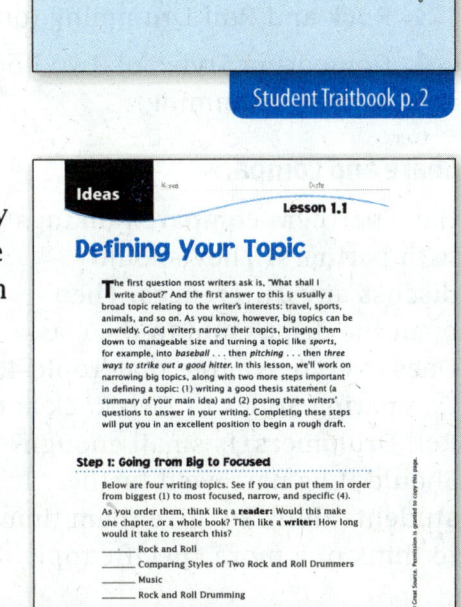

Student Traitbook p. 2

Student Traitbook p. 6

Planning takes the place of the many drafts that are usually necessary without adequate planning.

—Donald M. Murray
A Writer Teaches Writing

Coach's Corner
Your writers' responses do not have to match our list exactly. This is NOT a test! What matters is the recognition that writers do not just think of a general topic, such as weather, and start writing. They figure out what aspect of this big, general topic interests them (or their readers) and what very specific message they want to deliver.

Bringing everyone in . . .   Differentiated Instruction

It's critical to recognize that writing process, even though we talk about it and describe it, truly is different for every single writer on the planet. There are writers who can begin with a broad topic and narrow it in their minds as they write, working out a thesis and conceptualizing probable readers' questions as they go. But these writers are not typical. For most, planning time is well spent. Even for those who perform some of these steps almost subconsciously, it's helpful to be aware of how good writers think and plan.

Ideas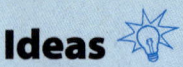

Practice Trait
Lesson 1.1

Coach's Corner

If writers have any difficulty with this task, remind them of our key questions. As writers, they can ask how long it would take to research a topic. Researching music would take a lifetime, while researching styles of two drummers might only take hours. As readers, they can ask whether a topic would fill one chapter or a whole book. The styles of two drummers could be covered in a chapter, perhaps less. A topic like Rock and Roll would easily fill a book, and the topic of music would fill many books.

Coach's Corner

Topic choice is important! Writers will be working with their same topics throughout the lesson. Encourage them to choose wisely!

Teaching the Lesson

Step 1: Going from Big to Focused

Review the directions. Be sure students understand the task: ranking the four writing topics from biggest (1) to most narrow and specific (4). They should work on this task individually, but they will have a chance to compare rankings in the next part of this lesson.

Most should rank them as follows:

1. Music (this is the broadest topic)
2. Rock and Roll (one kind of music)
3. Rock and Roll Drumming (one aspect of Rock and Roll)
4. Comparing Styles of Two Rock and Roll Drummers (a focused look at drumming)

Share and Compare

Have partners compare rankings with partners. They should discuss any differences. Then open the discussion to the class. Does everyone agree that Topic 4, Comparing Styles of Two Rock and Roll Drummers, is small enough? Should it be narrowed further? If students think so, give them time to think of a more specific topic.

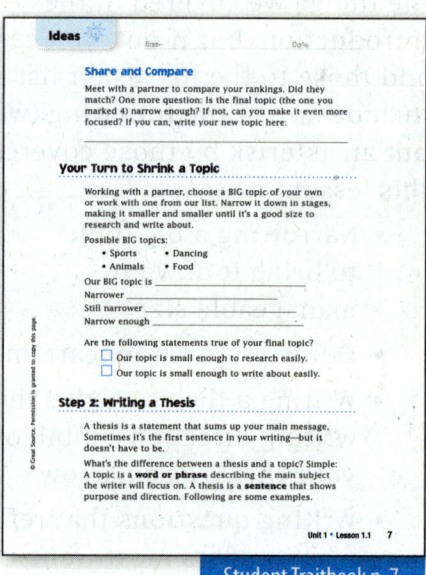

Student Traitbook p. 7

Your Turn to Shrink a Topic

Students will work with partners on this task. Share the directions. Then encourage them to choose a topic both partners find interesting. They can choose one from our list, but we encourage students to think of a topic on their own. They should

- write the BIG topic in the blank provided.
- shrink it step by step until it feels small enough to handle comfortably.
- answer the question to be sure the topic is focused enough.

When everyone has finished, share a few of the small topics with the whole class.

Bringing everyone in... **Differentiated Instruction**

> It is enormously helpful to some writers to see where others began and how they managed to bring a huge topic down to size. Have one or two teams share their process, showing the rest of the class the topic with which they started and the discussion they had or questions they raised to shrink that topic down to size. Have other writers comment on how many steps this took and how the writers knew the topic was small enough to write about.

Step 2: Writing a Thesis

This portion of the lesson focuses on the difference between a topic (a word or phrase) and a thesis (a statement). It is important for students to recognize that a thesis sums up the writer's main point or message, and therefore it gives direction to the writing. Students have now had significant practice working with someone else's topic. It's time to turn their attention to their own writing.

Review the directions and discuss the examples about cats and food. Answer any questions students may have. Give them 2–3 minutes to create thesis statements relating to the following topics.

- Driving
- Seventh grade

When they finish, have them share some of their topic sentences and answer any questions. Then have them work with partners to write an original topic sentence of their own (based on their own narrow topic from Step 1).

Turning Your Topic into a Thesis

All teams should take a minute to write their thesis statements. Each statement should be a complete sentence summing up the main message to readers.

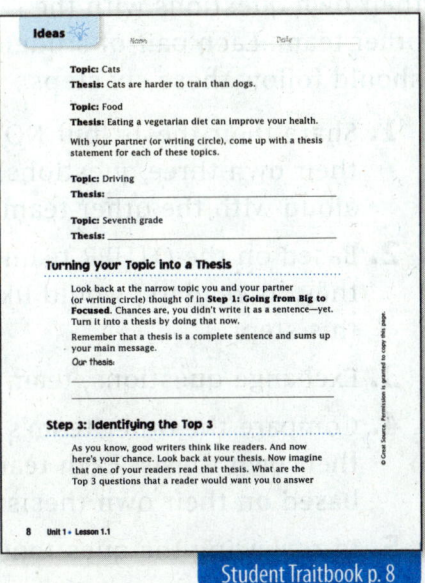

Student Traitbook p. 8

Coach's Corner

Theory, idea, opinion, view, and *argument* are all synonyms for *thesis*. A good thesis gives direction to a piece of writing, but, even more important, it gives direction to the writer. It clarifies the message in the writer's own mind. Sometimes a thesis is implied rather than stated outright. But writing a thesis can be helpful to the writer all the same. It's like looking at a map when starting a journey. It helps the writer know where he or she is headed.

Ideas

Practice Trait
Lesson 1.1

Bringing everyone in... Differentiated Instruction

The word *thesis* is intimidating to many young writers. It sounds so formal. Describe it as a "one-sentence summary of your message." This is the same idea, sans formality. More advanced writers will quickly discover that a thesis can change as the writer writes, just as a traveler can start out heading for Italy and wind up in Egypt. Unpredictability is one of the beauties of writing. But a good writer, like a seasoned traveler, usually has a destination in mind.

Coach's Corner

Note: If you are dividing this lesson into two parts, **Day 2 begins here.**

Coach's Corner

The questions should be suggested by the writers' own thesis. If no questions come to mind, it may be that their thesis is not explicit enough. Ask writers this simple question: What is your main message to the reader?

Coach's Corner

The purpose of this activity is to give each team a chance to see if others would think of the same readers' questions they did, given the same thesis. If the other team comes up with even one dramatically different or more intriguing question, that could influence the upcoming writing in a creative way.

Step 3: Identifying the Top 3

Review the directions, reminding students to think like readers as they come up with their Top 3 questions. These are, in fact, the three questions they think readers would most want them to answer. Be sure students hold on to these questions. They will need them for the writing portion of this lesson—coming right up!

Share and Compare

Give students time to look over the directions on their own. Then give them about 6–8 minutes to meet in writing circles (two pairs per circle). They will be sharing thesis statements and writing three more readers' questions, this time based on the OTHER team's thesis. They will not share their own questions with the other team. Each pair of students should follow these six steps:

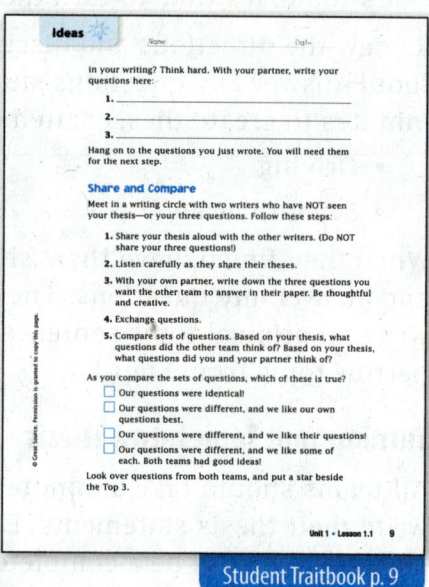
Student Traitbook p. 9

1. Share their thesis (but NOT their own three questions) aloud with the other team, and listen to their thesis, too.

2. Based on the OTHER team's thesis, write down three questions they, as readers, would like answered. Use scratch paper for this step.

3. Exchange questions, team to team.

4. Compare the other team's questions with those they wrote on their own thesis. Each team now has a total of six questions based on their own thesis.

5. In reviewing the questions, decide which three of the six they like best.

6. Star those Top 3 questions.

24 Unit 1

The 12-Minute Skeleton Draft

Give students time to look over the directions on their own and ask any questions. Then give them just 12 minutes (no more) to create a skeleton draft on scratch paper. This draft is NOT meant to be complete by any means. It is, as the name suggests, a barebones beginning to what can become a longer, expanded piece. You can time each part, if you wish, and push students to write very quickly.

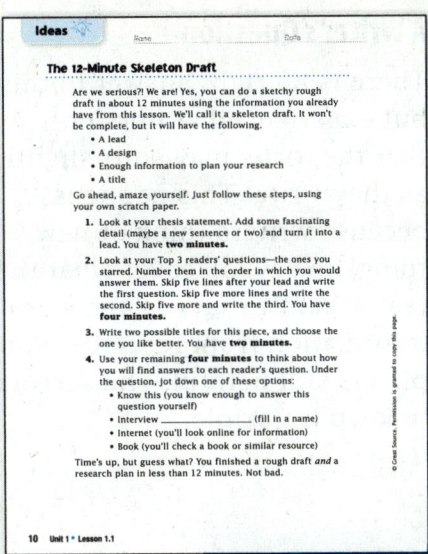

Student Traitbook p. 10

Step 1 (two minutes)

Add a detail or two to the thesis statement and turn it into a dramatic lead.

Step 2 (four minutes)

Identify the Top 3 readers' questions (the ones with stars), number them in the order they should be answered, and write them into the text, skipping five lines after each (this space is important).

Step 3 (two minutes)

Write two possible titles and choose the favorite.

Step 4 (four minutes)

- Begin to answer each of the three readers' questions.
- Write a sentence or two to add detail, or jot down where you could find the information you need: Internet, written resources, interviews, etc.

Bringing everyone in... Differentiated Instruction

This activity does wonders for writers who feel overwhelmed by the size of an informational writing task, or for those who tend to procrastinate. There is something about having a first draft behind you (however rough) that inspires many writers. And even though the draft is skeletal, the focus is identified, and the content is laid out in order, with a plan for research. Just a quick glance at this draft tells the writer what to do next.

Coach's Corner

Writers need to work very quickly, but the good news is they do not need significant knowledge of the topic to complete this step. They just need to be organized. Most will be amazed to discover how much they can accomplish in only 12 minutes!

Ideas

Practice Trait
Lesson 1.1

A Writer's Question

There is no right answer to this, but experienced writers notice that the focus may shift slightly as they write. This happens because writers think of new things to say, discover what they really want to say, or uncover new information from research. But a plan is still helpful. The secret is to keep it flexible.

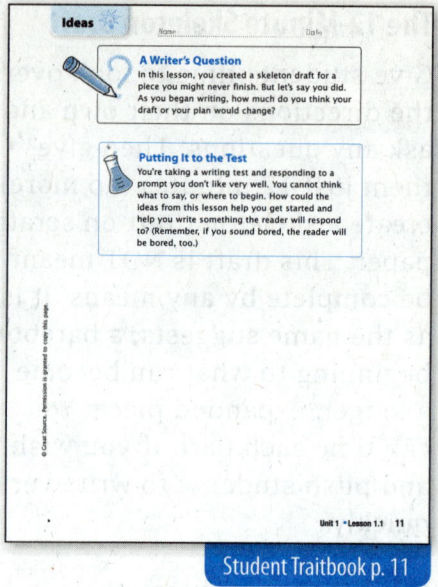

Student Traitbook p. 11

Putting It to the Test

In an on-demand situation, it's a good idea to remember that the prompt you (as a writer) dislike intensely was someone's idea of a good question to ask! The prompt writer had something in mind. What was it? An excellent approach is to imagine what the writer of the prompt might like to know: What three questions would that person ask if he or she were standing in front of you? Write those questions on scratch paper, and use them to guide the response.

Extending the Lesson

- You can extend the power of this lesson by refining your 12-minute draft. This time, have students turn their three readers' questions into statements and expand what they had to say about each one. Even a 12-minute time frame allows for quick research of one question, and that's a start. Even if writers never finish these drafts, it is worthwhile for them to see how much a writer can accomplish with even 12 minutes of focused effort.

- Create an interactive website and open a discussion on skeleton drafts. Invite students, teachers, writers, and parents to contribute. What other ideas do people have for spending those first 12 minutes wisely?

- Do an Internet search on the trait of Ideas. How else do writers define this trait? What's important to strong ideas?

- Have writers create two-minute podcasts on procrastination. What tips do they have for overcoming that initial inertia?

LESSON 1.2

Cutting Through the Fog

Student Traitbook pages 12–17

Ideas

Introduce Trait
Practice Trait
Lesson 1.1
Lesson 1.2
Lesson 1.3
Lesson 1.4
Conventions & Presentation
Apply Trait

Fog is wonderfully mysterious and moody in the opening scene of a Sherlock Holmes or Jack the Ripper movie. In writing, it's just annoying. In this lesson, students have a chance to notice the kinds of details that sweep the fog away, then practice revising some foggy writing by adding details of their own.

Objectives

Students will
- identify details that make writing clear and impressions vivid.
- compare a crystal clear and a foggy version of the same piece.
- choose one of three foggy passages to revise.

 Time Frame

Allow 50 minutes for this lesson. We suggest dividing it into two parts.

- **Part 1:** Students review an example from literature, identify strong details, and compare the original to a foggy revision of the same example.
- **Part 2:** Students choose one of three vague passages to revise, and rewrite it, adding detail they invent.

Unit 1   27

Ideas

Practice Trait
Lesson 1.2

Setting Up the Lesson

Open the lesson by telling students that you want to share a newspaper article with them. Open a copy of a local or any prominent paper and pretend to read an actual article on any topic: current events, sports, entertainment, or whatever. Only, instead of reading the actual article, read your foggy version of it, which might (in the case of a sports story, for instance) sound something like this: One team played against the other team, and at the end they had a final score. Some of the fans were pretty happy, all right! But others were disappointed. Another event is scheduled to happen soon, somewhere nearby.

Student Traitbook p. 12

Your students are almost certain to question whether you are reading the real deal, but in the unlikely event that they don't, do ask them to comment on the article: what they learned, whether they thought the writer did a good job of bringing the game to life, and so on. Have them tell you what questions remain in their minds, or what other information they felt the reporter should have shared. Then, read the original article for comparison, making sure to share the name of the reporter. Ask students whether the original article leaps the river in the trait of Ideas. Why? After this discussion, share the introduction in the Student Traitbook aloud.

Bringing everyone in . . . Differentiated Instruction

Students will appreciate our defogging references in this lesson much more if they know what fog is like. Perhaps you live in an area that experiences fog frequently. If so, talk about it—what it's like to walk or drive in fog, what you see when you look out the window. Have any of them been in a plane looking down on fog? For those who have not seen it, you might want to share photos, or even the beginning of a film that opens with a foggy scene. Talk about how fog is used in films to set the mood. Why is it so perfect for mysteries? And not so perfect for, say, comedies? Not being able to see where you're going can definitely set the stage for a mystery story, it but can leave readers unable to decode a writer's message. Just to clarify, detailed writing is the opposite of foggy writing.

Teaching the Lesson

Sharing an Example: *Stuck in Neutral*

Share the directions and read the passage from Terry Trueman's book *Stuck in Neutral* aloud, or have one of your writers share it (following a chance to preview and rehearse). Remind students to think carefully, as they listen, about whether Trueman's writing creates a fog that clouds meaning, or it uses vivid details that invite the reader right inside the story.

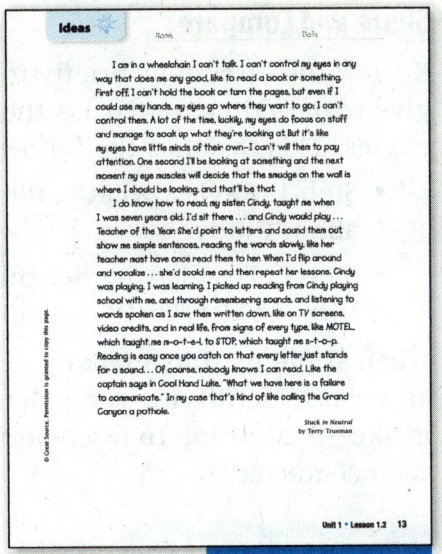

Student Traitbook p. 13

Reflection

Share the directions or have students read them. Then give them 2–3 minutes to record their responses to the Trueman passage. Take time to discuss their general reactions before they meet in writing circles.

- Did they like the passage?
- Did it make them curious about the speaker?
- Would they like to read more?

Student Traitbook p. 14

What Did You Learn?

For this portion of the lesson, have students meet in writing circles. When they are grouped, review the directions to make sure everyone understands the task.

- One or two people in the circle will focus on the narrator, writing down what they learned.
- One or two people will focus on the narrator's sister Cindy, writing down what they learned.

> **Coach's Corner**
>
> This passage comes from *Stuck in Neutral* by Terry Trueman. Some of your writers may wish to have you share more of the book, or may want to read more on their own.

Ideas

Practice Trait
Lesson 1.2

Coach's Corner

Explain that readers draw conclusions about characters (and other things) all the time, using both details (direct evidence) and inference (conclusions based on hints, intuition, and guesses). Both are important in pulling the full meaning from a text. The narrator suffers from cerebral palsy. His family cannot know that Shawn is actually a genius; capable of an active internal life he has no power to reveal to them.

Coach's Corner

Some synonyms for *infer* include *deduce, suppose, conclude, conjecture, surmise, assume* and *understand.*

Share and Compare

Review the directions briefly to see if there are questions. Then give writers time to discuss the two characters in their writing circles. This task has the following two steps.

- Step 1: Review what readers learn about the narrator and about Cindy.
- Step 2: Decide whether this information was shared directly through *details* (D) or is *inferred* by the reader (I).

When students finish talking in groups, briefly discuss the passage as a class, identifying some details that show what each character is like—in addition to interesting inferences writers made about each character.

Bringing everyone in . . .   Differentiated Instruction

Some students may not be familiar with the terms *infer* or *inference.* Take a minute or two to explain that an inference is a best guess based on information that's available. Sometimes clues that support an inference are obvious—if you see a person dressed in a firefighter's uniform, you infer that he or she is indeed a firefighter—and most likely that's the case. Sometimes the clues are subtle. Maybe a person shows unusual concern over fire safety regulations. It's possible to infer that he or she is a firefighter, but there's no direct evidence. The inference could certainly be wrong.

Fog Alert!

Review the directions to be sure everyone understands the task. Then, invite one of your writers to read the revised Trueman passage aloud. Clearly, it is very different from Trueman's original, and not just because it's shorter.

Give writers a few minutes to work with partners or in writing circles to list as many of the missing elements (from the revised version) as they can think of.

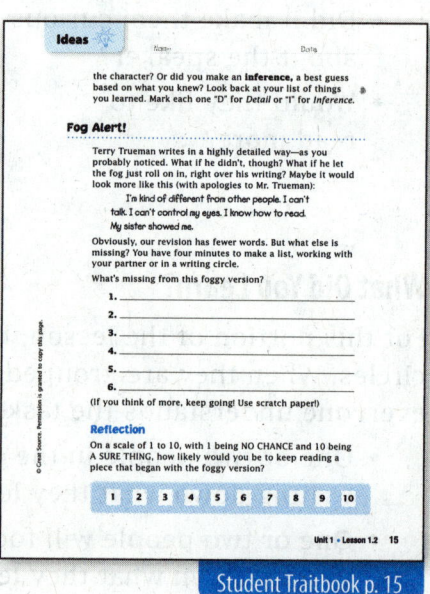

Student Traitbook p. 15

Discuss results as a class. Following are a few elements we think are missing from the foggy revision.

- Specific details—e.g., "my eyes go where they want to go"
- A real sense of the interaction between Shawn (the narrator) and Cindy

- Scenes we can picture: Shawn trying to focus, Cindy playing "Teacher of the Year"
- A sense of how smart Shawn really is, and how aware of the world around him
- Awareness that family members underestimate Shawn
- The fact Shawn doesn't feel sorry for himself, he just shares how things are
- A sense that Shawn is a curious person who loves to learn
- A sense that Cindy has no strong personal relationship with Shawn, but uses him to practice teaching skills
- Voice and feeling—Shawn's personality coming through in the narrative

Reflection

Have students rate this selection, showing the following.

- How likely it is (on a 1 to 10 scale) that they'd keep reading a book that began with the foggy version
- How likely it is (on a 1 to 10 scale) that they'll check out Trueman's actual book

Defogging

Remind students of your discussions from the first part of the lesson, particularly the contrast between Terry Trueman's original example of writing and our foggy revision. Remind them of the details that distinguished one from the other.

Then, review the directions for this section in the Student Traitbook to make sure students understand the task. They should follow these five steps:

1. Read all three examples to get a sense of the message.
2. Choose one to revise.
3. Review the example again, pencil in hand, making notes.
4. Create a new draft, on scratch paper or on the computer.
5. Strive to defog the message by adding any details that will bring it to life.

Give students 15 minutes or more for their revisions, encouraging them to go back more than once to add details or expand the piece.

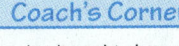
Student Traitbook p. 16

Coach's Corner

Note: If you are dividing this lesson into two parts, **Day 2 begins here.**

Coach's Corner

In revising, students are welcome to invent any details they wish. Don't let them feel too locked in to the original paragraph. It's just an idea starter. They can change the focus, the speaker, anything. The goal is to fill the writing with detail that will lift readers out of the fog.

Unit 1 31

Ideas

Practice Trait
Lesson 1.2

> **Bringing everyone in . . .**   **Differentiated Instruction**
>
> For advanced writers or those wanting to try something different, have them write two paragraphs in two different voices. For example, Example 2 might be written both from the speaker's perspective (Paragraph 1) and from the pet's (Paragraph 2). Example 3 might be written from the bully's perspective (Paragraph 1) and from that of the person being bullied (Paragraph 2). Writers who finish quickly should be encouraged to try more than one example.

Share and Compare

Give writers time to meet in writing circles to share their revisions. They may wish to choose one revision to read aloud to the class. Remind them to also discuss their strategies for revising. Process counts as much as product.

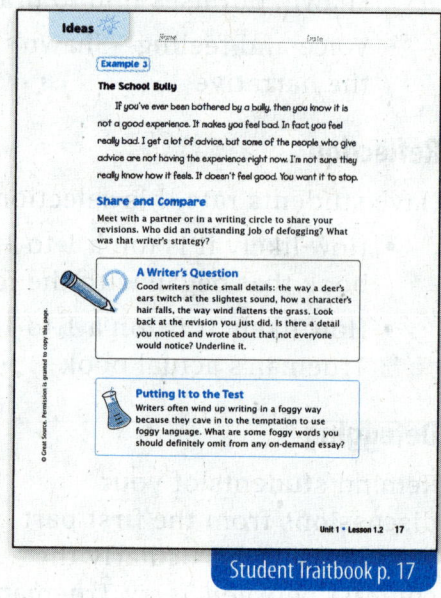

Student Traitbook p. 17

A Writer's Question

How many of your writers included detail that not everyone would notice? Have them scan their revisions to see. Share a few aloud.

Putting It to the Test

Foggy writing does indeed come from foggy language. Brainstorm some words that writers who value clarity should strive to avoid. Your writers may mention *nice, good, stuff, great,* and so on. Keep a list posted and add to it. Remember, there's no rule stating that writers cannot use these words, ever. The idea is not to *rely* on them.

Extending the Lesson

- Read more of Trueman's book *Stuck in Neutral* aloud. Have writers think about how their first impressions of Shawn and his sister Cindy are confirmed or expanded (or changed) as you read. Talk about the role detail and inference play in creating these characters. Share the fact that this was Trueman's debut book, and that his own son has cerebral palsy. How might this influence his writing?

- Have writers explore their own favorite literature for passages with rich detail. Create a book of favorites, or an online booklist to share with other writers.

- Search online for favorite quotations about details and create a collage.

- Initiate a blog discussion on inference and the role it plays in helping appreciate literature.

- Start an online discussion of *Stuck in Neutral*.

Ideas

Introduce Trait
Practice Trait
- Lesson 1.1
- Lesson 1.2
- **Lesson 1.3**
- Lesson 1.4
- Conventions & Presentation

Apply Trait

LESSON 1.3

From Sketch to Portrait

Student Traitbook pages 18–23

This lesson builds on what writers learned in Lesson 1.2 by asking them to focus on the importance of detail in creating a character. In this lesson, we use the word **sketch** to refer to quick brushstrokes, which are broad, general details that give a quick impression about a character. We use the word **portrait** to describe a true-to-life description that creates a unique individual—someone who seems real and alive. Detail, of course, is applicable to every kind of writing, from personal portraits to science reports.

Objectives

Students will

- understand the importance of detail in creating a realistic character.
- realize that carefully chosen details help readers know the person behind the words.
- review several examples to assess whether each is more of a sketch or portrait.
- create an original, vivid portrait of any character, real or fictitious.

 Time Frame

Allow 50 minutes for this lesson. We suggest dividing it into two parts.

- **Part 1:** Students review a portrait of writer E.B. White written by Kathleen Krull and rank three character sketches based on the quality of the detail each provides.
- **Part 2:** Students choose a person to describe and create an original, vivid portrait.

34   Unit 1

Setting Up the Lesson

Read the introduction from the Student Traitbook aloud. Then let students know that this lesson is about turning a vague sketch into a clear portrait.

Preview the examples they'll be reading and discussing shortly.

The published passage for this lesson (from Kathleen Krull's *Lives of the Writers*) is written in third person, and it's about writer E.B. White. The other examples are written in first person. Either way, what matters is the detail, and what we learn about the person who is the focus of the passage. Does that person seem real, and if so, what is it that makes the character come to life?

Student Traitbook p. 18

If you wish, extend this introduction by sharing one or more vivid character portraits from any literature. Following are a few suggestions. As you share, ask your students what sort of person or character each one is. How do they know?

- *Notes from a Liar and Her Dog* by Gennifer Choldenko: Chapter 2, first paragraph
- *Bull Run* by Paul Fleischman: any chapter—first paragraph or the whole piece
- *Flipped* by Wendelin Van Draanen: first few paragraphs of the first two chapters (this story is told in alternating voices)
- *Guys Write for Guys Read*, edited by Jon Scieszka: any chapter (each a personal portrait or story written by a favorite author)
- *Charlotte's Web* by E.B. White: second half of the chapter titled "Charlotte"

Coach's Corner

This is a good time to talk about third person (*he, she, they*) versus first person (*I, we*). Portraits can be written in either third person, about someone else, or first person, from the character's own perspective. Both can be effective. Also explain that with first person portraits, the writer is not always writing about himself or herself. Sometimes a writer assumes the voice of another character in order to create the sense that an experience is immediate and personal. Some writers have a gift for writing in multiple voices, and it can be a highly entertaining way to write.

Unit 1 35

Ideas

Practice Trait
Lesson 1.3

Coach's Corner
Suggest that writers underline or highlight details that help them know what E.B. White was like.

Teaching the Lesson

Sharing an Example: *Lives of the Writers*

Review the directions. Then share the passage from *Lives of the Writers* aloud, or ask one or two volunteer students (allowing them time to rehearse) to read it aloud to the class. Remind students to

- listen carefully as the passage is read aloud.
- think about the *character* E.B. White.
- think about the details that create that portrait.

> **Bringing everyone in . . .** **Differentiated Instruction**
>
> Many of your students are likely familiar with the author E.B. White and his famous book *Charlotte's Web*. Ask how many have read this book and whether they recall the characters. Some may also know of his other works, both fictional and informational: *Stuart Little*, *The Trumpet of the Swan*, *The Elements of Style* (with William Strunk), *Here Is New York* (with Roger Angell), *Letters of E.B. White*, *Farewell to Model T*—and various magazine writings.

Reflection

Share the directions aloud or have students read them carefully. Have them fill in their responses and rate the passage. Most should rate it fairly high. We learn many things about E.B. White. Your writers may mention any or all of the following.

- He was worried about making an impression
- He was very shy
- Eileen found him appealing and charming—despite his shyness
- White was the youngest of six children
- His friends called him Andy
- He was a happy child
- He didn't mind being alone
- He held numerous jobs that had little to do with writing
- He was squeamish about some of his work as a reporter
- Apparently (this is an inference), he liked Shakespeare

Coach's Corner
If you shared one or more character portraits to open this lesson, students may naturally compare Krull's passage to those you read aloud earlier. Encourage this, by all means. They do not need to choose a favorite, necessarily. What really matters is to identify strategies various writers used to bring characters to life.

Student Traitbook p. 19

Bringing everyone in . . . **Differentiated Instruction**

Some students are likely to be surprised that this portrait doesn't include any physical details. We don't find out how tall White was, whether he was thin or husky, whether he was athletic or had big feet or freckles or a large nose. We could never pick him out of a line-up. You may wish to talk about the fact that literary portraits sometimes include physical features and sometimes do not. Is it always important? When the writer does not provide any physical details, what happens in our readers' minds?

Sketches or Portraits?

Review the directions to be sure students understand the task: to read and rate three portraits, all written in first person. They must decide whether each portrait is

- so sketchy they can hardly tell anything about the person,
- strong enough to provide just a hint or two, or
- strong enough to make the reader feel he or she knows the character.

You may wish to read the three examples aloud, or call on student volunteers to read them. We recommend having students read all three silently first, forming initial impressions, and then hear them read aloud to see if they change their minds about any ratings.

Coach's Corner

Once students have read and rated all three examples, discuss the specific details or words that give us a true picture of each character. Most students should see Example 1 as the strongest, and Example 3 as the sketchiest. Why is Example 1 strongest? Is it partly the voice? Which details contribute to that voice?

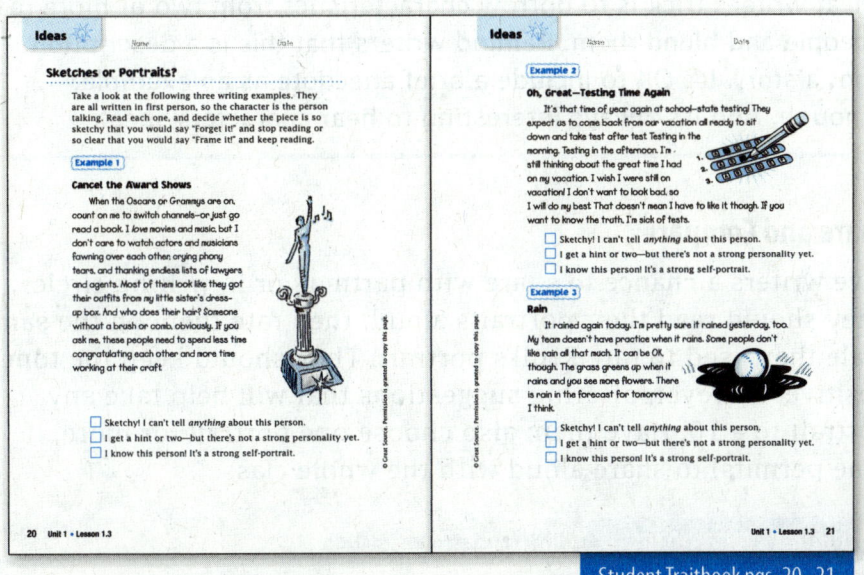

Student Traitbook pgs. 20–21

Unit 1   37

Ideas

Practice Trait
Lesson 1.3

Coach's Corner

Note: If you are dividing this lesson into two parts, **Day 2 begins here.**

Coach's Corner

We strongly suggest that writers choose someone they know well. This makes creating the portrait much easier because they can picture the character in their minds, and have seen him or her "in action." Also, this is a good time to remind writers about the difference between first and third person.

Creating Your Own Portrait

Remind students of your discussion from the first part of this lesson, and direct their attention once more to the three portrait examples.

Review the directions for this portion of the lesson to make sure they are clear: Students choose a character they know well and create a vivid portrait, using detail to bring him or her to life.

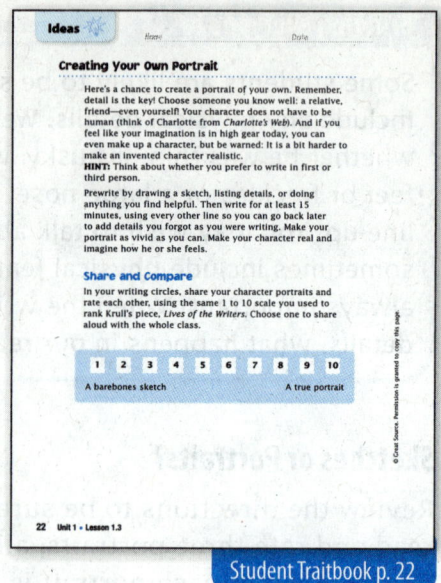

Student Traitbook p. 22

Bringing everyone in... — Differentiated Instruction

Drawing the character is a good way to get started. A list of characteristics can help, especially if it goes beyond the physical. Encourage students to avoid age, height, or weight unless those things are somehow linked to the character's personality. Have them think instead about how the character thinks, moves, speaks, etc. What does he or she love or fear? Creating a fictitious character is harder because the writer must (usually) invent everything. A neat writer's trick is to borrow characteristics from two or more real people and blend them. Remind writers that this is a description, not a story. It's OK to include a brief anecdote as an example, though. And it's always interesting to hear characters speak.

Share and Compare

Give writers a chance to share with partners or in writing circles. They should read their portraits aloud, then rate them on the same scale they used to rate Krull's portrait. They should keep the tone positive, however, offering suggestions that will help take any portrait to a 10. Have them also choose one portrait (or more, if time permits) to share aloud with the whole class.

Bringing everyone in... — Differentiated Instruction

Rating each other's work is tricky business. Suggest that writers give each other five points for simply creating a portrait, then add a point for each thing readers learn about the character. Naming the specifics they learn is much more helpful to the writer than saying, "This is good" or "This needs work." Writers should also avoid saying, "You need to . . ." A positive way of phrasing suggestions is something like, "I'm still curious about . . ."

A Writer's Question

We've already pointed out that Krull's portrait of E.B. White includes no physical detail, but we do know that she's describing a young man. In our example portraits, we do not directly say whether each speaker is male or female, or how old the speaker might be. Talk about the person your writers picture behind the words. Is that portrait more vivid when the voice is stronger? Why? Could listeners figure out these details from your writers' own portraits, even if they didn't state them directly?

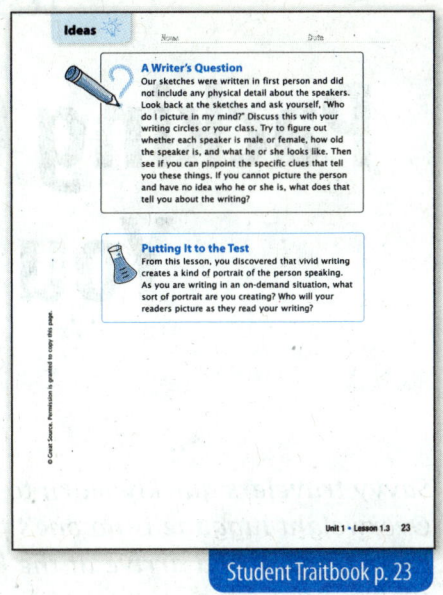

Student Traitbook p. 23

Putting it to the Test

This is a personal question, but a good one on which to reflect. Each piece of writing definitely creates an impression. Think about having students do a written reflection about this in their notebooks. Who is the person behind his or her own words? What sort of portrait would they like to create? This question matters because most of the time—outside of the classroom—readers do not know a writer personally.

Extending the Lesson

- If you did not have time to share all the examples you would have liked during your introduction to this lesson, share some now, or have students share some from their own favorite literature.
- Have students try writing a short narrative in two (or more) voices, using *Bull Run* as a model.
- Create an online journal for a character you invent as a class, and have each writer create one daily entry. Watch how your character evolves over time. What details do people choose to share to define who this person is?

Ideas

Introduce Trait
Practice Trait
Lesson 1.1
Lesson 1.2
Lesson 1.3
Lesson 1.4
Conventions & Presentation
Apply Trait

LESSON 1.4

Packing Only What You Need

Student Traitbook pages 24–30

Savvy travelers quickly learn to pack only what they need. Overweight luggage is no one's friend. At the same time, it's possible to underpack and arrive at the beach without the snorkel and flippers. Balance is the trick in packing—or in writing. Writers need to include enough details to make the writing meaningful and intriguing but leave out what isn't helpful or relevant. It takes a lifetime of writing to achieve this balance. This lesson is a beginning.

Objectives

Students will

- understand the importance of omitting filler, while including important details.
- assess a published piece, looking for strong detail and filler.
- Revise an overpacked example to eliminate filler (and add any detail they wish).

Time Frame

Allow 50 minutes for this lesson. We suggest dividing it into two parts.

- **Part 1:** Students will review two examples, learning to recognize filler and distinguish it from important detail.
- **Part 2:** Students revise an example that contains substantial filler, with the goal of cutting it in half.

40   Unit 1

Setting Up the Lesson

Share the introduction to this lesson from the Student Traitbook. It discusses packing a backpack for school. Use a backpack or a small suitcase as a model to discuss what is, and isn't, filler. You can simply make a list, but of course, if you want to go to the trouble of having props, you can make the game more fun. Together with your students, list (or show) some things that should and should not make the cut when someone is packing wisely. Here are just a few suggestions. Your students will think of many more! (Note that your lists will change slightly, depending on the weather and if you're packing for a trip or a day at school.)

Student Traitbook p. 24

Essentials for the Backpack: Snacks, water, cell phone, jacket, books, regular umbrella

Non-essentials: Rock collection, video games, beach umbrella, folding chair, small television, deck of cards

Have some fun talking about the many nonessentials people tend to pack—whether for a simple trip to school or a longer trip to another country. What are some of *your* favorite nonessentials, the ones you know you should leave at home but can't bear to do without?

Bringing everyone in . . . Differentiated Instruction

Some students have probably traveled by plane and know how strict weight requirements for luggage can be. As you talk about packing and overpacking, they may enjoy hearing about current guidelines and how they force travelers to redefine what they consider essential. Writers sometimes have to do this, too, especially when there's a word or space limit, or when they're asked to focus exclusively on one topic.

Ideas

Practice Trait
Lesson 1.4

Coach's Corner
This passage is from *Stowaway* by Karen Hesse. Some of your writers may wish to have you share more of the book, or may want to read more on their own.

Coach's Corner
Writers who underline or highlight details they consider significant will find the next portion of this lesson easier.

Coach's Corner
Note that writers may not consider any of Hesse's details filler. We agree completely! However, we set up the lesson this way so that they would have a chance to weigh each bit of information carefully—without imposing our prejudgment. A good way to decide if something is filler is to ask, "Would I enjoy reading this piece just as much if this little tidbit were missing?" Of course, not everyone agrees. One person's juicy detail is another's extra baggage.

Teaching the Lesson

Sharing an Example: *Stowaway*

Review the directions to be sure they're clear. Then give students time to read through the example passage from *Stowaway* on their own. Remind them to ask themselves whether author Karen Hesse achieves a good balance when it comes to detail. Does she

- give us enough detail to help us picture what's happening and feel part of the experience?
- give us so much detail we feel weighed down?

Identifying Important Details

Review the directions to be sure they are clear. Then give writers time to go back through the passage and do the following two things.

- Identify those details they think are especially important (these should go in the center of the circle)
- Identify details (if any) that they consider filler (these should go outside the circle)

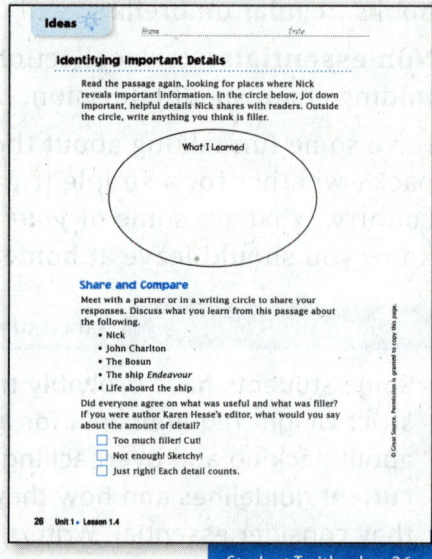

Student Traitbook p. 25

Student Traitbook p. 26

42   Unit 1

Share and Compare

Give students time to share their graphics with a partner or in a writing circle. Also encourage them to talk briefly about what they learn from the passage about Nick, John Charlton, the Bosun, the ship *Endeavour*, and life aboard the ship.

Also discuss their editor response to Hesse's passage. We think the amount of detail is just right. Each detail does count, and we would cut nothing. Your writers are free to disagree!

Hey! No Fair Peeking!

Review directions so that students understand the task. They should

- work individually.
- read the passage with a pencil in hand.
- mark anything that appears to be filler.
- trust their own eyes and ears, without looking back at the original!

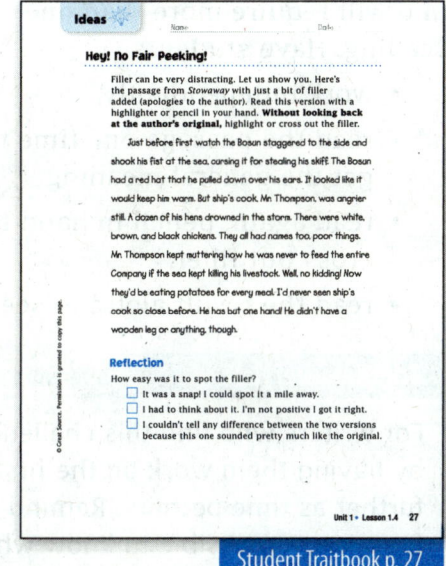

Student Traitbook p. 27

Coach's Corner

Bosun is a shortened version of the word *boatswain* (both are pronounced bōss'n), a noncommissioned officer who is in charge of maintaining a ship and its equipment. Students may be unfamiliar with this term, which you may have them look up in a dictionary.

Reflection

Students likely found it easy to spot the filler. Have them compare their revision with the author's original to be sure they deleted only filler!

HINT: Since *we* wrote the filler, can your writers hear a shift in voice?

Refer to the filler below for easy reference.

- *The Bosun had a red hat that he pulled down over his ears. It looked like it would keep him warm.*
- *There were white, brown, and black chickens. They all had names too, poor things.*
- *Well, no kidding! Now they'd be eating potatoes for every meal.*
- *He didn't have a wooden leg or anything, though.*

Unit 1   43

Ideas

Practice Trait
Lesson 1.4

Coach's Corner
Note: If you are dividing this lesson into two parts, **Day 2 begins here.**

Coach's Corner
It is fine to change the wording to make the piece read smoothly. Students may also notice that some parts could use additional detail—they're a bit sketchy. We will get to that in a moment. For now, they should just work on eliminating excess baggage.

Filler, Beware!

Remind writers of the work they completed in the first part of this lesson, distinguishing between critical details and filler. Then review the directions for this section to make sure the task is clear: editing a piece to delete filler. This is a longer piece and will require more than one reading. Have students

- work independently.
- read the passage one time to get the general meaning.
- read again, pencil in hand to cross out filler.
- read the result aloud to see if what remains makes sense.

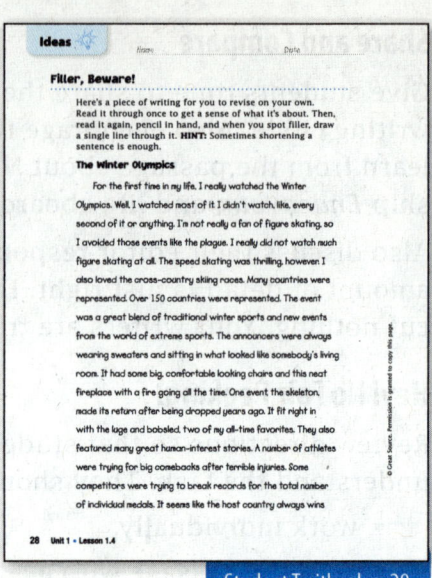

Student Traitbook p. 28

Bringing everyone in... | Differentiated Instruction

For writers who find this challenging, reduce the size of the task by having them work on the first half of the piece, then going further as time permits. Remind them to identify the main message first. It is impossible to know what is filler without knowing what message details are intended to support. Also remind writers that even though this piece is written as one large paragraph, it may cover several subtopics, each of which needs its own paragraph. Finally, encourage them to read aloud as they work, asking of each sentence, "Does this add something new and important?"

Share and Compare

Review the directions, and give students time to compare revisions with partners and to identify the statement that most closely matches their revision. We hope most crossed out about half, or close to that amount. When they finish, have them go back for one more look and insert a caret where more information is needed (they do NOT need to fill it in—just mark where it should go). Ask students what the next revision step might be.

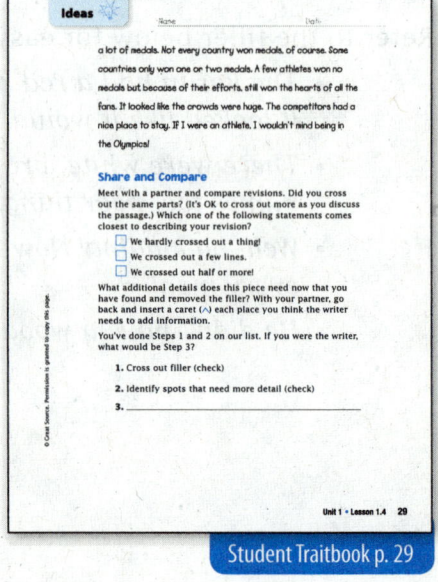

Student Traitbook p. 29

44 Unit 1

The original Olympics piece is **262 words long.** Following is our suggested revision, which runs **121 words.**

> **The Winter Olympics**
>
> For the first time, I really watched the Winter Olympics. Over 150 countries were represented. The event was a great blend of traditional winter sports and new events from the world of extreme sports.
>
> The speed skating and cross-country skiing races were especially thrilling. One event, the skeleton, made its return after being dropped years ago. It fit right in with the luge and bobsled, two of my all-time favorites. They also featured many human-interest stories. A number of athletes were trying for big comebacks after terrible injuries. Some were trying to break records for the total number of individual medals. A few athletes won no medals but, because of their efforts, still won the hearts of all the fans.

There are numerous informational holes, however. The writer needs more information on the following.
- What he means by "extreme sports"
- Why the speed skating and cross-country races were thrilling
- What the skeleton event is all about, and why it fits in with luge and bobsled
- Which athletes were trying for comebacks or records
- Who, specifically, won the hearts of fans—and how

Next steps in revising might include the following.
- Filling in those informational holes
- Watching a video on the Olympics to inspire new details
- Doing online research on one or two athletes
- Thinking of a new, more exciting title

Ideas

Introduce Trait
Lesson 1.4

Writing became such a process of discovery that I couldn't wait to get to work in the morning: I wanted to know what I was going to say.

—Sharon O'Brien
Writer

A Writer's Questions

If you accidentally put soy sauce into your chocolate cake, it's pretty hard to get it out. But in writing, details don't become permanent until publication. Filler in a rough draft is not a sign the writer is doing something wrong! It's often a sign the writer is exploring an idea. Drafting is the time to get everything out there. Exploration helps the writer rethink his or her real message, which can be pared down during revision.

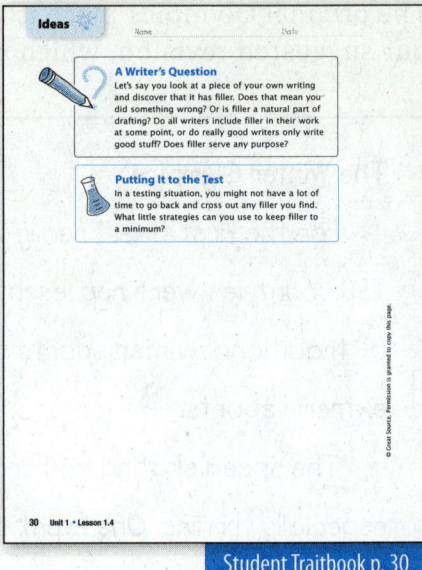

Student Traitbook p. 30

Putting It to the Test

On-demand writing is different from most real-world writing in that the first draft may also be the final! When this is the case, it is important to do everything possible to stay focused right from the start. It helps many writers to print out their main message on a piece of scratch paper and keep it visible as they write. It's less tempting to wander if the message is right there, like a warning sign. It also helps to have a planning list of details or questions to answer.

Extending the Lesson

- Talk about the genre of historic fiction. Which parts are most likely historically accurate and which does the writer invent? What is appealing about this genre to readers or writers?

- Using passages from *Stowaway* as an example, have writers create an online historic journal to reflect current events or any period in history through the eyes of one or more characters, each of whom must date and sign his or her journal entries. This can be a fascinating way to share information about a time in history, and is an appealing alternative to the more traditional history report.

- Post a piece of your own writing online—one that's still in very rough form. Invite students to revise it online by taking out filler and indicating the informational holes. See how many different versions you get back. Talk about how writers may see or hear filler differently.

- Learn more about Nicholas Young, Captain Cook, and the *Endeavour* by reading the rest of *Stowaway* and looking them up online.

Notes

Unit 1   47

Conventions & Presentation

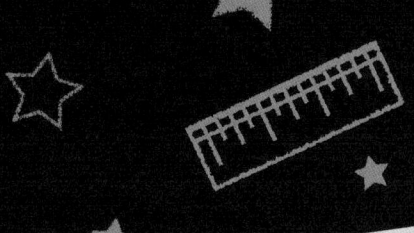

Overview

Good conventions and presentation are a courtesy to the reader. Ifawriterrunswordstogether or mispeals wrods, the message can be lost. Similarly, missing punctuation or punctuation that, is, put, in, where, it, is, not, needed can be interruptive to the flow of ideas—not to mention downright annoying.

During C&P Lessons, you will be helping students to

- understand that conventions help make text **clear, readable, and meaningful.**
- understand that presentation makes a message **visually appealing** and also directs a **reader's eye** to information he or she needs.
- see that Conventions and Presentation does not work in isolation, but **in harmony with other traits,** making each stronger.
- learn skills they can use to **strengthen conventions and presentation** in their own writing.

TRAIT DEFINITION

Conventions include anything and everything that a copyeditor would deal with: spelling, punctuation, grammar and usage, capitalization, and paragraphing. **Presentation** is layout—the look of the message on the page and the visual appeal it has for a reader. It includes such things as use of color, fonts, illustrations, white space, and overall design. Presentation ensures that the message gets noticed in the first place—and makes key information easy to spot.

Vicki & Jeff

Student Rubric for Conventions and Presentation

Students will be familiar with a rubric after working with the Student Rubric for Ideas. Explain that the Conventions and Presentation rubric focuses on good editing and effective design. Give students time to read and discuss the rubric. Answer any questions they may have about differences in levels or the language used.

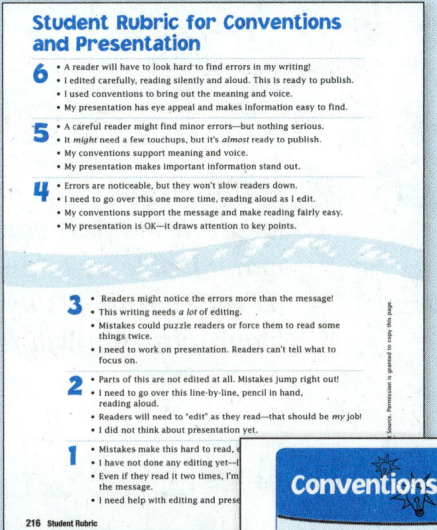

Student Traitbook p. 216

The Conventions & Presentation Poster

Before revealing the Conventions and Presentation poster on your wall, have students complete page 31 of the Student Traitbook. Things the writer does to build strong Conventions and Presentation appear on the left. Students will have to think about the impact of each item on the reader, and see if they can fill in the blanks on the right. After you have discussed each of the four elements, share the actual poster, putting it on the wall so that students can refer to it often. We recommend keeping the poster on the wall so students understand that Conventions and Presentation support all the other traits.

Student Traitbook p. 31

Ideas

Introduce Trait
Practice Trait
Lesson 1.1
Lesson 1.2
Lesson 1.3
Lesson 1.4
Conventions & Presentation
Apply Trait

Conventions and Presentation

Student Traitbook pages 32–40

In this lesson, students explore two ways of supporting the trait of Ideas. In the first part of the lesson (Level 1), students make editing manageable by taking it step by step. In the second part of the lesson (Level 2), students use factual information to create an interesting biography that will fit the back panel of a book cover.

Objectives

Editing Level 1: Conventions

Students will understand that

- careful editing eliminates small errors that create roadblocks to understanding.
- taking editing step by step can make a big task more manageable, and also increase editing efficiency.

Editing Level 2: Presentation

Students will understand that

- biographies (bios) answer many questions readers have about their favorite authors.
- bios can be informative, personal—even whimsical and humorous, but they must often fit into a limited space, so format counts.

 Time Frame

Allow 50 minutes for this lesson. We suggest dividing it into two parts.

- **Part 1:** Students apply step-by-step editing skills to proofread and correct five short passages.
- **Part 2:** Students revise a long bio, then write an original bio of their own.

50 Unit 1

Editing Level 1: Conventions
Making Editing Manageable
Setting Up the Lesson

Editing Level 1 focuses on Conventions. This lesson is designed to help any writers who struggle a bit with editing, showing them a way of making a big task manageable by breaking it into steps.

Students will warm up with a short passage that contains numerous errors. This practice helps editors become more aware of the kinds of errors that are easy for them to spot, and those that give them more trouble. Following this warm-up, they will edit a series of progressively more challenging passages.

For this lesson, students will need access to resources editors use:

- Dictionary
- Thesaurus
- Writing Handbook
- Copyeditor's Poster from this program

Some of these resources may be online. That is fine, too.

Begin with these steps:

- Read the introduction in the Student Traitbook.
- Have students define *conventions* and *presentation* in their own words. Use examples (covers of books) to illustrate various features of presentation so the distinction is clear for writers.
- Explain that this portion of the lesson will focus on conventions and its connection to Ideas, the primary trait you have been studying. Conventions support Ideas by ensuring that a message is not buried under distracting errors.
- Ask who has an editor's eye. What is the last conventional error they recall seeing (in a newspaper, in a textbook, or in their own writing)?
- Ask if there are certain kinds of errors that give them trouble, and share any of your own editing difficulties, too.
- Review the Copyeditor's Poster. Make sure all the marks are familiar to your writers and that they feel comfortable writing and using these marks to edit copy.

Bringing everyone in . . . Differentiated Instruction

Have your writers ever avoided editing because it just felt too overwhelming? Have you? (If so, be sure to share that experience!) Explain that this lesson is specially designed to show ways of making a big editing task more manageable by breaking it into steps.

Practice Trait
Editing Level 1: Conventions

Coach's Corner
Students will be editing hard copy, marking it with editor's symbols from the Copyeditor's Poster. Be sure everyone can see this clearly. Also, as you review the lesson or model editing of examples, it helps to project them electronically.

Coach's Corner
Encourage writers to think of conventions as anything a copyeditor would deal with or correct: spelling, punctuation, capitalization, usage and grammar, and paragraphing. Presentation is the look of print on the page: font style and size, use of open space, illustrations, and general design and placement.

Conventions & Presentation

Practice Trait
Editing Level 1: Conventions

Teaching the Lesson

A Warm-Up

Review the directions, taking care to review the five steps carefully. Encourage writers to choose one of the following approaches that will work best for them.

- Very confident editors can edit for several things at once—even for all five.
- Editors who think it might be helpful should start by focusing just on spelling, then going back to check punctuation, grammar, and missing or repeated words.
- Regardless of approach, all editors should read once for meaning before marking anything.
- All editors should also review the passage a final time AFTER editing, to be sure they didn't miss anything. Commend any editors who find even one more error by doing this.

Share and Compare

Give students time to talk with partners and compare the errors they found. Then share the total number of errors in the passage prior to having them take a final look. They should find 20 errors in all.

Coach's Corner

Many professional writers edit step by step, focusing first (or sometimes last) on the errors they find most challenging—often, that's spelling. Your writers may want to consider what is hardest for them and either get it out of the way up front or save it until they've spotted and corrected other errors.

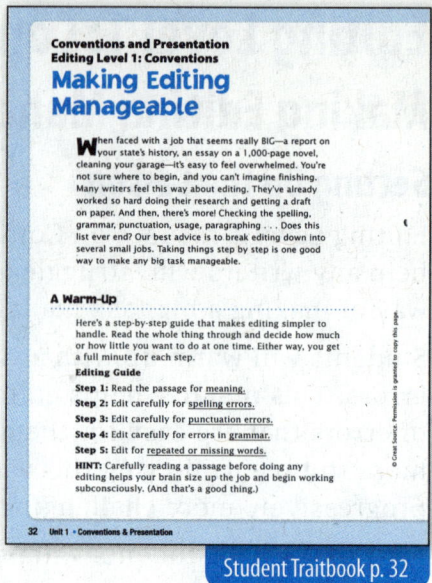

Student Traitbook p. 32

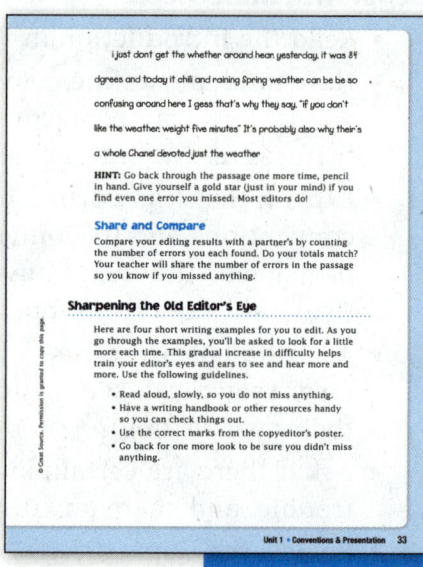

Student Traitbook p. 33

Here is the corrected passage, with corrections shown in blue.

> I just don't get the weather around here. Yesterday, it was 84 degrees and today it is chilly and raining. Spring weather can be so confusing around here. I guess that's why they say, "If you don't like the weather, wait five minutes." It's probably also why there's a whole channel devoted just to the weather.

Coach's Corner

After students coach you, talk about the errors that were especially easy to miss, such as the missing word *to* in the last sentence or use of *chili* (a real word) instead of the intended *chilly*. Reinforce the importance of knowing your own problem areas so you can be on the lookout for those kinds of mistakes, and also reading any text more than one time to help you catch the small things.

Bringing everyone in . . .   Differentiated Instruction

People who struggle with spelling or punctuation often have highly original ideas and compelling voice. The problem is, both ideas and voice can be camouflaged by distracting errors that vie for the reader's attention. On the other hand, really strong conventions support meaning and voice. Editing matters because the message matters! Student volunteers may be willing to project a line or two of their own writing electronically to give others practice in spotting errors. This can benefit everyone, and is much less scary if you (as the teacher) are also one of the volunteers!

Sharpening the Old Editor's Eye

In this portion of the lesson, writers edit four passages. The difficulty progresses as more kinds of errors are included each time. The idea is to train their editors' eyes and ears to look and listen for more and more with each round.

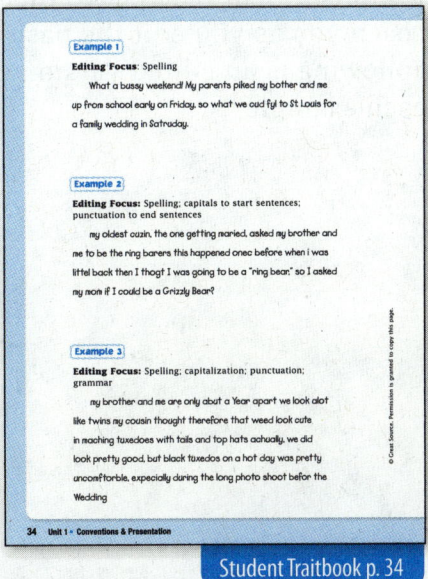
Student Traitbook p. 34

Unit 1   53

Conventions & Presentation

Practice Trait
Editing Level 1: Conventions

Coach's Corner

We recommend pausing after each passage to share and compare, rather than waiting until all four passages are finished, but you should use your own judgment about this, setting up the lesson as you wish. Either way, be sure to model correction of each passage, projecting them electronically if possible, and having students coach you. See edited passages under **Share and Compare**, below.

Coach's Corner

As you model the editing of these passages, resist the temptation to simply show writers what to do. Ask, "What's next?" so that they lead the discussion and point out the errors.

Bringing everyone in . . .   Differentiated Instruction

If doing all four passages in one lesson is too much for your writers, feel free to make four short lessons, and even do them across a span of four days. It's better to have short, frequent editing practice than to wear your editors out!

Students should

- work individually.
- read aloud, slowly, so they do not miss anything.
- feel free to use a writing handbook, dictionary, or any other resource.
- read once more AFTER editing to look for additional errors.

Passages are short. Most writers will likely complete the first two in about three minutes each and the next two in four to five minutes each.

Bringing everyone in . . .   Differentiated Instruction

Reminders of what to look for are provided at the beginning of each editing practice in this section. If students have any difficulty, be sure they are taking things step by step, checking spelling first, then capitals, then punctuation, and so on. If students need more then a few minutes for any passage, by all means extend the time. Those who finish quickly can be coaches.

Share and Compare

Again, we recommend reviewing passages one by one as students complete them. Then have them coach you as you edit the passage. Following is an edited version of each example.

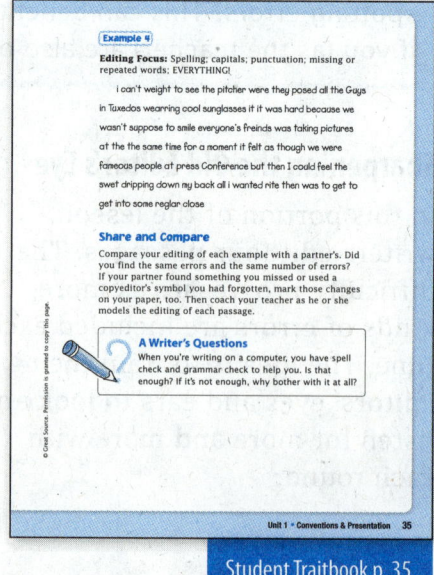

Student Traitbook p. 35

Example 1

What a ~~bussy~~ busy weekend! My parents p^ciked my ^rbother and me up from school early on Friday, so what we ~~cud~~ ^tol ~~fyi~~ fly to St. Louis for a family wedding ~~in Satruday~~ on Saturday.

Example 2

^M~~my~~ oldest ~~cuzin~~ cousin, the one getting ma^rried, asked my brother and me to be the ring ~~barers~~ bearers⊙ ^This happened ~~ones~~ once before when ^Ii was ~~litter~~ little⊙ ^Back then I ~~thogt~~ thought I was going to be a "ring bear," so I asked my mom if I could be a Grizzly Bear⊙?

Example 3

^M~~my~~ brother and ~~me~~ ^I are only about a ^year apart⊙ ^We look a#lot like twins⊙ ^My cousin thought therefore that ~~weee~~ we'd look cute in matching tuxedo^es with tails and top hats ~~achually~~⊙ Actually, we did look pretty good, but black tuxedoes on a hot day ~~was~~ were pretty ~~uncomftorbie~~ uncomfortables, expecially during the long photo shoot befo^er the ~~W~~edding⊙

Example 4

I can't ~~weight~~ wait to see the ~~pitcher were they~~ picture where they ~~posed~~ posed all the ~~Guys~~ in ~~Tuxedos~~ wea~~r~~ring cool sunglasses. It it was hard because we ~~wasn't~~ weren't suppose to smile. Everyone's ~~freinds~~ friends ~~was~~ were taking pictures at ~~the~~ the same time. For a moment it felt as though we were fam~~i~~ous people at a press ~~C~~conference but then I could feel the swe~~a~~t dripping down my back. all I wanted ~~rite~~ right then was to get ~~to get~~ into some reg~~u~~lar ~~close~~ clothes.

A Writer's Questions

The truth is, computerized "editors" cannot—as yet—compete with the human variety. They are programmed to look for certain spellings and word patterns, and such things as innovative sentence structure or fragments put them into a tizzy. But, they do provide a good beginning. A spell check program does catch many errors. (It just can't tell, ewe sea, if words are used correctly.) Similarly, programs designed to check grammar are anything but infallible, but like spell check programs, they give the writer a reason to take a second look.

> **Coach's Corner**
> Spell check suggests capitalizing ewe sea—making it Ewe Sea. Ah, that's better!

Editing Level 2: Presentation
Getting to Know You (in a Nutshell)

Setting Up the Lesson

This part of the lesson is about creating a short bio that will fit on the back panel of a book jacket. The purpose of the lesson is to show why bios are important and to give writers practice in putting together an interesting bio that will fit in a small space.

To prepare for this lesson, collect examples that illustrate well-written bios. You can find many online. Also look at book jackets in your library or media center. We've listed a few here. Though most bios are very straightforward, listing awards and/or other works for which the writer is famous, some offer extra features:

- Kate DiCamillo in *The Tale of Despereaux* (intriguing account of how this classic came to be)
- Sid Fleischman in *Escape: The Story of the Great Houdini* (a great job of linking bio to book)
- Patricia Polacco in *January's Sparrow* (notice there is also a bio for her researcher, Mary McCafferty Douglass)
- Melanie Watt in *Scaredy Squirrel at the Beach* (extends this writer's delightful humor right into the bio)

As you create your collection, consider what you will be asking students to look for: content, length, voice, effective illustrations (sketches, photos, graphics), complete and clear information, easy access to important details such as other works or websites, and arrangement of information on the page.

Begin with these steps:

- Remind students that presentation is all about how writing looks on the page. Does it have eye appeal? Does it help readers find the information they are looking for?
- Discuss the importance of good presentation in advertisements. Sellers must catch the attention of potential buyers and give them the information they need to make a purchase.

Conventions & Presentation

Practice Trait
Editing Level 2: Presentation

Unit 1 57

Conventions & Presentation

Practice Trait
Editing Level 2: Presentation

Coach's Corner

If students have access to their own favorite literature, encourage them to look at the bio for the author, which they may have overlooked up until now.

Coach's Corner

Ask how many of your writers regularly read author bios when reading a book. Do you? Talk about how knowing the author (even a little) can enrich the reading experience. Ask how many of them plan to routinely read this important section in the future.

Coach's Corner

Be sure students feel free to delete any copy, reword sentences, invent information (it's a fictitious person, after all), reorder details, or do anything to improve the piece. Writers who have computer access will likely find this task easier. Encourage writers to work quickly. This is only a warm-up for the writing in **Presentation Matters**.

Teaching the Lesson

A Warm-Up

Review the directions to be sure everyone understands the task.

Share your examples with students in any way you wish. For example, you might use a document projector. Or you might pass several examples to students in small groups, then have them exchange after a brief period.

As students go through the examples, have them record the "Must-Include" features they find for effective author bios. We made space for ten features, but they should list as many as possible.

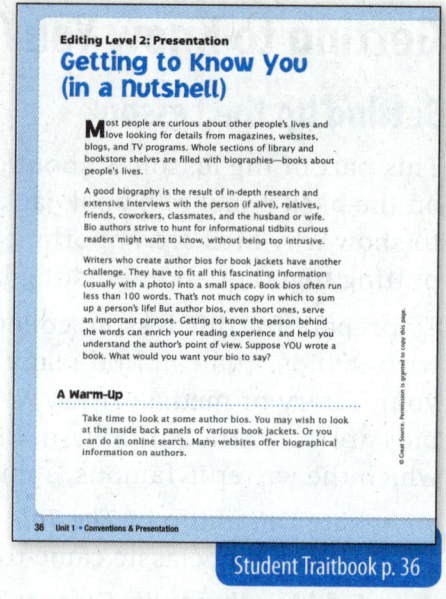
Student Traitbook p. 36

Share and Compare

Discuss the students' list as a class. If they hear an important feature they did not think of, remind them to add it to their own lists.

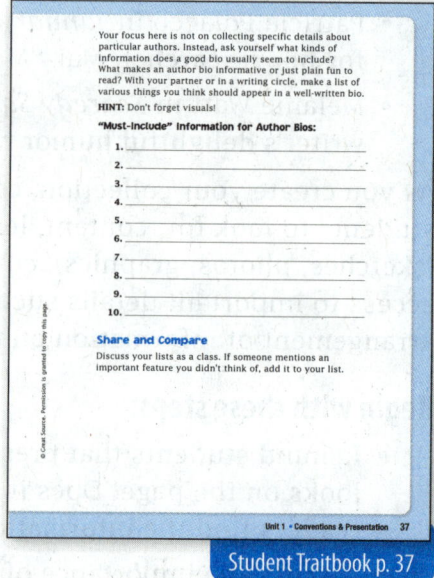
Student Traitbook p. 37

Whittling a Bio Down to Size

In this part of the lesson, students will review and revise a rough bio for a fictitious author. (Any resemblance to an actual author is completely unintentional.) Have students

- decide which details are important to keep.
- reduce the total word count from 226 words to 120.

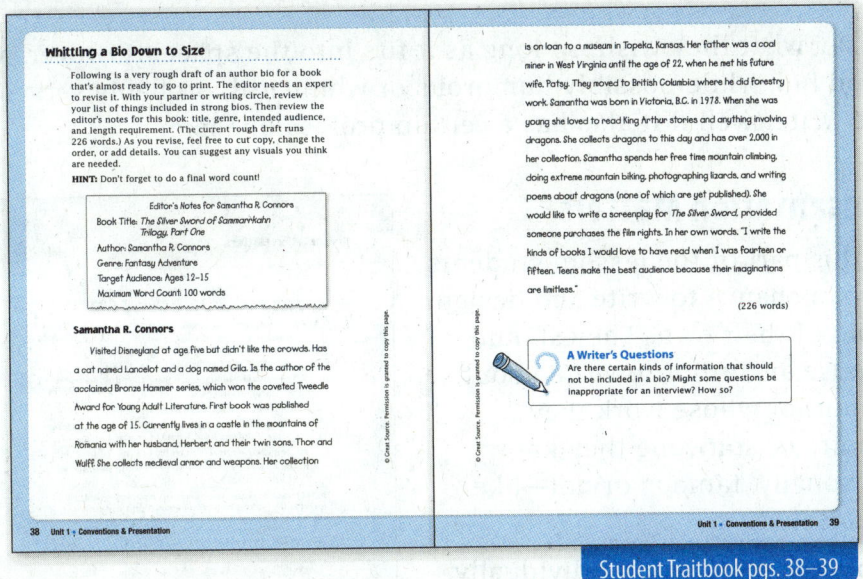

Student Traitbook pgs. 38–39

Share revisions as time permits. There is no correct revision. We chose to make ours quite short. Here it is, for purposes of comparison:

> Samantha R. Connors is the author of the acclaimed Bronze Hammer series, which won the coveted Tweedle Award for Young Adult Literature. She lives in a mountain castle in Romania with her husband, Herbert, their twin sons, Thor and Wulff, her cat Lancelot, and her dog Gila. She collects medieval armor and weapons, along with dragons (she has over 2,000). A daredevil at heart, Sam enjoys mountain climbing and extreme mountain biking. Having published her first book at 15, she says, "I write the kinds of books I would love to have read when I was fourteen or fifteen. Teens make the best audience because their imaginations are limitless."
>
> (109 words)

A Writer's Questions

Some information may be too private to include in a bio, especially if someone else writes it. (Interviewers need to ask interesting, important questions without being intrusive. All people, authors included, have a right to privacy.) Many authors, as your writers have discovered, write their own bios, and they are usually free

Conventions & Presentation

Practice Trait
Editing Level 2: Presentation

Coach's Corner

Writers who choose to write about themselves obviously have an advantage in that all information is at their fingertips. If writers choose to write about someone in the class, it is best if they do so in teams, with each writer doing a bio of the other. This makes coordination of the interviewing process easier. Note that interviews can be short (3 minutes at most). Writers only need a few interesting details to make a bio intriguing. Research of famous writers can be done online, and will likely require time outside of class.

to say what they wish, so long as it fits into the space. However, a good bio, while possibly humorous or whimsical, probably serves the writer well if it also has a certain professionalism.

Presentation Matters

In this part of the lesson, students have a chance to write and design a bio of their own. They should choose an author to write about: an author whose work they admire or someone they know personally, famous or not—like themselves!

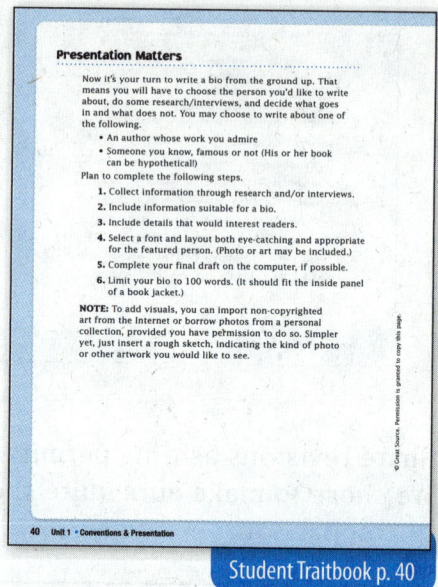

Student Traitbook p. 40

Writers should work individually, making notes (in the space provided), then completing their final design on paper or poster board or, alternatively, on the computer. This writing does not need the polish of a final draft, but should include the following.

- Specifications for eye-catching fonts
- Plans for use of color
- A clear and effective general design (most bios appearing on book covers are rectangular, and follow a portrait layout)
- Clear plans for placement of sketches or photos
- Effective, voice-filled copy introducing the author to readers

Allow about ten minutes for planning and making notes. During this time, writers may wish to research a favorite writer online or interview someone from the class.

Allow an additional 15–20 minutes for writing and design.

Coach's Corner

Whenever possible, allow students 2–3 days away from their own work prior to editing. This creates a detachment that is not possible immediately after writing, and will make editing stronger.

Bringing everyone in . . . Differentiated Instruction

Some writers may not have time to complete their bios in one lesson. That's fine. Have them complete their planning in one lesson and their writing in the next. Consider dedicating one class period to planning, interviewing, and researching, and a second class period to design and writing.

When writers finish their bios, provide time for sharing in writing circles or with the whole class. You may also wish to display them.

Extending the Lesson

- Group students into editing circles (groups of 3 or 4) to identify their own editing challenges and create short (3–5 sentence) practice passages for one another. This is easy to do on the computer by copying a passage from any text, then going back to insert one or more errors. Editing circles can decide which errors they will focus on and how many errors they will include in each practice. (Encourage them to keep the number under ten at first.) Then they can exchange practice passages with another circle, and coach one another. Students will gain editing skills from creating and completing lessons, as well as from coaching.

- Include writer bios in future pieces of your writers' work. They can write their own, or choose a writer from the class to help.

- As you share literature, continue to check out both the summaries (usually found on the inside front panel) and author bios (usually found on the inside back panel). Have writers comment on which are especially effective—and why. Encourage your students to preview a book by reading both parts. They will gain insight about what to look and listen for.

- Create final bios based on the work writers completed in this lesson, working online to experiment with fonts, colors, and photos (if available and not copyrighted).

- If any of your writers had difficulty with the editing lessons, wait a few weeks and repeat them. Consider repeating them later in the class year also, and comparing performances.

- If your students have computer access, continue asking them to work with creative design, making book covers, greeting cards, posters, or other written materials that fit your curriculum. Consider after-school sessions in which you or anyone with technical design skills provides direct instruction on how to incorporate these elements of design into writing.

- Start a blog discussion or create podcasts offering suggestions about good editing. What strategies can make the process more efficient, even for beginners?

Coach's Corner

When you create editing practice for students, focus on the errors you see in their work. Try to keep practices short enough to complete in five minutes or less, and focus on one kind of error at a time: spelling OR punctuation OR grammar. Be sure to have them edit their own work immediately after finishing the practice.

Proofread carefully to see if you any words out.
—Author unknown

UNIT 1
Ideas

Introduce Trait

Practice Trait

Apply Trait

Final Curtain Call 63
- Preview pages 63–71

50 min. **Assessing and Revising Sample Papers** 64
- Have students apply what they have learned about the trait of Ideas
- Have students revise Sample paper 4 for the trait of Ideas

Sample Paper 3: *Sharks: Misunderstood Inhabitants of the Sea*
   Score and Rationale

Sample Paper 4: *Stop Smoking Now!*
   Score and Rationale

Revising Sample Paper 4: *Stop Smoking Now!*

50 min. **Revising and Editing a Personal Draft** 69
- Have students revise and edit their own writing for Ideas and Conventions and Presentation
- Assess students' growth as writers

Parting Thoughts 71
- Conclude the trait of Ideas

62   Unit 1

Final Curtain Call

It's time to give students a chance to apply what they have learned. Each of the following steps also provides *you* with an opportunity to assess their growth. Have students demonstrate their knowledge of Ideas, as well as Conventions and Presentation, by doing these two things.

1. **Apply knowledge of Ideas by assessing and revising the writing of others.**

    Your students will read and assess Sample Papers 3 and 4. This time, they will work independently, using what they have learned to
    - decide for themselves which piece is stronger.
    - score each sample, using the Student Rubric for Ideas.
    - brainstorm ways of improving the weaker paper.
    - use the Student Rubric and/or Revising Checklist for Ideas to revise the weaker paper.

    Assessment Component: Base your assessment of growth on students' revision of Sample Paper 4: *Stop Smoking Now!* The revised version should advance one point or more on the rubric, achieving a final score of 4, 5, or 6. Assess each student's final draft of *Stop Smoking Now!* using the Teacher Rubric for Ideas.

2. **Apply knowledge of Ideas by assessing and revising personal writing.**

    Students will now pull their original drafts from their folders to revise and edit, applying everything they have learned from
    - reading and using the rubrics, checklists, and posters.
    - discussing and assessing the writing of other students.
    - reading or hearing literature that exemplifies strengths in the trait of Ideas.
    - completing five lessons to build skills in this trait.
    - assessing and revising weak samples: *My Most Scary Experience* and *Stop Smoking Now!*

    Assessment Component: Base your assessment of students' growth on their revision of their own writing. How much has it changed from rough draft (look at the score you assigned earlier) to final? Do not base your assessment exclusively on changes in scores, however. Look closely at the quality, nature, and extent of writers' revisions. How creative were they? What risks did they take? Add additional points for good editing or creative presentation.

Coach's Corner

Compare students' revision of this paper with their earlier revision of Sample Paper 1: *My Most Scary Experience* (at the opening of this unit). Do you see differences in the amount or quality of revision? What new insights do they have about the trait of Ideas?

Coach's Corner

Every positive change, however small, counts as revision. Give writers simple tips that make revision manageable, trait by trait.

Coach's Corner

If a student's final score does not leap the river in Ideas or in Conventions and Presentation, provide an option to revise or edit further, using one or both checklists to create a workable plan. Presentation is more applicable to some types of writing than to others. If a student is designing a cover or TOC for a report, consider presentation. For a simple story, offer credit for fonts, use of subheadings, etc.

Coach's Corner

Check out the Assessment Guidelines for a more detailed discussion of effective ways to assess your student writers' performance and growth.

Ideas

- Introduce Trait
- Practice Trait
- **Apply Trait**
- **Assessing and Revising Sample Papers**
- Revising and Editing a Personal Draft

Assessing and Revising Sample Papers

Student Traitbook pages 41–45

Sample Paper 3: *Sharks: Misunderstood Inhabitants of the Sea* and Sample Paper 4: *Stop Smoking Now!*

1. Explain that this activity will give students a chance to see how they have grown as assessors and revisers with respect to the trait of Ideas.
2. Refer them to the Student Rubric for Ideas.
3. Pair students up, and then refer them to Sample Papers 3 and 4.
4. Remember that at this point you will let students be a little more independent by
   - giving them both papers at one time.
   - having them read the papers to each other—in any order.
   - telling students to decide through discussion which is stronger in the trait of Ideas.
   - scoring the two papers together, thereby using comparisons to help zero in on the best score for each.
5. As students score the papers, they should think about these

   ### ❓ Key Questions . . .
   - *Does the paper have a clear main message?*
   - *Does the writer focus on that message?*
   - *Is the writer's main idea narrow and focused enough to be manageable—or too big to handle?*
   - *Does the writer share helpful, unusual, or interesting details?*
   - *Do those details create a vivid picture in your mind?*
   - *Does the writer seem to know the topic well—or rely on generalities?*
   - *Is all of the information important, or is some of it filler?*
   - *As a reader, do you learn anything new from the paper?*
   - *If appropriate, are there sensory details?*
   - *As a reader, do you feel as if your most important questions are answered?*

Coach's Corner

Students can work with partners or in writing circles for this activity. Keep in mind that larger teams usually require somewhat more time for discussion. However, hearing multiple opinions about a piece of writing is obviously advantageous. If students work with just one partner, consider changing partners to let them hear a new coaching voice. Note that students can and should vote on scores individually, even when discussing with others.

Coach's Corner

Sharks is an informational paper; *Stop Smoking Now!* is a persuasive essay. The writer of *Stop Smoking Now!* struggles with minimal information, relies on generalities and common wisdom about addictions, rarely addresses the main topic. By contrast, the writer of *Sharks* has clearly taken time to get to know his topic. One good way to think about it is this: Which piece shares new or helpful information?

6. When students finish scoring, discuss the papers as a class. Talk about which is stronger in the trait of Ideas and why. Once students have agreed on the best scores for each piece, compare their scores with ours (See *Scores and Rationales*).

7. Have students identify strong features from *Sharks*. What does this writer do well, in terms of the trait of Ideas? Have them identify specific problems with *Stop Smoking Now!* What specifically would the writer need to do to make this piece stronger in the trait of Ideas?

Score and Rationale for Sample Paper 3:
Sharks: Misunderstood Inhabitants of the Sea

Most students should see this paper as **strong.** This writer knows a great deal about sharks and writes with confidence. The paper opens with a strong thesis sentence and every detail within the paper connects in some way to the idea that sharks are misunderstood and we should educate ourselves about them. Readers who have not studied sharks will be intrigued to discover that they are lazy, that they do not pursue humans (as depicted in popular films), that most eat small fish, and, most interesting and shocking of all, that we kill 100 million of them per year. That raises the question: Are sharks endangered? The writer implies that they might be but does not address this question openly. One of the real strengths of this piece is that it is written in such a clear, forthright manner. Every part is easy to understand and follow. The organization and voice are also strong. (You may wish to return to this piece when studying those traits.) Details are well selected and teach us a great deal about the topic. This paper would receive a **score of 6 in the trait of Ideas.**

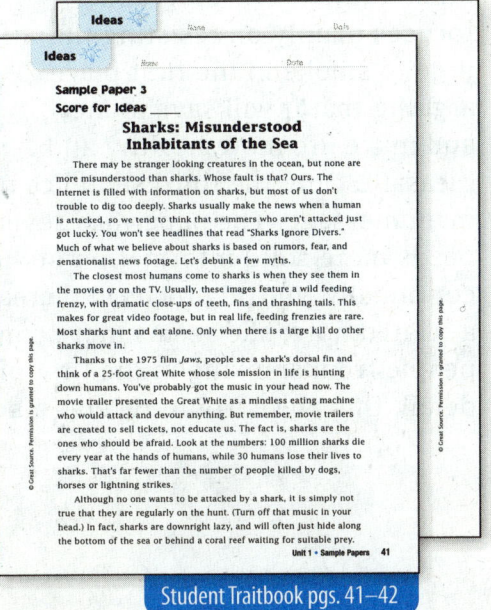
Student Traitbook pgs. 41–42

Ideas

Apply Trait
Assessing and Revising Sample Papers

Coach's Corner

Both papers have source lists, and both lists contain conventional errors. Remember, this would be scored under the trait of Conventions and Presentation. If you wish, you can create an extension lesson in which writers use an approved handbook to check formatting of one or both lists and make editorial corrections. This is excellent practice, but because of the time involved, we do recommend doing it as a separate lesson.

Score and Rationale for Sample Paper 4: *Stop Smoking Now!*

Most students should agree that this paper **needs significant revision** in the trait of Ideas. The writer opens with a strong statement, "Quitting smoking can be very hard," then falls back on a litany of generalities and clichés about addictions in general. The second paragraph addresses the likelihood of becoming a smoker in the first place, then wanders off on a discussion of other addictions. Paragraph 3 focuses mainly on resisting the urge to smoke in the first place, arguing that it will save money and make life more healthy and pleasant. Only the third sentence of that paragraph addresses the main message. The paper has several problems. First, the writer needs more solid information on her topic. Second, she wanders continually, shifting focus and creating confusion. And finally, on a related note, she seems more concerned with preventing young people from smoking in the first place. Because it lacks focus *and* detail, this piece would receive a **score of 2 in the trait of Ideas.**

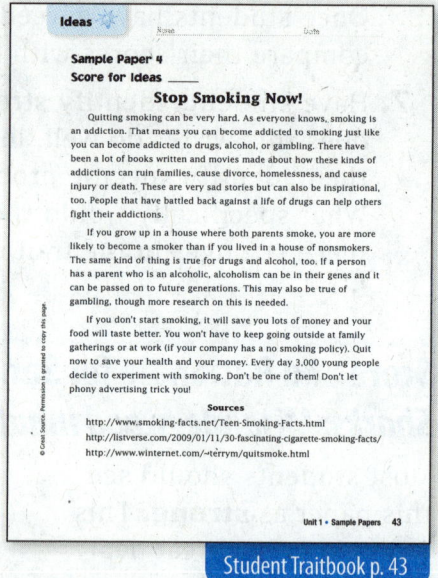

Student Traitbook p. 43

Revising Sample Paper 4:
Stop Smoking Now!

Have students revise the sample paper with the lower score in the trait of Ideas: *Stop Smoking Now!* Their goal is to raise the score from a 3 to a 4 or *higher*. This revision challenge tests students' knowledge of the trait of Ideas and helps prepare them to revise their own writing.

1. Remind each student to refer to the Revising Checklist for Ideas or the Student Rubric for Ideas (their preference) as they revise.

2. Tell students to try recalling (on their own—without looking at a rubric) the most important features of strong Ideas. As they call out features, record them. Their list should include things such as the following (in students' own words).

    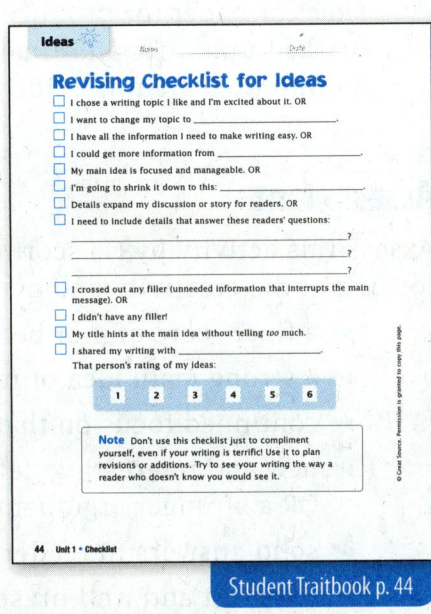

    Student Traitbook p. 44

    - *A clear main idea or message*
    - *Helpful, interesting details that support that message*
    - *Sensory details as appropriate*
    - *Answers to readers' questions*
    - *Absence of unrelated details or filler (unneeded information)*
    - *Focus (writing stays on message)*

3. Remind student writers that each of them is in charge of his or her revision. It is all right to shift the focus (which also means a new title), add or delete information, start or end in a different place, or make any other changes that improve the piece. They are in charge!

Coach's Corner

In preparation for revision, writers will need to begin by choosing a focus: reasons (or methods) to stop smoking OR reasons not to smoke in the first place.

Unit 1   67

Ideas

Apply Trait
Assessing and Revising Sample Papers

Coach's Corner

Even minimal research will strengthen a writer's revision of this piece. You may wish to allow one class period just for this. Encourage students to work together in teams (with a partner or in a writing circle) to gather information to support a strong revision.

Coach's Corner

It is OK for students to delete large portions of this paper because they are too general or because they do not support the reviser's new thesis. The paper is weak enough to merit almost a total rewrite. Information on alcohol, drugs, gambling, divorce, and homelessness has no relevance to this topic. NOTE: The general topic of addiction is far too big for a paper of this scope.

Coach's Corner

Students may wish to use what they know of good presentation to design a cover for the final draft or incorporate illustrations (so long as they are not copyrighted). By all means encourage this, and provide additional points for strong presentation, including a well-presented source list. Remember to also refer students to the **Revising Checklist for Conventions and Presentation** on page 45 of the Student Traitbook.

4. Give students a chance to collaborate prior to revising. Take time for a brief class discussion on smoking. Students can work together to look up information on the web or in the media center, and to determine a focus for the piece: how to stop smoking, reasons to stop smoking, OR reasons and ways to fight the urge to begin smoking.

5. Have students mark up the rough draft, crossing out or adding information, and then copy their final onto a clean sheet of paper (or produce it on the computer). Their original marked up drafts and final copy should be stapled together to go into their writing folders.

Assessment

Assess this activity by (1) scoring the final draft for Ideas and (2) looking at the creativity and overall extent of the revision. Look for

- a final score of 4 or better in the trait of Ideas.
- a strong main idea or message (possibly a strong thesis).
- continued focus on that message throughout the piece.
- new and interesting details about not becoming a smoker OR a stronger argument about ways and reasons to stop.
- solid answers to readers' questions about smoking.
- a correct and well-presented list of sources, including any new sources students consult or cite.

Bringing everyone in... Differentiated Instruction

All originals in this program have been edited for spelling, punctuation, and grammar so that errors will not be distracting as students focus on other features of writing. But as students revise, they will need to edit any new text; they will also need to cite sources correctly. Be sure students have copies of the **rubric and checklist for Conventions and Presentation,** a dictionary, and an approved writing handbook that shows how to cite sources in their writing, both within the text and in end notes.

Ideas

Introduce Trait
Practice Trait
Apply Trait
Assessing and Revising Sample Papers
Revising and Editing a Personal Draft

Revising and Editing a Personal Draft

Applying Knowledge of Ideas by Revising Personal Writing

The revision your students just completed on Sample Paper 4: *Stop Smoking Now!* provides a good warm-up for revising and editing their own writing effectively. Everything in the unit has been directed toward this goal: helping student writers become strong, independent revisers of their own work.

1. Have students recall the personal writing they created after the literature connection (*When Zachary Beaver Came to Town*). This should still be in rough draft form in their folders.

2. Have them remove that writing from their folders and assess it for Ideas and for Conventions and Presentation, using the student rubrics for those traits. As they assess, they should ask themselves these

   ❓ **Key Questions . . .**
   - *Does this paper leap the river in each trait?*
   - *Did I highlight any problem areas or write myself notes?*
   - *What could I do to make my writing stronger?*

3. Based on their answers to these key questions, students should revise and edit their writing. Their goal is to make the paper leap the river (scores of 4, 5, or 6) in both traits or, if the writing is already strong, to make even small revisions that improve it further. As with Sample Paper 4, they should mark up the rough any way they wish, and copy the final onto new paper or enter it on the computer. Rough and final should be stapled together, so that you have a visual representation of any changes or expansions.

Coach's Corner

In assessing their own writing, students do NOT need to come up with scores. This is not about grading or scoring; it's about preparing for revision. They only need to ask themselves, "Is my writing effective? Does it work? And if not, where are the weak spots? How can I make my writing more appealing?"

Coach's Corner

The importance you place on presentation must depend in part on the resources you have available to support this trait. To really challenge and expand students' presentation skills, you need to provide students with computer access, together with some direct instruction in selecting fonts, or using such design features as italics, boldface, boxes, columns, and so on. Allow additional time if presentation is important.

Unit 1 69

Ideas

Apply Trait
Revising and Editing a Personal Draft

Coach's Corner

As you go through this progarm, your students will gain new skills in both drafting and revising. A portfolio is one way to capture that growth. A rough and final draft stapled together make an excellent addition to a portfolio because good assessment does not focus only on the final draft, but also on the journey the writer took to get there.

Assessment

Assess this activity by scoring students' final drafts and also comparing the rough draft (that you scored earlier) with the final. Look for

- a final score of 4 or more in each trait,
- an improvement of at least one point in each trait, OR
- any revisions or editorial changes that make a difference.

Bringing everyone in . . . Differentiated Instruction

When you have writers who aren't sure how to begin, tell them to star (in the margin) one thing they are unhappy with, and then have a conference, with you or another student. A good coach (whether adult or student) encourages forward motion step by step. A writer may need to work on something, confer, then work again—and confer again. Some writers will finish their revision within one class period, while others may need an additional period or time outside of class. Though working in time for revision may sometimes be difficult, in-class revision has significant advantages. Students can work together and support each other's efforts, and you can observe and coach.

Parting Thoughts

All writing begins with ideas—with a message to share. We can't really talk about the trait of Organization until there is something to organize. We can't really talk meaningfully about the trait of Voice until the writer has something definite to say. That's why it's critical to spend extra time with the foundational trait of Ideas, encouraging young writers to find personally important topics, do any research needed to fully explore that topic, and select details that will grab and hold readers' attention. The better a writer knows a topic, the easier it becomes to choose details that help writers "come inside" the writer's world. Inexperienced writers often begin drafts with no more than a surface acquaintance with a topic. It doesn't work. They wind up relying on common knowledge, or wandering off the topic to discuss something more comfortable and familiar. When it comes to the trait of Ideas, knowledge is everything. Strength in ideas comes partly from imagination, but it's also the direct result of paying close attention to the world around you, observing, recording, remembering, and above all, having the curiosity to ask good questions and seek the answers.

In a writer there must always be two people— the writer and the critic.
—Leo Tolstoy

Vicki & Jeff

UNIT 2
Organization

Overview

Unit 1 focused on Ideas, the writer's message. Unit 2 is all about **Organization,** the trait that supports Ideas by presenting the writer's message in an understandable, memorable way. Together, these two traits form the foundation of strong writing. As students will see throughout this unit, organization shifts to fit the message—never the reverse. Everything from a simple paragraph to a complex website requires a design unique to its particular content and purpose. When organization is working as it should, readers have such an easy time processing text that it's as if they're on a guided tour of the writer's thinking.

In this unit, you will be helping students to

- put details in a **logical order.**
- keep the **spotlight on the main message.**
- use **transitional words** to clearly connect ideas.
- **organize information** effectively, step by step.
- understand how strong **Conventions and Presentation** support **Organization.**

TRAIT DEFINITION

Think of **Organization** as design and order. As with architecture, design depends on function. A school and a museum are designed differently; so are a business letter and a mystery novel. Still, good organization nearly always includes these features: a strong lead to pull readers in, transitions that make connections clear, logical order, and a conclusion that wraps things up. Good organization makes information easy to find and follow—but doesn't draw attention to itself. It supports and showcases the writer's primary ideas.

Vicki & Jeff

Unit at a Glance

Introduce Trait

Discussing Sample Papers 76

Making the Literature Connection 82

Writing a Personal Draft 85

Practice Trait

Lesson 2.1: Organization's a Joke 90

Lesson 2.2: Avoid the Wandering Spotlight...................96

Lesson 2.3: Staying Connected 103

Lesson 2.4: Putting the Puzzle Together 110

Conventions and Presentation......................................116

Apply Trait

Assessing and Revising Sample Papers......................128

Revising and Editing a Personal Draft 133

Unit 2 73

UNIT 2
Organization

Introduce Trait

The Opening Act 75	• Preview pages 75–86
Discussing Sample Papers 76	• Introduce trait language and rubric
15 min. Sample Paper 5: *How to Shop* Score and Rationale	• Analyze weak and strong writing
15 min. Sample Paper 6: *Shopping by Computer* Score and Rationale	
50 min. Making the Literature Connection 82	• Model the trait of Organization in literature: *If the World Were a Village*
	• Connect reading and writing
50 min. Writing a Personal Draft 85	• Coach students in creating a piece of personal writing
	• Assess students' drafts to create benchmark scores

Practice Trait

Apply Trait

The Opening Act

Introduce the trait of Organization by first describing the concept. Organization is design, the structure of the piece—like the skeleton of an animal or the framework of a building. It includes the lead (beginning), the order in which ideas are presented, transitions (connections between ideas), and the conclusion (ending). Organization holds the writer's ideas together.

Let students see and hear this trait in action—first in two writing samples and then in a piece of literature (*If the World Were a Village*) in which good design transforms an overwhelming list of factual details into an easy-to-follow set of short essays about who inhabits planet Earth. Following the Literature Connection, students will have a chance to create an original piece of writing on a topic of their choice. They will revise and edit this piece down the road, using what they have learned about Ideas, Organization, and Conventions and Presentation. Here's the Opening Act in more detail.

1. **Discuss and assess the sample papers.** Expand students' understanding of Organization by discussing two sample papers: *How to Shop* (in which strong organization guides the reader step by step to better shopping habits) and *Shopping by Computer* (in which the writer's tendency to wander makes it difficult to focus on the main message).
   As before, encourage students to talk, to mark up sample papers by making notes or highlighting features, and to refer often to their student rubrics. Remind students that
   - **strong writing samples** give writers ideas for strategies *they* can try—while
   - **weaker samples** show problems to avoid and offer opportunities to practice revision.

2. **Connect the trait to literature.** Continue your conversation by showing how professional writers use a lead to get readers hooked, chunk information to make it "digestible," connect smaller ideas to a larger message, keep the informational flow going, and wrap things up with a conclusion that leaves readers thinking. Our featured text for this unit is *If the World Were a Village: A Book about the World's People* by David J. Smith. Share this or *any text* strong in Organization. Remember to allow a full class period (or more) for the literature lesson.

3. **Complete a personal draft.** Following the Literature Connection, have students write a personal draft on *any topic of their choice*. The writing may be inspired by *If the World Were a Village,* but it does not have to be. Writers should put their first drafts into folders for a time in order to create the "mental distance" needed to see their own writing as another reader might see it. They will revise and edit their work at the close of the unit, using skills gained through the five lessons that follow.

Coach's Corner

Students now have two rubrics: one for Ideas and one for Organization. Because these two traits work so closely together (it's the writer's ideas that determine the design, after all), keep both rubrics close at hand and encourage students to think about main idea and detail as they discuss organizational effectiveness.

Coach's Corner

As in the previous unit, we share writing samples in pairs—one strong, one problematic. Contrast is important in defining a trait, but it isn't necessary to represent the full range (1 and 6) of performance. As you share other writing examples, look for one that seems virtually ready to publish and one that needs significant revision.

Coach's Corner

We encourage you to use your own literary mentor texts to illustrate a host of things about organization: leads, conclusions, overall design, and so on. Don't forget to have students select and share examples of their own. And look beyond books—to letters, ads, films, whatever.

Organization

- Introduce Trait
- **Discussing Sample Papers**
- Making the Literature Connection
- Writing a Personal Draft
- Practice Trait
- Apply Trait

Discussing Sample Papers

Student Traitbook pages 47–49, 217

Student Rubric for Organization

Prior to presenting the introductory sample papers to students, read each aloud to yourself so you feel ready to share it aloud with students. You can also ask student volunteers to read the papers aloud, provided you give them time to rehearse. It is important that writers assess with their ears as well as their eyes. We suggest questions to ask with respect to each paper, but please raise additional questions of your own and encourage students to do that, too.

1. Have students turn to the Student Rubric for Organization in the *Student Traitbook*. Remind everyone that

   - a score of 6 indicates **strong performance**— but NOT perfection.
   - a score of 1 indicates a **beginning level of performance**— NOT failure.
   - the "river" divides writing in which **strengths outweigh problems** from writing that needs significant revision because **problems outweigh strengths.**

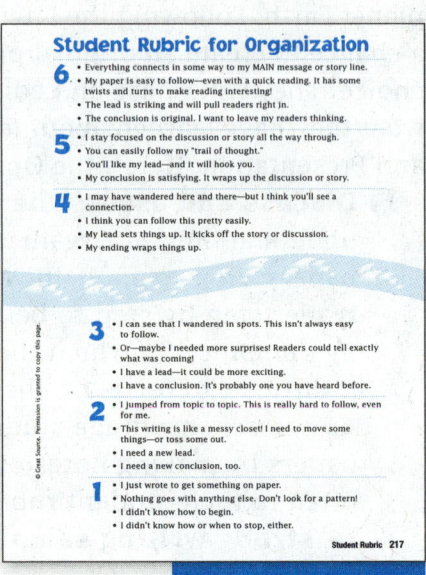

Student Traitbook p. 217

2. Encourage students to ask questions about anything that is unclear.
3. Explain that for this lesson, students will read and rate two pieces of writing: *How to Shop* and *Shopping by Computer*. They will work with partners, scoring each paper and defending their scores, using the language of the rubric.

Coach's Corner

Whether your students are working with partners or in writing circles, you may wish to think about mixing things up by having students work with someone new. Students gain considerable assessment skill from hearing a range of perspectives on writing.

Bringing everyone in... **Differentiated Instruction**

Ideas and Organization work together to ensure that the writer's main message takes center stage and that all supportive details are clearly connected to that message. Because these two traits are so closely aligned, it's easy to confuse them. However, you can explain the difference metaphorically, using anything that requires organization—such as a book store. Imagine the books themselves as the writer's ideas. Just piling them into a heap would make individual titles very hard to find. Some organizational designs are better than others, though. For example, if books were organized by color, or size, or date of publication, the result wouldn't be a whole lot better than putting them into a pile. Organizing them by content and genre, however—and then alphabetically within sections—makes any title simple to locate. And that's just how the right organizational design supports a writer's ideas.

Sample Paper 5: *How to Shop*

1. Read *How to Shop* aloud (or have a student read it), and as you read, tell students to think about these

    ### ❓ Key Questions . . .

    - Does the writer have a clear main message?
    - Does the writer stay focused on that message—or jump around?
    - Does the paper have a strong lead? Or does it just start in?
    - Do the details come in an order that makes the paper easy to follow?
    - Are ideas clearly connected to each other—and to the main message?
    - Does the writer use transitional words to build bridges, idea to idea?
    - As a reader, do I ever feel lost or confused? Do I need to reread?
    - Does the paper have a satisfying conclusion that effectively wraps up the discussion? Or does it just stop?

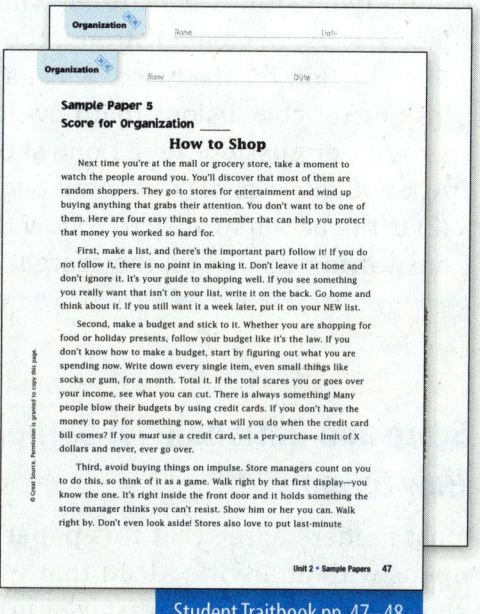

Student Traitbook pp. 47–48

Coach's Corner

Students sometimes struggle to identify the lead and conclusion. This can be tricky because there is no standard length for these features—some run only a sentence, others much more. Underlining the lead and conclusion is a good habit. You try it, too. Then compare your definition of a paper's lead and conclusion with that of your students. This will help them get a grip on these somewhat elusive features that writers need to know well.

Unit 2   77

Organization

Introduce Trait
Discussing Sample Papers

Coach's Corner

Remind students to first consider whether or not the paper "leaps the river" (strengths outweigh problems) before assigning a specific score.

2. Have students mark up the sample paper in any way they wish: underlining the lead or conclusion, or writing notes in the margins (remember, you can use sleeve protectors and dry erase markers for this).

3. Have students score the paper, 1 through 6, using the Student Rubric for Organization.

4. After scoring, have students discuss their scores and reasons with partners.

5. When partners finish talking, vote as a class (with a show of hands or by moving to corners) and tally scores. Tell students to
   - think about the key questions listed under Step 1 above.
   - state whether or not they think this paper leaps the river in Organization.
   - defend their scores using the Student Rubric for Organization.

> **Bringing everyone in...** *Differentiated Instruction*
>
> The lead and conclusion are like the "bookends" of writing. If those two features are strong, what comes between is usually (not always, of course) strong, too. That's because the lead sets the direction for the piece, while a strong ending usually reveals insights or conclusions that flow logically out of the preceding story or discussion. Here's one shortcut for scoring Organization. Ask two questions: (1) Are the beginning and ending both strong? (2) Is the paper so easy to follow that I never feel lost? If the answer to both is yes, the score is usually high.

Coach's Corner

Sample Paper 5 is a personal essay, an exploration of a topic from a personal perspective, based on both experience and observation. To succeed in this genre, the writer needs a clear message and evidence that he or she has learned something important to share with the reader. Are those things true of this piece?

Score and Rationale for Sample Paper 5: *How to Shop*

Most readers agree that this paper is **strong** in Organization. It opens with an inviting lead that will pull any reader who has ever shopped right into the discussion. The writer then sets up the rest of the paper beautifully by telling us that he will give us four strategies for saving money—and he follows through by presenting them clearly and in order, step by step. Each one clearly connects to the main idea: Don't be a random shopper. The concluding paragraph wraps things up effectively, echoing ideas presented in the lead without being repetitive. This paper would receive a **score of 6 in the trait of Organization.** It is also strong in both Ideas and Voice.

Sample Paper 6: *Shopping by Computer*

1. Answer any new questions about the Student Rubric for Organization.

2. Continue to have students work in pairs or in writing circles, giving them new partners if you wish.

3. Read *Shopping by Computer* aloud (or ask a student to read it) and as you read, tell students to think about these

   ### ❓ Key Questions . . .

   - *Does the writer have a clear main message?*
   - *Does the writer stay focused on that message—or jump around?*
   - *Does the paper have a strong lead? Or does it just start in?*
   - *Do the details come in an order that makes the paper easy to follow?*
   - *Are ideas clearly connected to each other—and to the main message?*
   - *Does the writer use transitional words to build bridges, idea to idea?*
   - *As a reader, do I ever feel lost or confused? Do I need to reread?*
   - *Does the paper have a satisfying conclusion that effectively wraps up the discussion? Or does it just stop?*

4. As before, have students underline the lead and conclusion, and write notes in the margins.

5. Have students score the paper, 1 through 6, referring to the Student Rubric for Organization.

6. After scoring, have students discuss the paper and the score with partners.

7. When partners finish talking, vote as a class (with a show of hands or by moving to corners) and tally scores. Tell students to

   - think about the key questions listed under Step 3 above.
   - state whether or not they think this paper leaps the river in Organization.
   - defend their scores using the Student Rubric for Organization.

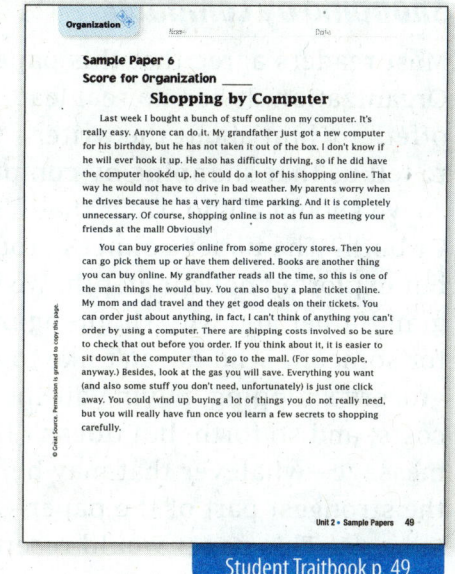

Student Traitbook p. 49

Coach's Corner

Shopping by Computer is an expository piece—a how-to paper. Such a piece should offer a full and clear explanation of a concept or process with examples that will help a reader perform a task or understand something better. Does this paper do that?

Coach's Corner

Even though students are working with partners or as part of a writing circle, they should vote individually. The purpose of their discussion is to raise questions and issues about writing that sharpen each person's thinking. If possible, pairs or groups should strive for agreement within a point, but each writer gets a vote.

Organization

Introduce Trait
Discussing Sample Papers

Coach's Corner

Shopping by Computer is a perfect example of how difficult it is to organize information until the main idea is clear. This writer has not fully come to grips with what she wants to say—and until that is clear, it is impossible to organize supporting details or examples.

Coach's Corner

As a reminder, there is no expectation that your scores will agree exactly with ours. However, in general, your students should agree with our assessments of which pieces tend to be strong and which tend to be problematic and in need of serious revision. What writers' can assess, they can revise. Seeing problems is the first step in solving them.

Score and Rationale for Sample Paper 6: *Shopping by Computer*

Most readers agree that this paper **needs significant revision** in Organization. It has no real lead; it just starts in. The title doesn't offer any hint about the writer's main point or thesis. Is she trying to tell us that shopping by computer is easy and convenient, so we should all do it? Or that it's SO easy we may overspend? Or both? The paper bounces around, raising numerous issues but exploring none in depth. We learn a little about the writer's grandfather and why shopping by computer might be advantageous for someone who doesn't like to drive. The writer also mentions grocery shopping, buying airline tickets, watching out for shipping costs, and so forth, but doesn't link any of these ideas to her main message—whatever that may be. The final two sentences form the strongest part of the paper—and might offer a good place to begin. This paper would receive a **score of 2 in the trait of Organization.**

Creating a Baseline Assessment

Have students revise *Shopping by Computer* (the weaker of the two introductory papers) working individually. Assess the *revised* drafts (using the Teacher Rubric for Organization) to provide baseline scores reflecting students' revision skills for this trait. Record those scores. At the close of the unit, following direct instruction in Organization, you can compare these early revisions to the revisions your students do on their own writing and on Sample Paper 7: *Going Organic*. This comparison will tell you how much students have grown as revisers with respect to the trait of Organization. (See **Extending the Lesson** for some suggestions on setting up this revision activity.)

Extending the Lesson

- Take one more look at *How to Shop.* Have students identify any specific strategies this writer uses that they might try in their own writing.

- Have students revise *Shopping by Computer* so that it has a strong central message, inviting lead, and effective conclusion. Students should work individually, but it is fine to do any planning with a partner or in a writing circle, discussing online shopping and its advantages or disadvantages. Encourage students to make notes and to use those notes as they write. A T-chart with pros on one side, cons on the other, can be enormously helpful. Expect planning and revising to fill one full class period.

- Have students check favorite books to see how authors they admire chose to begin or end their writing.

- Another way to approach revision is to focus on one portion of the writing, such as the lead or ending, and create multiple versions. This not only gives students practice, but helps them understand that there are literally thousands of ways to write anything. There's no magic formula for good organization. It grows out of what the writer has to say. For tips on many ways to write leads, see the book *A Writer Teaches Writing* by Donald Murray, Chapter 2.

- 🖱 Look up "leads" or "conclusions" online for numerous tips on writing both—and also for examples of effective leads or conclusions.

- 🖱 Start your own blog discussion on writing a good title, lead, or conclusion—or on any other topic relating to the trait of Organization.

Coach's Corner

Some of your writers may have strong opinions, pro or con, about online shopping. Instead of writing a how-to piece (which can seem very bland when it covers a topic the writer knows *too* well), writers might like to turn it into a persuasive essay, taking one side or the other, and presenting reasons people should or should not do the majority of their shopping online. Revising is more fun and more effective when the writer believes in what he or she is saying.

We know that a reader takes three to five seconds—or less—to decide to read an article. Professionals know how quickly they have to capture the reader, and the journalistic term "lead" comes from the need to lead the reader into the story.

—Donald M. Murray
A Writer Teaches Writing

Organization

- **Introduce Trait**
  - Discussing Sample Papers
  - **Making the Literature Connection**
  - Writing a Personal Draft
- **Practice Trait**
- **Apply Trait**

Coach's Corner

When choosing books to teach Organization, look for strong leads and/or conclusions, and transitions that clearly link ideas. Also look for a design that makes information easy to follow and remember. Share a variety of structures: chronological, question and answer, comparison-contrast, step-by-step, argument and rebuttal, and so on. Picture books are particularly wonderful for teaching design because you can share the whole book. But a book with multiple chapters or sections offers a chance to share a whole series of titles, leads, or conclusions. Sometimes you'll want to share a whole publication, and sometimes just one feature.

Coach's Corner

Be sure to check out Smith's note, "Teaching children about the global village," as well as his extensive list of sources in the back of the book.

Making the Literature Connection

RECOMMENDED BOOK — *If the World Were a Village: A Book about the World's People* by David J. Smith

Our emphasis in Unit 2 is on using design effectively to support the writer's message. For this lesson, we have chosen David J. Smith's *If the World Were a Village*, a nonfiction treatise for younger readers on "world-mindedness." The book is based on an intriguing premise: If the world were a village of 100 people, who would those people be? How many, for example, would speak particular languages, be members of a particular race, go to school, have enough food or water—or electricity? How much money would "rich" people have to spend? How much would the poorest have? An impressive array of information is neatly divided into sections introduced with guiding questions, then expanded and explained using well-researched statistics. The book will have students eager to offer their own guesses on a host of topics, and its effective design will show one way to present factual content without putting readers' heads on data overload.

Sharing the Text

1. Show students the book *If the World Were a Village* and share the title and author. Let students know it was published in 2002, but the information was updated in 2008.

2. Preview the book's main idea: *What if we thought of the entire world as a single, representative village of 100 people?* The author proposes that by learning about these villagers—their nationalities, languages, ages, religions, and resources—we would learn about the realities of our current world and perhaps be better prepared for many problems our future world will confront.

Bringing everyone in . . . — Differentiated Instruction

Most likely, your class includes students from diverse backgrounds. Ask students how many have experiences living in or traveling to another country. Their experiences, if they are comfortable sharing, can provide an important human context for the numbers presented in the book.

3. Let students know you are going to read several sections from this book—we would suggest the introduction, along with the sections on nationalities, age, food, schooling, money, and possessions as starting points. It is not necessary to read the sections in order. If you prefer, you can share the table of contents and have students choose the sections they would most like to hear. Each section presents a great deal of statistical information that could overwhelm readers if covered too quickly. So take time to linger.

4. Take a few moments to talk geography—locations of countries, languages spoken, landforms, rivers, climate zones—to get students ready for the world's eye view that is key to the book's premise.

5. Read the suggested sections, taking your time so your students aren't overwhelmed by statistics. Be sure everyone understands that the 100-person village is representative of the world. If you are familiar with the book, feel free to set up and share a favorite section of your own.

6. With your students' help, recount some of the numbers that seem most surprising, least surprising, unsettling, or startling.

7. Discuss what some of the numbers seem to be saying about work that needs to be done in the future.

8. Discuss the organization of each section: introductory or transitional sentences, usually followed by a framing question, followed by statistical data.

Coach's Corner

We encourage you to involve your students directly by inviting them to make guesses about some of the information you share. They are likely to be surprised by some of the data. You may also wish to check out the current total world population so that students can appreciate what percentage of people are represented by the number 100.

Coach's Corner

Do you teach social studies—or do you work closely with a colleague who does? If possible, use a globe or map or locate some specific countries or areas of the world mentioned in the book. And if possible, have someone on hand who can discuss the most populated and least populated portions of the globe, and the distribution of various resources that influence access to food, water, electricity, and so forth.

Coach's Corner

Much of the data in this book is presented in list form, with writing preceded by a number. If you have a document camera, share this method of formatting information, asking students to comment on its effectiveness. Is this a format they could use in their own writing? When might this format be useful?

Organization

Introduce Trait
Making the Literature Connection

Other Books You'll Love

Throughout this program, we rotate recommendations by genre:

- **Classic**—both traditional and contemporary
- **Poetry**—an individual poem or collection
- **Nonfiction**—picture book or longer text
- **Fiction**—picture book or longer text

Please keep in mind that your *own favorite books* are almost certain to include examples of strong organization: an enticing lead, smooth transitions, logical flow, design suited to the writer's purpose, and an appropriate, satisfying ending. Meanwhile, here are three more texts to explore:

1. **Poetry:** "The Panther" by Rainer Maria Rilke (in the book *The Selected Poetry of Rainer Maria Rilke*)

   Written during Rilke's years in Paris, "The Panther" represents a new lyrical style, perhaps influenced by the visual arts and Rilke's association with the sculptor Auguste Rodin. This poem offers a great opportunity for students to experience the way in which organization can allow an author to reveal information and inspire insight, bit by bit. It has several slightly different translations (look them up online by typing in "The Panther"), offering students the chance to select a favorite interpretation. This poem is a fine piece to use in choral reading.

2. **Fiction:** *Tangerine* by Edward Bloor

   Organized as main character Paul Fisher's journal entries, the structure provides an almost daily glimpse into Paul's family, school, and sports life. The story, set in the strange community of Tangerine, Florida, hovers around a dark secret involving Paul's mysterious eye injury—he must wear thick glasses—that is finally revealed in a dramatic conclusion. A great tale, part sports book, part American gothic, this book makes an excellent read-aloud or book to discuss as a class or within a reading group (perhaps online). Both the overall design and the powerful conclusion make it a good choice for the trait of Organization.

3. **Classic:** *The Westing Game* by Ellen Raskin

   Great mysteries require superior organization if the writer is to keep all of the characters and plot elements in line. This Newbery Medal winner manages to effectively juggle the events surrounding a large cast: 16 characters involved in solving the puzzle-mystery of Sam Westing's will. Humor, wordplay, and surprise twists will keep readers engaged.

Writing a Personal Draft

1. Let students know that they will now have a chance to create a personal piece of writing on a topic of their choice. Give them a few minutes to confer with a partner about possible writing topics. They can check their writing journals or choose a topic suggested by *If the World Were a Village*, such as:

   - An original story about members of a "world" village like the one described in the book (narrative fiction)
   - Experiencing life in another part of the world's village (informational, narrative)
   - Traveling outside one's home country (narrative, expository, poetry)
   - "Home"—what the concept means (narrative, expository, poetry)
   - The plight of hungry people—locally or in the world (informational, persuasive, expository)
   - Living without electricity or running water (informational, expository, narrative)
   - Statistical report on any topic—presenting data in a similar format (informational)
   - Life in the world village 1,000 years ago—or sometime in the future (imaginative)
   - Report on a country—language, geography, economy, religion—mentioned in *If the World Were a Village:* China, Brazil, Pakistan, Indonesia, and so on (informational, expository)
   - Biography of David J. Smith (informational)
   - Review of the book *If the World Were a Village* (response to literature, persuasive)

2. Give students 5–8 minutes to discuss topics. This vital component of prewriting helps many writers gain a strong sense of direction—and encourages them to think of topics that extend beyond our list.

3. You may wish to record some writing ideas for whole-class reference (from our list or from students' suggestions—or both), then offer individual coaching as needed. Remind writers that they may choose any topic that suits them—whether inspired by *If the World Were a Village* or not.

Organization

Introduce Trait
Discussing Sample Papers
Making the Literature Connection
Writing a Personal Draft

Practice Trait

Apply Trait

Coach's Corner
If your technical resources permit, offer students the option of presenting their information in a format that includes audio, video, PowerPoint, or a combination of all three.

Coach's Corner
This is an excellent time to model topic selection—by choosing one of your own. Even if you don't finish the piece, modeling how you decide what to write about and how you get started will provide invaluable help to your writers.

Unit 2   85

Organization

Introduce Trait
Writing a Personal Draft

4. We recommend providing about 5 minutes for prewriting and an additional 20–30 minutes for initial drafting (in addition to prewriting time), but please use your own judgment.

Bringing everyone in . . . **Differentiated Instruction**

Students are likely to need very different amounts of writing time, based on stamina and topic selection. Some may easily finish a rough draft in 20–30 minutes, but researched pieces or essays may take longer. Provide as much flexibility as possible by offering alternative activities for those who finish quickly and additional writing time for those who need it.

5. Remind students to double or triple space (even if they are composing on the computer) and to allow wide margins so there will be ample room for revision later.

Bringing everyone in . . . **Differentiated Instruction**

Students who need additional information through research will benefit by using this time to create a "skeleton" draft as they did in Lesson 1.4 (Unit 1), a lean framework of main points or questions that they hope to cover. Each point in the skeleton draft may be followed by four to eight lines of blank space. In that space, students can write questions they will attempt to answer through research—which might involve reading, surfing the web, interviewing people, and so on. Though sketchy, a skeleton draft IS a first draft—and represents a writing milestone. Remind students that they have from now until the end of this unit to gather information.

6. When students feel they have a finished their rough drafts, have them confer with partners or meet in writing circles of three or four, reading their writing aloud to listen for a strong lead; smooth, easy-to-follow organizational flow; and (if present yet) a satisfying conclusion. It is fine to make any changes that occur to them, but there will be time for more comprehensive revisions later, following direct instruction in Organization.

7. This draft should now be placed in students' writing folders. They may revise or expand it at any time—but will have a chance for thorough review and revision before it is assessed.

Coach's Corner

Once students have finished their rough drafts, use the Teacher Rubrics for Ideas and Organization to create baseline scores for these drafts. Later, after you ask students to revise, you will base grades on your assessment of their *revised drafts*—as well as on the extent and quality of the revision. Also score Conventions and Presentation, if you wish. This will help you compare the rough draft to the later edited version.

Coach's Corner

Planning is hard for many students. Assist them by doing a little "backwards planning" as a class. Begin with the due date for the final draft. Then, determine how many days you have between now and then. Let's say a writer plans to answer three research questions. By planning backwards, he or she can set a personal "due date" for each one. This makes a big project manageable.

Notes

UNIT 2
Organization

Introduce Trait

Practice Trait

	Shifting the Spotlight..................89	• Preview pages 89–125
50 min.	**Lesson 2.1**..................90 Organization's a Joke	• Explore order and timing • Focus on "set-up" and "punch line"
50 min.	**Lesson 2.2**..................96 Avoid the Wandering Spotlight	• Keep the spotlight on the main idea • Create an original focused draft
50 min.	**Lesson 2.3**..................103 Staying Connected	• Recognize transitions • Revise to eliminate transition overload
50 min.	**Lesson 2.4**..................110 Putting the Puzzle Together	• Review the basics of organization • Write an organized piece
50 min.	**Conventions and Presentation**..................116 Paragraphs: The Building Blocks of Writing Information on the Level	• Organize copy into paragraphs • Create multi-level information trails

Apply Trait

Shifting the Spotlight

Your students have had a chance to begin defining Organization in their own minds by assessing and discussing two sample papers: *How to Shop* and *Shopping by Computer*. They have also seen and heard Organization in action through your sharing of the book *If the World Were a Village*.

It is time to shift the spotlight, giving students a chance to practice specific skills they can use in revising writing—their own or anyone's—for Organization. Several important features of Organization are covered in the focused lessons that follow. Once students have completed *all* of the focused lessons, they will apply what they have learned by (1) revising *someone else's* writing and (2) revising and editing *their own* writing. Follow these two steps:

1. **Complete Lessons 2.1 through 2.4.** Allow two days for each lesson. Through these lessons, students will learn strategies for
   - putting ideas in order, loosely adapting the set-up to punch line structure of a joke.
   - keeping the spotlight focused on the main message.
   - using transitions to clearly connect ideas—but remembering not to overdo it.
   - combining all organizational elements to create an easy-to-follow draft.

2. **Link Organization to Conventions and Presentation.** Allow a full class period for each part (one for Level 1, one for Level 2). Students will learn that Conventions and Presentation supports strong Organization through: (1) good paragraphing that effectively "chunks" information (Conventions) and (2) creation of multiple informational trails that let readers access a message on several levels (Presentation).

Students have seen the format of the Ideas poster. Encourage them to continue thinking like readers by looking at the Organization poster. Again, various things the writer does appear on the left. Tell students to think about the impact of each item on the reader and to see if they can fill in the blanks on the right (*So the READER . . .*). After you have discussed all four elements, display the actual poster so that students can refer to it often. Don't forget to add ideas your writers think of on their own, both now and throughout the year.

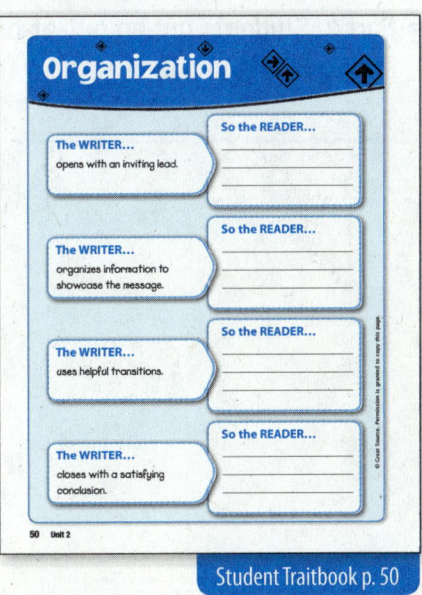

Student Traitbook p. 50

Organization

Introduce Trait

Practice Trait
- Lesson 2.1
- Lesson 2.2
- Lesson 2.3
- Lesson 2.4
- Conventions & Presentation

Apply Trait

LESSON **2.1**

Organization's a Joke

Student Traitbook pages 51–55

Not really. Organization is serious business. But then, so are jokes. Actually, they take some highly skilled writing. A joke needs to be set up well and expanded just enough so the listener "gets it." Most important, it has to end with an effective punch line, delivered in a timely fashion. When it comes to jokes, order and timing are everything. What's more, most jokes are fairly short, so the writer has to accomplish everything in just a few lines. Small wonder that the humble joke makes such a good model for effective organization.

Objectives

Students will
- recognize the importance of good sequencing.
- identify sequencing problems in an example passage.
- organize an out-of-order piece to make the sequencing logical and effective.
- work on two important elements in organizational design: set-up (lead) and punch line (conclusion).

Time Frame

Allow 50 minutes for this lesson. It can be broken into two parts.
- Part 1: Students discuss sequencing and work on identifying some sequencing problems.
- Part 2: Students put an out-of-order piece in order, then write a strong lead and conclusion for the piece.

90   Unit 2

Setting Up the Lesson

The purpose of this lesson is to help students understand the importance of good sequencing—and also to use the three parts of a joke (set-up, expansion, punch line) as a rough model for organizing longer pieces of writing.

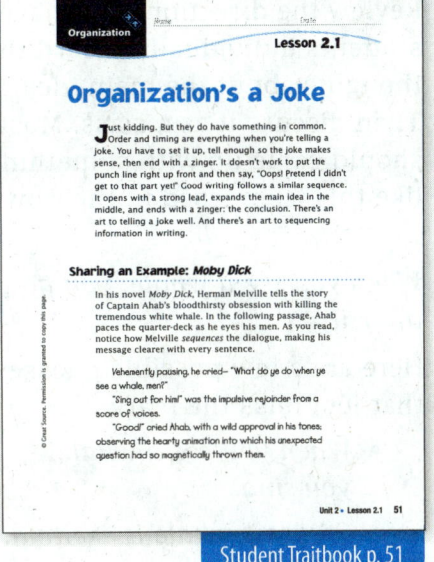

Student Traitbook p. 51

Once students have read the unit and lesson introductions, introduce this lesson with a joke or two. If you have a funny, appropriate joke to share with your students, you can begin with that. You can also have student volunteers share pre-approved jokes. As another option, check your media center for an age-appropriate collection. There are literally dozens of joke books for children and pre-teens. Share two or three and have students "dissect" the jokes by identifying the parts (set-up, expansion, punch line).

Most jokes follow a pattern:

- an opening line that sets up the joke
- another line or two (sometimes less) that expand the opening or gives the listener any information needed to "get" the joke
- the closing line or zinger—the point of the joke

Talk about the link between the organizational structure of a joke and that of most writing—whether the writer is creating a paragraph, report, essay, or story. Though we're over-simplifying here for the sake of comparison, there's a lot to be learned about good organization by studying the skeletal structure of a joke:

- the opening line = the lead in a longer piece
- the expansion = expanding paragraphs that develop an idea
- the punch line = the conclusion

Teaching the Lesson

Sharing an Example: *Moby Dick*

Review the directions. Then, share the passage from *Moby Dick* aloud or have a student (after rehearsing) share it. As they listen, students should focus on the sequence of events, thinking about how each line makes the picture of what is happening just a little bit more clear in their minds—almost like watching details gradually added to a painting.

Coach's Corner

The jokes you choose to share do NOT have to be hilarious. This isn't stand-up comedy, so feel no pressure! Even if students consider them "pretty dumb," you can use them to illustrate the general format—the pattern most jokes follow. This is helpful because jokes are small, and it's easy for young writers to remember the three key parts: set-up, expansion, punch line.

Unit 2   91

Organization

Practice Trait
Lesson 2.1

Coach's Corner

This passage is clearly not intended to be humorous. Yet it does have the three elements you and your students earlier identified as central to a good joke. Can students find them in the passage? NOTE: If they can, that's a sign that the passage has a good lead and conclusion—which it does.

Coach's Corner

It's very tempting to look back while doing this. But that misses the point. The idea is to see whether or not readers see and hear problems without comparing this draft to the original. So—no peeking.

Coach's Corner

Many students likely found this an easy task—but it's possible some found it extremely challenging. The key is logic. The full meaning of each sentence in this passage depends heavily on the sentence that comes before it. That's why pulling even one sentence out, or putting even one out of order, disrupts the "sense" of the piece.

Quick Reflection

Review the directions and have students individually record their thoughts about the main idea. Then discuss it as a class. Most should come up with something like this (expressed in their own words):

When you see a whale, you go after it.

Here are a few possible guesses that just miss the mark:

- *When you see a whale, you sing.*
- *Seeing a whale is exciting.*
- *Whales can sink boats.*

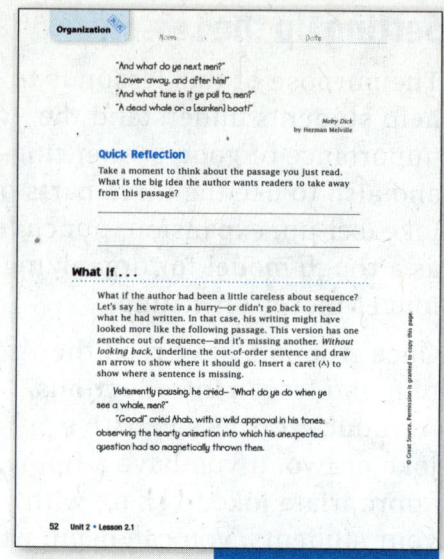

Student Traitbook p. 52

What If . . .

Review the directions to be sure everyone understands the task. Have students work individually, and remind them NOT to look back at the original passage as they work (have them cover it with a piece of paper)—just to trust their eyes and ears to help them identify some problems with sequencing. They should notice

- an out-of-order sentence (underline it and draw an arrow to show where it should go).
- a place where a sentence is missing (mark it with a caret).

IMPORTANT: Move on to the next section—**Quick Reflection**—*before* you discuss students' response to the passage and how easy (or difficult) it was for them to spot the problems.

Quick Reflection

Review the directions and give students time to mark their responses. Discuss them as a class. Then return to the **What If . . .** passage and talk about the problems you find there:

- The **second sentence** is missing; it makes no sense for Ahab to cry "good" without an answer to his question about what to do when a whale is spotted.
- The **sixth and seventh sentences** are out of order. The question about what tune to sing has to be asked before the men answer.

Students' marked up passage should look something like this:

> Vehemently pausing, he cried— "What do ye do when ye see a whale, men?"
> ∧ "Good!" cried Ahab, with a wild approval in his tones; observing the hearty animation into which his unexpected question had so magnetically thrown them.
> "And what do ye next, men?"
> "Lower away, and after him!"
> ↑"A dead whale or a [sunken] boat!"
> ⤶"And what tune is it ye pull to, men?"

Playing with Order

Remind students that you have been talking about logical sequencing. In this part of the lesson, they'll challenge themselves by putting nine sentences in an order that tells a logical and interesting story.

Review the directions, making sure everyone understands the task. Students should

- read all nine sentences before marking anything, just to get a sense of the story.
- work with a partner or in a writing circle to put the nine sentences in order.

Allow about 8 to 10 minutes for this activity.

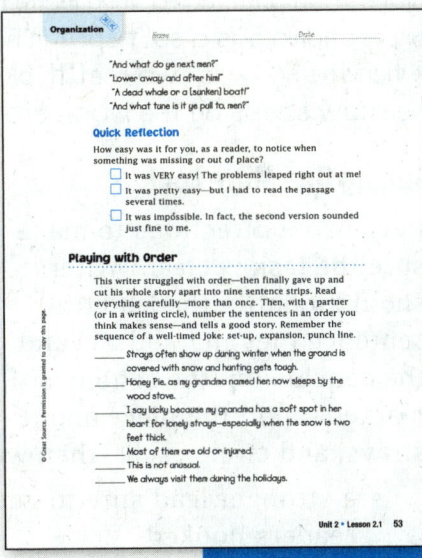

Student Traitbook p. 53

Coach's Corner

Note: If you are dividing this lesson into two parts, **Day 2 begins here.**

Bringing everyone in . . . Differentiated Instruction

This task will be far easier for many students if they can play with the sentences like puzzle pieces. Consider copying them and cutting them into sentence strips, then giving one set to each writing circle. This will encourage students to read and talk as they work, and to try out various arrangements, looking for the one that works best.

Organization

Practice Trait
Lesson 2.1

Once students finish, have several teams discuss the process they used to put the sentences in order (they should mention reading aloud and noticing which sentences flowed naturally and logically out of the others). Then, ask a volunteer team to read their story aloud. Though some variations are possible, we think the following is the most logical:

(1) My grandparents live on an 80-acre farm just outside Spokane. (2) We always visit them during the holidays. (3) Last year, about a week before our visit, a stray calico took up residence inside the horse barn. (4) This is not unusual. (5) Strays often show up during winter when the ground is covered with snow and hunting gets tough. (6) Most of them are old or injured. (7) This particular stray was no more than a kitten—a very lucky one at that. (8) I say lucky because my grandma has a soft spot in her heart for lonely strays—especially when the snow is two feet thick. (9) Honey Pie, as my grandma named her, now sleeps by the wood stove.

Taking One More Look

Review the directions to make sure the task is clear. Writers should identify the lead (the sentence they marked #1) and the conclusion (the sentence they marked #9) in the piece about strays, and circle each—then write

- a stronger lead sure to get readers hooked.
- a stronger conclusion that leaves a lingering thought or image in the reader's mind.

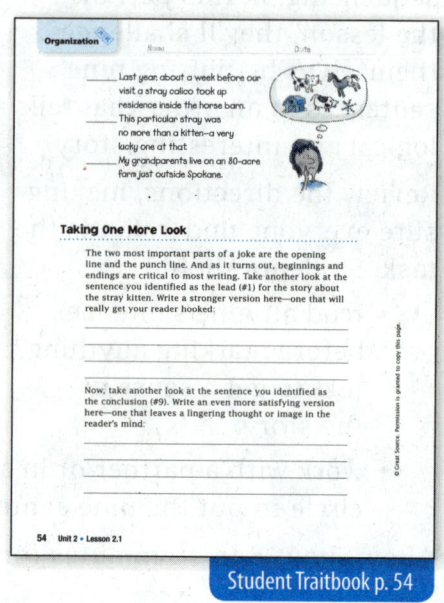

Student Traitbook p. 54

Allow about 6–8 minutes for this activity. Writers who finish early should be encouraged to write more than one lead or ending.

Share and Compare

Give students time to share their writing with partners or in writing circles. If time permits, some may wish to share with the class as a whole.

Here are our revisions—just for purposes of illustration (you may share them if you wish—but students will prefer to see yours):

New Lead: When the holidays come, I can't wait to head for my grandparents' 80-acre farm. Something surprising always happens.

New Conclusion: Honey Pie, as my grandma named her, now sleeps by the wood stove—and as she dreams, sometimes I imagine I can see her mouth curve into a smile.

Coach's Corner

Have writers work alone for this part of the lesson. Part of the point is that many leads or conclusions are possible—it's important for writers to see and hear some variety in the final result. Remind them that it is fine to change any details they wish. For example, they may or may not mention the town of Spokane in the lead.

Coach's Corner

This is a very good time for you to model your own writing by sharing a lead and/or conclusion of your own. If you wrote more than one, share them all—and have students identify the one they like best. They will love comparing your versions with their own.

A Writer's Questions

Pieces of writing can almost always be put together in a number of ways—so playing with design makes very good sense. Sometimes, for example, the conclusion in a rough draft winds up as the lead in the final draft. Design changes with the writer's thinking.

Putting It to the Test

Actually, there is a little trick even professional writers use—and it's very simple. They read everything aloud—as they write, not just at the end. It isn't necessary to reread with every single sentence, but doing so two or three times while writing helps ensure that the flow is logical and orderly. (And as we'll see in Unit 5, it's also a wonderful way to test sentence fluency.)

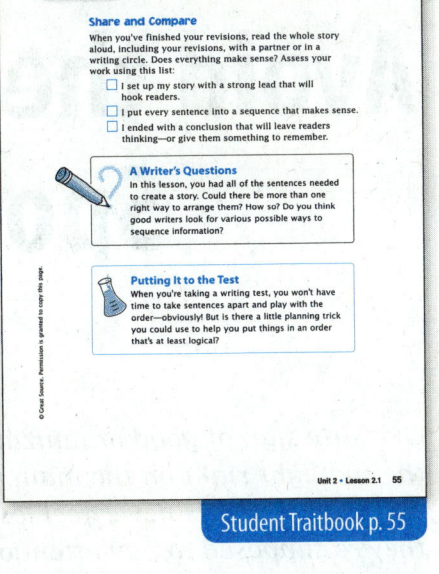

Student Traitbook p. 55

Extending the Lesson

- Have writers, working in writing circles, create an original piece of writing that runs from five to eight sentences, writing it as a list. Make sure writers review and revise so the order is logical enough to recapture. Then have them cut their writing into strips, shuffle them, clip the set with a paper clip, and pass it to another group. How quickly can groups re-order one another's writing? And—here's the real test—can the writers themselves re-order it correctly?

- Look through any newspaper. How strong are the leads and conclusions? Does what comes between lead and conclusion work well to expand information and inform readers?

- If you have not done so previously, look up leads and conclusions online for a host of examples and tips on how to write both.

- Create an online writing "puzzle" based on an original piece in which sentences are out of order. See how many different ways readers think of to arrange it.

The perfect ending . . . is like the curtain line in a theatrical comedy. We are in the middle of a scene (we think) when suddenly one of the actors says something funny, or outrageous, or epigrammatic, and the lights go out. We are startled to find the scene over, and then delighted by the aptness of how it ended.

—William Zinsser
On Writing Well

Unit 2   95

Organization

- Introduce Trait
- **Practice Trait**
  - Lesson 2.1
  - **Lesson 2.2**
  - Lesson 2.3
  - Lesson 2.4
  - Conventions & Presentation
- Apply Trait

LESSON **2.2**

Avoid the Wandering Spotlight

Student Traitbook pages 56–60

One sure sign of good organization is the writer's ability to keep the spotlight right on the main message. When a writer does this diligently, readers never feel lost and never wonder what it is they're supposed to pay attention to. Like a skillful director, a good writer minimizes distractions so that key lines will be heard and remembered.

Objectives

Students will

- read a writing example to determine the main idea.
- revise the example to improve the focus.
- choose a topic and create an original, focused piece of writing.
- share personal writing and offer feedback to others.

Time Frame

Allow 50 minutes for this lesson. It can be broken into two parts.

- Part 1: Students read and assess an example of writing, then revise it to improve the focus.
- Part 2: Students choose a topic and create an original piece of writing, making sure all details stay focused on the main message.

96 Unit 2

Setting Up the Lesson

Share the introduction to Lesson 2.2.

Then illustrate the "wandering spotlight" using any powerful flashlight. (Unless your room can be partially darkened, you'll need one with a very bright light.) Have students imagine you are going to make a video right there in your classroom. They need to guess what the main message is. (Let's say it's writing instruction—but you can choose your own subject.) Move your light from spot to spot, focusing at first on things that have a clear connection to your main message: resource books, posters, writing materials, computers (if you have them), a stack of papers on your desk, your own writing, trade books—or the students themselves!

Encourage students to guess what your message or theme might be. They should be able to do this fairly quickly. Once they catch on, get a little more random, shifting the light to things that have NO clear connection to your writing theme: a plant, the window sill, your shoes, the door. Insist, at first, that these are all connected to writing instruction. As your students protest, confess that they're right—there really is no obvious connection. You've made your point: When the spotlight wanders and the connection is unclear, viewers—or readers—become confused. Tell students to keep this wandering spotlight in mind as they review the writing example in this lesson—and as they do some writing of their own.

Teaching the Lesson

Sharing an Example: "Night Sky"

Review the directions for this first section. Then, give students time to read the piece called "Night Sky," quietly, to themselves. Remind them to think about the spotlight as they read. Is it focused on one clear main idea—or does it bounce around?

Student Traitbook p. 56

Coach's Corner

Connections in writing are not always obvious. Sometimes a subtopic seems totally unrelated to the subject at hand until the writer explains the connection. But writers have a choice to make. Either they need to make the connection crystal clear—or let that idea go for the time being.

Coach's Corner

Do you and your writers ever do freewriting as a way of searching for topics? If so, you might point out that in freewriting, randomness works to the writer's benefit. The difference is that freewriting is not (usually) done for an audience; it's done for the writer, as a way of exploring his or her own thinking. In such writing, one topic suggests another—and another. This stream-of-conscious thinking is an outstanding way of identifying potential writing topics (and building fluency).

Coach's Corner

If you prefer, you can share the text aloud—or have a student volunteer who has rehearsed it do so. It is helpful to many students to hear the text as well as see it.

Unit 2   97

Organization

Practice Trait
Lesson 2.2

Bringing everyone in... Differentiated Instruction

It is important for students to understand what constellations are and to know that Orion, Cassiopeia, Taurus, and Draco are constellations named after ancient mythological characters. This knowledge will help them make sense of the passage. You may also wish to ask how many are familiar with O. Henry's story "The Gift of the Magi." This story is *not* central to the writer's main idea (stargazing); however, it is more difficult to judge that without knowing what the writer is talking about.

Reflection

Give students time to record their reflections. Make sure they fill in the blank to show what they think the writer's main idea might be. Wait until after students have talked to partners or writing circle teams (in the next step, **Share and Compare**) to discuss the passage as a class.

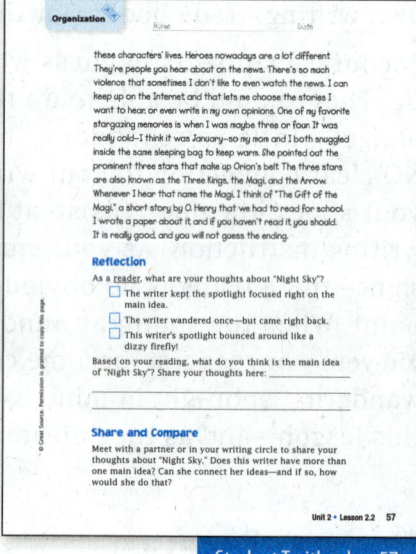
Student Traitbook p. 57

Share and Compare

Give students time to discuss their impressions of the passage with a partner or in a writing circle. Most should agree that

- the writer's spotlight bounced around.
- the main idea is that it's rewarding to watch the stars—because there's more to the night sky than one might think at first.

Coach's Corner

Could the writer of "Night Sky" connect her wanderings to her main idea? Probably. But she would have some work to do. The focus might have to shift from stargazing to kinds of heroes.

Refocusing

Review the directions to make sure everyone understands the task: They will read "Night Sky" again, pencil in hand, drawing a line through anything that wanders and might best be saved for another time.

When they finish, have students assess their own work. Point out that if they have cut enough, the piece will need a new ending. Encourage students to write a conclusion of a sentence or two.

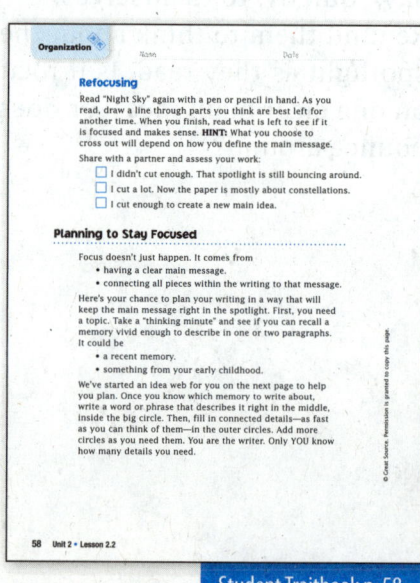
Student Traitbook p. 58

98   Unit 2

Here, for the sake of comparison, is our version. Your students' revision need not match ours:

Night Sky

Ever since I can remember, my mother has told me about the constellations and their stories. Orion, Cassiopeia, Taurus, and Draco have always been my favorites. When I see them now, I don't just see the stars; I see the tragedy or the heroism behind these characters' lives. ~~Heroes nowadays are a lot different. They're people you hear about on the news. There's so much violence that sometimes I don't like to even watch the news. I can keep up on the Internet, and that lets me choose the stories I want to hear, or even write in my own opinions.~~ One of my favorite stargazing memories is when I was maybe three or four. It was really cold—I think it was January—so my mom and I both snuggled inside the same sleeping bag to keep warm. She pointed out the prominent three stars that make up Orion's belt. The three stars are also known as the Three Kings, the Magi, and the Arrow. ~~Whenever I hear that name the Magi, I think of "The Gift of the Magi," a short story by O. Henry that we had to read for school. I wrote a paper about it, and if you haven't read it, you should. It is really good, and you will not guess the ending.~~ [NEW SENTENCE] Because my mom knows so much about astronomy *and* astrology, I've learned to "read" the night sky, too.

Coach's Corner

Students may be wondering whether what they're cutting is "filler," as they did in Lesson 1.4 (Unit 1). Not exactly. Filler is—as its name implies—writing intended to take up space. It's fluff. Filler is usually when a writer says the same thing multiple ways just to fill the page. In this case, the writer has many worthwhile things to say; the question is, can they go together in one piece.

Organization

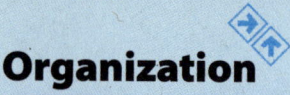

Practice Trait
Lesson 2.2

Bringing everyone in... Differentiated Instruction

Creative writers may wish to shift the focus of the piece so that it's about heroes instead of constellations. This is harder, but it can certainly be done and offers a challenge for those who find this task too easy. Shifting focus will, of course, influence what writers cut—and in addition, they'll probably need to rewrite or add details to smooth the flow.

Coach's Corner

Note: If you divide this lesson into two parts, **Day 2 begins here.**

Coach's Corner

There's a little trick to webbing, and it is to work quickly—not shutting any ideas out, but just letting them flow. A writer does not have to use every idea recorded in the web, but if it isn't there, it may be forgotten. So encourage writers to work rapidly and to add as many circles as they need to record details.

Coach's Corner

Let writers transition from prewriting to drafting at their own pace. Not everyone has to begin writing at the same time. Some writers can envision a whole piece within seconds of beginning to prewrite, while others need much more planning time to feel comfortable. Moving too quickly into drafting causes unprepared writers to slam on the brakes ("writer's block" often means "I wasn't ready"), so let them control the timing.

Planning to Stay Focused

Remind students of your discussion on staying focused—keeping the spotlight on the main idea. Let them know they will have a chance to be in control of that spotlight today—as writers.

Share the directions to make sure everyone understands the task. They should

- take a "thinking minute" to come up with a topic—any vivid memory.
- use the idea web to make a plan, recording all of the details that come to mind.

Creating a Focused Draft

Share the directions to make sure they are clear. Notice that we have suggested several different genres. Writers should feel free to write whatever they envision—character portrait, poem, story, essay, or whatever.

Allow 10–15 minutes for writing—or more, if you can. Writers should use their own paper for this.

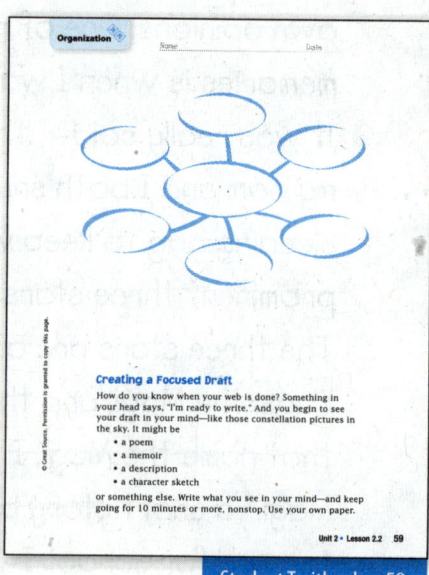

Student Traitbook p. 59

Share and Compare

When writers have had time to finish at least a very rough draft, have them meet with partners or in writing circles to share their memories—and offer one another feedback. They will need scratch paper or index cards for this. As each writer shares, listeners should record what they hear as the main message on paper or a card, fold it, and hand it to the writer. Writers should wait to look at the cards until everyone has finished reading aloud.

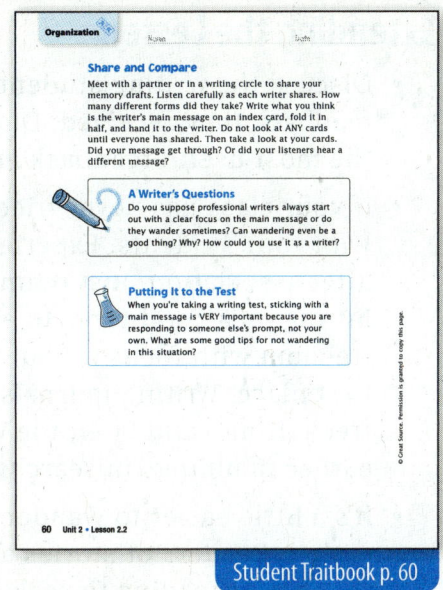

Student Traitbook p. 60

A Writer's Questions

Most professional writers *do* begin with a clear focus. But virtually all would agree that the focus often shifts in the course of writing—and that sometimes is a very good thing. Because writing is *thinking on paper*, we actually teach ourselves about a subject *as we write* about it—the very act of writing leads to insight. Writing also triggers memory—and association. Put all of these together, and you have a good recipe for a continually evolving (and shifting) message. But the writer always needs to have *some* vision in his or her head.

Putting It to the Test

In on-demand writing, the writer's ability to stick relentlessly to the topic at hand is often used as one measure of "success." So wandering is NOT a good idea. Period. One of the best ways to stay focused is to reread the prompt periodically while writing—and also to read over your own writing. Here's another tip: It isn't "wandering" IF you can make the connection clear. So, if you think of a terrific point to make, just be sure you can connect it in some way to your main message.

Organization
Practice Trait
Lesson 2.2

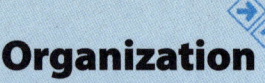

Extending the Lesson

- Discuss the writing students did for this lesson—as well as the feedback they received. Did any of it surprise them? What was the most useful feedback anyone got?

- If your class has never tried freewriting, try it. Freewrite *with* your students. Experience the joy of making association after association, just roaming with your writing—possibly hitting on a good topic to explore further. It's hard to compare freedom with focus if you've never experienced freedom in the first place. Writing journals make an excellent place to record freewriting—and later, the writer can go back and look through earlier ramblings in search of a possible topic.

- It's a little easier to wander in narrative writing and get by with it. Readers of stories are forgiving because—usually—they aren't reading to seek information as much as to be entertained. So look through nonfiction writing for examples of highly focused passages—and encourage your students to look, too.

- Watch any short documentary film with your students. Talk about how the writer and the director use a combination of words (in the voice-over script) and video to maintain continuity. Is it possible to identify a thesis—a strong main message? How do film makers continually reinforce this message throughout the production without being redundant?

LESSON 2.3

Staying Connected

Student Traitbook pages 61–66

Organization

Introduce Trait
Practice Trait
Lesson 2.1
Lesson 2.2
Lesson 2.3
Lesson 2.4
Conventions & Presentation
Apply Trait

When connections are clear, a piece of writing has coherence (an important feature of organization). Good writers use words and phrases called transitions to build bridges of thought from one idea to the next. As students will discover in this lesson, transitions can show changes in time or place, indicate cause and effect, set up a conclusion or example—and much more. They're extraordinarily helpful when used well—but when overused or misused, they can create turmoil for readers.

Objectives

Students will
- discuss the role of transitions in an example from literature.
- review a list of transitions to determine the kinds of connections they show.
- identify transitions in a second writing selection.
- revise a writing example by adding missing transitions and deleting or replacing any that do not work.

Time Frame

Allow 50 minutes for this lesson. It can be broken into two parts.

- Part 1: Students discuss the role of transitions in one example from literature, review a list of transition words, and look for transitions in a second example.
- Part 2: Students revise a piece by adding, deleting, or changing transitions.

Unit 2 103

Organization

Practice Trait
Lesson 2.3

Coach's Corner

This brainstorming is likely to start out slowly—unless your students are very familiar with transitions and have studied them before. Be patient. Gradually add a few of your own to the list, and soon it will expand. Later in the lesson, when students look at our list of transition words, they will be pleased to see listed there many that they thought of on their own.

Setting Up the Lesson

Share the introduction to Lesson 2.3.

In order to use transitions effectively, students need to understand what they are and how they function. Everyone uses transitions in speaking, of course—but not everyone is familiar with the term *transition*. For purposes of this lesson encourage students to think of it as a chain, linking one idea to another. Then see how many transitions your students know already and create a brainstormed list. Start students off with a few examples (use a document camera to project our examples below)—and keep adding:

meanwhile

next week

however

although

similarly

nearby

104 Unit 2

Teaching the Lesson

Sharing an Example: *Leaving Home*

Have students CLOSE THEIR BOOKS. This is important for this first part of the lesson because you are going to read aloud, and you do NOT want students to follow along with their eyes. That spoils the activity. Instead, you want students to just *listen* for the transitions they hear.

Read aloud the passage from Sneed Collard's book with plenty of expression. When you finish, have students

- identify any transitions they noticed. (Make a list of these on the board.)
- read the passage to themselves, paying special attention to the transitions in blue print.
- compare their impressions from listening (listed on the board) to what they see on the page (the blue words in the passage).

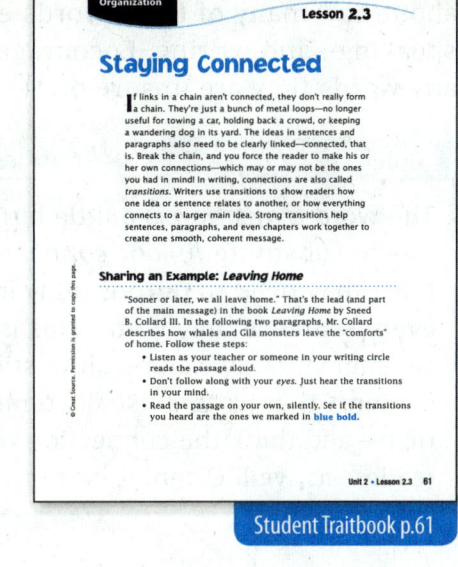

Student Traitbook p.61

Words That Connect

In this part of the lesson, students review a list of transitional words and phrases. Be sure students understand that this list is NOT intended to be complete. There are literally thousands of transitional expressions that do not appear on this list. The list is intended to expand students' understanding of transitions by

- giving them a range of examples.
- showing the *kinds* of connections transitions can make.

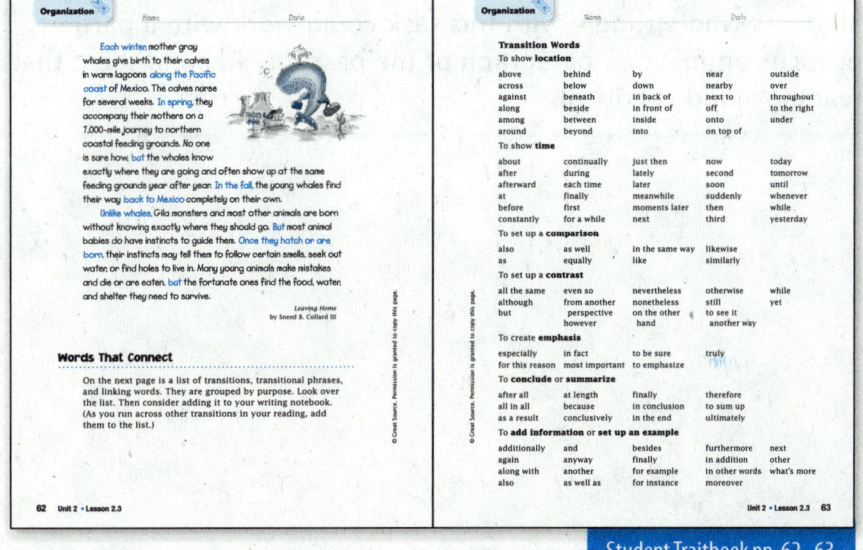

Student Traitbook pp. 62–63

Coach's Corner

How different would the Collard passage be if he had left out ALL of the transitional words and phrases? Have a volunteer try to read it aloud without any of the words in blue (a little spontaneous editing is required for this). What changes for readers or listeners?

Coach's Corner

If possible, make a copy of the Transition Words list for each student and have them slip it into their writing notebook for easy reference.

Unit 2   105

Organization

Practice Trait
Lesson 2.3

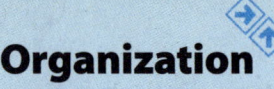

Have students read through the list with a partner and talk about how many of these words each of them uses in his or her speaking—and writing. Encourage students to ask for definitions of any words they are unsure of.

Bringing everyone in... Differentiated Instruction

The word *transition* is a little intimidating for some students. Feel free to substitute *link* or *connection*. Also, some students may think they need to purposefully insert a transitional phrase into every sentence they write. This is unnecessary—and as they will see momentarily, can result in stilted, unnatural writing. Remind students that writers usually omit transitions when they are in a rush—and think the connection that's obvious to them is obvious to readers as well. Often, it isn't.

Hunting for Connections

In this part of the lesson, students must identify the writer's transitions. They are not highlighted or otherwise marked.

Review the directions. Then have students go through the passage about training a dog, sentence by sentence, to look and listen for transitional words or phrases. Students should highlight (or otherwise mark) all they find.

Student Traitbook p. 64

Coach's Corner

Remind students that the writer may use transitions that do not appear on the Transition Words list. Those are only examples, not a complete collection. Students may refer to the list, certainly. But the key to identifying transitions is to listen for connections—which may occur at the beginning, middle, or end of a sentence.

Bringing everyone in... Differentiated Instruction

Students who struggle with this task could work with a partner or focus on just one paragraph of the passage. Remind them that reading aloud is critical.

Share and Compare

Give students time to compare transitions with partners or in a writing circle. Most should have found several. Have students coach you as you go through the passage and highlight the transitional expressions. Talk about the kinds of connections they show.

Following is the passage with transitional phrases highlighted. Did your students find any we missed?

> **As soon as** I adopted Jake from the shelter, I knew I had to train him to do two things: curb the drooling and sit. Jake was a droopy-mouth kind of dog, **however**, so my first goal was hopeless. I decided to focus on the second.
>
> **Before** we started sitting lessons, I had to hit the Web to figure out what to do. A food reward seemed like a safe bet, **as well as** plenty of time and patience.
>
> **The next day,** I armed myself with doggie treats and took Jake out to our neighborhood park for his first lesson. It was a beautiful day for some dog training. I removed his leash, wiped the drool from my hand, and **then** pushed down on his rear end.
>
> "Sit," I commanded. "Sit, boy."
>
> **Suddenly,** Jake spotted a squirrel. He let out a hearty bark and took off running, with me crying out behind him.
>
> **An hour later,** I was a sweating, exhausted mess. Jake had happily chased three squirrels, a Frisbee, and a flock of birds, but we were no closer to him actually sitting. **In the end,** I decided to skip the part where the treats were a reward and instead used them as a lure. **In other words,** I had to bribe my dog to sit.
>
> Hey, don't laugh. It worked.

> **Coach's Corner**
>
> It is not important for students to identify every single last transition in the passage. What matters is that they understand how transitions work—to connect ideas—and that they can identify many of them as they read or write.

> **Bringing everyone in . . .** **Differentiated Instruction**
>
> If some of your students have difficulty identifying any transitions, provide an additional mini lesson on this, using another passage rich with transitional expressions, but shorter than this one. Go through the passage one sentence at a time and have students identify the transitions as you go. Ask questions: *When did this happen? Where did this happen? Is this the same or different? What words tell you that?*

Organization

Practice Trait
Lesson 2.3

Coach's Corner

Note: If you are dividing this lesson into two parts, **Day 2 begins here.**

Making a Chain of Thought

To close this lesson, students will revise a piece by

- inserting needed missing transitions.
- crossing out transitions that are not needed.
- replacing transitions that do not make sense with transitions that clearly, logically connect ideas.

Review the directions and make sure the task is clear. Have students work individually on this portion of the lesson. Give them

- about 5 minutes to simply read the piece and figure out the meaning.
- about 10 minutes more to revise.

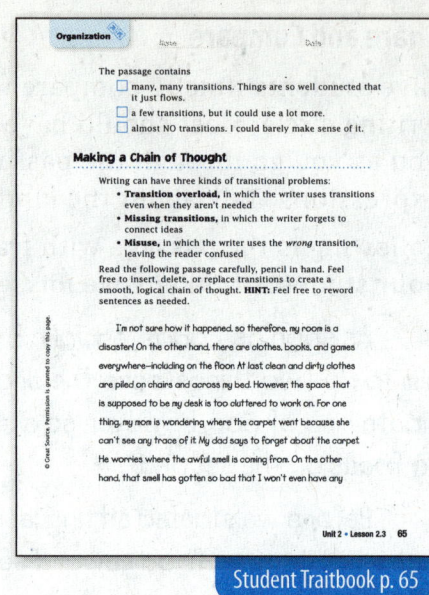

Student Traitbook p. 65

Bringing everyone in . . . | **Differentiated Instruction**

Some students struggle with this activity because they try to be too literal: take one word out, put one word in. There's a better, easier way. The first step is to figure out what the writer is trying to say. Once that is clear, it is much easier to figure out which transitions work—and which could go or be replaced. Also, it's better to "go light" on transitions than to overdo.

Share and Compare

When students finish revising, give them

- about 5 minutes to compare results with a partner—or in writing circles.
- an additional 5 minutes to coach you as you revise together.

Following is one suggested revision (your students' responses do NOT need to match ours), with new transitions shown in **blue**:

Coach's Corner

The best way to tell whether transitions work is to read the result aloud. We did that—and thought ours made sense. Did your writers do the same?

I'm not sure how it happened. ~~so therefore,~~ **but** my room is a disaster! ~~On the other hand,~~ There are clothes, books, and games everywhere–including on the floor. ~~At last,~~ Clean and dirty clothes are piled on chairs and across my bed. ~~However,~~ **Even** the space that is supposed to be my desk is too cluttered to work on. ~~For one thing,~~ **At this point,** my mom is wondering where the carpet went because she ~~can't~~ can **no longer** see any trace of it. My dad, **on the other hand,**

108 Unit 2

says to forget about the carpet. He worries where the awful smell is coming from. ~~On the other hand,~~ That smell has gotten so bad, in fact, that I won't even have any friends come over. ~~For example,~~ This very week I'm going to clean my room before I lose all contact with my friends, lose all my valuable stuff, or am grounded by my parents. ~~Nevertheless,~~ Worst of all, I could be cited for a fire hazard, and then, ~~at long last,~~ I will have even more trouble!

A Writer's Question

Have students look at any recent piece of their writing and highlight the transitions. Did they use any? Are they logical? Remember, the transitions "champ" isn't necessarily the writer who uses the *most* transitions—but the one who uses them well.

Putting It to the Test

All genres require a wide range of transitions, of course, but just the same, certain genres tend to rely on some kinds of transitions. For example, transitions indicating location are especially important to description. Those indicating time are important in narrative. Which categories might be especially important to a persuasive essay? How about advertising copy? Or explanation of steps in solving a math problem?

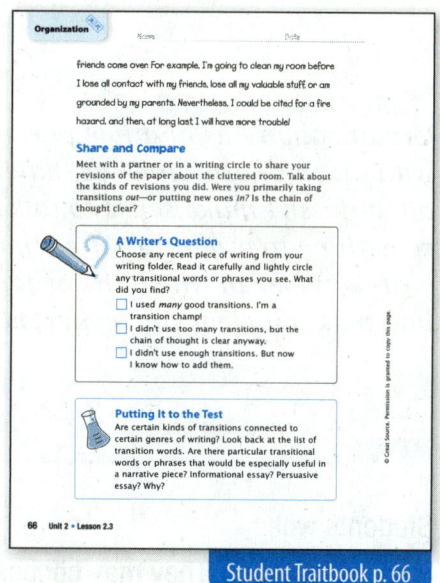

Student Traitbook p. 66

Extending the Lesson

- Have students try writing a piece without using *any* transitions. It's harder than it sounds! Have them give you a topic and see how far you can get without using a single transition. Caution students to keep an eye out and let you know if you "slip up." This is actually one of the best ways to learn just how important transitions are.

- Look and listen for transitions in literature you share. Add to your Transition Words list, using what your students find, and keep that list posted where they can refer to it, or make copies they can slip into a binder.

- Research transitions online. You will find many more lists—as well as tips for using transitions well and not overdoing it.

- Create a podcast on the effective use of transitions, answering such writers' questions as *How important are transitions?* or *How do I know when I've overdone it?*

Organization

Introduce Trait
Practice Trait
Lesson 2.1
Lesson 2.2
Lesson 2.3
Lesson 2.4
Conventions & Presentation
Apply Trait

LESSON **2.4**

Putting the Puzzle Together

Student Traitbook pages 67–71

Organization has multiple parts—and so does this lesson. We begin with an emphasis on Ideas, having students write a thesis. After all, it doesn't make sense to talk about organization until there is something to organize. After that first important step, writers will write a paper in which the organization fully supports the message and makes it clear and coherent for readers.

Objectives

Students will

- choose a topic. (They may choose our focus topic, the stonefish, or any topic of their own.)
- write a thesis sentence to give the topic focus and direction.
- do any necessary research to uncover intriguing details relating to the topic of choice.
- select the most striking details (from our list or their own).
- write an effective lead and conclusion for the piece.
- create an original paragraph about the stonefish—or another topic of choice.

Time Frame

Allow **50 + minutes** for this lesson. We recommend dividing it into **two or three** parts.

- Part 1: Students choose a topic, write a thesis, and assemble or narrow a list of details. (**Note:** Add one additional day for research if writers prefer to choose their own topics.)
- Part 2: Students write a strong lead and begin a draft on the stonefish (or any topic of their choice). Writers who finish will also draft an effective conclusion.

Setting Up the Lesson

Note: This lesson is set up, like most lessons in the Grade 7 program, to span two days. You ONLY need to add a third day up front (prior to Parts 1 and 2) if writers prefer to choose their own topics. We support this approach fully—but it is imperative to allow additional time for personal research on those topics.

This is a lesson about putting all organizational strategies together. Begin by asking students to list the keys to strong organization. (Have them do this *without looking* at their rubrics or checklists—or the first page of Lesson 2.4.) If you like, also make a list of potential organizational problems.

Once students finish, share the introduction to Lesson 2.4.

Finally, give students a few minutes to meet in writing circles to decide whether they will

- write about the stonefish (researched details are provided),
- write about a topic the whole writing circle chooses and combine research efforts, OR
- choose individual topics so that each writer does his or her own research.

Teaching the Lesson

What's My Thesis?

Review the directions. Then, give students time to go through the list of 20 details about stonefish—or their own list of details (on any topic). Do some details seem to go together to support a particular message? Have students write that message as a thesis in the space provided.

You may also wish to have students share this thesis with a partner to be sure it is focused and narrow enough to write about in two or three short paragraphs.

Student Traitbook p. 67

Student Traitbook p. 68

Coach's Corner

Writers may find this decision easier if they know just a little about the stonefish—including what it looks like. It's a highly venomous and fascinating creature with a face only fans will admire. Share a photo from online or from a source in your media center. Here are some book suggestions:

Stonefish: Needles of Pain
   by Meish Goldish

Fish (Eyewitness series)
   by Steve Parker

Seashore (Eyewitness series)
   by Steve Parker

Eye Wonder: Ocean
   by Mary Ling and Sue Thornton

Coach's Corner

Note: Please keep in mind that it is important for students to finish any necessary research **before** beginning the actual lesson: **What's My Thesis?** However, if all students are writing about the stonefish, additional time is not needed.

Unit 2 111

Organization

Practice Trait
Lesson 2.4

Coach's Corner

These choices (keep or toss) are critical because they determine whether a piece of writing will be a rehash of things the reader already knows—or a fascinating glimpse into a new world. Writers should be cautious about overloading themselves, too. Better to go into a draft armed with four knockout details than a hundred generalities.

Keep It or Toss It?

Share the directions. Then give students time to review our list (20 details on the stonefish) or their own list of details—with their thesis statement in mind. Details that are helpful and interesting are keepers and should be starred. Encourage students to omit any details that

- do not fit the thesis,
- are too general,
- will not interest readers, or
- are common knowledge.

Allow about 5–6 minutes for students to review their lists and make choices.

Student Traitbook p. 69

Bringing everyone in . . . | Differentiated Instruction

Even writers who choose to write on the stonefish may well uncover some new details by reading or doing online research. They may add those details in the next part of the lesson. If a writer is unsure whether a detail is a keeper or a throw-away, ask this: If you were reading about the stonefish (or whatever), would *you* find this interesting? If so, your reader likely will, too!

Add to the List

Share the directions. Then give writers 3–4 minutes to add any new, intriguing details to the existing list. Writers do not *have* to add anything, but a writer who digs up even one intriguing detail we missed takes ownership of the writing.

Coach's Corner

Experienced writers continue to do research right up until the moment a piece is finished—or goes into production. It is never too late to add a fascinating detail.

Grab the Reader's Attention...

Writers will spend some time writing just the lead. That's all they need to work on in this portion of the lesson. Share the directions to be sure everyone understands the task. Then have writers

- look through their list of details to find something so intriguing that readers won't be able to resist it.
- spend 3–5 minutes writing a terrific lead.

...and Keep Ideas Flowing!

Share the directions—without interrupting writers' train of thought too much! Let them know how much time (approximately) they have to keep the flow going. Then turn them loose. Remind writers that they do not need to use every detail, and there is no minimum length. They should keep writing until the piece feels finished— then end with a dynamite conclusion (this calls for another terrific detail).

Student Traitbook p. 70

Bringing everyone in... — Differentiated Instruction

Are you using this time to write with your students? If so, good for you because it is one of the best ways to motivate them—and to model how a writer looks at work. It is easier, for example, to ask for relative quiet (writing workshop is almost never *totally* quiet) if YOU are busy writing, too. It also gives you a sense of how much time is realistic for each task. And when you share your writing, students can compare their leads, conclusions, choice of detail— and so on. A hundred things you don't have time to say you can "say" by sharing your writing.

Coach's Corner

Note: If you are dividing this lesson into parts, **Day 2 or Day 3 begins here.** (This is Day 3 IF you allowed an extra day right up front for research.)

Coach's Corner

We offer one example of an ineffective lead: *This will be a report about the venomous stonefish.* Your writers can probably think of other less than stellar leads. Have them do that. Make a list. Knowing how NOT to begin can be a wonderful kick starter.

Coach's Corner

Remember to give writers a two-minute warning when writing time is nearly over. This allows them to conclude the current thought— and either write a quick ending or write themselves a note about where to pick up next time.

Unit 2   113

Organization

Practice Trait
Lesson 2.4

Coach's Corner

Remind students that there's an art to good commentary. It's the writer, not the listener, who is responsible for revision or next steps. So criticisms are not really useful—and can even be counterproductive. What is helpful, however, is the listener's honest response: *I could just picture . . . It made me feel . . . Here's what I saw in my mind . . . I'm still wondering . . . .*

Sharing Your Efforts

Review the directions and give students time to share with partners or in writing circles, your preference. If you are a writer too, by all means join one of the groups. Remind listeners to listen carefully for

- a strong lead.
- an easy-to-follow sequence.
- a spotlight that stays on the main idea (so it stands out).
- smooth transitions that link ideas or sentences.
- an ending that wraps things up in a satisfying way.

Bringing everyone in . . .   *Differentiated Instruction*

Volunteers who wish to share with the whole class should be encouraged to do that. A writer often discovers with a partner, or in a small writing circle, that listeners respond well to his or her work—and that gives the writer courage to share with a bigger audience. Writers will also be encouraged by your willingness to share your own writing (and process) aloud.

A Writer's Questions

Have writers actually write down their very next steps and then share them by making a class list. You will likely discover two things: (1) your writers are better planners than even *they* realized, and (2) writers are at different places in the process and have very different ideas about what to do next. Terrific. That kind of diversity is one indicator of a successful workshop.

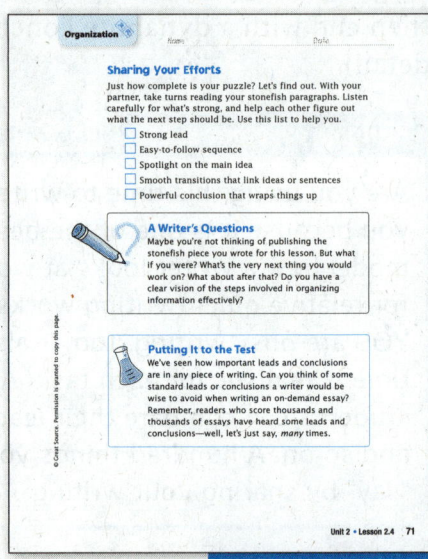
Student Traitbook p. 71

Putting It to the Test

Why is this so important? Because the beginning and ending of any piece get the most attention from readers. If they're clichés, if the writer sounds bored by the topic, scores are likely to drop. You may already have brainstormed some leads to avoid. Do the same with conclusions. Then ask for volunteers to read just their leads or conclusions aloud. Which ones are especially effective? Do they sound different from everyone else's?

Extending the Lesson

- Wait two days and then have students complete or revise their paragraphs on the stonefish (or whatever their topic may be). Encourage additional research in the interim.

- Spend time discussing titles, encouraging writers to come up with good titles for the pieces they have written. Explain that a good title, like a strong lead, gives the reader a sense of direction. Share titles your writers come up with.

- Read your own paragraph on the stonefish—or any topic on which you may have written recently. Invite students to assess it for the trait of Organization. Does it have all of the essentials in place? What did *you* think was your main organizational strength? Do your students agree?

- Expand students' feedback skills by offering online help for other students in your school who may be struggling with organization. Feature a different topic each week: writing a thesis, choosing details, keeping the spotlight on your message, writing a lead, using transitions, writing a conclusion, and so on.

- Look up "leads" or "conclusions" online for numerous tips and activities you and your students will find helpful.

Keep in mind that the person to write for is yourself. Tell the story that you most desperately want to read.

—Susan Isaacs
Actor and
Best Selling Author

Organization

- Introduce Trait
- **Practice Trait**
  - Lesson 2.1
  - Lesson 2.2
  - Lesson 2.3
  - Lesson 2.4
  - **Conventions & Presentation**
- Apply Trait

Conventions and Presentation

Student Traitbook pages 72–80

In this lesson, students explore two ways of making Organization stronger. In the first part of the lesson (Level 1), students "chunk" a list of details into paragraphs—deciding for themselves how many paragraphs there should be. In the second part of the lesson (Level 2), students explore ways writers present information on multiple levels, then create three to five multi-level pages for a nonfiction picture book.

Objectives

Editing Level 1: Conventions

Students will understand that

- paragraphs "chunk" information, thereby making it easier to follow.
- there's more to the definition of a paragraph than "sentences on the same topic."
- writers need to decide when to begin a new paragraph.

Editing Level 2: Presentation

Students will understand that

- in many publications, information is presented on several levels.
- having choices makes information accessible to more readers.
- ordering information in levels takes knowledge of one's audience.

Time Frame

This lesson has two parts. Allow a full class period for each.

- Part 1: Students explore paragraphs and reorder information into paragraphs.
- Part 2: Students explore multi-level presentation of information and create an example for a nonfiction picture book.

Editing Level 1: Conventions
Paragraphs: The Building Blocks of Writing

Setting Up the Lesson

Editing Level 1 focuses on Conventions. In this part of the lesson, students will explore the nature and structure of paragraphs, then reorder factual information on vultures into an unspecified number of paragraphs (whatever number they feel is right).

Begin with these steps:

- Have students read the lesson introduction, or read it aloud.
- Explain that in this lesson, you will be reviewing paragraphs.
- Have students define the word *paragraph* as they think of it now. Record some of their thoughts and notice if this initial definition expands or changes throughout this lesson.
- How many of your writers consider themselves skilled at deciding when to begin a new paragraph? How many struggle with it? Share your own experiences with this, too

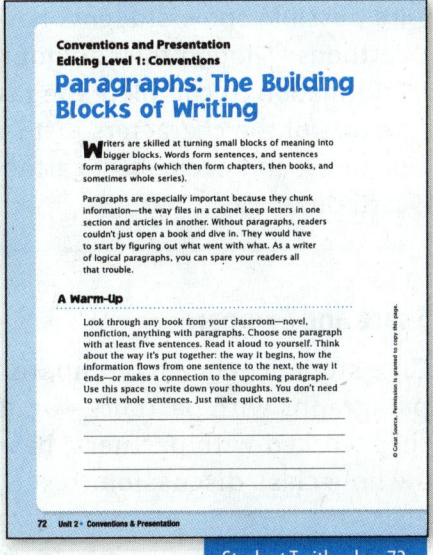
Student Traitbook p. 72

Teaching the Lesson

A Warm-Up

Review the directions for the **first part** of the warm-up, calling for students to explore paragraphs of five sentences or more, noticing how they are structured, and following the general flow of information. Students should look for the following as they make notes:

- The **opening sentence:** Does it signal the topic of the paragraph or get readers engaged in some other way?
- The **general flow** of other sentences: Are they connected well? Do they focus on a key message?

Coach's Corner

Paragraphs can be tricky. Many of us were taught to begin a new paragraph when we "changed topics." But in fact, even a tiny shift (same topic but different sub-topic) can signal the need for a new paragraph. Moreover, some paragraphs don't have a topic all to themselves; they serve as transitions between two other "content" paragraphs. And paragraphs are also used to mark speech.

Coach's Corner

Note: Students can explore any sort of book for **A Warm-Up**: textbooks, trade books, novels, or nonfiction. Anything written in paragraphs will do, but you may wish to **preview books prior to the lesson** in order to have a range of strong examples.

Coach's Corner

Students are likely to notice that paragraphs are structured in multiple ways. Also, some writers use many more paragraphs than they might need. They do this deliberately to create open space. Why would they do this?

Unit 2   117

Conventions & Presentation

Practice Trait
Editing Level 1: Conventions

- The **closing sentence** of the paragraph: Does it offer a closing thought—*or* does it lead the reader into the paragraph coming up?

Take a few minutes to discuss your students' findings and answer questions they may have. Did they discover anything that might influence their personal definitions of a paragraph?

When you finish your discussion, go on to the **second part** of the warm-up, which asks students to put five sentences about Road Runner cartoons into a paragraph. Give students about 3–4 minutes to complete this task, working with partners.

> **Bringing everyone in . . .** Differentiated Instruction
>
> It's possible some students have not heard of the Road Runner cartoons. Though they do not really need this background information to complete the task, you may want to show them a picture of the characters just for fun. You can find information, pictures, and even short cartoons online under "Road Runner cartoons."

Share and Compare

Give students time to compare paragraphs with partners—or, if they worked with partners, have a whole class discussion to see if everyone agreed.

Here are the five sentences reordered into paragraph format, numbered for easy reference:

> (1) Have you ever seen a Road Runner and Coyote cartoon? (2) If you have, then you know that Coyote spends each cartoon trying to capture the Road Runner. (3) He invents or sends away for all sorts of exotic machines and methods to catch Road Runner, but they never work. (4) Road Runner always outsmarts Coyote in the end and runs away. (5) Beep-beep!

Student Traitbook p. 73

Coach's Corner

We indented this example paragraph, and most students think of indentation as THE way to mark a paragraph. It's one way, but not the only one. Look carefully at your examples, and you're likely to see that many first paragraphs run "flush left," or aligned with the left margin, not indented. Publishers sometimes call this "block style." Paragraphs can also be set apart by spacing—vertical spacing, horizontal, or both. Some paragraphs are part of a list and may be bulleted or numbered. And the paragraph you're reading right now is boxed. Paragraphs come in many styles and shapes.

Things to notice:

- The **first sentence** is a question—and it effectively pulls the reader in.
- The **next three** sentences answer this question, so they're definitely connected to the main idea: what happens in a Road Runner cartoon.
- The **next-to-last** sentence is really the wrap-up, the definitive answer to the question.
- The **final** statement—Beep-beep!—is just for fun, an echo of Road Runner's "theme song."

12 Sentences = X Paragraphs

In this section, students have a more challenging task: ordering 12 sentences into an unspecified number of paragraphs (hence the "X"). Students may decide to make just one paragraph—or more than one. **NOTE:** There may be more than one effective way to order this information. The key is finding "chunks" that help readers make their way through the information as easily as possible.

Review the directions to make sure students understand the task. Then have them work with partners or in writing circles to

- read all 12 sentences, getting the scope of the information on vultures.
- put the sentences in an order that makes sense—also grouping them in paragraphs.
- continue to read aloud as they work in case they change their minds about the order.

> **Coach's Corner**
>
> Encourage students to think about chunking information in a way that will make it easy for readers to understand and remember. The best way to do this, of course, is by being a reader yourself.

> **Bringing everyone in . . .** **Differentiated Instruction**
>
> Many students have an easier time with tasks of this type if the sentences are cut into separate strips so that they can manipulate them. You may wish to consider this option. It is almost impossible to "see" a document in list form, especially when things are out of order.

Share and Compare

Have volunteers share their vulture paragraphs with the rest of the class—and discuss any disagreements about the arrangement of information. You are likely to see and hear some variety and that is just fine. What matters is coming up with an arrangement that makes sense. On the next page is one possibility.

Conventions & Presentation

Practice Trait
Editing Level 1: Conventions

Coach's Corner

For additional information on vultures, see: ecoworldly.com or lifestyle.iloveindia.com

Vultures are nature's scavengers and clean the environment by eating dead animals. It may sound gross, but they are able to eat and process animal carcasses in any condition, including diseased, rotting, or badly decayed. They are not bashful eaters, either. Vultures have been known to eat up to 20 percent of their own body weight during one feeding.

Luckily, considering their diet, vultures are naturally equipped with acids in their digestive systems able to eliminate disease bacteria like anthrax and cholera. As natural garbage disposals, vultures help keep many of these diseases from spreading to other animals and even humans.

It's probably also fortunate that vultures don't have a great sense of smell. But they do have amazing eyesight. In fact, a flying vulture can spot a three-foot dead animal from four miles away!

Vultures have a few other strange behaviors and abilities to go along with their interesting food preferences. If a vulture needs to cool or even disinfect itself after feeding on rotten flesh, it urinates on its legs. Unless you are a vulture, do not try this at home.

NOTE: What do your writers think about our question? Is there only one right answer to the equation?

A Writer's Questions

Did any of your writers choose to put all 12 sentences into one big paragraph? That's one possible decision—after all, they're all about vultures. The problem is, this writer has several slightly different things to say about vultures:

- They're scavengers who eat grotesque amounts of food.
- They have specialized digestive systems.
- They have (luckily) a terrible sense of smell despite remarkable vision.
- They have, to say the least, unusual habits.

By dividing those separate issues (all relating to vultures) into separate paragraphs, the writer makes it easier for a reader to focus on one detail at a time—and remember it.

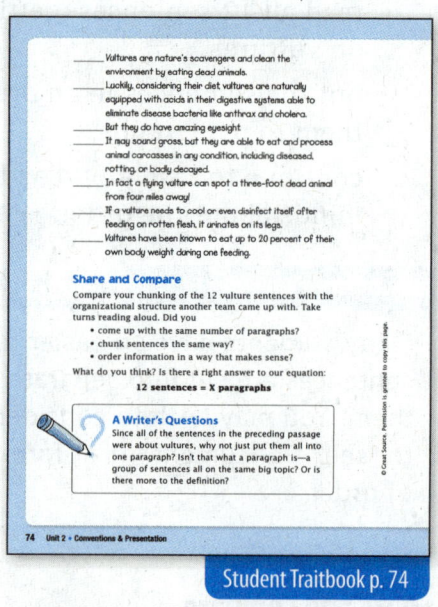

Student Traitbook p. 74

Editing Level 2: Presentation
Information on the Level

Setting Up the Lesson

Editing Level 2 focuses on Presentation—making information eye catching and accessible. This level of editing is the final step in preparing a document for publication. One of the big questions a document designer needs to ask is, "Where will the reader's eye go first?" In some cases, as we'll see in this lesson, that depends very much on the kind of information the reader is looking for. It's quite possible to create various informational trails—on various levels.

Begin with these steps:

- Share the introduction to the lesson.
- Remind students that Presentation is all about making information both eye appealing and accessible, so that readers can quickly find what they're looking for.
- Spend some time reviewing the three primary levels of information (some books have other informational trails, as well):
  - the **Big Idea** level (big print, main ideas, key facts)
  - the **Graphic** level (photos, drawings, charts, other illustrations)
  - the **In-depth** level (smaller print, detailed or special interest information)
- Tell students to imagine themselves opening a textbook at random. What would their eyes settle on first? Next?
- Discuss some of the possibilities. Some readers look at titles and subtitles. Some start right in reading. Others look at pictures or graphics—or anything in boldface print. Designers know about these options and use them to make various informational trails.

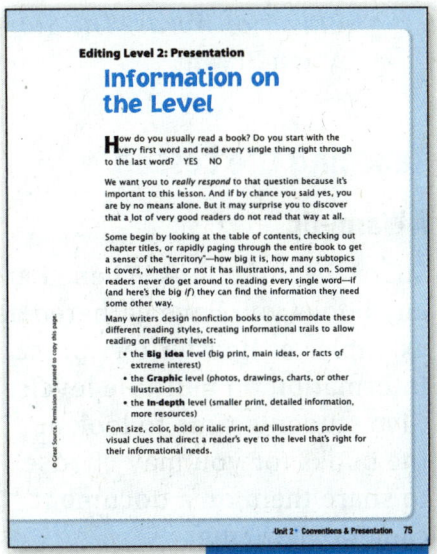
Student Traitbook p. 75

Conventions & Presentation

Practice Trait
Editing Level 2: Presentation

Conventions & Presentation

Practice Trait
Editing Level 2: Presentation

Coach's Corner

A few of our recommended books are intended primarily for younger readers. But remember, this lesson is not about content per se; it's about *format*. We have suggested nonfiction picture books for this **Warm-Up** because this is the kind of text your writers will be creating at the end of the lesson.

NOTE: To facilitate **A Warm-Up** (see below), you will need examples of books that offer varied informational trails. Many textbooks do this. The book you are holding in your hands does this, too! We also recommend any of the following books:

- *Animals Hibernating* by Pamela Hickman
- *Leaving Home* by Sneed B. Collard III (and other books by this author)
- *Surprising Sharks* by Nicola Davies
- *Name That Style: All About Isms in Art* by Bob Raczka (and other books by this author)
- *Oh, Rats!* by Albert Marrin
- *The Story of Salt* by Mark Kurlansky
- *A River of Words: The Story of William Carlos Williams* by Jen Bryant

Teaching the Lesson

A Warm-Up

Share the directions. Then share any books you have gathered as examples of how writers present information on multiple levels. Give students time to look at the books (or you may choose to share them on a document camera), noticing

- the different levels of information and how they are formatted.
- use of presentation devices such as bullets, numbers, boxes, colors, and so on.
- additional informational trails we did not mention—such as bios or lists of resources.

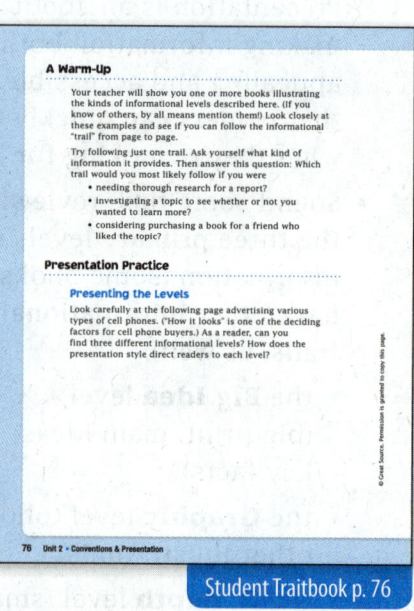

Student Traitbook p. 76

The point is to see that information is not just presented in sentences or paragraphs, all in the same size and style of font. Some information appears in italics or bold, in a different or larger font, boxed or shaped in interesting ways, and so on.

Discuss the kinds of informational trails that would be most useful for:

- Research (**In-depth** level)
- Investigating a topic (**Big Idea** level)
- Considering purchase of a book (all levels)

Coach's Corner

Your students may notice that creating different informational trails not only makes certain types of information (such as names or key facts) easy to find, but also tends to make pages more visually interesting. Of course, designers have to be careful. Too many different trails—photos here, maps there, bulleted lists, boxes, boldfaced definitions—can create chaos instead of ready access. Good design is an art.

122 Unit 2

Presentation Practice

Presenting the Levels

In this portion of the lesson, students have a chance to critique an informational page on cell phones. Share the directions. Then give students time to:

1. Review the example ad for cell phones.

2. Talk with a partner (or members of a writing circle) about what they like or what could be improved.

3. Discuss the four questions that follow the cell phone ad page.

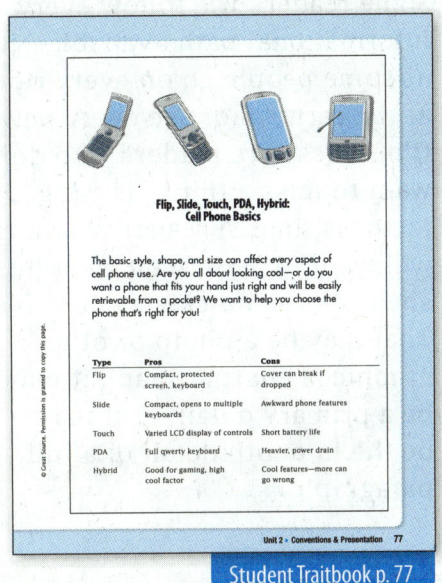

Student Traitbook p. 77

Discuss their responses as a class. Here are a few of the things students may notice:

- The phones in the pictures are not labeled.

- Though five types of phones are described in the chart, only four are pictured.

- The paragraph introduction sets up a contrast between "cool" phones and those that "fit your hand." But it's hard to tell which are which.

- This ad may be most useful to people who already know a lot about cell phones—though it does prepare a potential buyer to ask questions.

- The ad as a whole is not very visually appealing. Will people who hadn't previously thought of getting a new cell phone look at it?

- On the positive side, the various informational levels are easy to spot and use.

- The fonts are readable—though not especially dramatic.

- The designer makes good use of space. Things aren't crowded together.

Coach's Corner

Students may notice some things we missed—or we may have listed one or two things they did not notice. Either way, coach them to do a thorough review and to identify things they might do differently if they were designing this ad. Is this piece ready to go to press? We vote no, but what do your students think?

Unit 2   123

Conventions & Presentation

Practice Trait
Editing Level 2: Presentation

A Writer's Questions

Some readers *will* follow every informational path available—just as some people go on every ride at the carnival or see every new film. These are readers who don't want to miss a thing. The big factor is time. A reader in a hurry will want to zero in on what he or she needs as quickly as possible. That may be a photo or other graphic (a chart or map), it may be a primary detail, or it may be the in-depth detail of a full paragraph.

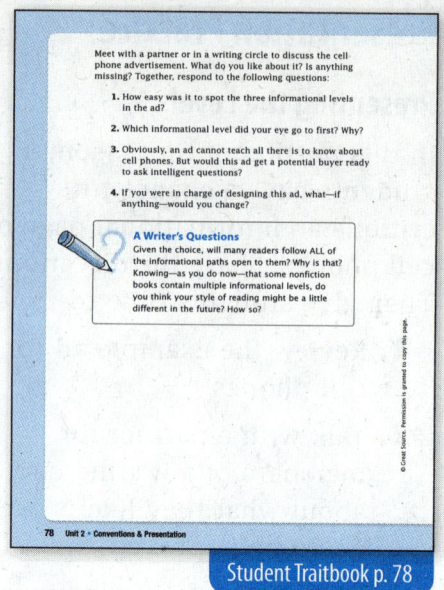

Student Traitbook p. 78

Coach's Corner

Encourage students to choose a topic fairly quickly. It should be one that members of the group know well so they will not need to do much, if any, research.

Presentation Matters

In this part of the lesson, students will work with partners or in writing circles to write and design a portion of a nonfiction picture book on a topic of their choice. They can divide the work to make it manageable, and they do NOT need to complete full illustrations. They can do rough sketches or describe the illustrations they would like to see an artist create.

Review the directions and tell students to read through them carefully.

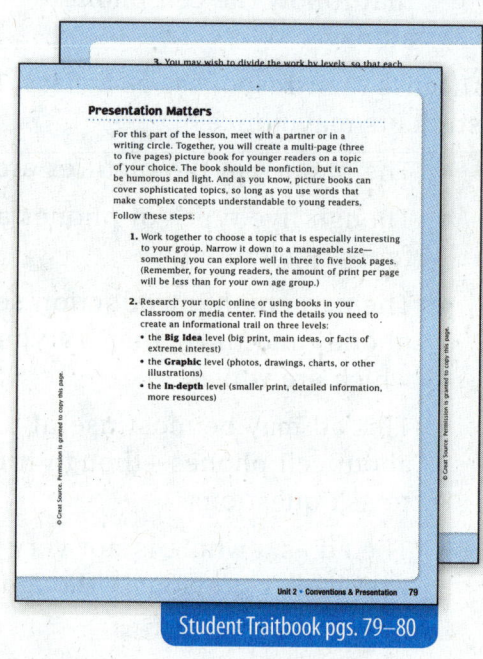

Student Traitbook pgs. 79–80

Then give students 20 minutes or more to work. They should

- work with a team if possible (or at least with a partner).
- choose a topic familiar to everyone on the team.
- divide the work. (Point 3 in the *Student Traitbook* suggests one way to do this with a four-person team. Teams of different sizes will need to make adjustments.)
- write copy and design rough sketches.
- put everything together in a "final" copy, using clean paper.

When students finish, share and discuss results, and if possible, put pages on display where your students or others can view them.

Coach's Corner

Another way to divide the task is to give each team member one or two whole pages to do—all levels. This approach creates excellent continuity *within each page*—but less continuity *page to page*.

124 Unit 2

Extending the Lesson

- Have writers edit any piece of their own work, using skills they developed in this and the preceding unit.

- Have writers review the definitions of *paragraph* they wrote at the beginning of this lesson. Do they think about paragraphs differently now?

- Give students an example of well-paragraphed text—only don't mark the paragraphs. Can they decide where each paragraph should begin? Does their decision have to match that of the writer?

- Complete the books you began in **Presentation Matters**—or create new ones on another topic.

- Present your books to a primary audience and ask for their feedback.

- Discuss the kinds of books for which multiple levels are especially helpful. Would you be as likely to see them in a novel as in a nonfiction book, for example? *Could* a novel or fairy tale picture book incorporate multiple levels, though? If so, how?

- Watch any movie trailer. What different informational trails does the producer create to give the viewer complete information—and to get the viewer to want to see the film?

UNIT 2
Organization

Introduce Trait

Practice Trait

Apply Trait

Final Curtain Call 127	• Preview pages 127–135
Assessing and Revising Sample Papers 128	• Apply what students have learned by assessing Sample Papers 7 and 8
Sample Paper 7: *Going Organic* Score and Rationale	• Revise Sample Paper 7 for Organization
Sample Paper 8: *The California King* Score and Rationale	
Revising Sample Paper 7: *Going Organic*	
Revising and Editing a Personal Draft 133	• Have students revise their own writing for Ideas, Organization, and Conventions and Presentation
	• Assess students' growth as writers
Parting Thoughts 135	• Conclude the trait of Organization

(50 min.) for Assessing and Revising Sample Papers
(50 min.) for Revising and Editing a Personal Draft

Final Curtain Call

It's time to give students a chance to apply what they have learned—and to give you a chance to assess their growth as writers and revisers. Have students demonstrate their knowledge of Ideas and Organization, as well as Conventions and Presentation, by following these steps:

1. **Apply knowledge of Organization by assessing and revising the writing of others.**

   Your students will read and assess Sample Papers 7 and 8. This time, they will work independently, applying what they have learned to
   - decide for themselves which piece is stronger.
   - score each sample paper, using the Student Rubric for Organization.
   - brainstorm ways of improving the weaker paper.
   - revise the weaker paper for Organization.

   Assessment Component: Base your assessment of growth on students' revision of Sample Paper 7: *Going Organic.* The revised version should advance at least one point on the rubric, achieving a final score of 4, 5, or 6. Assess each student's final draft of *Going Organic* using the Teacher Rubric for Organization.

2. **Apply knowledge of Organization by assessing and revising personal writing.**

   Have students pull their rough drafts from their folders to revise and edit, applying everything they have learned from
   - reading and using student rubrics, checklists, and posters for Ideas, Organization, and Conventions and Presentation.
   - discussing and assessing the writing of others.
   - reading or hearing literature that exemplifies strengths in Ideas and Organization.
   - completing lessons to build skills in three traits: Ideas, Organization, and Conventions and Presentation.
   - assessing and revising weaker writing samples.

   Assessment Component: Score each revised draft and compare those scores to the baseline scores you assigned to writers' rough drafts earlier. Do not base your assessment *exclusively* on the differences between these scores, however. Look carefully at the quality, nature, and extent of each writer's revision. How creative were they? What risks did they take? Add additional points for good editing or creative presentation.

Coach's Corner

Remember to check out the Assessment Guidelines (in the back matter) for additional suggestions on effective ways to assess your student writers' performance and growth.

Coach's Corner

If a student's score on the final draft does not leap the river in any given trait, provide that student with an option to revise or edit further, using one or more checklists for revision to create a workable plan.

Coach's Corner

Continue to give students some simple tips that make revision manageable. **Ideas:** Add one or two intriguing details. Make sure the main message is clear. **Organization:** Make sure the lead and conclusion are strong. Be sure the order is easy to follow. **Conventions:** Wait until the final draft to edit or design layout. Read all text twice, once silently, once aloud, pencil in hand. Refer to a dictionary, personal notes, and a handbook. **Presentation:** Consider small features that can make a document attractive: carefully chosen fonts, well placed headings and subheads, good use of open space, illustrations or graphics, a table of contents, and a well designed list of sources, if applicable.

Organization

- Introduce Trait
- Practice Trait
- **Apply Trait**
  - **Assessing and Revising Sample Papers**
  - Revising and Editing a Personal Draft

Assessing and Revising Sample Papers

Student Traitbook pages 81–85

Sample Paper 7: *Going Organic* and Sample Paper 8: *The California King*

1. Explain that this activity will give students a chance to see how they have grown as assessors and revisers with respect to Organization.
2. Refer each student to the Student Rubric for Organization.
3. Pair up students and then refer them to Sample Papers 7 and 8.
4. At this point, let students be a little more independent by
   - passing out both sample papers at once.
   - having students read the papers aloud to each other—in any order.
   - having them decide for themselves which paper is stronger in Organization. (Most teams should choose *The California King*.)
   - scoring the two papers together, thereby using comparisons to help zero in on the best score for each.
5. As students score the two papers, they should think about the following

❓ Key Questions . . .
- Does the writer have a clear main message?
- Does the writer stay focused on that message—or jump around?
- Does the paper have a strong lead? Or does it just start in?
- Do the details come in an order that makes the paper easy to follow?
- Are ideas clearly connected to each other—and to the main message?
- Does the writer use transitional words to build bridges, idea to idea?
- As a reader, do I ever feel lost or confused? Do I need to reread?
- Does the paper have a satisfying conclusion that effectively wraps up the discussion? Or does it just stop?

Coach's Corner

Students may also work in writing circles (three to four students) to discuss and score sample papers, if you prefer. They may still score papers individually, but groups (like pairs) should come to agreement within one point on the 6-point scale, if possible.

Coach's Corner

The two papers selected for this activity are both informational. Both writers did some research to learn about their topics and collect details that might make a report interesting. Clearly, one was more successful than the other. Comparing two papers written in the same genre helps students identify specific things that make writing successful.

6. When students are finished scoring, discuss the papers as a class. Talk about which is stronger in Organization and why. Once students have agreed on the "best" scores for each piece, compare their scores with ours (see Scores and Rationales).

7. Have students identify strong features from *The California King*. What does this writer do well, in terms of Organization? Have students identify specific problems with *Going Organic*. What specific revisions would make this piece stronger in Organization?

> **Coach's Corner**
>
> When an informational piece is well organized, the reader's understanding of the topic grows throughout the discussion. In addition, the reader's primary questions about the subject are thoughtfully addressed. Is that the case with each paper?

> **Coach's Corner**
>
> In order to organize well, writers must have a clear message in mind. Clearly, the writer of *The California King* knows his topic well, and has identified some excellent details to share. The writer of *Going Organic*, by contrast, has identified some of the questions relating to organic food. However, we're missing a lot of answers! This is much like the skeleton draft writers created in Lesson 1.4—except that it lacks logical order! This deck of detail cards is well shuffled!

Score and Rationale for Sample Paper 7: *Going Organic*

Most readers see this paper as **needing significant revision** in Organization. The lead starts out strong with the first sentence, then dissolves into a heap of indecision with sentence 2. The primary problem is lack of a clear main message. Phrases like *nasty chemicals* and *less likely to get certain kinds of cancers* suggest that the writer is a champion of organic food, but she needs to say this more directly. In addition, the writer raises a number of questions for which she has no answer— or only a partial answer: Is it science or common sense? What do farmers need to do to be certified? Why is it so hard to grow your own organic food? And finally—the topper because it poses as a conclusion—Is organic food really more healthy? The old "time will tell" or "more research is needed" conclusion is always a weak out for a writer who hasn't done the research. More information, orderly presentation, and a stronger lead and conclusion will boost this paper several points on the scale. Right now it would receive a **score of 2 in the trait of Organization**.

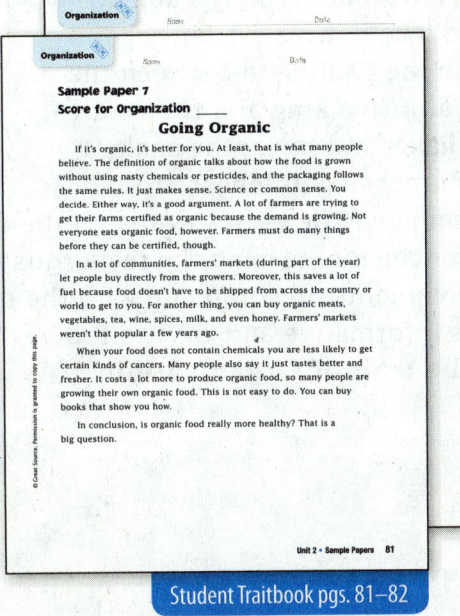

Student Traitbook pgs. 81–82

Unit 2   129

Organization

Apply Trait
Assessing and Revising Sample Papers

Coach's Corner

Both sample papers have source lists—and both lists contain conventional errors. Remember, this would be scored under the trait of Conventions and Presentation. If you wish, you can create an extension lesson in which students use an approved writing handbook to check formatting of one or both source lists and make editorial corrections. This is excellent practice, but because of the time involved, we do recommend doing it as a separate lesson.

Score and Rationale for Sample Paper 8: *The California King*

Most readers agree that Sample Paper 8 is **very strong** in Organization. It starts with a strong lead and right up front lets readers know that this is a report on "one very tough customer," not the "surfer dude" we might have expected, given the title. Each paragraph provides new and well coordinated information: first on hunting habits and the king's ability to face down a rattler, second on the confusion between the California king and the coral snake, and third, the snake's supposed gentleness around humans. The writer wraps up the discussion with an excellent conclusion, teasing the reader just a bit and echoing earlier comments on confusion with the deadly coral snake. The paper is informative and easy to follow. It would receive a **score of 6 in the trait of Organization**.

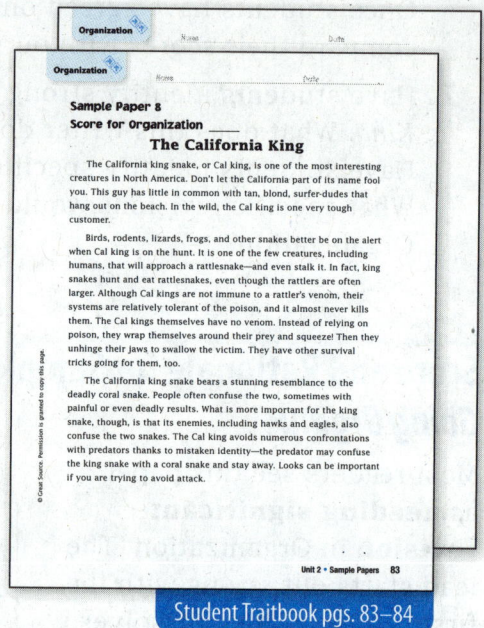

Student Traitbook pgs. 83–84

130 Unit 2

Revising Sample Paper 7: *Going Organic*

Have students revise the paper with the lower score in Organization: *Going Organic*. Their goal is to raise the score from a 2 to a 4 or higher. This challenge tests their knowledge of Organization and their creativity in solving various writers' problems. It is also excellent preparation for revising their own writing.

Follow these steps:

1. Remind each student to refer to the Revising Checklist for Organization or the Student Rubric for Organization. Most will want to work from one or the other—their choice.

2. Tell students to look carefully at Sample Paper 7: *Going Organic*. Remind them that all helpful revisions are welcome, but their primary focus for this lesson should be on Organization. They may work individually—or in teams to plan. They will write individual drafts.

3. Remind students that they are free to add or delete details, move things around, change the wording, add a new title— *anything at all*. They are in charge!

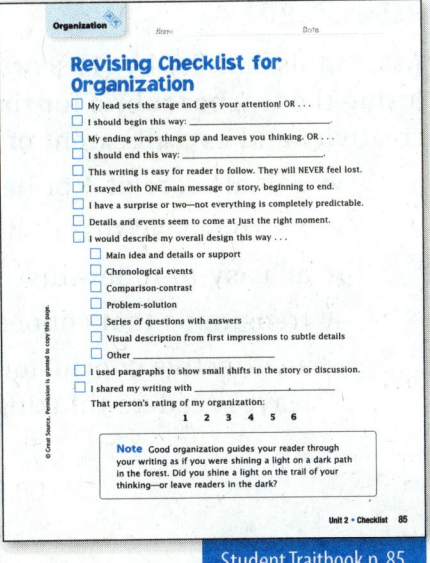

Student Traitbook p. 85

Coach's Corner

Working with partners is helpful in identifying problems, planning revision, and—as needed— dividing the task of research. It is fine for partners to share information, so long as they write individual drafts.

Coach's Corner

You may wish to remind students that revising for organization is always easier once the writer has a clear main message in mind. This writer does not. Individually, or as a group, students must decide what that message should be.

Bringing everyone in... Differentiated Instruction

Not all students will be familiar with organic food, and clearly, even basic information will greatly enhance this revision. Start with a class discussion to see what students know already. Together, you may be able to answer some of the questions the writer raises about chemicals or certification. If not, consider a brief time for online research to gather the details that will result in strong revisions.

Unit 2 131

Organization

Apply Trait
Assessing and Revising Sample Papers

4. Have students mark up the sample paper with cross-outs, inserts, and arrows—and add longer inserts by stapling or taping them on.

5. If you wish, provide time for students to share their rough drafts before making a final copy.

6. Final copy may be handwritten or word processed and should be stapled or clipped to the rough draft before it is handed in.

Assessment

Assess this activity by (1) scoring the final draft for Organization (using the teacher rubric for that trait) and (2) looking at the creativity and overall extent of the revision. Look for

- a final score of 4 or better in Organization.
- a strong lead that pulls readers into the discussion.
- an easy-to-follow discussion in which key points stand out.
- transitions that connect ideas in a clear, logical way.
- an effective conclusion that wraps up the discussion and leaves readers thinking.

Revising and Editing a Personal Draft

Applying Knowledge of Organization by Revising Personal Writing

The revision your students just completed on Sample Paper 7: *Going Organic* provides a good warm-up for revising their own writing effectively. Everything in this unit has been directed toward this goal: helping writers become strong, independent revisers of their own work.

1. Ask students to recall the personal writing they created after the Literature Connection (*If the World Were a Village* by David J. Smith). This should still be in rough draft form in their writing folders.
2. Have them remove that writing from their folders and assess it for both Ideas and Organization, as well as Conventions and Presentation, using the student rubrics for those traits. As they assess, students should ask themselves these

   ❓ **Key Questions . . .**
   - *Does this paper leap the river in each trait?*
   - *Did I highlight any problem areas or write myself notes?*
   - *What could I do to make my writing stronger?*

3. Based on their answers to these key questions, students should revise their writing, marking up their rough drafts any way they wish. Their goal should be to make the paper leap the river in *all three traits:* Ideas, Organization, and Conventions and Presentation (scores of 4, 5, or 6).
4. Final drafts may be copied onto new paper—or entered into the computer.
5. **Rough drafts and final drafts should be stapled together**, so that you can easily make comparisons and track the planning and flow of their revision.

Organization

- Introduce Trait
- Practice Trait
- **Apply Trait**
  - Assessing and Revising Sample Papers
  - Revising and Editing a Personal Draft

Coach's Corner
Remember that assessment takes many forms. Students are not scoring their writing, but simply using what they know about each trait to identify problems and plan revision. What's most helpful to a reviser is a "to do" list written right into the rough draft and addressing primary problems: e.g., write a stronger lead, show how this connects (underline the sentence), add more detail here (with a caret to indicate the spot), and so on.

Coach's Corner
While students will do their actual revising independently, they should feel free to talk in teams and to borrow revision ideas from one another.

Coach's Corner
If you have a rough draft you are working on, use it to model the first few steps of your own revision. In only one or two minutes, you can rework a lead and make one or two marginal notes—perhaps comment on the title. The impact will be dramatic.

Organization

Apply Trait
Revising and Editing a Personal Draft

Assessment

Assess this activity by (1) scoring the final draft for Ideas, Organization, and Conventions and Presentation (using the teacher rubric for each trait) and (2) looking at the creativity and overall extent of the revision. Look for:

- A clear main idea
- Details that expand or enrich that idea
- Focus: spotlight on the message, beginning to end
- Lead that invites readers in
- Transitions that connect ideas
- Easy-to-follow design
- Conclusion that wraps things up
- Title that gives the piece direction—much like a good lead
- Conventions that support meaning and voice
- Presentation that is eye appealing and/or makes information accessible

Bringing everyone in . . .   **Differentiated Instruction**

When writers aren't sure how to begin revising, start with the foundation: the central idea. Is it clear? Build from there. Are there two or three intriguing details to share with the reader? If writers need more information, help them discover sources. If it's a topic they know well, a good next step is making a list of questions a reader might wish to have answered. This gives the writer an easy plan to follow. The next step is a strong lead. Once that's in hand, it often points the way to what comes next. Then the trick is to keep the pencil moving! Last steps: strong conclusion and title. The best titles are written *last*.

Parting Thoughts

Organizing begins with the message—with having something to say. That message forms the core, the center of the writing, and all details revolve around it, like planets around the sun. A clear message also fuels the lead, which is simply the writer's way of getting the reader to join in the conversation—as well as the conclusion, which is the writer's way of keeping the discussion or story alive in the reader's mind even after the last sentence has been read. One key to becoming proficient in organizing information is to take chances—the way a decorator might in arranging a room. No one ever put a sofa there? Or a bookshelf over there? Terrific. Let's be the first ones to try it and see what happens. New arrangements can transform our perspective. Experimentation is a good way to approach writing, too. Experimental writers test leads, conclusions, and titles to see how the world looks from the other side of the room. Instead of giving our writers prescribed outlines to follow, we want to push them to try what hasn't been done before. We need to trust that through their discoveries, they will teach themselves to think—and perhaps teach us, as well.

It turns out that many writers actually discover what they have to say in the process of writing it. The writer's challenge is to keep this sense of discovery intact; this keeps writing fresh and vibrant.

—Ralph Fletcher
What a Writer Needs

Vicki & Jeff

UNIT 3
Voice

Overview

Already students have looked at the two traits that form a strong foundation for writing: Ideas, the writer's message, and Organization, the writer's way of ordering details to make the message logical and appealing. In this unit, students explore **Voice**, the trait that connects writer and reader. Voice is the writer's presence on the page—part personality, part audience awareness, part conviction. Because voice is highly individual, it varies writer to writer and also shifts slightly with genre, though something of the person behind the words always lingers, whether the writing takes the form of a poem or a report. There is no divorcing voice from passion; that's why voice is always strongest when writers choose their own topics or shape them from a personal perspective.

In this unit, you will be helping students to

- **create a personal definition** of voice.
- match **voice with purpose.**
- use knowledge of a topic to **write with confidence.**
- **refine voice** to reach a particular audience.

TRAIT DEFINITION

No one would mistake the writing of Maya Angelou for that of Jerry Seinfeld or Edgar Allan Poe. The something that tells us who is speaking is called **voice**. Voice is often called "fingerprints on the page" because it is unique to each person. Voice combines individuality, energy, and conviction. It's the writer's way of pulling readers in, the quality that makes a story or discussion impossible to put down, as the saying goes. The message is what the writer has to say, and voice is how he or she says it. The trait of Voice is deeply influenced by language, detail, and personal style. But much of it comes from within, sharing from the heart what matters most to the writer.

Vicki & Jeff

Unit at a Glance

Introduce Trait

Discussing Sample Papers 140

Making the Literature Connection 146

Writing a Personal Draft 149

Practice Trait

Lesson 3.1: Creating a Personal Definition 154

Lesson 3.2: Linking Voice to Purpose 161

Lesson 3.3: The Voice of Confidence 169

Lesson 3.4: Knowing Your Audience 175

Conventions and Presentation 180

Apply Trait

Assessing and Revising Sample Papers......................192

Revising and Editing a Personal Draft 197

UNIT 3
Voice

Introduce Trait

	The Opening Act 139	• Preview pages 139–150
15 min.	**Discussing Sample Papers** 140	• Introduce trait language and rubric
	Sample Paper 9: *A Close Call* Score and Rationale	• Analyze weak and strong writing
15 min.	Sample Paper 10: *Toughest Thing on Two Legs* Score and Rationale	
50 min.	**Making the Literature Connection** 146	• Model the trait of Voice in literature: *Science Verse*
		• Connect reading and writing
50 min.	**Writing a Personal Draft** 149	• Coach students in creating a piece of personal writing
		• Assess students' drafts to create benchmark scores

Practice Trait

Apply Trait

138 Unit 3

The Opening Act

Explain that voice is energy, enthusiasm, personal perspective on a topic, confidence, and personal style—the writer's individual, unique way of expressing his or her ideas. Let students see and hear this trait in action, first in two student writing samples and then in a piece of literature in which the voice is strong, comical, and distinctive. Following the literature connection, students will have a chance to create an original piece of writing on a topic of their choice. Later they will revise and edit it, using what they know about Ideas, Organization, Voice, and Conventions and Presentation. Here's the Opening Act in more detail.

1. **Discuss and assess the sample papers.** Expand students' understanding of Voice by discussing two sample papers.
   - *A Close Call* (in which a potentially exciting tale is told in a monotone voice)
   - *Toughest Thing on Two Legs* (a character portrait that rings with voice)

   Encourage student writers to talk, to read samples aloud to each other, to highlight moments that are strong in the trait of Voice, and to refer often to their student rubrics. By this time, students likely recognize that
   - **strong samples** suggest strategies writers can use in their own writing.
   - **weaker samples** suggest problems to avoid and also offer a chance to practice revision on someone else's work.

2. **Connect the trait to literature.** Continue your conversation by letting students hear the voice of one or more professional writers. Our featured text for the unit is *Science Verse* by Jon Scieszka. Use this or *any text* strong in Voice. Remember to allow a full class period (or more) for the literature lesson. We recommend sharing multiple voices that differ widely in tone, culture, perspective, and genre. This will help students see that Voice is expansive and complex, that it has infinite variety, and that this diversity is in itself partly what defines the trait.

3. **Complete a personal draft.** Following the literature connection, have students write a personal draft on any topic of their choice. The writing may be inspired by *Science Verse*, but it does not have to be. Writers should put their rough drafts into folders for a time in order to create the mental distance needed for strong revision. They will revise and edit the piece at the close of the unit, using skills gained through the five lessons that follow.

Coach's Corner
In discussing or scoring writing samples for this unit, focus on the trait of Voice first. But include other traits in the discussion, noticing in particular how much detail influences not only Ideas but Voice.

Coach's Corner
Keep in mind that students may add to or revise their writing at any time. Some may want to add information bit by bit, particularly if it involves research. However, there will also be time for a last reflective look at the close of the unit. Their growth will be measured, in part, by the difference between the early rough draft and the final.

Voice

Introduce Trait
Discussing Sample Papers
Making the Literature Connection
Writing a Personal Draft

Practice Trait
Apply Trait

Coach's Corner

Reading aloud is especially important in teaching Voice. It helps listeners feel the power and impact. Writers need to hear the voices of as many writers as possible in order to appreciate the infinite forms voice can take. Reading aloud with expression is one important way of learning to *write* with voice.

Coach's Corner

By this time, students are learning that pieces of writing are individual and no rubric can describe everything about them. A rubric isn't meant to do that. What the rubric can do is provide very good indicators about whether a paper is strong in a trait and, if not, what some of the primary problems are likely to be.

Coach's Corner

Throughout this unit, have students work with partners or in writing circles. You can mix this up, doing some of each. Having one partner ensures that everyone will talk, but listening to many perspectives expands a writer's thinking about what makes writing work, and that's the main point of any assessment exercise.

Discussing Sample Papers

Student Traitbook pages 87–89; 218

Student Rubric for Voice

Prior to presenting the two introductory sample papers to students, read each one aloud to yourself so you can hear the voice and read the piece with expression. If you ask student volunteers to read the papers aloud, be sure they have time to rehearse. It is important that writers assess with their ears as well as their eyes. We provide questions to ask with respect to each paper, but add your own questions and those of your writers to our list.

1. Have a student lead a discussion of the Student Rubric for Voice. By now, everyone should know that in this rubric

   - a score of 6 indicates **very strong** performance—but NOT perfection.
   - a score of 1 indicates a **beginning level** of performance—NOT failure.
   - the river divides writing in which **strengths outweigh problems** from writing that needs significant revision because **problems outweigh strengths.**

2. As students review the rubric, have them ask questions about anything that is unclear.

3. Explain that for this lesson, you will have students read and rate two pieces of writing: *A Close Call* and *Toughest Thing on Two Legs*. They will work with partners (or in writing circles), scoring each paper and defending their scores, using the language of the rubric.

Bringing everyone in... Differentiated Instruction

Several things can make your students' assessment of the trait of Voice easier. First, encourage them to read any piece they assess aloud, even if you have already done so. Performing text brings out nuances of voice that listening alone does not always capture. Second, ask them whether they would be likely to read the piece aloud to someone else for fun. Writing that is strong in the trait of Voice begs to be shared. Third, have them identify specific moments within the text where the voice seems particularly strong. They may have other criteria, too—part of the personal rubric we form in our minds through experience as writers and readers.

Sample Paper 9: *A Close Call*

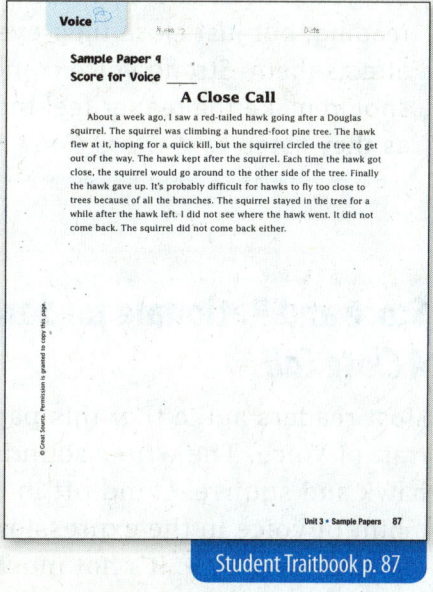

Student Traitbook p. 87

1. Read *A Close Call* aloud (or have a student read it). As you read, ask students to think about these

   ### ❓ Key Questions...

   - Is this paper fun to read or listen to?
   - Would you like to read more by this author? Why?
   - Does this writer put a lot of energy into the writing?
   - Do you think he chose this topic personally?
   - If you wrote on this topic, could you make the voice stronger?
   - What word best describes the voice in this paper?
   - Is this writer sharing his honest opinion about homework? How do you know?
   - Can you point to specific places in the paper where the writer's voice comes through?
   - How about places where the writer definitely needs to say things differently?

2. Have students mark up the papers by underlining moments that have strong voice (or moments where voice fades).

Coach's Corner

Chances are, your writers will not find many moments to highlight in this piece. That's fine! Have partners or writing circles save their responses (even if the paper has no marks on it) so they can compare it with Sample Paper 10: *Toughest Thing on Two Legs*, once they've had a chance to respond to that piece.

Unit 3 141

Voice

Introduce Trait
Discussing Sample Papers

3. Have students score the paper, 1 through 6, using the Student Rubric for Voice.
4. After scoring, have them discuss their scores and reasons with partners or in their writing circles.
5. When they finish, vote as a class (with a show of hands or by moving to corners) and tally scores. Have students
   - think about the key questions listed under Step 1 above.
   - state whether they think this paper leaps the river in the trait of Voice.
   - defend their scores using the Student Rubric for Voice.

> **Bringing everyone in . . .** Differentiated Instruction
>
> Suggest that listeners *not look* at the text while someone else is reading, but just close their eyes and think about how the writing affects them. Strong voice comes from emotion in the writer, and should make the reader feel that emotion, too. What do readers feel as they listen to *A Close Call*?

Score and Rationale for Sample Paper 9: *A Close Call*

Most readers agree that this paper **does NOT leap the river** in the trait of Voice. The writer sounds just a shade more interested in the hawk and squirrel stand-off in the first part of the paper. We hear a hint of voice in the expressions *going after, hoping for a quick kill,* and *kept after*. It's not much, but it keeps us mildly engaged, hoping for the excitement to build as the squirrel makes a valiant escape, or is ultimately plucked from the tree by the determined hawk. Instead, neither happens. Both main characters just go away. That's what we feel like doing at the end. This paper would receive a **score of 2 in the trait of Voice**.

Coach's Corner

A Close Call is intended as a personal narrative. A good narrative tells what happened, but it is more than a list of events. There's a reason for the telling—a point to the story. Often this point is revealed at the end, when the writer tells something he or she has learned or will always remember—or still has to resolve. Is this piece a true story or more of a list?

Sample Paper 10: Toughest Thing on Two Legs

1. Answer any new questions students have about the rubric.

2. Have students change partners for this discussion.

3. Tell them to follow along as you read *Toughest Thing on Two Legs* aloud (or have a student read it, after a little rehearsal). As you read, remind students to think about these

   ### ❓ Key Questions . . .
   - *Did the writer choose a topic that he has strong feelings about?*
   - *Did you enjoy it? Would you like to read more by this writer?*
   - *Do the writer's feelings come through? Is he being honest?*
   - *What word would describe this voice?*
   - *Can you point to moments where the voice is really strong?*
   - *Are there moments where the voice could be stronger?*
   - *If you wrote about this topic, how could you add more voice?*
   - *Would you read this paper aloud to a friend? Why?*

4. As before, have students underline or highlight moments that are strong in the trait of Voice.

5. Have them score the paper, 1 through 6, referring to the Student Rubric for Voice.

6. After scoring, have them discuss the paper and the score with partners or in writing circles. When they finish talking, vote as a class (with a show of hands or by moving to corners) and tally scores. Have students
   - think about the key questions listed under Step 3 above.
   - state whether they think this paper leaps the river in the trait of Voice.
   - defend their scores using the Student Rubric for Voice.

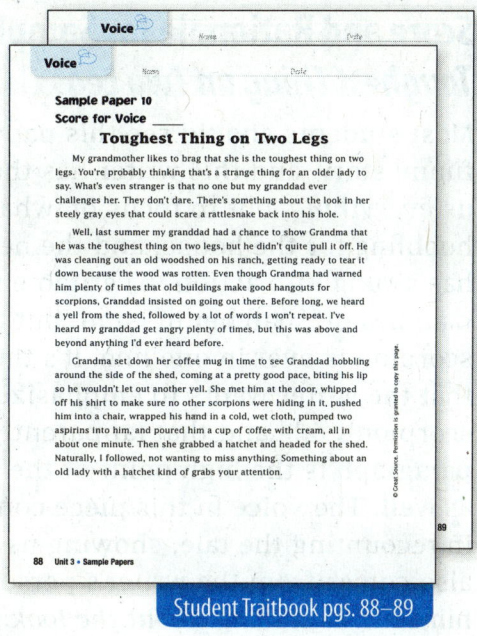

Student Traitbook pgs. 88–89

Coach's Corner

In a really strong piece, the voice never fades completely, but it may go up and down, rather like a roller coaster. Have students compare their highlighted copy of *A Close Call* with that of *Toughest Thing on Two Legs*. The visual contrast should be striking, and the difference in scores needs to reflect that.

Voice

Introduce Trait
Discussing Sample Papers

Coach's Corner

Toughest Thing on Two Legs is a blend of two genres—personal narrative and character portrait. It definitely tells a story with a message, but it's also meant to reveal the characters of Grandma and Granddad.

Coach's Corner

As you go through this unit, your writers will find their own words for describing voice, and may go beyond the rubric. Weave their voices into that document, and make it your own. Remember too that the more literature you share aloud, the stronger, wiser, and truer your writers' personal definitions of voice will be.

Coach's Corner

Though this revision activity is optional, we strongly recommend taking one class period for it. Rehearsing revision on the work of someone else is low-risk because the draft is already problematic, and it doesn't belong to your students. They have less of a personal stake, therefore, in trying new strategies.

Score and Rationale for Sample Paper 10: *Toughest Thing on Two Legs*

Most students should see this paper as **strong**. It recounts a funny story, and this writer has the remarkable sense not to tell us *everything*, but to focus on what matters. We see Granddad hobbling for the house, and the next thing we know, Grandma has swung into action, a veritable nurse on turbo power. She marches off, hatchet in hand, but the actual dispatching of the scorpion is over in one line. It's the confrontation with Granddad that the writer wants to emphasize: the smallness of the attacking scorpion's tale and that (apparently) fake limp. The next to last paragraph is the high point of the story, and the character portrait as well. The voice in this piece comes largely from writer's honesty in recounting the tale, showing us the story behind the story. It also comes from the writer's personal, individual way of expressing himself: *something about the look in her steely gray eyes that could scare a rattlesnake back into his hole.* Notice the vivid details and strong verbs that also contribute to the voice. This paper would receive a **score of 6 in the trait of Voice.**

 ## Creating a Baseline Assessment

Have students revise *A Close Call* (the weaker of the two introductory papers) working individually. Assess the *revised* drafts (using the Teacher Rubric for Voice) to provide baseline scores reflecting students' revision skills for this trait. Record those scores. At the close of the unit, following direct instruction in the trait of Voice, you can compare these early revisions to the revisions your students do on their own writing and on Sample Paper 11. This comparison will tell you how much they have grown as revisers with respect to the trait of Voice. (See **Extending the Lesson** for some suggestions on setting up this revision activity.)

Extending the Lesson

- Talk about other strengths in *Toughest Thing On Two Legs*. Are the details carefully chosen? Is there a strong main idea? Look carefully at the lead and conclusion. Did this writer do a skillful job? Look again at the verbs the writer uses to describe Grandma's triage in the third paragraph. What is the effect?

- Writing with voice is partly about topic choice. Spend time talking about the things you love to write about. Share your favorites, and encourage writers who aren't already doing so to keep a list of favorite topics in their writing journals.

- Suppose that the writer of *A Close Call* wrote this paper during an on-demand writing assessment. The prompt was: "A story involving an animal." How could the writer have personalized this prompt to make the writing work? Let's also suppose that the writer was determined to write about the squirrel and the hawk. Could he have changed the story in any way to give it more voice? Would it be all right to depart from what really happened in order to make the writing a trifle more exciting?

- As a class or in teams, devise a plan for revising *A Close Call*. Discuss the topic as a class or give students time in writing circles to talk about various approaches. Following are some prompting questions you can ask.
    - Why is the story called *A Close Call*?
    - Is the writer on the side of the hawk or the squirrel?
    - How else could this story end?
    - What important details (if any) are missing?
    - Could this story be told from another point of view? Whose?

Bringing everyone in . . . Differentiated Instruction

For a slightly different approach to revision, have students meet in writing circles to discuss the paper, then assume various roles—the writer, another human observer, or even the hawk or squirrel. Have them write about the day's events in character in first person, then share the results in reader's theater fashion.

- Look up favorite authors online. Does anything about their lives connect to the topics they chose to write about?

- Listen to any author read his or her own work aloud on CD. Can the author bring out voice in a way no one else can?

- Start a blog discussion on the trait of Voice. Include definitions, authors with strong voice, tips for putting voice into writing—anything.

Coach's Corner

We know that voice comes, in part, from how the writer is feeling as he or she writes. How is this writer feeling? How does the writer need to feel? What will make that happen? NOTE: If a story is a little on the dull side, but it is the story the writer is determined to tell, being inventive with detail is not a bad idea. This writer isn't under oath; he's trying to entertain readers.

Coach's Corner

The original piece is very short, yet still contains unneeded information. The revisions can be short, too. Length is not the goal. Voice is the goal. If writers can tell this story in 4–6 sentences, terrific. Note that if the ending changes, the title may need to change as well!

Voice

Introduce Trait
Discussing Sample Papers
Making the Literature Connection
Writing a Personal Draft
Practice Trait
Apply Trait

Coach's Corner

When choosing a book to teach the trait of Voice, look for books that touch your heart or ignite your curiosity. Choose books you *love*, the ones you return to again and again. It is not always necessary to share the whole book. Share any *moment* that makes you laugh or grow nostalgic. Don't forget the importance of sharing *many* voices to let your students hear a wide range of cultures and genres.

Coach's Corner

We have suggested that you read the whole book—it's not long and students may ask you to anyway. Certain poems may need to be reread to get every ounce of humor. There will most likely be science topics your students have encountered in class. You might even want to give the science teachers a heads-up. This book may create a great across-the-curriculum writing opportunity!

Making the Literature Connection

 **RECOMMENDED BOOK** *Science Verse* by Jon Scieszka

If there were a recipe for voice, it would have to include a large helping of honesty, a heap of passion for the topic, and a generous serving of individuality. All are wrapped together in the book chosen for this lesson: Jon Scieszka's *Science Verse*. It's the playful story of a student who cannot seem to pay attention, told through personal voice-filled imitations of familiar poems and designed to get readers to hear the "poetry of science in everything."

Sharing the Text

1. Show students the book and share the title and author. Let them know it was published in 2004. Ask if any of your students are familiar with the book or with Jon Scieszka's other books, including *The Math Curse, The True Story of the Three Little Pigs, The Stinky Cheese Man and Other Fairly Stupid Tales,* and *Knucklehead: Tall Tales and Almost True Stories of Growing Up Scieszka.*

2. Preview the book's main idea: An unnamed student is zapped by his teacher, Mr. Newton, with—not a math curse—but a curse focusing on the poetry of science. From that moment, he begins to see and hear everything about science as poetry. You (and some of your students) may hear the echoes of Poe, Frost, Carroll, Wadsworth, Longfellow, folk songs, nursery rhymes, limericks, and schoolyard chants.

3. Ask if students are familiar, by title, with any of the poems on which the author's imitations are based: "The Song of Hiawatha," "The Raven," "Jabberwocky," "Casey at the Bat," "Stopping By Woods on a Snowy Evening," "The Night Before Christmas," and so on.

Bringing everyone in... **Differentiated Instruction**

Your students will appreciate this book far more if they know some of the poems on which Scieszka's imitations are based. All are listed in the back of the book in a section titled "Observations and Conclusions." You may not wish to read all of the original poems, but you could read one or two and have others available for students to explore on their own.

4. Let your students know you are going to read the whole book, and to be listening for references to familiar science topics or areas of personal interest.

5. With your students' help, recount some of the science topics cursed by poetry. Perhaps one of your students has extended knowledge of a topic based on a personal interest.

6. Talk with your students about any other rhyme or poetry styles that come up in the book. How did they come to know them? Ask if they have favorite poems. Are there any they would like to read aloud—individually or with a group? Take time for that.

7. Have students identify moments in which they feel the voice is particularly strong. Talk about features that contribute to that voice: word choice, rhythm, strong feelings, details, and so on.

Coach's Corner

Students will enjoy the wacky illustrations, which definitely contribute to the voice of the book. If possible, share them as you read, and ask for students' comments on artist Lane Smith's style. Note the short, comical bios on the back inside panel of the book jacket (with a good clue about pronouncing Scieszka).

Voice

Introduce Trait
Making the Literature Connection

Other Books You'll Love

Throughout the program, we will rotate recommendations by genre:

- **Classic**—both traditional and contemporary
- **Poetry**—an individual poem or collection
- **Nonfiction**—picture book or longer text
- **Fiction**—picture book or longer text

Keep in mind that your own favorite books are almost certain to include vibrant, quotable passages that make them ideal for teaching the trait of Voice. The more literature you share, the stronger your students' understanding of this trait will be. Here are other books to explore:

1. **Classic:** *Kidnapped* by Robert Louis Stevenson.
   Young David Balfour, who tells the tale in the first person, sets off to his uncle's house carrying a letter from his recently deceased father. David has reasonable expectations of some form of inheritance to perhaps set his course in life. His expectations are shattered upon meeting his uncle, "... a mean, stooping, narrow-shouldered, clay-faced creature ..." This is a grand story filled with action and mystery but also a sense of humor, distinguishing it as a blend of adventure, romance, epic, and picaresque tale.

2. **Nonfiction:** *Tracking Trash: Flotsam, Jetsam, and the Science of Ocean Motion* by Loree Griffin Burns.
   This book focuses on the efforts of oceanographer Dr. Curtis Ebbesmeyer to understand ocean currents. His methods are a bit unorthodox, even unusual in his chosen field of study. To understand ocean currents, Dr. Ebbesmeyer, along with his team of mostly amateur ocean enthusiasts, has become an expert on flotsam and jetsam, the floating trash that is either accidentally lost or cast overboard from ocean-going vessels. His unique methods (rubber ducks were employed in one of his best-known experiments) are fascinating. The voice also comes from his sharing of startling findings about massive plastic "islands" that threaten ocean creatures—and us.

3. **Fiction:** *A Stone in My Hand* By Cathryn Clinton.
   Like any strong piece of historical fiction, this book is the result of great passion and meticulous research. The story is told by young Malaak, whose perspective is enhanced by seeing imaginatively and vicariously through her dove, Abdo, who flies free above the Gaza City. The story takes place in Gaza during 1988–1989, the time period of part of the first intifada. Malaak's voice is authentic (aided by a glossary) and powerful without being overtly political.

Voice

Introduce Trait
Discussing Sample Papers
Making the Literature Connection
Writing a Personal Draft
Practice Trait
Apply Trait

Writing a Personal Draft

1. Tell your students they will now have a chance to create a personal piece of writing on any topic of their choice.

2. Give students a few minutes to confer with partners about possible writing topics. Tell them to make a list as they talk and to be prepared to share it with the class. Possible topics suggested by the book *Science Verse* include the following.
   - An original story imitating a classic or other familiar story (narrative fiction)
   - Imitative original poetry based on a well-known poem (poetry)
   - A reflection on a memorable teacher (narrative, expository, poetry)
   - A past, present, or future science project (informational, persuasive, expository)
   - An experience with the wonder of discovery (narrative, expository, poetry)
   - An original story with a science theme (imaginative)
   - Report on one of the topics covered in *Science Verse*: astronomy, matter, the universe, single-celled organisms, etc. (informational, expository, poetry)
   - Biography of Jon Scieszka (informational)
   - Review of the book *Science Verse* (persuasive, response to literature)

3. Give students 5–8 minutes to discuss topics. This conversation will set them up to begin their prewriting and drafting.

4. Tell writers who have thought of an original writing idea to share their thoughts with the class. Be sure all writers understand that they may choose *any* topic that suits them, whether inspired by *Science Verse* or not.

Coach's Corner
Consider posting a copy of this list while students are having their discussions. That way, they can refer to it as they talk. As much as possible, encourage students to choose topics and genres they like and about which they have strong feelings. This will make a striking difference in the amount of voice you hear in their writing.

Coach's Corner
This is an excellent opportunity to write with students, and to model topic selection. If you decide to do this (and we hope you do) be sure to emphasize the importance of choosing a topic you have strong feelings about, or something you have always wanted to research. Even if you do not finish the piece of writing, modeling topic selection is invaluable for your writers.

Unit 3 149

Voice

Introduce Trait
Writing a Personal Draft

Coach's Corner

This time is adjustable, according to your personal schedule, and you may wish to extend drafting into another class period, especially if you have many writers who need to do research or who just need additional writing time. Writers may also need to do some writing outside of class.

Coach's Corner

As students likely know by now, taking a mental break from any writing allows a writer to see his or her own work more objectively, and makes editing far more effective as well. At the same time, those writers who are doing research may need to visit their drafts periodically as they uncover new details. Each time writers return to a draft, remind them to begin by reading what they have written so far. This awakens the memory.

Bringing everyone in . . . **Differentiated Instruction**

Topic choice is critical in writing with voice. Help writers who struggle by guiding them toward a genre with which they feel comfortable. Remember that all of us (adults, too) tend to feel more comfortable writing what is familiar. Young children often write stories because so many stories are read to them. Be sure your writers have multiple genres available as readers. If you read nonfiction aloud regularly, you'll encourage your writers to try it.

5. Students should spend about five minutes prewriting: sketching, making a web, writing a list of questions or details, and so on.

6. Provide students with 20–30 minutes (in addition to pre-writing time) for drafting.

7. Remind students to double or triple space (even if they are composing on the computer) and to allow wide margins so there will be ample room for revision later.

8. When students feel they have a finished rough draft, have them confer with partners, reading their writing aloud to listen for voice. It is fine to make any changes that occur to them at this time, but there will be time for more comprehensive revisions later, following direct instruction in the trait of Voice.

9. Rough drafts should now be placed in their writing folders. At the close of the unit, they will have time to look at them again and to create revised drafts. It's those revisions that will be assessed.

Notes

UNIT 3
Voice

Introduce Trait

Practice Trait

Shifting the Spotlight..................153	• Preview pages 153–189
Lesson 3.1..................154 Creating a Personal Definition	• Describe voices and revise a weak example • Create a personal definition of voice
Lesson 3.2..................161 Linking Voice to Purpose	• Find words to describe voice and purpose • Revise to match voice and purpose
Lesson 3.3..................169 The Voice of Confidence	• Listen for confidence in nonfiction • Use knowledge to write with confidence
Lesson 3.4..................175 Knowing Your Audience	• Match voice to audience • Write similar letters to two audiences
Conventions and Presentation..................180 The Triple Threat The Play's the Thing	• Use conventions to create voice • Write a short play

(Each lesson: 50 min.)

Apply Trait

Shifting the Spotlight

Your students have now
- assessed two papers for Voice: *A Close Call* and *Toughest Thing on Two Legs.*
- seen and heard voice in action through your sharing of *Science Verse* by Jon Scieszka.

It is time to shift the spotlight, giving students a chance to practice specific skills they can use in revising and editing their writing. Several important features of voice are covered in the focused lessons that follow. Once students have completed all focused lessons, they will apply what they have learned by (1) revising *someone else's* writing and (2) revising and editing *their own* writing. Follow these two steps.

1. **Complete Lessons 3.1 through 3.4.** Allow two days for each lesson. Through these lessons, students will learn strategies for
   - defining the trait of Voice in their own terms.
   - matching voice with purpose.
   - creating the confident nonfiction voice that comes with knowledge.
   - fine tuning voice to reach a particular reader.

2. **Link Voice to Conventions and Presentation.** Allow a full class period for *each part* of this lesson. Students will learn how Conventions and Presentation supports strong Voice through: (1) use of particular conventions that bring out the voice in dialogue (Editing Level 1: Conventions) and (2) design of a script that guides actors through a performance (Editing Level 2: Presentation).

Give your students additional practice in *thinking like readers* by having them complete page 90 in the Student Traitbook. Various things the writer does to make voice strong appear on the left. Have students fill in the blanks on the right by imagining how each of these things affects the reader. Once you have discussed all four elements, display the Voice Poster where students can refer to it often.

Student Traitbook p. 90

Voice

Practice Trait

Introduce Trait

Lesson 3.1
Lesson 3.2
Lesson 3.3
Lesson 3.4
Conventions & Presentation

Apply Trait

LESSON 3.1

Creating a Personal Definition

Student Traitbook pages 91–96

Over time, writers encounter many definitions of the trait of Voice, including those in this program. In the end, though, each writer needs to define this important trait on his or her own. That personal definition springs mostly from reading—hearing and feeling the power of other voices. As writers encounter new voices in literature, and experiment with their writing voices, those early definitions change and grow. That's a reflection of the trait itself; Voice is a complex trait that reveals itself in infinite ways.

Objectives

Students will

- assess several writing examples to begin defining voice on their own terms.
- revise a selected example to make it stronger in the trait of Voice.
- reflect on examples they have heard and shared to create a personal definition.

Time Frame

Allow 50 minutes for this lesson. We suggest breaking it into two parts.

- **Part 1:** Students assess and discuss examples provided within the lesson.
- **Part 2:** Students revise a weak example and create a personal definition for voice.

154 Unit 3

Setting Up the Lesson

Give students time to read the unit introduction in the Student Traitbook. Respond to any questions or comments.

Then share the introduction to Lesson 3.1.

Students will be working in writing circles for at least a portion of this lesson. Since this lesson is about defining voice, begin by sharing excerpts from books or journals you think have strong voice. Keep them short so that you can share three or more. Talk in a personal way (not using a rubric) about why each voice speaks to you and what you find special about it. Go for variety. For example, you might share a voice from another time (Edgar Allan Poe or Shakespeare), some poetry or a short passage from a novel, a nonfiction voice, and perhaps a line or two from a personal letter or email. Talk about the writers who have moved you or influenced your own writing the most.

Once you finish sharing favorite authors, do a quick brainstorm definition of voice. Do NOT refer to rubrics or checklists as you do this. Just jot down notes from your own thinking as rapidly as students call them out.

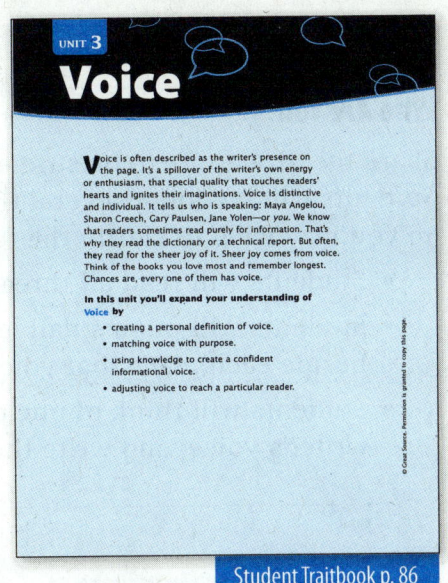

Student Traitbook p. 86

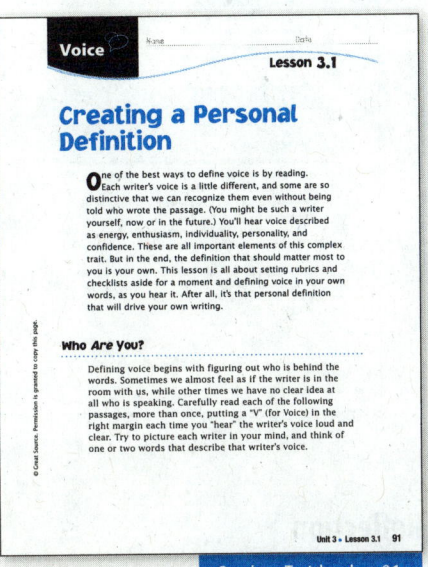

Student Traitbook p. 91

Coach's Corner

Encourage your writers to share their favorite authors, too. As an extension of this lesson, have them look for read-aloud passages of their own. What you model in **Setting Up the Lesson** will influence their search, so if you want them to look beyond trade books, be sure you do that, too!

Coach's Corner

You may wish to keep this brainstormed list visible throughout the lesson, but encourage students to add any new thinking to it as the lesson evolves.

Voice

Practice Trait
Lesson 3.1

Coach's Corner

You may choose to have writers read examples on their own, or you can read each one aloud, then pause as writers mark the examples and write describing words in the space provided. Either way, we suggest allowing 3–4 minutes per example.

Teaching the Lesson

Who *Are* You?

Share the directions to be sure everyone understands the task. Students will be doing several things in this portion of the lesson, so you may wish to clarify the following.

- Students will read all three examples more than once.
- Students will put a small letter "v" in the right-hand margin beside each place that voice really shines.
- Students will think of one or more words to describe each writer's voice, and write those words in the space provided.

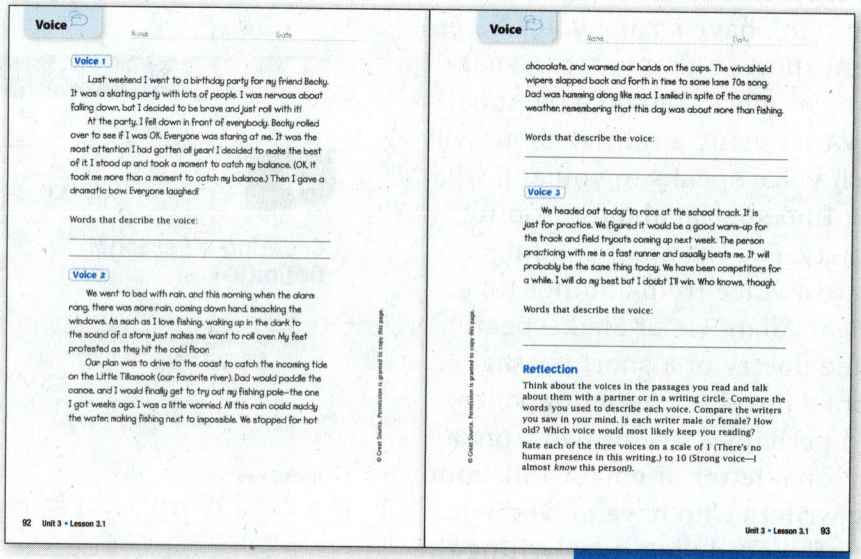

Student Traitbook pgs. 92–93

Reflection

Share the directions and group students into writing circles. Give them time to share their responses to each of the three examples and to rate each one on a scale of 1 to 10:

1 = No human presence in the writing
10 = I feel as if I know this person

When they finish, discuss the three voices as a class.

> **Bringing everyone in . . .**   **Differentiated Instruction**
>
> By now your readers are sufficiently familiar with the examples that many of them can probably read them aloud with comfort and with appropriate expression. This is a good time to ask for volunteer readers as you respond to each example.

When everyone has finished responding to all three examples, talk about which one is strongest and why, and remind students to be thinking about the personal definitions of voice they will write toward the close of this lesson.

There are no correct answers to the ratings of the three passages. Your writers' responses to each example may differ.

Voice 1
Our Rating: 9 or 10

Descriptive Words: *Comical, excited, confident, surprised, upbeat, energetic, distinctive, lively, candid, direct*

Voice 2
Our Rating: 7 or 8

Descriptive Words: *Honest, open, reflective, resigned (to the bad weather), weary, thoughtful, insightful, caring*

Voice 3
Our Rating: 2 or 3

Descriptive Words: *Vague, faint, quiet, weak, dim, pale, fading*

Giving Voice a Boost

Students will begin this portion of the lesson in writing circles, choosing a piece of writing to revise and discuss. Remind writers of the three examples they rated during the previous lesson, and have them choose one (most likely the weakest) to revise. They may write individual revisions or create one group revision, working together.

Share the directions for this section, helping students understand that they will be revising one of the three examples they just read (individually or as a group). Take time to review a few revision possibilities (they are not limited to the following).

- Changing wording
- Adding detail
- Writing from a different point of view
- Writing in two voices
- Changing the genre to a poem or drama

Student Traitbook p. 94

Coach's Corner
We asked students to mark those moments where the voice is particularly strong. This is a totally personal response, yet readers often agree. If possible, project the three examples to show where you hear the voice emerging. This is also a highly effective way of responding to students' everyday writing, and makes a great basis for discussion in a conference.

Coach's Corner
Note: If you are dividing this lesson into two parts, **Day 2 begins here.**

Coach's Corner
Be sure students understand that they are not required to do any of these things in revising. These are only suggestions. The goal is to increase the voice to a 10 on the scale, if possible.

Voice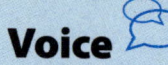

Practice Trait — Lesson 3.1

Allow about 15–20 minutes for this revision activity. Remind students that they should be prepared to share their revisions with the class.

> **Bringing everyone in... Differentiated Instruction**
>
> Writers who have not produced a group draft before may need a little guidance on how to go about this. The first step is to decide on some revision strategies—adding details or writing a poem, for example. Then it is often helpful to have one person be the designated recorder and do the actual writing as others offer suggestions. The recorder also needs to read the piece aloud periodically during revision so the rest of the team can hear what they have so far. This process takes a little coordination, but it offers writers a chance to synthesize multiple revision strategies. It is intense but also very instructive. It does tend to take more time than individual revision, so be as flexible as you can.

Share and Listen

Give several volunteers an opportunity to share their revisions aloud, encouraging listeners to take any notes that may be helpful to them in writing their final definitions—coming right up!

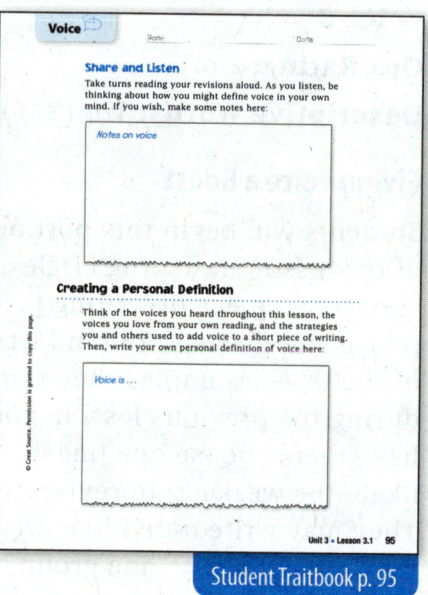

Student Traitbook p. 95

> **Bringing everyone in... Differentiated Instruction**
>
> It may not have occurred to some of your writers how much reading influences the way each of us writes. Take a minute to talk about this, sharing writers who have most influenced you. The echo of a favorite voice may be the result of conscious imitation, but it's just as likely to be completely unintentional, a subconscious mimicry of a tone, style, or attitude to which we're drawn. For an interesting and hilarious description of how this works, see Stephen King, *On Writing*, the section titled "On Writing," Part 1.

Creating a Personal Definition

This is an opportunity for writers to pull all their thoughts together and think of a personal definition that reflects how they think of voice right now. Allow about 5–6 minutes, encouraging them to

- review the brainstorming you did together as a class (in **Setting Up the Lesson**).
- reflect on the passages they've heard and rated.
- look over any notes they made as they listened to classmates share their revisions.

Writers should work independently to complete these definitions, and if they keep writing journals, they should enter their definitions there. That way, they can return to them, and expand or revise them as their thinking changes.

A Writer's Questions

We all read things we *have* to read: lists and reminders, tax codes, rules or laws, contracts or other legal documents, and so on. Someone has to write these, and the people who do so are writers every bit as much as novelists. Further, some people *do* aspire to write things such as legal documents. Others hope to write novels, picture books, or poems. What are your writers' goals?

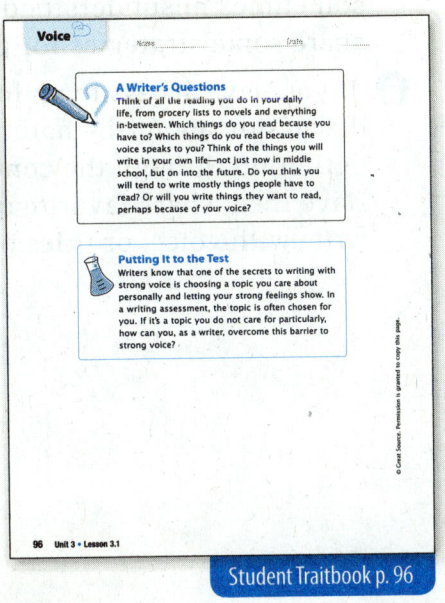
Student Traitbook p. 96

Putting It to the Test

Actually, almost any topic can bend to a writer's preferences if the writer takes time to personalize it. For example, suppose a prompt says: "Write about the importance of recycling." A writer who tackles this on a world level is likely to wind up writing vague platitudes like "Recycling is good for the planet." Everyone agrees, and nobody wants to read about it. But suppose a writer brings the topic down to a personal level, thinking, "What happens in *my* family? What little things do we do, and what do we resist doing because it's too much trouble?" Now we have the makings of an interesting exploration of recycling strategies and roadblocks, complete with insight because the writer is now writing what he or she knows.

Coach's Corner

If time permits, have some of your writers share their definitions aloud. As an alternative, write them on sentence strips and create a definition collage.

Unit 3 159

Voice

Practice Trait
Lesson 3.1

If you want to be a writer, you must do two things above all others: read a lot and write a lot. There's no way around these two things that I'm aware of, no shortcut.

—Stephen King
On Writing: a Memoir of the Craft

Extending the Lesson

- Encourage writers to return now and then to the definitions of voice that they entered in their writing journals. Every writer redefines voice in his or her own mind forever—and recording current thinking helps keep the ever evolving definition alive.

- Share your own definition of voice. Is it similar to your writers' definitions? Feel free to borrow from one another.

- Continue to read aloud from favorite pieces with strong voice. Have students talk about how they respond to each voice, what sets it apart, or what qualities they might wish to incorporate into their own writing. Be sure to share passages strong in voice throughout the year, not just during this unit.

- Voice in email messages (or other electronic media) is sometimes misunderstood. Why is this? Talk about it, and share some strategies for projecting the right voice.

- If you have access to an interactive website, start a blog discussion about the nature of voice. Continue to refine your definition through the contributions of other participants! Have them share favorite quotations, names of authors who write with voice, or titles of works that have strong voice.

LESSON 3.2

Linking Voice to Purpose

Student Traitbook pages 97–102

Voices are distinctive and individual, and a strong voice is recognizable regardless of whether the writer is drafting a letter or email, writing a report, or creating a picture book. Nevertheless, just as we temper our speaking voices to suit the occasion (one for the wedding, one for the football field), we also refine our writing voices to suit the purpose. That's one reason a news report and a letter to a friend sound so different. In this lesson, writers practice matching voice with purpose.

Voice

Introduce Trait
Practice Trait
Lesson 3.1
Lesson 3.2
Lesson 3.3
Lesson 3.4
Conventions & Presentation
Apply Trait

Objectives

Students will
- recognize the importance of matching voice with purpose.
- analyze two examples from literature to determine the purpose.
- refine the voice in a third example so it better suits the intended purpose.

Time Frame

Allow 50 minutes for this lesson. It can be broken into two parts.
- **Part 1:** Students discuss two examples and use voice to determine the writer's purpose.
- **Part 2:** Students revise a third example, refining the voice so it better suits the purpose.

Voice
Practice Trait — Lesson 3.2

Setting Up the Lesson

This lesson is about refining voice to suit purpose, but also (on the flip side) using voice as a clue about the writer's intention. Readers do this constantly—listening consciously or subconsciously for humor, an authoritative tone, confidence, or other indicators that suggest how a writer wants his or her message to be interpreted. Begin by sharing the introduction to Lesson 3.2 in the Student Traitbook. Then, set up this lesson with two quick activities:

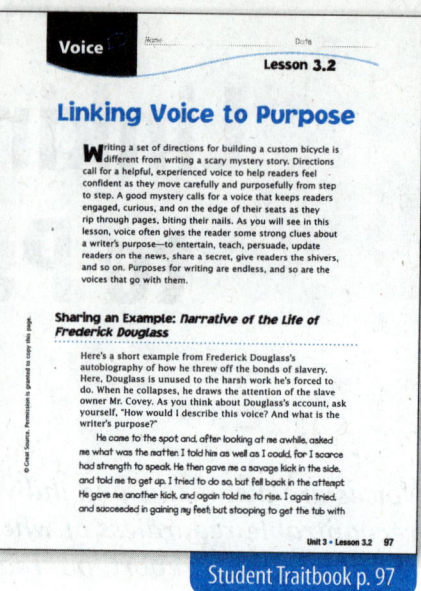

Student Traitbook p. 97

Warm-Up Activity 1
Read two (or more) very short examples with extremely different voices. Don't tell students where the writing comes from (e.g., a letter, a novel, an encyclopedia) because that will give away the purpose. Just read the example aloud and have them guess. Be sure the purposes of your examples are different: e.g., to entertain, to make people laugh, to teach readers something, to warn readers of possible dangers, and so on.

Warm-Up Activity 2
List several types of writing and have your students tell you the kind of voice they would expect from each. Following are some suggestions, but please feel free to create your own list.

- Greeting card
- Encyclopedia entry
- Email
- List of school rules
- Introduction to a math textbook
- Mystery novel
- Recipe for apple pie
- Script for a TV sitcom
- Script for a TV drama
- Picture book for kindergarten children

Coach's Corner
Keep the examples brief so you have time to share at least half a dozen. That way, students will hear a variety of voices, and they will hear some sharp contrasts.

Teaching the Lesson

Sharing an Example: *Narrative of the Life of Frederick Douglass*

Review the directions. Then read the example from *Narrative of the Life of Frederick Douglass* aloud or have them meet in writing circles and choose a reader to share the example aloud.

> **Bringing everyone in . . .** **Differentiated Instruction**
>
> Some readers need to hear a passage first, then go back and read it on their own. It's often helpful to underline moments where the voice is strong, and make marginal notes about the kind of voice they hear. This will set them up for the next part of the lesson.

Voice and Purpose

Share the directions. Have writers discuss the passage in their writing circles and

- circle each word from our chart that they feel describes the voice from *Narrative of the Life of Frederick Douglass.*
- add other descriptive words.
- check each statement that reflects the writer's purpose.
- add any other purposes we didn't think to put on our list.

Once everyone finishes, discuss the passage and your students' responses. Your writers' responses do not need to agree with ours.

Student Traitbook p. 98

Our Response:

Words to describe this writer's voice: *nervous, sad, terrified*

Based on this voice, what is the writer's purpose?

- To make us nervous and tense (a little—not enough to stop reading)
- To paint a vivid picture in our minds
- To show how some slaves were treated
- To reveal what Mr. Covey is like (it's a beginning)
- To make us curious about American history
- To make us feel sorry for Frederick Douglass (or at least give us sympathy for him)

Coach's Corner

Remind listeners to think about the voice as they hear the passage. Who is speaking? How is the speaker feeling? How do we, as listeners, feel? What is this writer's purpose?

Coach's Corner

It's important to keep in mind that writers often have multiple purposes. Further, voices can shift slightly, even within a passage. So a reader who is very tuned in may hear more than one quality coming through in the writer's words.

Voice

Practice Trait
Lesson 3.2

NOTE: We don't have enough information to really learn much about life in the 1800s, and the piece is not humorous. But the mood is tenser because of the pain being inflicted on Frederick Douglass. Some readers *might* wish to live in the 1800s, but there's no obvious intent on the part of the writer to make us feel this way.

Different Voice—Different Purpose(s)

Share the directions to make sure everyone understands the task. This time students are on their own to think of words to describe the voice, and to come up with a list of purposes. Have students

- read the passage aloud in their writing circles.
- reread the example, looking and listening for voice and linking it to purpose.
- list as many words as they can think of to describe the voice in the space provided.
- list as many purposes for this piece as they can think of.

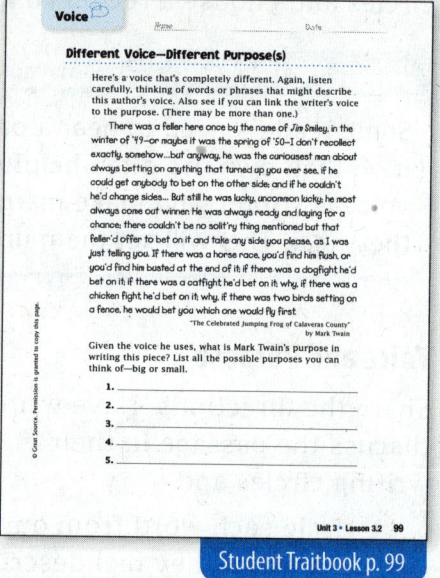

Student Traitbook p. 99

Once writers have finished responding to the passage, discuss it as a class. Feel free to share our responses, but be careful not to present them as the answers. We offer them only for purposes of comparison.

Coach's Corner

Alternatively, you can read the passage aloud if you prefer. Realize, however, that one of the challenges for writers is to hear the voice in any passage they read to themselves. If you are the reader, they will hear the voice as you interpret it.

Bringing everyone in . . .   Differentiated Instruction

The Mark Twain passage is challenging because of the way the narrator speaks. Take a few minutes to discuss the dialect and any words your students are unsure about, and encourage them to write notes on their copy. Words that may be stumbling blocks for some readers include *feller, curiousest, solit'ry,* and *busted.*

Our Response:

Words to describe this writer's voice: *casual, convincing, passionate, nostalgic*

Based on this voice, what is the writer's purpose?

- To share his excitement about Jim Smiley's luck
- To entertain his audience
- To paint a vivid picture of Jim Smiley's betting shenanigans
- To help readers see how determined Jim Smiley was to win a simple bet

A Good Match?

Remind writers of the two example passages you reviewed and discussed in the first part of this lesson. Explain that today they will use what they have learned to revise a passage to better suit its intended purpose.

Share the directions for this section to make sure the task is clear. If you have a student volunteer to share "What a Blackout!" have him or her read it aloud just as if presenting a story on the evening news.

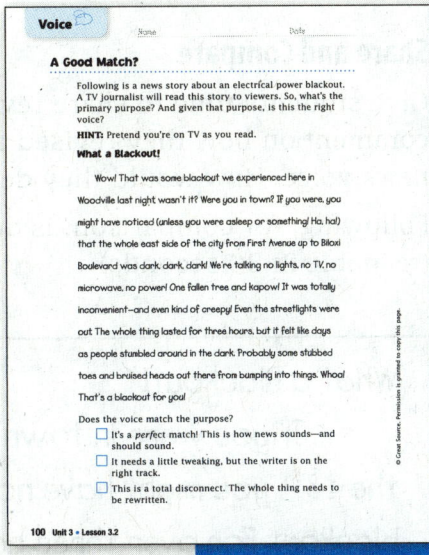

Student Traitbook p. 100

Have listeners fill in their responses. Most should agree that the voice—gushy, emotional, and far too excited—is all wrong for the news (though it could work in a note or email).

Emergency in the Newsroom!

Share the directions so that everyone understands the task. Then have writers work individually, with partners, or in writing circles to revise the passage so that it *is* right for a newscast. They should remember to read aloud as they go. It is fine to revise right on the copy. They do not need to rewrite unless they prefer to do so.

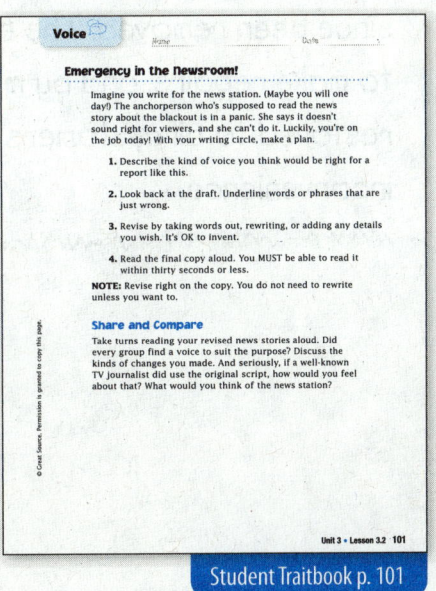

Student Traitbook p. 101

Coach's Corner

Note: If you are dividing this lesson into two parts, **Day 2 begins here.**

Coach's Corner

The next section opens with an analysis of the passage called "What a Blackout!" If you would like to have a student volunteer share this passage aloud, set this up now by choosing someone and asking him or her to rehearse it in preparation for the conclusion of that section.

Coach's Corner

News stories tend to be short for a very practical reason. News anchors have many stories to cover and limited time in which to do it. So one of the challenges of this exercise is making sure the final copy can be read aloud in 30 seconds or less.

Unit 3   165

Voice

Practice Trait
Lesson 3.2

Coach's Corner

Unlike most voices your writers have heard or studied throughout this unit, a news voice is intended to be objective and anything but individual. It should be impossible to tell who wrote a particular news story. The idea is to present information in a factual and unbiased manner, free from the personal touch that usually characterizes strong voice.

Bringing everyone in . . . | **Differentiated Instruction**

It's hardly a news flash that not every middle school student is an avid viewer of the news! With this in mind, you may wish to take a minute to talk about the right voice for a news story. How do news anchors try to present their stories? What tone of voice and facial expression do they typically use? If you have access to a short film, you might share it. In the world of news, by the way, *story* doesn't necessarily (or even usually) mean narrative. This term is used in journalism to refer to anything from an announcement to a full-blown report, and it often implies a researched piece.

Share and Compare

Give students time to share revised versions of the newscast and to comment on how they revised and the difference they hear in the news voice. How would they describe this new voice?

Following, for comparison, is our revised version of the newscast (readable in 30 seconds).

What a Blackout!

If you were in town around 9 p.m. on Tuesday the 18th, you might have noticed or even experienced a blackout. For over three hours, the whole east side of the city from First Avenue up to Biloxi Boulevard was without lights or power. Even streetlights were out. The fallen tree responsible for the power outage has since been removed. The electrical company scrambled to make repairs, and by midnight, power had been restored to all customers. The city apologizes for any inconvenience.

A Writer's Questions

Some writers feel that journalists sometimes editorialize too much. They may also feel that voices on the Internet can be too personal, inappropriately comical, or sarcastic. Share your thoughts and invite theirs. Above all, help them understand that readers, viewers, and listeners do judge writers by the voice they hear.

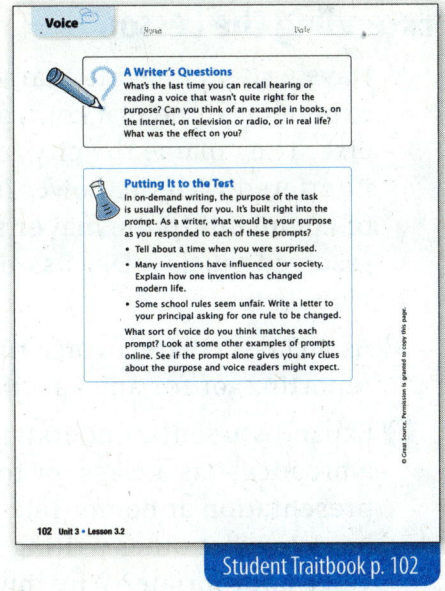

Student Traitbook p. 102

Putting It to the Test

An intended genre or purpose is usually built right into a prompt, provided the reader looks closely and reads carefully. Sometimes this takes inference, and the reader has to look for key words that suggest what the prompt writers are looking for:

- <u>Tell about a time</u> when you were surprised. (This calls for a **story**.)
- Many inventions have influenced our society. <u>Explain</u> how one invention has changed modern life. (An explanation calls for **expository or informational** writing.)
- Some school rules seem unfair. Write a letter to your principal <u>asking for a change</u> in one rule. (This calls for a **persuasive letter**—something to change the principal's thinking.)

Unit 3   167

Voice

Practice Trait
Lesson 3.2

Coach's Corner

Rubrics do not have to be genre-specific, but with a trait as vast and diverse as voice, it's hard to have one rubric fit all. Your writers are likely to find that voice shifts a little with every genre, and the rubric (written or internal) must shift, too.

Extending the Lesson

- Have writers imagine that they live in the area that experienced the blackout, and suffered along with everyone else. They blame the city for not taking down trees that clearly interfered with the power lines. Have them draft a short note of complaint to the mayor suggesting that this problem be resolved quickly. Discuss the right voice for a complaint letter. What is it?

- As a class, create a voice rubric appropriate for journalistic reporting, or for any specific genre of your choice.

- Expand students' understanding of a news voice by watching a broadcast as a class, or telling them to watch a news presentation at home. Talk about the voice they do or do not hear. In what other writing situations is an objective news voice appropriate? Why might it not work to write in this sort of voice all the time?

- Create your own rubric for voice in news writing and post it online.

- Listen to any book on CD and brainstorm words that describe the voice—and a list of writer's purposes.

- Look up a few prompts online and evaluate them to see if you and your writers can figure out the intended purpose. What sort of response is the prompt writer looking for?

LESSON 3.3

The Voice of Confidence

Student Traitbook pages 103–108

Voice

Introduce Trait

Practice Trait

Lesson 3.1
Lesson 3.2
Lesson 3.3
Lesson 3.4
Conventions & Presentation

Apply Trait

Can informational writing have voice? How? Professional writers know this well. Nonfiction books that lack voice aren't likely to get published, and if by chance they do, they're not likely to sell. Voice isn't just a gimmick or extra, like a sunroof. It's the writer's way of reaching out to the reader, getting that reader involved and excited, and most important, presenting information in a way that makes it memorable. To put it another way: Informational voice is good teaching on paper.

Objectives

Students will
- recognize the importance of voice in good informational writing.
- understand that such voice is a mark of confidence, which comes from knowing a topic well.
- analyze several passages for voice.
- create an original paragraph with strong voice.

Time Frame

Allow 50 minutes for this lesson. It can be broken into two parts.
- **Part 1:** Students analyze several passages for voice and talk about the voice they hear in each one.
- **Part 2:** Students do ten minutes of research on a chosen topic, then create an informational paragraph with strong, confident voice.

Unit 3   169

Voice

Practice Trait
Lesson 3.3

Coach's Corner

In the first part of this lesson, students are asked to select a brief nonfiction passage with strong voice to share aloud within a writing circle. You may allow time overnight for them to identify a passage. It can come from any source: book, magazine, newspaper, online article, etc. Remind them to rehearse reading aloud so they can bring out the voice. They will also do ten minutes worth of research on a topic of choice for Part 2 of the lesson; this research may be based on the same source.

Coach's Corner

Voice in informational writing comes primarily from two things. The first is passion for the topic, so topic choice is vital. The second is knowing enough about the topic to select interesting details, leave out what doesn't matter as much, and never, ever sound as if you're reaching desperately for anything to fill the page. Ironically enough, the very act of research often creates an interest in the topic that the writer didn't originally feel.

Setting Up the Lesson

Share the introduction to Lesson 3.3 in the Student Traitbook.

This lesson is about writing with confidence, which in turn leads to voice. Confidence comes, of course, from knowing a topic well. Begin by asking students where writers get information. There are many answers to this question, including online research, reading, films or other electronic media—even hands-on experience. Then try a little experiment. Have students write for just one minute (no more) on each of two topics:

- **Topic 1:** Life in the seventh grade
- **Topic 2:** Difficulties with organic farming

When they finish, ask which topic was easier to write about. How many writers were unable to write even one sentence about Topic 2? Explain that it is all but impossible to write with voice and confidence about something you know little or nothing about. Then ask how much easier it might be to write about organic farming if they knew even one or two of the following facts.

- Organic farming is now a $50 billion + industry and growing rapidly.
- Organic farming is growing fastest in the U.S and Europe, but Australia loves it, too.
- Organic farming is so-called because it does not make significant use of chemicals.
- One of the biggest problems with organic farming is pest control.
- Farmers control pests by covering plants with bags or bringing in carnivorous insects like lady bugs and praying mantises to eat others.

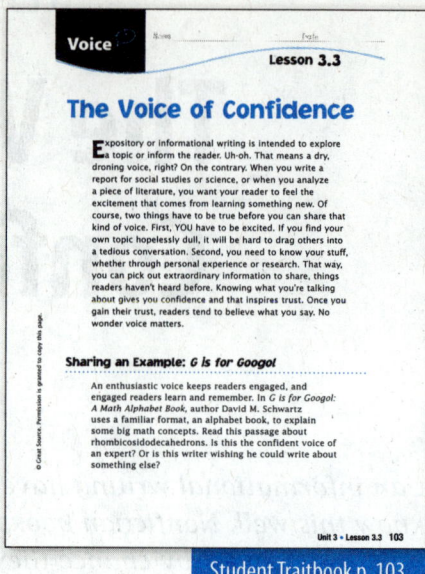

Student Traitbook p. 103

170 Unit 3

Teaching the Lesson

Sharing an Example: *G is for Googol*

Share the directions. Then share the example from *G is for Googol* while students follow along. Remind them to

- listen for the voice: Is this writer connecting with readers?
- question whether the author, David M. Schwartz, knows his stuff. Is he writing with the confidence that comes with knowing a topic well?

> **Bringing everyone in . . .**   **Differentiated Instruction**
>
> Some of your writers will benefit from knowing what a *polyhedron* is. See if they can define it: a three-dimensional geometric figure with multiple faces. If you have a copy of Schwartz's book, you may also share other passages. Writers will enjoy hearing more of this writer's voice—he is clearly enchanted with math concepts. (And yes, knows them well.)

Coach's Corner

> The passage is from *G is for Googol: a Math Alphabet Book* by David M. Schwartz. We recommend that *you* read the passage aloud yourself. It is a little challenging, mostly because of that word *rhombicosidodecahedron*. Practice saying this word together.

Reflection

Give writers a minute or two to fill in their responses, and discuss them as a group. Most should find this voice appealing and even wish that other textbooks were written with as much enthusiasm.

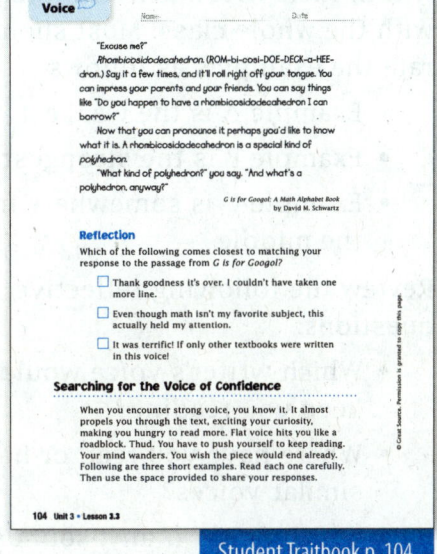

Student Traitbook p. 104

Coach's Corner

> We have used the word *confident* to describe this kind of voice. What other words fit? Perhaps *secure, poised, knowledgeable, expert, well-informed, assured.*

Searching for the Voice of Confidence

Share the directions aloud to be sure everyone understands the task. Then group students into writing circles and give them time to share Examples A, B, and C. Suggest that they do the following.

- Skim them quickly on their own
- Choose a reader to read each one aloud
- Listen as each example is shared, then fill in their responses

Allow 12–15 minutes (4–5 minutes per example) for this task.

Coach's Corner

> Remind students that even though they are working together in a group, they do not need to agree on their responses to any piece of writing. They should think and respond individually, then compare notes if they wish. Voices are distinctive, and so are reader responses.

Unit 3 171

Voice

Practice Trait
Lesson 3.3

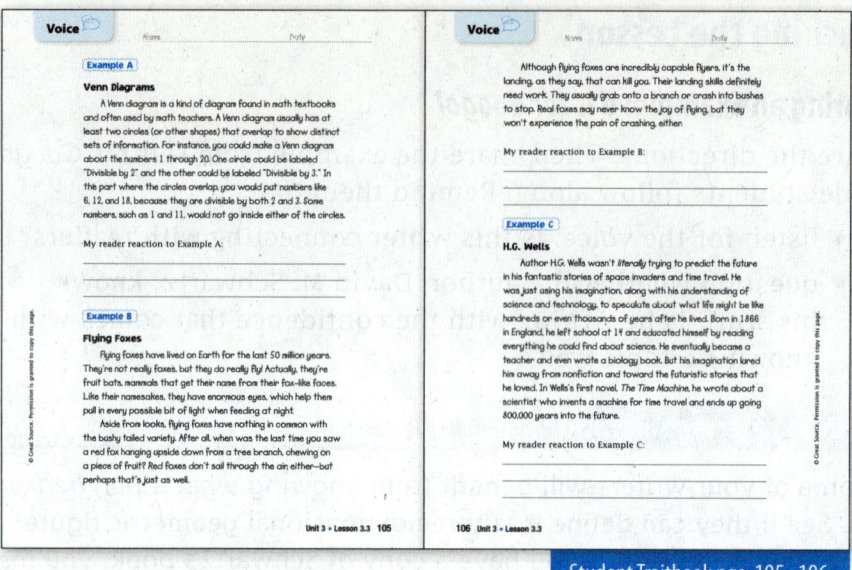

Student Traitbook pgs. 105–106

Coach's Corner

A good way of getting at the strength of a particular voice is to ask, "If this were just the first part of a 100-page book, how much would you look forward to reading more?" Voice in informational writing is important precisely because it keeps readers engaged, which keeps them learning.

Share and Compare

Give students time to share their responses to the three passages within their writing circles, then with the whole class. Most should rate the examples as follows.

- Example A is the weakest
- Example B is the strongest
- Example C is somewhere in the middle

Review the following reflective questions.

- Which writer's voice would keep you reading?
- Where have you read or heard similar voices?
- Which voice, if any, sounds like you?

Student Traitbook p. 107

Coach's Corner

You can also set this activity up within your classroom by providing a range of nonfiction books, newspapers, and journals for writers to explore. Nonfiction book writers known for strong voice include Gary Paulsen, Paul Fleischman, Sid Fleischman, Ben Hillman, and David Quammen. Add your favorites, along with favorite journalists, to the mix.

Sharing Another Confident Voice

Share the directions and make sure everyone understands the task and has a voice to share. If you have prepared them for this ahead of time, they have passages selected. (If not, you can delay this portion of the lesson, giving them time over night to locate a passage to share.) When everyone is ready, have them complete the following.

172 Unit 3

- Meet in writing circles to share their nonfiction passages
- Take turns reading aloud
- Discuss the voices that they hear
- Choose one voice from the group to share with the whole class

I'm the World's Leading Expert

Refresh students' memories about your previous discussions on informational voice and the link to confidence—and knowledge of the topic. Invite comments and questions.

Then review the directions for this portion of the lesson, and give students twenty minutes to complete the following.

- **Choose** a topic.
- Do some quick, light research to **uncover three intriguing details**.
- **Record those details** in the space provided.
- Use this information to **write draft paragraphs** on the topics.

Paragraphs need not be polished, but they should sound confident! Have writers use their own paper.

Share and Compare

Give writers time to share their paragraphs with partners or in writing circles. They should listen for the moment with the strongest voice, and let the writer know what that is. If listeners hear different strong moments, so much the better!

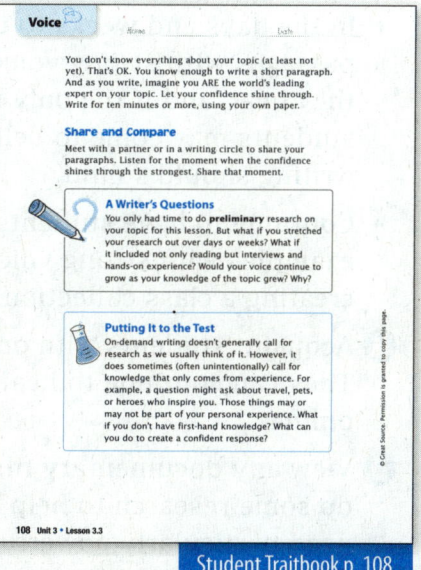

Student Traitbook p. 108

Coach's Corner

Note: If you are dividing this lesson into two parts, **Day 2 begins here.**

Coach's Corner

Students can look to any resource for information, but we recommend that they consider the source from which they drew the share-aloud passage. If they liked that topic enough to read about it, they might want to write about it, too—at least one paragraph. This also reinforces the reading-writing connection: Writers often borrow content, voice, and genre from the reading they love.

Coach's Corner

The purpose of this activity is NOT to produce a thoroughly researched piece, but only to demonstrate how much power even a tiny bit of knowledge can lend to voice. As writers share, be sure they listen for that confidence, and give their classmates supportive feedback.

Unit 3   173

Voice

Practice Trait
Lesson 3.3

A Writer's Questions

While there is no right answer to this question, we believe that voice does grow with knowledge. Most serious nonfiction writers research topics for days—even months. And as their understanding grows, so does their confidence and ability to choose the most unusual, little-known details. Readers love writers who truly teach them something new.

Putting It to the Test

Lack of personal experience can be a roadblock, but sometimes there's a way around it. When faced with a question outside your range of experience, you can try to recall any second-hand experience: a conversation, film, television show, or book. Sometimes, even with a few clues, you can invent enough details to make your writing convincing. Imagination helps, too. After all, the reader won't know whether you've actually owned a dog yourself or you're just pretending, based on a friend's experience or a movie you saw. Finally, confidence makes a big difference. Write as if you *are* the world's leading expert, even if you don't feel that way. You might be surprised how convincing a confident attitude can be!

Extending the Lesson

- In the days and weeks to come, share additional nonfiction passages with strong voice. Writers tend to imitate the voices they hear, and if the only nonfiction models are textbooks, students may come to believe that is how their own nonfiction writing should sound.
- Continue to have students search for nonfiction (and other) examples with strong voice. Share them aloud and consider creating a class collection.
- Acquaint students with one or two of your favorite journalists. They can continue to hear those voices in newspapers or online.
- View any documentary film with strong voice. Have students do some research to help you make a selection. Film scripts need particularly powerful voice because the narration has to compete with visuals that are often striking and dramatic. This is no easy task. After viewing the film, discuss the special challenges that face script writers. Is this a job any of your writers might aspire to?

If students are going to write, they need to regularly experience the best modern voices in the land, the voices of their time.

—Tom Romano
Crafting Authentic Voice

LESSON 3.4

Knowing Your Audience

Student Traitbook pages 109–114

Voice

Introduce Trait
Practice Trait
Lesson 3.1
Lesson 3.2
Lesson 3.3
Lesson 3.4
Conventions & Presentation
Apply Trait

Readers, like fish, don't all respond to the same bait. A wiggly 5-year-old with a passion for video games, an energetic 16-year-old football player, and a dignified 60-year-old theater director may be looking for very different things as readers. The writer who knows his or her audience well will stand a better chance of capturing and holding their attention.

Objectives

Students will
- understand that voice must sometimes be refined to suit the audience.
- analyze a passage to see how one character adjusts his voice for the audience.
- write a brief note with a specific audience in mind.
- write two similar persuasive letters to two very different audiences.

Time Frame
Allow 50 minutes for this lesson. We suggest breaking it into two parts.
- **Part 1:** Students discuss an example and write a short note to a specific audience.
- **Part 2:** Students create two similar letters to two different audiences.

Unit 3 175

Voice

Practice Trait
Lesson 3.4

Coach's Corner

In everyday life, we change voices to suit the audience all the time. Ask how many of your writers have overheard someone speaking on the phone, and known just from the tone of voice who was most likely on the other end of the line. What gave it away?

Setting Up the Lesson

Share the introduction to Lesson 3.4 in the Student Traitbook.

For this introduction, play a game called Name That Audience. To do this, you will need at least three examples of writing from different sources. (Use more if you have time to locate them.) Be sure you do not share book covers or magazine or newspaper titles—that makes the game too simple. Just read 2–4 sentences from each source, and see if students can guess the intended audience. Use any sources you like. Following are some suggestions.

- A picture book for young readers
- A novel for readers of your students' age
- An encyclopedia for a general audience
- A magazine article for adult readers
- A recipe for young cooks
- An advertisement for the general public
- A film review for the general public
- A passage from a textbook for elementary students
- A passage from a letter or email you've received recently

As you share, talk about how your writers know who the intended audience is. What about the voice gives it away? Language? Sentence structure? Tone? Or a combination?

Teaching the Lesson

Sharing an Example: "Sugarcane Fire"

Share the directions and the excerpt "Sugarcane Fire" from *Crazy Loco* by David Rice, or if you prefer, have a volunteer (with some rehearsal) share it aloud. Remind students to listen for the subtle way Romero adjusts his voice to get what he wants from the high school students.

Student Traitbook p. 109

Coach's Corner

This passage is from "Sugarcane Fire" in *Crazy Loco* by David Rice. Note that we do not hear Romero speak in the beginning of the passage, but based on what the bullying high school students say to him, we can infer how he might be feeling, and how his voice might sound if he did not work hard to modify it.

176 Unit 3

Reflection

Give students time to discuss the passage with partners or in writing circles. When they finish, have them share comments with the whole class, referring to some or all of our reflective questions:

- How was Romero feeling inside?
- What sort of voice might have come out if he'd let those feelings show?
- What sort of voice *did* he use (after giving it some thought)?
- Why did the high school students give him the tickets?

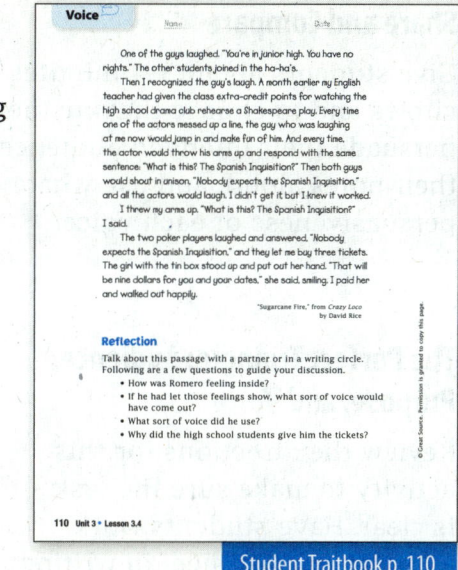

Student Traitbook p. 110

Bringing everyone in . . . **Differentiated Instruction**

Have any of your students been in a similar situation? You may have a student who identifies with Romero and is willing to share his or her experience. Or, you may have an experience of your own to share. Have you ever had to deal with bullies?

A Different Audience

Review the directions to make sure everyone understands the task. Students will imagine that *they* are in the position of wanting to buy tickets, and you, their teacher, are the person selling the tickets. You are NOT supposed to sell those tickets to younger students, so they will need to make their notes very convincing. Give them 3–4 minutes to write.

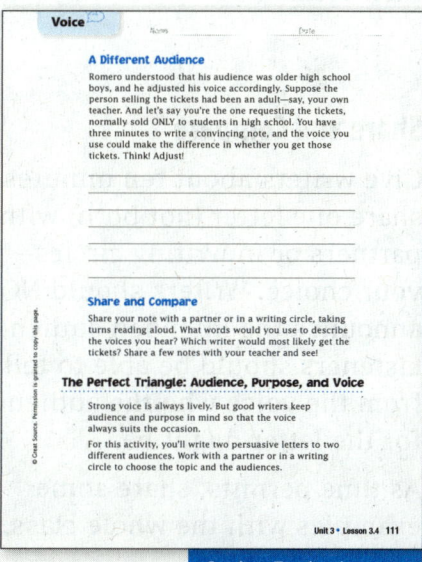

Student Traitbook p. 111

Coach's Corner

Be sure students understand that the key to success is voice. They cannot change the rules, and you are not supposed to bend them. This is a hypothetical situation, and not necessarily reflective of what you would REALLY decide under these circumstances!

Unit 3 177

Voice

Practice Trait
Lesson 3.4

Coach's Corner
Respond in a simple yes-no fashion: the note would persuade you or it wouldn't. What matters is feedback on what did or did not make each note persuasive. If none of the notes persuade you, specify the kind of voice you were hoping for.

Coach's Corner
Note: If you have divided this lesson into two parts, **Day 2 begins here.**

Coach's Corner
Have writers choose any topic. Our list is only intended to jump start their thinking.

Coach's Corner
Writers should choose two audiences that are totally different—in age, for example, or in perspective. The whole point is to modify the voice to suit each audience.

Share and Compare

Give students about 3–4 minutes to share their notes in writing circles and to choose the one they think is most likely to persuade their intended audience: you! Then have them read their notes aloud, and use whatever method you wish to rate the persuasiveness of each voice.

The Perfect Triangle: Audience, Purpose, and Voice

Review the directions for this activity to make sure the task is clear. Have students work with partners or meet in writing circles to choose two audiences. Then have them choose a topic (from our list or one of their own).

Give them about 5–6 minutes to discuss the task and make their choices. Once they are ready, give them about 10–12 minutes to write their letters (5–6 minutes per letter). Writers should work **individually** when composing their letters.

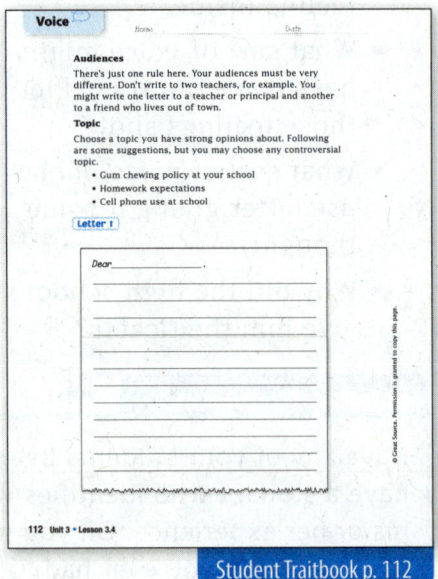

Student Traitbook p. 112

Share and Compare

Give writers about ten minutes to share one letter (not both) with partners or in writing circles—your choice. Writers should NOT announce the intended audience. Listeners should be able to tell from the voice who the audience for the letter might be.

As time permits, share some examples with the whole class.

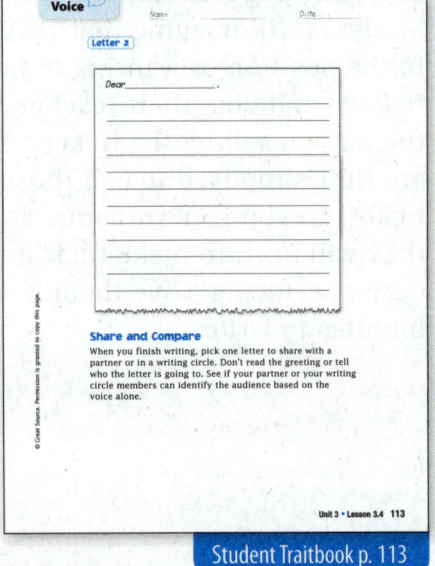

Student Traitbook p. 113

A Writer's Questions

When the audience changes, the purpose sometimes shifts a little, too. For example, let's say the topic is cell phone use in school. A student might write to a principal to persuade him or her to allow more leniency in cell phone regulations in the name of safety. That same student might write to a friend basically to express frustration at having to keep a cell phone turned off for much of the day. Though the topic remains constant, both voice and purpose shift with audience.

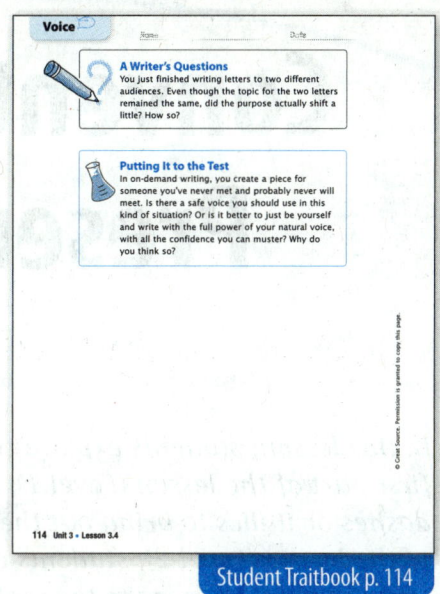

Student Traitbook p. 114

Putting It to the Test

There is no simple answer to this question. This is precisely the sort of decision writers and teachers are talking about when they discuss the importance of taking risks. A safe voice never offends anyone, but is unlikely to receive high scores in that trait either. A writer who uses a comedic or sarcastic voice runs the risk that readers won't like it. But if they do, they *really* like it. And the reward is likely to be a high score. Sometimes, shooting for the moon pays off.

Extending the Lesson

- Have students return to the definitions of voice they wrote in Lesson 3.1. Would they add or change anything now? Post some of their refined definitions.
- Review the Student Rubric for Voice. Does it sufficiently capture the strategies writers really use? If we left something important out, revise the rubric to make it more useful for you and your students.
- Letter writing is a great way to practice voice. Have students compose emails for various audiences and keep a running journal entry about the various subtle ways they shift voice as they do so.
- Create a blog inviting participants to share specific strategies for putting voice into writing. In particular, discuss the impact of purpose and audience on voice.

I've sought to help students write clearly, succinctly, and vividly with detail, drama, and verve. They know when they've written this way. Sometimes a quiet sureness comes over them. Sometimes they light right up, so transforming is the experience of writing with voice.

—Tom Romano
Crafting Authentic Voice

Voice

Introduce Trait
Practice Trait
Lesson 3.1
Lesson 3.2
Lesson 3.3
Lesson 3.4
Conventions & Presentation
Apply Trait

Conventions and Presentation

Student Traitbook pages 115–124

In this lesson, students explore two ways of bringing out voice. In the first part of the lesson (Level 1), students use conventions such as dashes or italics to bring out the voice in dialogue. In the second part of the lesson (Level 2), students examine the format of a stage play and use what they learn to create a mini play of their own.

Objectives

Editing Level 1: Conventions
Students will

- understand that dashes, exclamation marks, and italics influence the way text is read.
- practice reading aloud, reflecting on how these conventions affect their performance.
- edit an example of dialogue, introducing conventions that bring out the voice.

Editing Level 2: Presentation
Students will

- understand that a play is formatted differently from dialogue in a novel or short story.
- review layout from an actual play script.
- create a mini play, using what they have learned about appropriate format for a script.

 Time Frame

Allow 50 minutes for this lesson. We suggest breaking it into two parts.

- **Part 1:** Students explore the use of conventions in creating or enhancing voice.
- **Part 2:** Students review a play script and create a mini play of their own.

Editing Level 1: Conventions
The Triple Threat

Setting Up the Lesson

In this part of the lesson, students explore the use of exclamation marks, italics, and dashes to influence voice in any writing—most notably dialogue. Be sure the Copyeditor's Poster is plainly visible so they can see how to insert various marks.

Begin with these steps:
- Share the introduction to this lesson in the Student Traitbook.
- Ask how many of your students use exclamation marks, italics, or dashes in their writing.
- Be sure they know what each mark is and how it is used.

Bringing everyone in . . . **Differentiated Instruction**

It is important for students to understand throughout this lesson that while some conventions (capital at the beginning of a sentence, subject-verb agreement) are about right and wrong, many conventions are less about correctness and more about finding subtle ways to bring out meaning and voice. Truly skillful use of conventions goes far beyond simply getting it right.

Teaching the Lesson

A Warm-Up

Read through the directions for this section together, pausing to review the examples that show use of the dash and hyphen. Emphasize the difference between the dash and the hyphen by doing the following things.

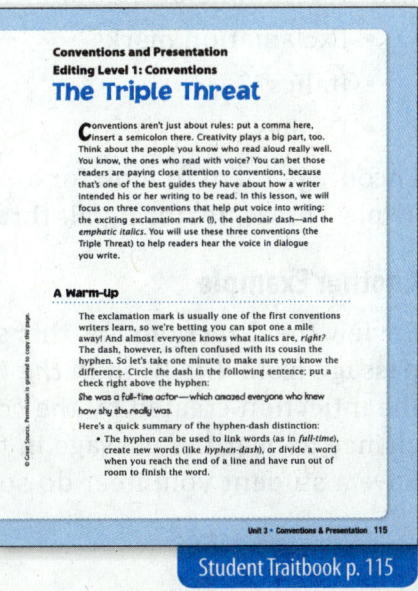
Student Traitbook p. 115

Conventions & Presentation

Practice Trait
Editing Level 1: Conventions

Coach's Corner

Be prepared to model use of exclamation marks, italics, and dashes. Ideally, you will have students locate their own examples, using books they bring to class or publications you provide. You want examples with good dialogue.

Unit 3   181

Conventions & Presentation

Practice Trait
Editing Level 1: Conventions

- Look carefully at the initial example and have students identify the hyphen and the dash:

  She was a full-time actor—which amazed everyone who knew how shy she really was.

- Discuss what each mark shows and have students read this sentence aloud to hear and feel the effect of the dash. Ask how the use of the dash in this sentence makes us read it just a little differently than a comma would. (It gives it more emphasis.)
- Review the explanations in the warm-up, and be sure the distinction between hyphen and dash is clear.
- Make sure all your students are comfortable with the use of exclamation marks (which should not be overdone) and italics (which create emphasis).

Take a Look

For this part of the warm-up, writers should spend some time skimming books that contain dialogue. We recommend grouping students in writing circles so that they can share and discuss any examples they find. Have them continue looking until each group has found an example of dialogue with at least one of the following.

- Exclamation marks
- Italics
- Dashes

Encourage them to look for a Triple Threat, featuring all three!

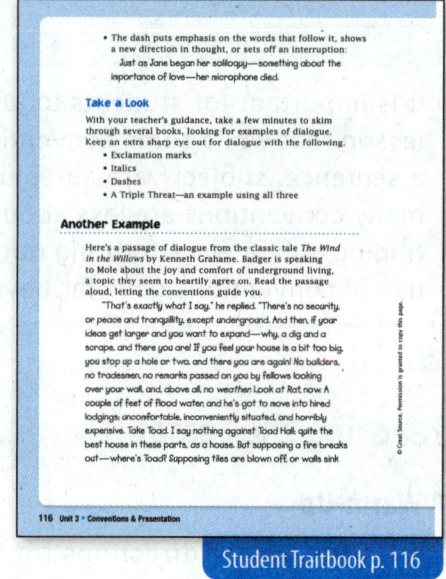

Student Traitbook p. 116

Another Example

Review the directions for this section, and have students read the passage from *The Wind in the Willows* silently, on their own, hearing the inflection created by the conventions. Once they have had a chance to hear the passage in their own minds, read it aloud, or have a student volunteer do so.

Coach's Corner

Students will appreciate the impact of these conventional marks far more if they read the dialogue aloud—and also try to imagine how it would sound if the marks were not in place. Tell them to think of these marks as cues to the reader, showing how a passage should be interpreted.

Coach's Corner

It is important for the reader (whether it's you or a student) to pay close attention to use of exclamation marks, italics, and dashes in this passage so that listeners *hear* the marks. We suggest NOT having readers follow along. Instead, have them try to envision the conventions based on how the person reads the text.

182 Unit 3

Share and Discuss

Review the directions briefly. Then give readers time to go back and highlight any conventions that helped them figure out how to read the passage. Also ask whether they might (as writers) have used additional italics or other conventions in this text, based on their own reading.

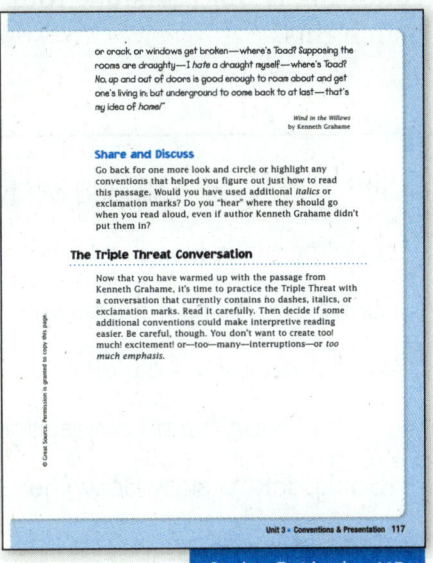

Student Traitbook p. 117

Coach's Corner

Do expressive readers tend to create their own conventions as they read aloud—or even silently? Do any of your students do this? Take a moment and discuss how expressive oral reading sometimes works this way.

The Triple Threat Conversation

Now that students are warmed up, it's time for them to do some editing of their own, adding dashes, exclamation marks, or italics to create voice in dialogue.

Review the directions to make sure everyone understands the task. Then have them read the passage about Chandra and Alex on their own, playing with conventions to create the voice they hear. Encourage them to

- read the passage more than one time.
- experiment by reading aloud, trying various things until they find a "sound" they like.
- test those conventions by reading aloud, softly.

Coach's Corner

Remind writers that this is a different sort of editing from much of what they have done in the past. They are not looking for errors. They are using conventions to reflect the voice they hear in dialogue, and to show readers how to interpret a passage in an expressive way.

Share and Compare

Have writers meet with partners or in writing circles to compare their work. Encourage them to read aloud, line by line, as they do so. They should not spend too much time trying to resolve disagreements, but simply consider different ways of reviewing the text. When they finish, have them coach you as you mark up all or part of the text.

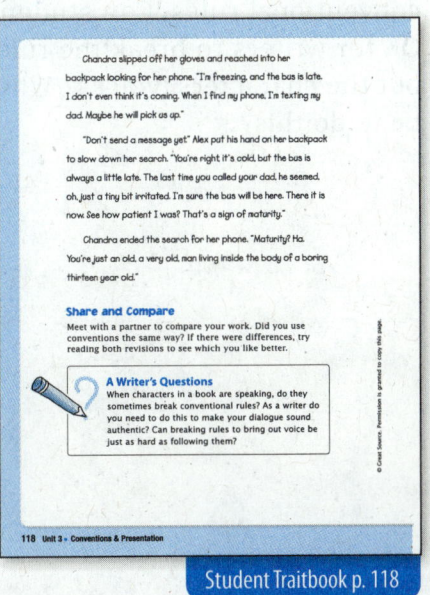

Student Traitbook p. 118

Unit 3   183

Conventions & Presentation

Practice Trait
Editing Level 1: Conventions

Following is our revision. Your students' work does NOT need to match this.

> Chandra slipped off her gloves and reached into her backpack looking for her phone. "I'm freezing!! The bus is late—I don't even think it's *coming*. When I find *my* phone, I'm texting *my* dad. Maybe *he* will pick us up."
>
> "Don't send a message *yet*." Alex put his hand on her backpack to slow down her search. "You're right, it's cold, but the bus is *always* a little late. The last time *you* called *your* dad, he seemed—oh, just a *tiny bit* irritated. I'm sure the bus will be here—there it *is!* See how *patient* I was? That's a sign of *maturity*."
>
> Chandra ended the search for her phone. "*Maturity?!?* Ha! You're just an old—a *very* old—man living inside the body of a *boring* thirteen year old!"

A Writer's Questions

Discuss whether students think characters in books break conventional rules. Can students think of any examples? Is it OK for writers to break the rules if they feel it is necessary to bring out the characters' voices? Why or why not? How difficult might it be to do this?

Editing Level 2: Presentation
The Play's the Thing

Setting Up the Lesson

In this lesson, students have a chance to see that dialogue or discourse in a play is formatted quite differently from that in a novel or short story. A script includes stage directions and cues to guide the actors, transforming simple speech into a multi-dimensional performance. Students will compare the dialogue between Chandra and Alex (from Level 1 of this lesson) to a play version, review a second script, and create a mini play of their own.

Bringing everyone in . . . Differentiated Instruction

Perhaps you have a drama class or group at your school. But if not, some students may have never seen a theater production. Find out if any have, and give them a few minutes to share their experiences. You may wish to share your own, too. If you have computer access, you can watch a few minutes of a performance (perhaps something from *Hamlet*, in tribute to our title) so that students can picture the way actors move as they say their lines. Also consider researching current theater productions in your area or sharing playbills from those or other productions.

Teaching the Lesson

A Warm-Up

Review the directions for this part of the lesson. Then have students read and discuss the dramatic version of the Chandra and Alex conversation, either with partners or in writing circles.

Tell students to notice as many differences as possible between this play version and the original dialogue in the Student Traitbook. They should write their comments in the numbered list provided.

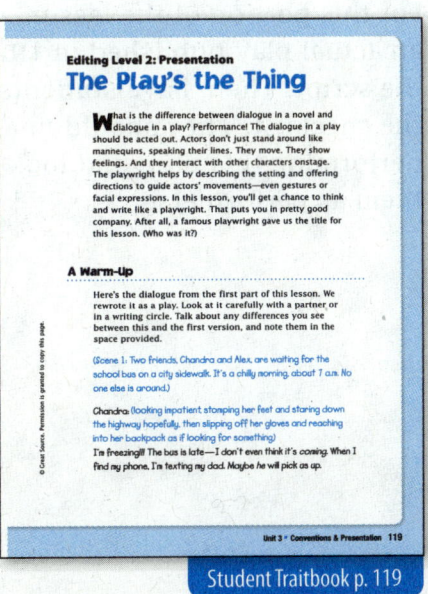

Student Traitbook p. 119

Conventions & Presentation

Practice Trait
Editing Level 2: Presentation

Coach's Corner

Actors on a stage can incorporate an expressiveness that is difficult for a reader sitting in a chair to attain. Take a minute to discuss how the ability to move and gesture in dramatic ways can influence the way dialogue is received by an audience. How are performance and voice connected?

Unit 3   185

Conventions & Presentation

Practice Trait
Editing Level 2: Presentation

> **Bringing everyone in...** **Differentiated Instruction**
>
> Students may enjoy performing this play, and it will give them practice for the writing they do later. Students cannot really appreciate the benefit of stage direction until they experience it as actors, who rely on that direction to know how to conduct themselves on stage. Have a narrator read the first part, which sets the stage.

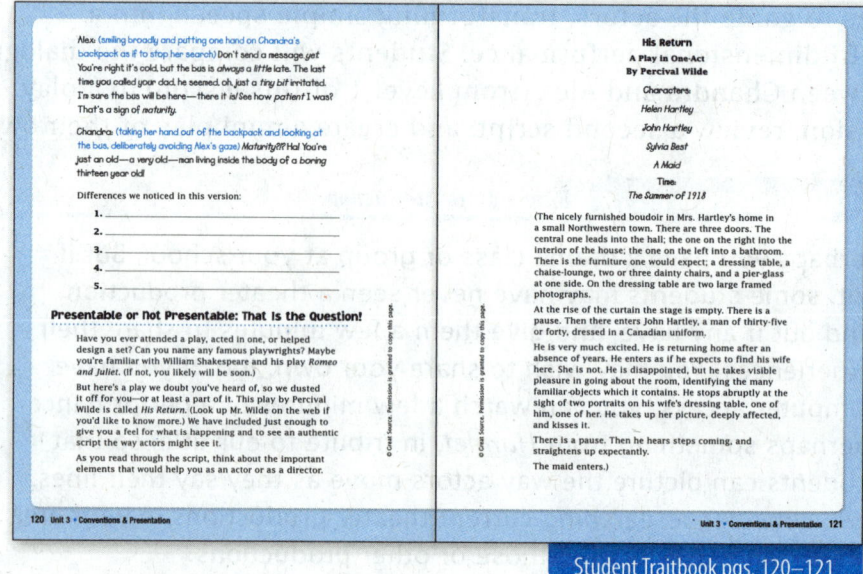

Student Traitbook pgs. 120–121

Presentable or Not Presentable: That Is the Question!

For this portion of the lesson, students will examine a script for an actual play published in 1922. Review the directions preceding the script. Then, have students read through the play, up to the checklist. They should imagine how it feels to be an actor performing this play, and look for anything that would be helpful to them as performers.

Checklist

Have students work with partners or in writing circles to complete the following.

- Review the script.
- Check each item on the list that this script includes.
- Add any other helpful items we may have forgotten.

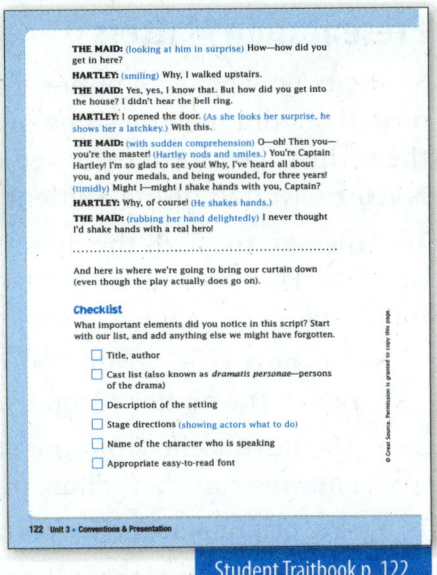

Student Traitbook p. 122

Share and Compare

When students finish, take time to review the script and go over their thoughts. What is helpful? Is there anything the scriptwriter might have done differently to make rehearsal and performance even easier for the actors?

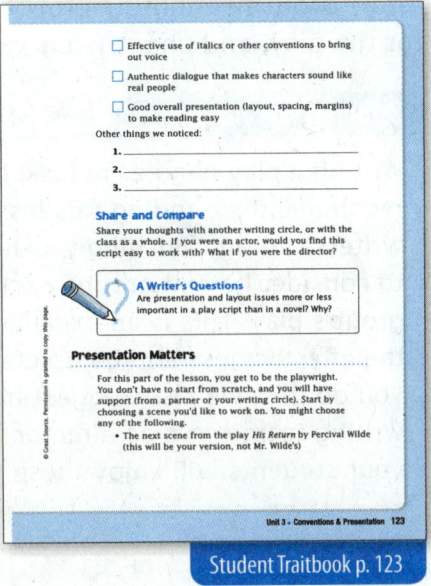

Student Traitbook p. 123

Coach's Corner

If time permits, perform this play as well. This may delay your students' writing of their own script for another day, but it does provide excellent preparation for that closing activity (see **Presentation Matters**).

A Writer's Questions

Most people would likely agree that presentation issues are more important in a play script than in a novel because a play is meant to be performed, not just read. This is why people so often say they never really understood or appreciated Shakespeare until seeing it on the stage. Performing requires "reading" with your whole body, not just your eyes, ears, and voice.

Conventions & Presentation

Practice Trait
Editing Level 2: Presentation

Coach's Corner

Remind writers to refer to the Checklist periodically to be sure they are not leaving anything important out of their scripts. They should write the play as if it were going to be performed by someone else—someone outside their circle. There's no minimum length, but it is helpful if each character speaks several times.

Presentation Matters

Students now have an opportunity to write a short play of their own. It should include some of the elements they have noticed in the scripts they have reviewed (see **Checklist** in the **Presentation Matters** section of the Student Traitbook).

Together, go through the directions so that everyone understands the task. They can choose to base their play on any of the following.

- The next scene from the play "His Return" (it does not need to match the actual second scene of the original play)
- The next scene from the story of Chandra and Alex (set anywhere of their choosing)
- Any original scene involving two characters

We suggest that writers work in writing circles of three or four students for this activity, but they may also work with partners. Allow about five minutes for them to choose a subject and setting for the play, and about twenty minutes more for writing.

Bringing everyone in . . . | **Differentiated Instruction**

Writing a play is no easy task! If you can be flexible with time, we recommend extending this lesson into another class period so that writers can put finishing touches on their plays. You may also wish to consider having groups exchange scripts and perform another group's play. This is an excellent (and very fun) way to check out the effectiveness and completeness of the stage directions. If you do this, we also suggest having one person from the original writing team serve as director for the performing group. You and your students will enjoy these performances!

Checklist

Have students work with partners or in writing circles to complete the following.

- Review the script.
- Check each item on the list that this script includes.
- Add any other helpful items we may have forgotten.

Student Traitbook p. 124

Extending the Lesson

- Have students edit any copy on which they are currently working, using skills they practiced in this and preceding lessons for the trait of Conventions and Presentation.
- Look for creative uses of conventions in any literature you are currently reading, and continue your discussion of how conventions affect voice.
- If you have not already done so, perform the plays you wrote as part of this lesson.
- Look for other plays or scenes your students can perform, and connect performance with the trait of Voice. How does this trait come alive on stage?
- Find a theater director or actor who might come to your class to discuss what makes for a good script, and how much actors depend on writers.
- Search online for other productions that are now public domain. If you find one that interests your writers, perform it—perhaps inviting an audience. (Use your presentation skills to design posters advertising the play, personal invitations, or both.)
- Watch any theater production, online, on video, or (best of all) in person. Talk about how stage direction likely influenced any part of the production.
- Check out websites for local theater groups to hear interviews with actors or directors, sometimes offered interactively.

When students write with voice, they put the indelible stamp of their personalities on the information—they make it their own.

—Ralph Fletcher
What a Writer Needs

UNIT 3
Voice

Introduce Trait

Practice Trait

Apply Trait

50 min.

Final Curtain Call 191	• Preview pages 191–199
Assessing and Revising Sample Papers 192	• Have students apply what they have learned about Voice by assessing Sample Papers 11 and 12
Sample Paper 11: *Annapurna: One of the 14* Score and Rationale	
Sample Paper 12: *The Little Black Dress* Score and Rationale	• Have students revise Sample Paper 11 for the trait of Voice
Revising Sample Paper 11: *Annapurna: One of the 14*	

50 min.

Revising and Editing a Personal Draft 197	• Invite students to revise and edit their own writing for Ideas, Organization, Voice, and Conventions and Presentation
	• Assess students' growth as writers
Parting Thoughts 199	• Conclude the trait of Voice

Final Curtain Call

It's time to give students a chance to apply what they have learned. Each of the following steps also provides *you* with an opportunity to assess their growth. You will have students demonstrate their knowledge of Ideas, Organization, Voice, and Conventions and Presentation by completing the following steps.

1. **Apply knowledge of Voice by assessing and revising the work of others.**

    Your students will read and assess Sample Papers 11 and 12. This time, they will work independently, using what they have learned to
    - decide for themselves which piece is stronger.
    - score each sample, using the Student Rubric for Voice.
    - brainstorm ways of improving the weaker paper.
    - use the Student Rubric and/or Revising Checklist for Voice to revise the weaker paper.

    Assessment Component: Base your assessment of growth on students' revision of Sample Paper 11: *Annapurna: One of the 14*. The revised version should advance several points on the rubric, achieving a final score of 4, 5, or 6. Assess each student's final draft of *Annapurna: One of the 14,* using the Teacher Rubric for Voice.

2. **Apply knowledge of Voice by assessing and revising their own personal writing.**

    Students will now pull their original drafts from their folders to revise and edit, applying everything they have learned from
    - reading and using *four* student rubrics, checklists, and posters.
    - discussing and assessing the writing of other students.
    - reading or hearing literature that exemplifies strengths in all four traits.
    - completing lessons to build skills in *each trait.*
    - assessing and revising a weak writing sample.

    Assessment Component: Score each final draft and compare those final scores to the baseline scores you assigned earlier to writers' rough drafts. Do not base your assessment *exclusively* on the differences between these scores, however. Look carefully at the quality, nature, and extent of each writer's revision. How creative were they? What risks did they take? Add additional points for good editing or creative presentation.

Coach's Corner

If a student's score on the final draft does not leap the river in a given trait, provide that student an option to revise or edit further, using one or more checklists for revision to create a workable plan. In scoring Conventions, look for correctness, but also the writer's skill in bringing out meaning and voice; consider Presentation based on the importance of design to the document. It's critical to a play or poem, for example—perhaps less so to a narrative.

Coach's Corner

Check out the Assessment Guidelines for a much more detailed discussion of effective ways to assess your student writers' performance and growth.

Voice

Introduce Trait
Practice Trait
Apply Trait
Assessing and Revising Sample Papers
Revising and Editing a Personal Draft

Assessing and Revising Sample Papers

Student Traitbook pages 125–128

Sample Paper 11: *Annapurna: One of the 14* and Sample Paper 12: *The Little Black Dress*

1. Remind students that you have now talked about the trait of Voice for some time. This activity will give them a chance to see how they have grown as assessors and revisers with respect to that trait.
2. Refer them to the Student Rubric for Voice.
3. Pair students up, and then refer them to Sample Papers 11 and 12.
4. Let students be a little more independent by
   - giving them both papers at one time.
   - having them read the papers aloud to each other—in any order.
   - having them discuss and decide which is stronger in Voice.
   - scoring the two papers together, thereby using comparisons to help zero in on the best score for each.
5. As students score the papers, they should think about these

   ❓ **Key Questions . . .**
   - Is this paper fun to read or listen to?
   - Would you like to read more by this same author? Why?
   - Does this writer put a lot of energy into the writing?
   - Do you think he or she chose this topic personally—and likes it?
   - If you wrote on this topic, could you make the voice stronger?
   - What word best describes the voice in this paper?
   - Is the writer sharing his/her honest thoughts and feelings? How do you know?
   - Can you point to specific places in the paper where the writer's voice comes through?
   - Are there places where the writer should say things differently?

Coach's Corner

Writers will likely be working in writing circles for this activity. They should strive to come to agreement (on the 6-point scale) within a point. However, each student should vote individually. The purpose of working toward agreement is to stimulate discussion. Remind writers to read aloud as they score.

Coach's Corner

The two papers selected for this activity are both informational. Both writers did research to learn about their topics and collect details that might interest readers. Clearly, the writer of Sample Paper 12 found enough information to be very selective about the details she shared with readers, and this made a difference in voice.

Coach's Corner

Remind students that it is helpful to highlight or underline moments of strong voice, especially when comparing two papers. (Remember those small "v's" in the right margin?) The visual difference in results makes scoring far easier.

6. When students are finished scoring, discuss which paper is stronger in the trait of Voice and why. Tell students to identify strong features from *The Little Black Dress*. Where and how does this writer's voice come through? Tell them to identify specific problems with *Annapurna: One of the 14*. What keeps this writer's voice in check?

7. Compare students' scores with ours (See *Scores and Rationales*).

Score and Rationale for Sample Paper 11: Annapurna: One of the 14

Most readers agree that this paper **is weak in the trait of Voice.** Ironically, this writer knows quite a lot about the topic, but does little with the information to make it enticing, shocking, or anything but strictly factual. It is about as emotion-free as a description of a dangerous mountain might conceivably be. Like a computer, the writer feeds us data about heights, climbers, and recorded deaths, never elaborating or giving us reason to feel anything—even curious. Nothing is explained. For example why was Annapurna given its name? (It seems ironic for a mountain that is clearly known more for danger.) Why did the first climbers go up, and what went wrong with all those who failed or died? A hint of vivid description, a brief personal anecdote, even a quotation from one of the climbers or a photographer would have given a human touch to a piece that's currently colder than the mountain snows. Some readers may argue that there is a slight hint of voice in the next to last paragraph (*You can suffer a fatal fall or die of hypothermia*), but this seems more matter of fact than personal, so we would give this piece a **score of 1 in the trait of Voice**. This writer is writing to finish, not to engage us.

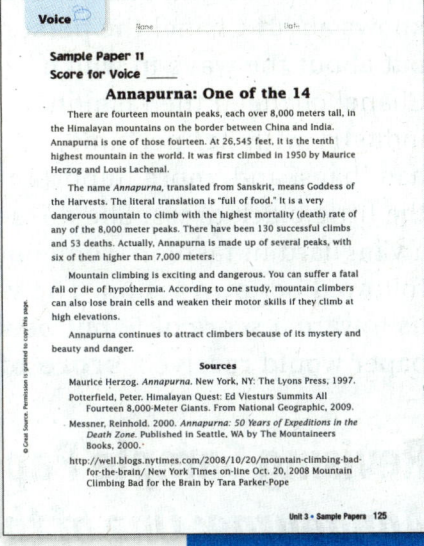

Student Traitbook p. 125

Coach's Corner

When an informational piece is strong in Voice, readers find themselves wanting to learn more. At this point, which topic would your students like to read more about, or research on their own: fashion or the Himalayas?

Coach's Corner

Readers have a lot of built-in topic bias. And there's no simple way around this. Some love race cars, some love box turtles. Caution readers that what they are scoring is not choice of topic per se, but the writer's skill in dealing with that topic, and perhaps sparking our interest in something we didn't know we cared about.

Voice

Introduce Trait
Assessing and Revising Sample Papers

Coach's Corner
Is there a gender divide between these two papers? Is it easier for females to hear voice in a paper about a fashion icon, or for males to hear voice in a piece on mountain climbing? Remind writers to look beyond the topic and to ask what the writer does with that topic. Even a reader who cares nothing about fashion is likely to hear the enthusiasm and total involvement the writer of Sample Paper 12 brings to this piece.

Coach's Corner
As you will note, both papers include lists of sources, and both source lists contain conventional errors. If you wish, you can focus one lesson on the conventions of setting up a source list correctly. Use whatever writing handbook your school approves (or one your writers are likely to use in college, such as the *APA Style Manual*) as a model for checking conventions and formatting of sources.

Score and Rationale for Sample Paper 12: *The Little Black Dress*

Most students should see this paper as **strong in the trait of Voice.** The writer's enthusiasm is evident from the very first line; opening with a quotation is an outstanding way to begin because we meet Coco Chanel right away. This humanizes the whole piece. What really gives this writing voice, however, is the writer's insight. She not only knows about Chanel the person, but about the ways in which Chanel changed the fashion industry with her perfume, handbags, and, more important, the little black dress. She does a fine job of portraying Chanel as a vanguard in fashion, someone who broke free of tradition and followed her own vision. The voice fades a little at the end, edging us toward a score of 5; but because the majority is strong, this paper would receive a **score of 6 in the trait of Voice.**

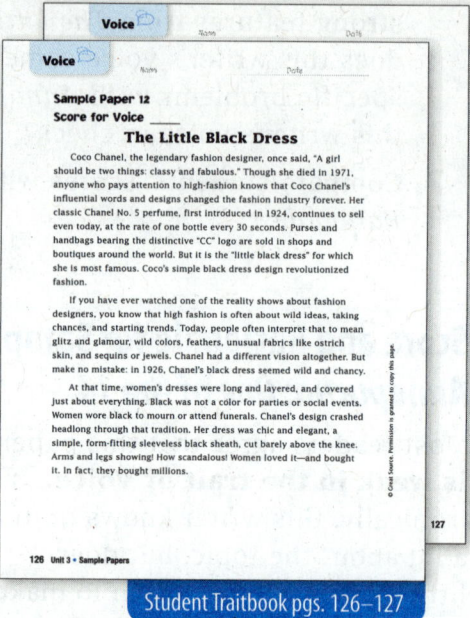

Student Traitbook pgs. 126–127

Revising Sample Paper 11: *Annapurna: One of the 14*

Have students revise the paper with the lower score in the trait of Voice: *Annapurna: One of the 14*. Their goal is to raise the score from a 1 to a 4 or higher. This challenge tests their knowledge of the trait of Voice, as well as their creativity in solving various problems, such as how to make readers care about a topic or how to present factual information in an interesting way. It is excellent preparation for revising their writing.

1. Remind students to refer to the checklist or the rubric for the trait of Voice as they work. It is easiest for most students to choose only *one*.

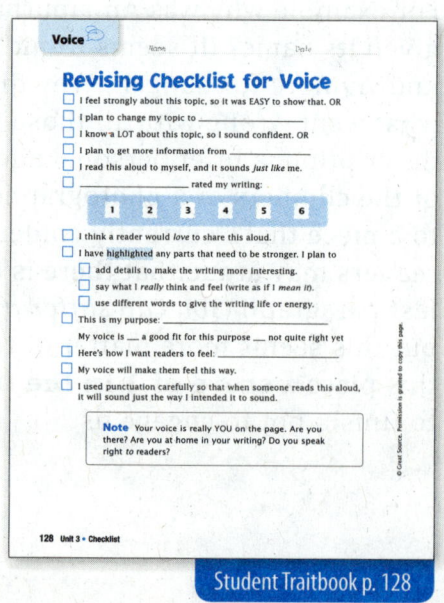

Student Traitbook p. 128

194 Unit 3

2. Have students call out the most important features of strong voice, making a list as they talk. The list should include the following (expressed in students' own words):
   - *If you knew this person, you could tell it was his or her writing*
   - *It's fun to share aloud*
   - *You can tell the writer really likes the topic—or finds it interesting*
   - *The writer sounds excited or curious*
   - *The voice is right for the purpose (to tell a story, to teach us something)*
   - *The writer knows the topic well enough to sound confident*
   - *The writer seems to talk right TO us*

3. Tell writers to look carefully at Sample Paper 11, *Annapurna: One of the 14*. The goal is to give this piece voice—to make it engaging and fun to read aloud.

4. Remind writers that it is all right to add or delete information, change the wording to express something in a stronger way, add a new title—*anything at all*. They are in charge!

5. Give students time to collaborate in planning their revision. They can brainstorm revision ideas, and coach each other about ways to find new information.

> **Bringing everyone in . . .** **Differentiated Instruction**
>
> If some writers wish to go more in depth, consider providing them with a full class period to research the Himalayas or the dangers of mountain climbing. Search your media center for resources on either topic. Following are sources offering information and photos. *Annapurna* by Maurice Herzog, *Above the Clouds: The Diaries of a High-Altitude Mountaineer* by Anatoli Boukreev, *Himalaya* (a novel) by Jonathan Neale, *The Abominable Snowman* by R.A. Montgomery (part of the *Choose Your Own Adventure* series), *The Wild Side: Extreme Sports* by Henry and Melissa Billings.

6. Tell students to mark up the rough with cross-outs, inserts, and arrows, and add longer inserts by stapling or taping them on. Final copy may be handwritten or typed, and should be stapled or clipped to the rough before it is handed in.

Coach's Corner

Your students have written their own personal definitions of voice, and should feel free to incorporate their perspectives into this list.

Coach's Corner

Students may work with partners or in writing circles to plan their revision. They may also borrow research details from one another. However, each writer is responsible for his or her own draft.

Coach's Corner

In revising for the trait of Voice, it can be helpful to imagine who the audience might be. You and your writers can decide this for yourselves. For example, it might be one short chapter in a book about extreme sports, designed for readers ages 12–14.

Coach's Corner

A quick Internet search will provide enough basic details on Annapurna to support a modest revision. Students who wish to write a stronger revision can. Keep in mind, though, that this revision is NOT a test of knowledge—it's practice in conveying information with voice.

Voice

Introduce Trait
Assessing and Revising Sample Papers

Assessment

Assess this activity by (1) scoring the final draft for the trait of Voice (using the teacher rubric for that trait) and (2) looking at the creativity and overall extent of the revision. Look for

- a final score of 4 or better in the trait of Voice.
- lively details readers will fine startling or intriguing.
- personal engagement with the topic.
- interpretation that puts simple facts into perspective.
- an effort to pull readers into the conversation.
- moments of strong voice a reader might highlight or share aloud.
- authority or confidence that comes from knowing a topic well.

Bringing everyone in . . .   **Differentiated Instruction**

Your writers might guess that this writer did not choose his own topic. And guess what—your students didn't choose to write about the Himalayas, either! It may or may not be a topic they find fascinating. But here's the thing about research. Even a cursory look into a topic usually uncovers one or two details the researcher did not know, and then cannot wait to share. Two or three striking details are enough to totally transform a passage of this length. Here's another tip: Facts are just one form of information. Sometimes an anecdote, a comparison, or a description that makes the reader feel as if he or she is on that mountain—and might not get back—can eclipse a whole bushel of raw data.

Voice

Introduce Trait
Practice Trait
Apply Trait
Assessing and Revising Sample Papers
Revising and Editing a Personal Draft

Revising and Editing a Personal Draft

Applying Knowledge of Voice by Revising Personal Writing

The revision your students just completed on Sample Paper 11: *Annapurna: One of the 14* provides a good warm-up for revising their own writing effectively. Everything in the unit has been directed toward this goal: helping writers become strong, independent revisers of their own work. Follow these steps:

1. Have students recall the personal writing they created after the literature connection (*Science Verse* by Jon Scieszka, illustrated by Lane Smith). This writing should still be in rough draft form in their folders.

2. Have them remove drafts from their folders and assess them for Ideas, Organization and Voice, as well as Conventions and Presentation, using the student rubrics for those traits. As they assess, they should ask themselves these

   ❓ **Key Questions...**
   - *Does this paper leap the river in each trait?*
   - *What are its strengths? How can I expand on those?*
   - *Did I highlight any problem areas or write myself notes in the margins?*
   - *What can I do to make this writing more effective?*

3. Based on their answers to these key questions, students should revise their writing, marking up roughs any way they wish. Their goal should be to make the paper leap the river (scores of 4, 5, or 6) in *all four traits:* Ideas, Organization, Voice, and Conventions and Presentation.

4. Final drafts may be copied onto new paper, or entered into the computer.

5. Roughs and finals should be stapled together, so that you can easily make comparisons and track the planning and flow of their revision.

Coach's Corner

As always, students do NOT need to score their writing. They only need to identify strengths to build on, or problems that need solving. They can also set up their revision with marginal notes to themselves: *more detail, quotation here, say this another way,* and so on. Remind them of the power of strong verbs and quality detail in boosting voice.

Coach's Corner

While students will do their actual revising independently, they should feel free to work with a partner or in a writing circle to review their rough drafts and identify the kinds of things they most want to focus on in their revisions.

Voice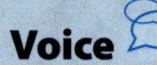

Introduce Trait
Revising and Editing a Personal Draft

Assessment

Assess this activity by scoring the final draft for the trait of Voice, as well as for Ideas, Organization, and Conventions and Presentation, using the appropriate rubrics. Also look at the creativity and overall extent of the revision. Following is a quick checklist of things to watch for.

- Clarity of the main idea
- Details that expand or enrich that idea
- Clear focus throughout the paper
- Inviting lead
- Effective transitions
- Overall organizational design that's easy to follow
- Conclusion that wraps up the story or essay
- Stand-out moments of voice
- Passages you might share aloud
- Engagement with the topic
- Voice suited to purpose and audience
- Creative and appropriate title
- Strong conventions that bring out meaning and voice
- Presentation that makes information accessible and gives the piece eye appeal

Bringing everyone in . . . | **Differentiated Instruction**

Use this or any checklist with flexibility. For example, if a student has written a journal or poem, it makes little sense to fret over leads or conclusions. Think of a checklist as a set of reminders that keep you from overlooking any strengths.

Parting Thoughts

Look carefully at any piece that is strong in the trait of Voice, and you'll find a clear message at the core. Like Organization, Voice is dependent upon Ideas (the foundational trait). Voice also comes from who we are and is therefore unique to each person. Its power comes from the writer's willingness to reveal that individuality. A writer can do many *little things* to increase the voice in a piece of writing: share intriguing details that come from careful observation, speak in a sure and confident way, and reveal heartfelt feelings. Nothing, however, takes the place of choosing a personally important topic—one the writer cares about deeply and knows well. Many people claim that research writing is voiceless. But that does not have to be the case. Informational writing can rock with voice, if the writer chooses a topic about which he or she has burning curiosity and takes the time and trouble to dig for information that answers his or her pressing questions. Voice is contagious; when the writer cares about a topic, we care, too.

Vicki & Jeff

UNIT 4
Word Choice

Overview

It's the word "choice" that explains what this trait is all about: considering, weighing, and carefully selecting words and phrases that make meaning clear—words that create the right mood or image. Sometimes, on very good days, words just seem to flow. But more often, it takes reflection and a little trial and error—like trying on shoes to find the right fit. It helps, of course, if the writer has a deep well of language from which to draw. That means a chance to read and hear the finest literature around, to experience how other writers use language to touch our hearts or make us think. Students who read frequently—and who are read to—have a strong foundation for choosing words that are both memorable and precise.

In this unit, you will be helping students to

- recognize **shades of meaning** and use a thesaurus wisely.
- find the right **words to suit the purpose.**
- revise in stages—first **de-cluttering, then adding vivid detail.**
- energize writing with **strong verbs.**
- understand how strong **Conventions and Presentation** support **Word Choice.**

Vicki & Jeff

TRAIT DEFINITION

Word Choice refers to the words and phrases a writer uses to create meaning or voice. Effective words are clear, precise, and sometimes memorable enough to quote. When word choice is impressive, readers find themselves going back to reread or underline a favorite passage. As with any trait, appropriate word choice depends on audience and purpose. The language of a legal contract is not the language of a poem. Still, most good word choice is marked by precision, strong verbs, original or thoughtful expression, judicious use of modifiers, and freedom from clutter.

Unit at a Glance

Introduce Trait

Discussing Sample Papers	204
Making the Literature Connection	210
Writing a Personal Draft	213

Practice Trait

Lesson 4.1: Shades of Meaning	218
Lesson 4.2: Words to Fit the Purpose	225
Lesson 4.3: The One-Two Revision Punch	231
Lesson 4.4: Harness the Power of Verbs	237
Conventions and Presentation	243

Apply Trait

Assessing and Revising Sample Papers	256
Revising and Editing a Personal Draft	261

Unit 4   201

UNIT 4
Word Choice

Introduce Trait

	The Opening Act 203	• Preview pages 203–214
15 min.	**Discussing Sample Papers** 204	• Introduce trait language and rubric
15 min.	Sample Paper 13: *A Good Place to Visit, But . . .* Score and Rationale	• Analyze weak and strong writing
	Sample Paper 14: *Most Embarrassing Moment* Score and Rationale	
50 min.	**Making the Literature Connection** 210	• Model the trait of Word Choice in literature: *The True Confessions of Charlotte Doyle* • Connect reading and writing
50 min.	**Writing a Personal Draft** 213	• Coach students in creating a piece of personal writing • Assess students' drafts to create benchmark scores

Practice Trait

Apply Trait

The Opening Act

Introduce the trait of Word Choice by first discussing the concept: using the "just right" word or phrase to convey an idea, or to create an image or mood. Let students see and hear this trait in action, first in two writing samples and then in a piece of literature in which precise and lively word choice gives historical fiction authenticity. Following the Literature Connection, students will have a chance to create an original piece of writing on a topic of their choice. They will revise and edit this piece down the road, using what they have learned about Ideas, Organization, Voice, Word Choice, and Conventions and Presentation. Here's the Opening Act in more detail.

1. **Discuss and assess the sample papers.** Expand students' understanding of Word Choice by discussing two sample papers: *A Good Place to Visit, But . . .* (in which lively word choice creates strong voice) and *Most Embarrassing Moment* (in which vague language keeps a potentially comic story from fulfilling its potential).

    Encourage students to talk, read the sample papers aloud to each other, highlight strong examples of Word Choice, and refer often to their student rubrics. By this time, your writers know to
    - look for language or strategies they might use in their own writing.
    - notice problems to avoid.

2. **Connect the trait to literature.** Continue your conversation by letting students hear the strong word choice in our featured text for the unit: *The True Confessions of Charlotte Doyle* by Avi. Use this or *any text* strong in Word Choice. Remember to allow a full class period (or more) for the literature lesson. We recommend sharing multiple examples from the book and providing time for students to share examples of their own.

3. **Complete a personal draft.** Following the Literature Connection, have students write a personal draft on *any topic of their choice*. The writing may be inspired by *The True Confessions of Charlotte Doyle,* but it does not have to be. Writers should put that writing into folders for a time in order to create the "mental distance" needed to revise effectively. They will revise and edit the piece at the close of the unit, using skills gained through the five lessons that follow. Your assessment of the rough and final drafts, and comparison of the two, will give you one important measure of your writers' growth.

Coach's Corner

Throughout this unit, you will want to help your writers connect the trait of Word Choice to other traits it influences significantly, particularly Ideas (strong word choice increases clarity) and Voice (strong word choice creates and reveals the writer's voice).

Coach's Corner

As always, writers may work on their writing at any time during the course of the unit. Some may need extra time for research. Knowing how to plan drafting and revision time wisely is one important key to success for many writers.

Word Choice

Introduce Trait
- Discussing Sample Papers
- Making the Literature Connection
- Writing a Personal Draft

Practice Trait

Apply Trait

Coach's Corner
We encourage you to have student volunteers read the sample papers aloud—but be sure to give them time to rehearse prior to doing so.

Discussing Sample Papers

Student Traitbook pages 130–132, 219

Student Rubric for Word Choice

Prior to presenting the two introductory sample papers to students, read each aloud to yourself so you can read it with expression and emphasize moments of strong (or problematic) word choice. It is important that writers assess with their ears as well as their eyes. We provide questions to ask with respect to each paper, but please add your own to our list.

1. Quickly review the Student Rubric for Word Choice. As always
   - a score of 6 indicates **strength**—but NOT perfection.
   - a score of 1 indicates a **beginning level of performance.**
   - the "river" divides writing in which **strengths outweigh problems** from writing in which **problems outweigh strengths.**

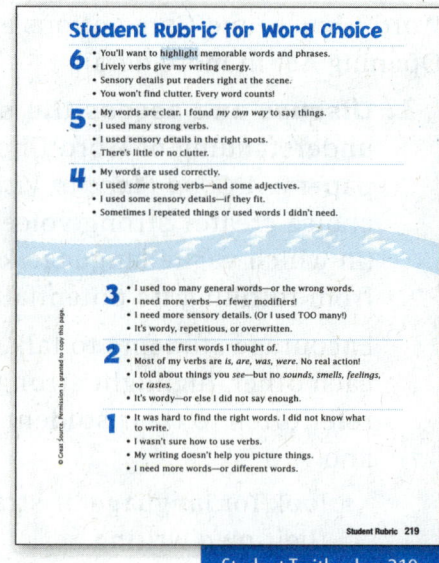
Student Traitbook p. 219

2. Respond to any questions.
3. Explain that for this lesson, students will rate two pieces of writing: *A Good Place to Visit, But . . .* and *Most Embarrassing Moment.* They will work with partners or in writing circles to discuss and score each paper, then defend their scores using the language of the rubric.

Coach's Corner
As you will see, we discuss the stronger paper (*A Good Place to Visit, But . . .*) first. However, feel free to flip the order if you prefer to begin with the problem piece.

Bringing everyone in . . . | **Differentiated Instruction**

Encourage students to highlight striking words or phrases as they score each sample paper for Word Choice. They should look for strong verbs, vivid descriptions, or just moments that make them say, "I like the sound of that" or "I wish I'd written that." Putting the two papers side by side, once they're highlighted, creates a striking visual contrast that makes scoring far easier.

Sample Paper 13: *A Good Place to Visit, But . . .*

1. Read *A Good Place to Visit, But . . .* aloud (or have a student read it), and as you read, tell students to think about these

   ### ❓ Key Questions . . .

   - *Are there striking words or phrases you would highlight?*
   - *Can you picture what it was like in the hospital?*
   - *Does the writer use words you might want to use in your own writing?*
   - *Did you notice any strong verbs? (Name one or two.)*
   - *Does the writer's word choice also make the voice stronger? If so, where?*
   - *Are there sensory details? (Words that make you see, hear, smell, taste, or feel things clearly?) If not, should there be?*
   - *Is the writing wordy? Would you cut anything?*
   - *Are there words or expressions that are overused?*
   - *Are any words used incorrectly?*
   - *Are there places where you would say something differently? If so, where?*

2. Have students mark up the papers by highlighting strong moments.

3. Have students score the paper, 1 through 6, using the Student Rubric for Word Choice.

4. After scoring, have students discuss their scores and reasons with partners or in their writing circles.

5. When they finish, vote as a class (with a show of hands or by moving to corners) and tally scores. Tell students to
   - think about the key questions listed under Step 1 above.
   - state whether or not they think this paper leaps the river in Word Choice.
   - defend their scores using the Student Rubric for Word Choice.

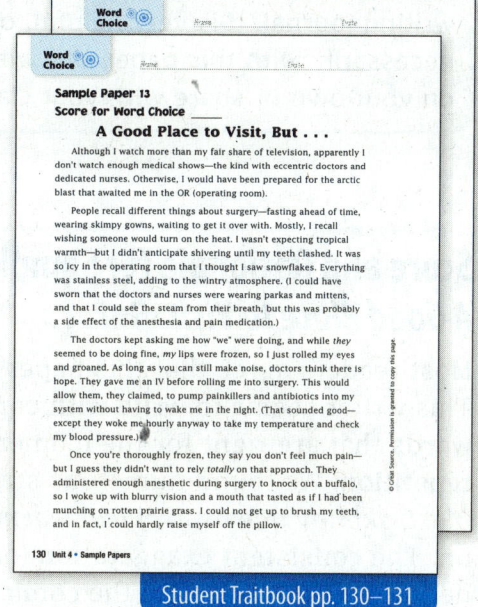

Student Traitbook pp. 130–131

Coach's Corner

Students should find many moments to underline or highlight in this paper. Remind them that they're not necessarily looking for new or unusual words. They're looking for everyday language used in a fresh, original, or memorable way. If it makes you nod or smile or see things in a new way, it's working.

Coach's Corner

A Good Place to Visit, But . . . is a mix of genres, part personal narrative, part descriptive essay. It tells a story, but the writer's intention is not to recount all of the events of his surgery; rather, he wants to describe the misery of feeling frozen throughout the procedure. This is an interesting organizational structure, relying loosely on a chronological story format, but taking big pauses to describe the surroundings.

Word Choice

Introduce Trait
Discussing Sample Papers

> **Bringing everyone in . . .** **Differentiated Instruction**
>
> Remind students to record favorite words or expressions in a writing journal. It is very helpful, of course; if you model this, not necessarily with this paper, but with any piece of writing you read on your own or share with your class.

Score and Rationale for Sample Paper 13: *A Good Place to Visit, But . . .*

Most readers agree that this paper is **strong** in Word Choice. This writer seems to write with considerable ease, always finding words that are right for the moment—and using remarkably little repetition. We found numerous striking words and phrases: *arctic blast, skimpy gowns, tropical warmth, wintry atmosphere,* and so on. The consistent exaggeration (or perhaps he's not exaggerating!) definitely contributes to the comical voice. Verbs are especially strong in the last part of the paper—which is appropriate since the writer is frozen (and presumably immobile) in the first part—notably *bungee jumping, down* (a dozen worms), *willed* (myself onto my feet), *propelled, bundled, rolled, soaking,* and *sneak.* Overall, the writer's word choice creates a dramatic recounting of his hospital experience, overflowing with sensory detail (especially feelings). This paper would receive a **score of 6 in the trait of Word Choice.**

Sample Paper 14: *Most Embarrassing Moment*

1. Answer any new questions about the Student Rubric for Word Choice.

2. Consider switching partners or regrouping writing circles so students hear a variety of perspectives as they discuss the sample paper.

3. Read *Most Embarrassing Moment* aloud (or ask a student to read it, after rehearsal), and as everyone else listens, remind students to think about these

   Key Questions . . .
   - Are there striking words or phrases you would highlight?
   - Do you sense the writer's embarrassment—and do you feel it, too?

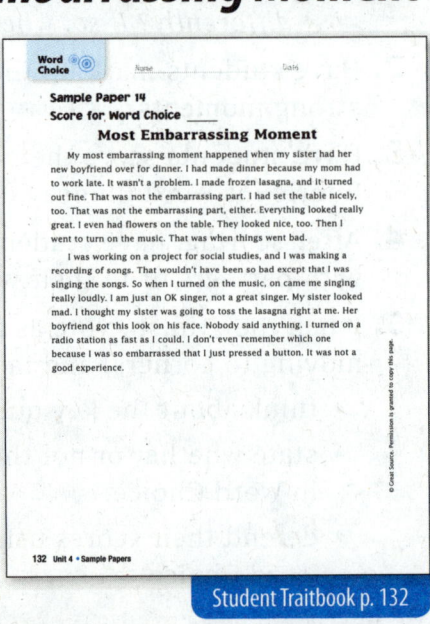

Student Traitbook p. 132

Coach's Corner

To really appreciate the problems this paper has with Word Choice, have students imagine that instead of reading this piece, they are listening to a friend tell this story—in precisely these words. What might they say at the end of the story? What questions might they have?

206 Unit 4

- *Does the writer use words you want to remember—or borrow?*
- *Did you notice strong verbs? If so, name one or two.*
- *Does the writer's word choice bring out the voice?*
- *Are there sensory details? (Words that make you see, hear, smell, taste, or feel things clearly?) If not, should there be?*
- *Is the writing wordy? Would you cut anything?*
- *Are any words or expressions used too many times?*
- *Are any words used incorrectly?*
- *Are some words or phrases too vague to give readers enough detail?*

4. As before, have students underline or highlight moments that are strong in Word Choice—then compare the highlighted copy to Sample Paper 13.
5. Have students score the paper, 1 through 6, referring to the Student Rubric for Word Choice.
6. After scoring, have them discuss the paper with partners or in writing circles.
7. When students finish talking, vote as a class (with a show of hands or by moving to corners) and tally scores. Tell students to
   - think about the key questions listed under Step 3 above.
   - state whether or not they think this paper leaps the river in Word Choice.
   - defend their scores using the Student Rubric for Word Choice.

Coach's Corner

Most Embarrassing Moment is a personal narrative. A good narrative usually leads up to a turning point, important event, or revelation. Clearly, the "embarrassing moment" is meant to be the highlight of this story. So—is it?

Score and Rationale for Sample Paper 14: Most Embarrassing Moment

Most readers agree that this paper **needs revision** in Word Choice. The premise of the story is excellent: the writer's singing skills (or lack thereof) revealed at an inopportune moment. The title creates some anticipation in readers, and we rush through the uneventful first paragraph, hoping for a funny high point that is a bit of a let-down: "on came me singing really loudly." That's it??!! Throughout the piece, the language is quiet and vague: *it wasn't a problem, it turned out fine, everything looked really great, they looked nice, things went bad, got this look on his face, not a good experience,* and so on. The writer's choice of words bleaches out the very details we're hungry for. We want to hear the people in this scenario speak—or shout. We want to picture the faces and hear the music, and cringe right along with the writer. On the positive side, the general message is clear. This paper would receive a **score of 3 in the trait of Word Choice.**

Coach's Corner

The main problem with *Most Embarrassing Moment* is that the writer seems to be holding back. General words like *fine, nice, bad, great, mad,* and *this look* tell us next to nothing. It's almost as if the embarrassment is still so strong it's inhibiting him. Simply letting go and filling in details will boost scores in Ideas and Voice—as well as in Word Choice.

Word Choice

Introduce Trait
Discussing Sample Papers

Coach's Corner

As you score and discuss other writing samples, students may notice strengths or problems in word choice that are not reflected in the rubric. Encourage them to note these—right on the rubric itself—and at some point, revise or expand the rubric so that it reflects your students' own thinking and discoveries.

Creating a Baseline Assessment

Have students revise *Most Embarrassing Moment* (the weaker of the two introductory papers) working individually. Assess the *revised* drafts (using the Teacher Rubric for Word Choice) to provide baseline scores reflecting students' revision skills for this trait. Record those scores. At the close of the unit, following direct instruction in Word Choice, you can compare these early revisions to the revisions your students do on their own writing and on Sample Paper 15: *Invaders of Our Land*. This comparison will tell you how much students have grown as revisers with respect to the trait of Word Choice. (See **Extending the Lesson** for some suggestions on setting up this revision activity.)

Extending the Lesson

- Talk about other strengths in *A Good Place to Visit, But . . .* Are the details vivid enough to give this piece a strong score in Ideas? Look carefully at the lead and conclusion. Are both effective? How strong is the voice? Would you consider sharing this paper aloud—just for fun—with a friend? Also notice the conventions. What punctuation does this writer use to bring out the voice of the piece?

- Share some writing examples for which strong word choice is critical. For example, look for verbs in a newspaper sports column. Check advertisements or menus for descriptive writing that plays to the senses—without being overdone. For word choice that stretches your writers' vocabulary, consider the work of Patricia Reilly Giff, Gennifer Choldenko, Phyllis Reynolds Naylor, Craig Childs, Toni Morrison, Paul Fleischman, Sid Fleischman, Truman Capote, Rebecca Stead, Kate DiCamillo, Jane Smiley, or Timothee de Fombelle. Be sure students have opportunities to find and share favorite passages of their own.

- As a class or in teams, devise a plan for revising *Most Embarrassing Moment*. Discuss the situation in preparation for this. How many of your students have had a similar experience? (It might not involve singing—any embarrassing experience will do.) Have you had such an experience? Without asking people to share more than they want to, discuss how it feels to be embarrassed in front of others. How do you feel physically? What goes through your mind? You may also wish to talk about the sister and her boyfriend. What are they probably thinking or saying during this episode? Should those details be included? Finally, suggest that students go through the piece and highlight words or phrases that are too vague to contribute to meaning or voice. (They should find many!) Replacing these with vivid details will be one important step.

Coach's Corner

Students might also take a moment to notice the verbs in *Most Embarrassing Moment*: happened, had made, wasn't, turned out, had set, looked, went, and so on. What happens when none of the verbs create action or energy? Why are verbs so important?

Bringing everyone in . . . **Differentiated Instruction**

Note that you can go about this revision in a couple ways. One is to rewrite *Most Embarrassing Moment* based on the scenario the writer lays out. The other is to create an original piece, based on a personal memory. Some writers are likely to favor the first because the central idea is already in place; others may prefer to base their writing on an experience they can recall because the details are vivid in their minds. We recommend offering a choice.

- Have students write online reviews of any book they feel has strong word choice—and tell them to mention word choice in the reviews.
- Start a blog discussion about good word choice. What's most important? Which authors have this trait down? Are there books students would recommend? Are there vague words or expressions to avoid as a writer?

Unit 4   209

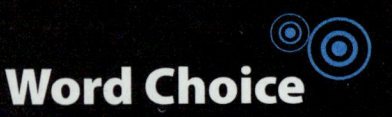

Word Choice

Introduce Trait
Discussing Sample Papers
Making the Literature Connection
Writing a Personal Draft
Practice Trait
Apply Trait

Coach's Corner

To teach Word Choice, look for any picture book, poetry, or chapter text with a focused message and striking words that bring that message to life. Share the whole book or any passage that illustrates clear phrasing, quotable moments, vivid imagery, original expression, effective use of sensory detail, strong verbs, or words you wish you'd thought of yourself. If possible, share some books above your students' reading level. Help them stretch!

Coach's Corner

For more information about the author, try:
  www.avi-writer.com

Coach's Corner

We have chosen an excerpt that is rich with detail created through strong word choice—in this case, words that bring the ship *Seahawk* into focus for both Charlotte and readers. Clearly, if your students are engaged by the book, you may wish to read the whole novel aloud or tell them to continue reading on their own (as you facilitate ongoing discussions).

Making the Literature Connection

 *The True Confessions of Charlotte Doyle* by Avi

Every word really does involve a choice and a *responsibility* for writers. Readers need clear pictures of people, places, and happenings, or the big idea of the story will slip away—along with the readers. Word choice is especially important in historical fiction, which requires writers to become experts on a particular period of time. The characters, events, and settings won't ring true without research on both topic and language. For this lesson, we have chosen Avi's Newbery Honor book *The True Confessions of Charlotte Doyle,* a high seas adventure rich in period detail, enlivened by language that makes life aboard ship both exciting and authentic.

Sharing the Text

1. Show students the book *The True Confessions of Charlotte Doyle* and share the title and author. Let them know it was published in 1990 and was a Newbery Honor Book for that year. (You may want to familiarize your students with the Newbery Medal.) Ask if any students are familiar with this or any of Avi's other books, including *Crispin: Cross of Lead, The Fighting Ground, Nothing But the Truth, Don't You Know There's a War On?,* and the *Tales From the Dimwood Forest* series.

2. Preview the book's main idea: Thirteen year old Charlotte Doyle has stayed in Liverpool, England to finish her school term, but now she must sail to Rhode Island unaccompanied by her parents. The year is 1832, and sea travel could take days or months. Charlotte is a mannered, obedient girl, used to deferring to authority. Onboard ship, she makes an unlikely friend, Zachariah, and from him, she learns the realities of life on board the *Seahawk* with Captain Jaggery—along with skills that will later save her life.

3. Let students know you are going to read an excerpt from this novel, chapters two and three.

> **Bringing everyone in...** **Differentiated Instruction**
>
> Some of the terminology may require explanation. Though the book has no glossary, there is an appendix explaining the ship's time, as well as a diagram of the *Seahawk* with many parts labeled. Many students will also benefit from a reading of the prologue, "An Important Warning." As you share this information, you may wish to point out how valuable a prologue or diagram can be in a novel that relies heavily on specialized information. If you share the whole book, consider having students create a glossary for it; this makes an excellent extension of the lesson.

4. Ask students if they are familiar with any sea stories, folktales, myths, or legends of crossing the ocean. Some may have experience with cruise ships, boats, or sailing.

5. Discuss historical fiction—what students know about the genre from previous reading experiences.

6. Read the suggested excerpt. If you are familiar with the book, feel free to set up and share a favorite passage of your own.

> **Bringing everyone in...** **Differentiated Instruction**
>
> Most students associate research with reports. It is worth spending a few minutes to talk about the importance of research in virtually ALL writing—including fiction. Fiction with one foot grounded in reality is more convincing—and therefore more fun to read. No wonder so many writers draw from personal experience even when inventing the actual stories they tell. For a fascinating example of how this worked in one writer's life, see Gary Paulsen's book *Guts*, a biographical review of personal experiences leading to the *Hatchet* books.

7. With students' help, recount some of Charlotte's first impressions of the *Seahawk* and its crewmembers. Balance these with any hints of foreshadowing suggested by the author.

8. Talk about the positive and negative impact of first impressions.

9. Have students identify moments in which they feel the word choice (especially new words or nautical terminology) is particularly strong or appropriate.

Word Choice

Introduce Trait
Making the Literature Connection

Coach's Corner

Don't forget the importance of having students identify their own favorite books or passages. You may wish to devote one class period to this kind of exploration, culminating in read-aloud sharing by individuals or groups. We also recommend taking time to compile a list of favorite authors your students consider to be experts in Word Choice (or any trait).

Other Books You'll Love

Throughout this program, we rotate recommendations by genre:

- **Classic**—both traditional and contemporary
- **Poetry**—an individual poem or collection
- **Nonfiction**—picture book or longer text
- **Fiction**—picture book or longer text

Please keep in mind that your *own favorite books* are almost certain to include strong verbs, striking descriptions, or words that will stretch your students' vocabulary. The more literature you share, the stronger your students' understanding of this trait will be—and the deeper the well from which they draw as writers. Here are several books to explore:

1. **Poetry:** *Heart to Heart: New Poems Inspired by Twentieth-Century American Art* edited by Jan Greenberg

   Each of the poems included in this collection was inspired by a work of art, also included. The poems are divided into sections: Stories, Voices, Impressions, and Expressions. The language of each poem has been carefully chosen by the writers to speak for the art, sending very personal and accessible messages to readers. Readers may even be inspired to write their own art-inspired poetry. (Don't miss David Harrison's poem "It's Me!" inspired by Andy Warhol's *Marilyn Diptych*.)

2. **Nonfiction:** *Look! Body Language in Art* by Gillian Wolfe (also by the same author: *Look! Zoom in on Art!* and *Look! Drawing the Line in Art*)

   This book (and each book in the series) is a double-bonus—students are exposed to great art and invited to make connections between the visual arts and writing. With each piece of art, students are specifically asked to study hands, mouths, body positions, and faces. The suggested art activities that follow lead easily into writing; for example, when students are asked to compare their hands with the hands of someone older, the lesson could easily evolve into descriptive writing with an emphasis on word choice.

3. **Classic:** *The Fellowship of the Ring: Being the First Part of the Lord of the Rings* by J.R.R. Tolkien

   Many students may be familiar with the film version of this classic fantasy—Frodo's mission to destroy the "one ring to rule them all." This volume and the ones that follow are not easy reads. Tolkien's eye leaves nothing to the imagination, describing every character, place, and object in great detail—along with their connection to the worlds and events of the story. The author even creates a language—elvish—to add an element of authenticity to the world of Middle Earth.

Writing a Personal Draft

Word Choice

Introduce Trait
Introduction to Word Choice
Making the Literature Connection
Writing a Personal Draft
Practice Trait
Apply Trait

1. Let students know they will now have a chance to create a personal piece of writing on a topic of their choice. Give them time to meet with a partner or in writing circles, checking their journals or considering various topics suggested by *The True Confessions of Charlotte Doyle,* such as:

   - An original "solo" adventure story—pitting yourself against the elements or the adult world (narrative fiction)
   - An experience traveling alone or being away from family (narrative, expository, poetry)
   - Experiencing the death or illness of a friend or relative (poetry, expository, narrative)
   - Standing up for yourself or a friend (narrative, expository, poetry)
   - "Roughing-it"—living without conveniences (narrative, informational, poetry)
   - Contrast between first impressions and reality (narrative, expository, poetry)
   - "Home"—what the concept means (narrative, expository, poetry)
   - The reality of ocean crossings in 1832 (informational, persuasive, expository)
   - A description of ships from the book's time period (informational, expository, poetry)
   - Myths of sea creatures (imaginative)
   - Report on the real geography of *The True Confessions of Charlotte Doyle*—Providence, Rhode Island; the Atlantic Ocean; Liverpool, England; and so on (informational, expository)
   - Sailing (informational, expository, poetry)
   - Biography of Avi (informational)
   - Review of *The True Confessions of Charlotte Doyle* (response to literature, persuasive)
   - Review of any classic sea adventure: *Sea Wolf, Treasure Island, The Odyssey, Master and Commander,* and so on (response to literature, persuasive)

2. Give students 5–8 minutes to discuss topics. This initial planning time will give many writers a much stronger focus and sense of direction as they begin drafting.

Coach's Corner

For students interested in more extended reading, please note that *The True Confessions of Charlotte Doyle* makes an outstanding companion book to *Treasure Island* (sea adventures from a young man's and a young woman's perspectives). It can also be paired with the High Seas Trilogy Books by Iain Lawrence: *The Wreckers, The Smugglers,* and *The Buccaneers.*

Unit 4 213

Word Choice

Introduce Trait
Writing a Personal Draft

Coach's Corner

Some writers may wish to incorporate technology into their writing. Audio or video—even PowerPoint—can greatly enrich any presentation, and is another genre to consider.

Coach's Corner

Writers who are incorporating technology into their work or who are doing research will obviously need more than 20–30 minutes to finish a draft. We encourage you to provide additional class time for this. Remind writers that though a first draft is meant to be rough, they should strive to be clear and to give themselves, as writers, a sense of direction. A good rough draft helps a writer picture what to do next.

Coach's Corner

A good way to close writing workshop is to have writers reflect on where they need to "go from here." Part of learning to write well is planning how to carry the process over day to day.

The difference between the right word and the almost right word is the difference between lightning and a lightning bug.

—Mark Twain
Author

---

3. Ask some writers to share their writing ideas, and record them for whole-class reference, offering individual coaching as needed. Remind writers that they may choose *any* topic that suits them—whether inspired by *The True Confessions of Charlotte Doyle* or not.

Bringing everyone in . . . **Differentiated Instruction**

Writers within writing circles may select a common topic—or a theme that each writer approaches from a slightly different perspective. Doing so has advantages. They can coach one another through drafting or revision and also share research responsibilities.

4. Encourage prewriting in addition to the opening conversation. Writers should spend about 5 minutes sketching, making a web, writing a list of questions or details, and so on.

5. Provide writers with 20–30 minutes to begin a draft. (A few may finish within this time.)

6. Remind writers to double or triple space (even if they are composing on the computer) and to allow wide margins so there will be ample room for revision later.

7. When writers feel they have finished a rough draft or a preliminary sketch of main ideas, have them confer with partners or in their writing circles to get a sense of "next steps." By the end of class, all writers should have a clear sense of their next writing task.

8. Writing—finished or not—should now be placed in students' writing folders. At the close of the unit, they will have time to look at this piece again and to revise it before it is assessed.

214 Unit 4

Notes

UNIT 4
Word Choice

Introduce Trait

Practice Trait

	Shifting the Spotlight 217	• Preview pages 217–252
50 min.	**Lesson 4.1** .... 218 Shades of Meaning	• Use a thesaurus wisely • Revise with carefully chosen synonyms
50 min.	**Lesson 4.2** .... 225 Words to Fit the Purpose	• Match language with purpose • Refine word choice in an original piece
50 min.	**Lesson 4.3** .... 231 The One-Two Revision Punch	• De-clutter wordy text • De-clutter—then add detail
50 min.	**Lesson 4.4** .... 237 Harness the Power of Verbs	• Identify strong verbs, revise weak ones • Use strong verbs in an original piece
50 min.	**Conventions and Presentation** .... 243 The Troublemakers Today's Specials	• Deal with homophones • Design a menu

Apply Trait

Shifting the Spotlight

Your students have now assessed two sample papers for Word Choice: *A Good Place to Visit, But . . .* and *Most Embarrassing Moment*. They have also seen and heard Word Choice in action through your sharing of *The True Confessions of Charlotte Doyle* by Avi.

It is time to shift the spotlight, giving students a chance to practice specific skills they can use in revising and editing their writing. Once students have completed *all* focused lessons, they will apply what they have learned by (1) revising *someone else's* writing and (2) revising and editing *their own* writing. Follow these two steps:

1. **Complete Lessons 4.1 through 4.4.** Allow two days for each lesson. Through these lessons, students will learn strategies for
   - recognizing shades of meaning and using a thesaurus wisely.
   - matching language with purpose.
   - revising in stages: de-cluttering, then adding detail.
   - using strong verbs to energize writing.

2. **Link Word Choice to Conventions and Presentation.** Students will learn that Conventions and Presentation supports strong Word Choice through: (1) careful use of the right homophone (Conventions) and (2) skillful combining of layout and wording to create copy (in this case a menu) that is descriptive and persuasive (Presentation). Allow a full class period for each part of this lesson.

Encourage students to continue *thinking like readers* by looking at the Word Choice poster in the *Student Traitbook*, considering each thing the writer does (left column) and filling in the impact on the reader (*So the READER . . .*). After you have discussed all four elements, display the actual poster, comparing students' responses to ours. Use sentence strips to continue adding your students' own ideas throughout the year.

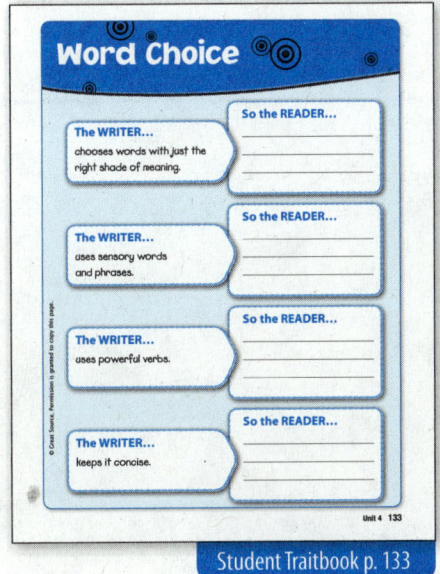

Student Traitbook p. 133

Unit 4 217

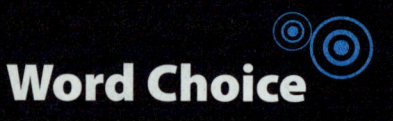

Word Choice

Introduce Trait

Practice Trait
- Lesson 4.1
- Lesson 4.2
- Lesson 4.3
- Lesson 4.4
- Conventions & Presentation

Apply Trait

LESSON 4.1

Shades of Meaning

Student Traitbook pages 134–139

There's an art to using a thesaurus well—as some of your writers may already know. Just looking up a word and substituting the first synonym listed is usually an unwise idea. It can result in some comical—and confusing—writing. On the other hand, careful use of a thesaurus, accompanied by some reflection, can help a writer find the word with just the right shade of meaning.

Objectives

Students will
- recognize that synonyms are diverse—even if they share a common bond.
- explore the nuances of meaning associated with various synonyms.
- revise an example of writing by choosing synonyms carefully.

Time Frame

Allow 50 minutes for this lesson. It can be broken into two parts.
- Part 1: Students explore shades of meaning in several sets of synonyms.
- Part 2: Students revise a passage by using a thesaurus and dictionary to find words that create the intended meaning and mood.

Setting Up the Lesson

Share the introduction to Lesson 4.1.

Begin with a quick review of what a thesaurus is and how to use it. Also have students distinguish between a thesaurus and a dictionary: What kinds of information are found in each? Ask students how many of them typically use a thesaurus—and how much time they spend choosing the word that will work best for the situation.

With students' help, explore synonyms for ONE common, everyday word. Here are a few suggestions to choose from:

- Nice
- Small
- Unusual
- Said
- Run
- Fly

Or feel free to choose your own word. Use any word you like—other than *big*. You'll be exploring the word *big* as part of the lesson.

List your synonyms (or some of them) and invite volunteers to use each one in a sentence. Record the sentences as well. Talk about the differences among the various synonyms. Are they interchangeable within the sentences your class created? (The answer to this question is the underlying focus of the lesson.)

Explain that in this lesson, you'll explore the importance of choosing the word with just the right nuance of meaning.

Teaching the Lesson

Sharing an Example: *Hope Was Here*

Share the directions to be sure everyone understands the task. Then share the passage from *Hope Was Here* by Joan Bauer aloud, or have a student share it.

Student Traitbook p. 134

Coach's Corner

It will be helpful for this lesson to have multiple dictionaries and thesauruses available for students to use. If they have their own copies, encourage students to bring those to class. Electronic editions will also work well, provided you have more than one computer.

Coach's Corner

Many students think the dictionary and thesaurus are interchangeable when actually they work in harmony. A good thesaurus will provide several synonyms—or more. But defining these words may require a dictionary. In addition, many writers like to challenge themselves. If the first search yields a synonym that's close to the intended meaning but not there yet, the writer will do a second search, seeking synonyms for that synonym.

Coach's Corner

If students read, remember to give them time to rehearse—and consider dividing the text into two parts, one for the **thief** synonyms, one for the **hope** synonyms. Remind readers to pause dramatically for each ellipsis.

Unit 4 219

Word Choice

Practice Trait — Lesson 4.1

Coach's Corner

If possible, write down definitions for each of the synonyms listed. That way, you can refer to them quickly and help students make good distinctions.

Reflection

Share the directions and give students time to talk with partners or in writing circles about the two sets of synonyms. Have them choose the ones they like best, using a dictionary to look up any words they are unsure about. Remind students that there are no right or wrong answers—but that choosing one word over another *does affect meaning.*

Using Your Thesaurus

Share the directions. Then use the example sentences to make sure students can distinguish between a noun (our **hope** for a win is high) and a verb (I **hope** it snows).

Give students time to look up three synonyms for *hope* used as a verb—then to choose one of those verbs and look up *more* synonyms.

Shades of *Hope*

Share the directions. Then give students just 2–3 minutes to write "I hope we win the game" in three different ways. Here are just a few possibilities:

- I **trust** we'll win the game.
- I **wish** we'd win the game.
- I **have faith** we'll win the game.
- I **dream** of winning the game.
- I'm **anticipating** we'll win the game.
- Winning the game is my **fantasy.**
- I **envision** us winning the game.
- My **goal** is to win the game.
- It's my **ambition** to win this game.
- I **long** to win this game.
- I **have a mind to** win this game.
- I **have my heart set on** winning this game.

Coach's Corner

There are literally dozens of ways to express this idea—or something close to it. So encourage students to go beyond just three. You might have them keep trying until you can list, as a class, at least eight or more possibilities. (We listed 12.)

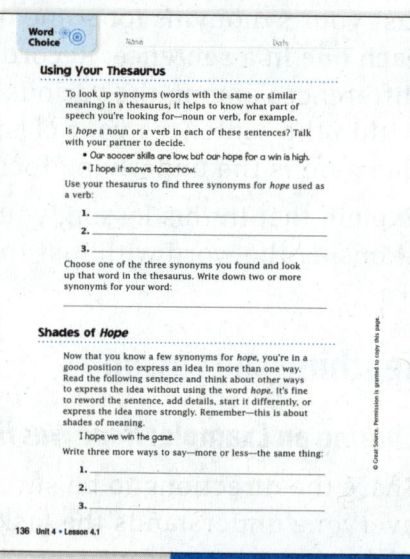

Student Traitbook p. 135

Student Traitbook p. 136

Shades of *Big*

In this portion of the lesson, we provide a list of synonyms, which students may add to, if they wish. After reviewing the list, have students decide if we have used the best synonym for *big* in each of the six sentences. Students can work with partners or in writing circles for this task.

Tell each team to

- look over the list of synonyms to make sure they are familiar with all of them.
- use a dictionary to check definitions of any words they do not know.
- read each of the six sentences carefully, paying special attention to the word in **bold.**
- use a thesaurus or dictionary to replace any words that do not seem to fit.

Allow about 12 minutes for this activity.

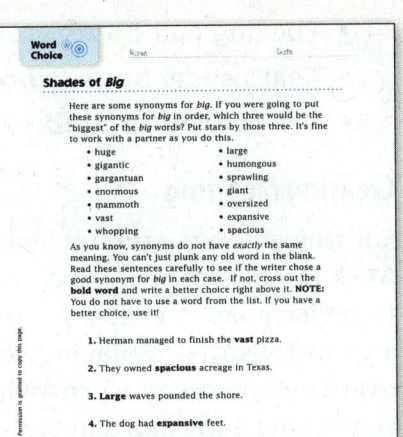

Student Traitbook p. 137

Coach's Corner

Remind students that our synonym list is only a convenience. They do not have to choose words from that list—and should feel free to stretch.

Bringing everyone in . . . | Differentiated Instruction

Words like *big* and *small* are what we might call "all occasion" words. We reach for them automatically because they can describe hats, pizzas, and tracts of land. But the whole point of word choice is to look for the word that fits the intended meaning. This takes a little time and patience—especially when there is no clear "right" answer. Encourage students to take their time and to talk through several possibilities for each sentence. They can take up to two full minutes per sentence (or more, if you wish).

Share and Compare

Give students time to compare their choices by having members of various groups share aloud. Expect to hear a range of possibilities. Our original choices were—we thought—a little off-target. But there are many viable ways to express each idea. Here are some:

- Herman managed to finish the **enormous/humongous/gargantuan** pizza.
- They owned **vast/sprawling/immense/sizable** acreage in Texas.
- **Massive/gigantic** waves pounded the shore.

Word Choice

Practice Trait
Lesson 4.1

Coach's Corner
Note: If you are dividing this lesson into two parts, **Day 2 begins here.**

- The dog had **huge/stocky/oversized/gigantic** feet.
- That's some **huge/whopping/enormous** fish you caught!
- Her **oversized/bulky/immense** hat blocked my view.

Creating Meaning

For this activity, students will work in pairs or writing circles to revise a short chapter from an adventure story, replacing some overused everyday words with something a bit more lively—but appropriate to mood and meaning. Students will need to make careful choices, using a dictionary and thesaurus to help.

Begin by reminding students of the focus in the first part of this lesson: choosing the best synonym for the occasion. Then share the directions for this section to make sure they are clear. Give students time to read Chapter 1 from *The Ship* to themselves—or read it aloud, if you prefer. Once they have finished reading, have students

Student Traitbook p. 138

- take a reflective minute to think about the mood they wish to create for this story.
- think about the setting—what they picture, how it would feel to be there.
- think about Dorcas—how she feels, what she sees, what she hopes to do.
- go through the passage carefully, replacing as many of the words in **bold blue** as possible with something more intense or dramatic.
- go as far as they can in about 20 minutes.

Remind students to imagine that this story will be made into a film—inspired by their writing!

Coach's Corner
Students should feel welcome, naturally, to use a dictionary or thesaurus as they work. However, if they rapidly think of an alternate way of saying something, they should go for it! If some words seem right as is, that's fine, too. Students should feel free to play with the wording if this helps them to work in a word or phrase they like.

Bringing everyone in... Differentiated Instruction

There are 23 bold blue words and expressions in the passage. You can simplify the task by having students (in pairs or teams) work on only a select number. Making good choices is more important than getting through all 23.

Share and Compare

As time permits, give writers an opportunity to share their revisions aloud. Comment on some of the word choices—and the mood or image created by those words. Here, for purposes of comparison, is our revision:

The Ship
Chapter 1

Dorcas stared up at the sky. Dark clouds were bunching in the west—a threatening storm was bearing down on the village. She grabbed her hat from the peg on the wall and tugged it down over her ears—then stepped out. The wind slammed the door behind her. It encircled her, almost ripping the coat right off her back.

Clutching her coat, Dorcas tore down the shadowy path. The wind was gusting—so there was no point lighting a candle. She couldn't see a thing—tree roots poked up everywhere, and sharp rocks grazed her feet. If only she could reach the village in time. Dr. Perfidy, the most menacing villain ever to sail the seas, was about to dock at their port! She was terrified, but there was no time to think of herself. Lightning exploded, and in the light, Dorcas saw the skeletal outline of the ship's mast and sails. She stopped worrying about falling and raced down the narrow trail, her feet smacking the dirt, and her heart hammering with every step.

Word Choice

Practice Trait
Lesson 4.1

A Writer's Question

Word choice definitely influences mood. If Dorcas were happy—and the scene were light and carefree—she might **pluck** her hat from the wall and **sail** down the path. The wind might **tickle** her face. She would be **thrilled**, not terrified, and lightning might **dance** across the sky. It isn't difficult to see and hear the impact of language on mood.

Putting It to the Test

A word like *good* can mean dozens of different things—from *proficient* to *high-quality, delicious,* or *well-behaved*. It all depends on context. The best way to know whether a synonym is right (if you do not know a word well) is to check the dictionary (most tests allow this). In addition, it's smart to plan your writing time so you have at least 2 minutes at the end to go back and reread what you have written, making sure it's sensible and right for the mood.

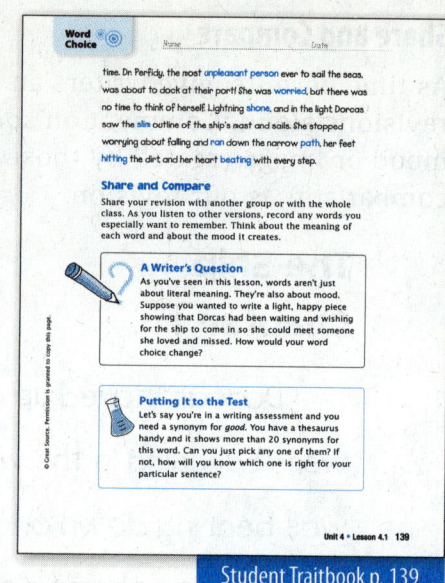

Student Traitbook p. 139

Extending the Lesson

- Give students time to do some literary exploration, looking for passages in which the word choice is especially strong.
- Revise the Dorcas passage to give it a cheerful—even comical—flavor. Discuss the changes in word choice required to do this.
- Provide extra credit to any writer who revises any published piece—even a single sentence—by replacing the language with something stronger, more vivid, or more precise.
- Extend the story of Dorcas online, inviting each writer who participates to add just a line or two—or as much as a whole paragraph. Talk about any word choice you especially like.
- Start a blog discussion about effective—and ineffective—use of the thesaurus.
- Do some online research on the history of the thesaurus.

LESSON 4.2

Words to Fit the Purpose

Student Traitbook pages 140–146

Word Choice

Introduce Trait
Practice Trait
Lesson 4.1
Lesson 4.2
Lesson 4.3
Lesson 4.4
Conventions & Presentation
Apply Trait

We always want words to be clear, correct, and precise. But the language of a poem is—usually—quite different from that of a technical manual. Voice shifts with purpose largely because language shifts with purpose. Sometimes words need to be formal, dressed in their no-nonsense attire; for other purposes, writers reach for language that is playful, dramatic, emotional—even outrageous. In this lesson, students explore the link between language and purpose, and create an original piece in which the two work in harmony.

Objectives

Students will

- recognize the link between word choice and writing purpose.
- identify specific words and phrases that help writers fulfill their purpose.
- create an original piece in which language and purpose work together well.

Time Frame

Allow 50 minutes for this lesson. It can be broken into two parts.

- Part 1: Students identify favorite words and expressions that reflect the writer's purpose—then revise example sentences so the language and purpose work in harmony.
- Part 2: Students create an original paragraph using language that suits the purpose: to explain, describe, or express feelings.

Unit 4   225

Word Choice

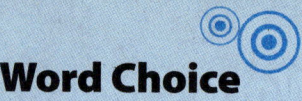

Practice Trait
Lesson 4.2

Coach's Corner

Note: To set up the lesson, we suggest you share diverse examples of writing, each with a different purpose. **Give yourself a day to look for three or four examples**—or more. If time permits, have students participate in the search. The more examples you have, the stronger your lesson will be.

Coach's Corner

As you make your class list, you may also want to discuss which purposes would call for more formal language—and which for informal, even playful, language.

Setting Up the Lesson

Share the introduction to Lesson 4.2.

This lesson is all about linking language and purpose. Use examples that help students understand and make this connection. Begin by asking them to list as many purposes for writing as they can think of. They can do this in writing circles or you may choose to do it as a whole class. Possible answers (there are many more):

- to entertain
- to describe something
- to share thoughts and feelings
- to teach someone something
- to explain a process
- to provide directions
- to announce an event
- to convince someone of something
- to tell a story
- to record history
- to socialize (keep in touch with friends)

Add your own thoughts to this list. For now, you just want students to see that writers write for many reasons—and to think about what some of those reasons might be.

For the second part of this introduction, share some of the writing examples you have gathered and have students make a guess about each writer's purpose. Make sure students do not see book covers or titles—this makes the guessing game far too easy.

If time permits, have a few student volunteers share examples they have brought in. They can do this in writing circles or with the class as a whole.

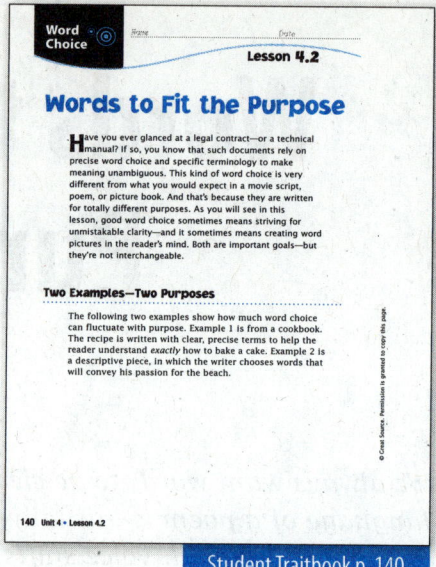

Student Traitbook p. 140

226 Unit 4

Teaching the Lesson

Two Examples—Two Purposes

Share the general directions to be sure they are clear.

Example 1

Then share the directions for Example 1 and give students time to read it silently. They should read once for meaning, then

- read the passage a second time, pencils in hand.
- underline any words or phrases that help this writer fulfill her purpose.

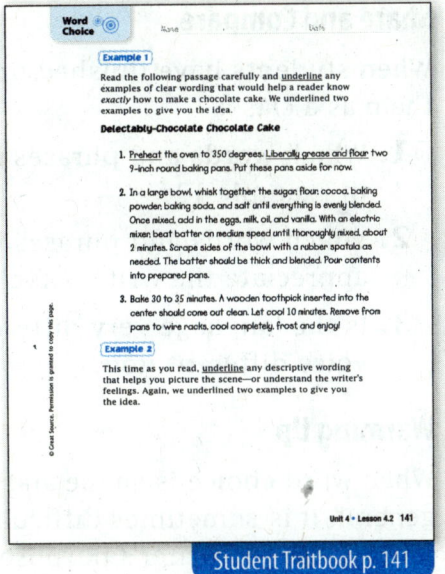

Student Traitbook p. 141

Coach's Corner

It's critical for students to be completely clear about the writer's purpose: to give us precise instructions. If we had not shared this purpose, would your students still have known what it was? How?

Bringing everyone in . . . Differentiated Instruction

How many of your students know anything about baking? Have any of them made a cake—or something similar—on their own? You may wish to point out that this activity may be slightly easier for those who are used to reading recipes. For those who aren't, it helps to think, "What little tips would make this easier for me?" Notice that the writer could have made her directions far more general. She wants readers to be successful, so she includes tiny details only an experienced baker would know. This is what makes her directions so good.

Example 2

When students finish marking up Example 1, go on to Example 2, following the same basic procedures. Remind students that the purpose for Example 2 is very different. Before proceeding, make sure everyone understands the writer's purpose (to describe a place and to share his feelings about it).

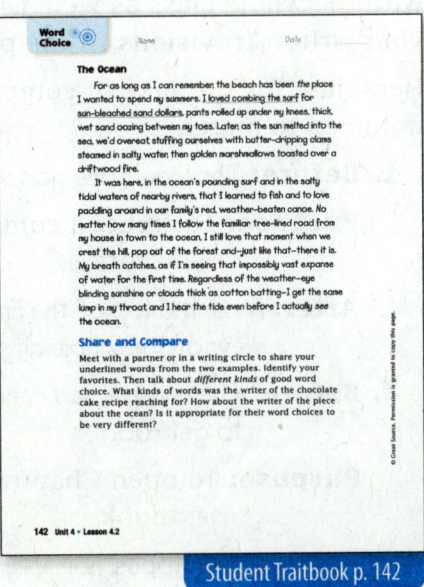

Student Traitbook p. 142

Unit 4 227

Word Choice

Practice Trait
Lesson 4.2

Coach's Corner

Encourage students to underline any key words or phrases they missed that come up in your discussion. Keep in mind that there are no right answers with this activity—however, a careful reader should find many examples of word choice that fit the purpose for each example. Note that Example 2 has two purposes: to describe and to share feelings. Most published writing has multiple purposes.

Coach's Corner

Writers should make their revisions sound authentic—but they can invent. They do not need to take time to research New York City or various sea creatures. Remind them, however, to think carefully about purpose. Sentence 2, for example, is the lead for a chapter in a textbook—not the opening to a horror film.

Coach's Corner

This portion of the lesson offers an excellent opportunity for modeling. After writers share with one another, show them how you would revise each sentence, talking aloud about your choice of words as you revise. Do all you can to link word choice to purpose.

Share and Compare

When students have finished marking up both examples, discuss them as a class:

1. Which words and phrases help make directions crystal clear in Example 1?
2. Which words and phrases help us picture the ocean scene or appreciate the writer's feelings in Example 2?
3. Is the language very different in these two examples? Is the voice different, too?

Warming Up

When word choice is vague and general, it is sometimes difficult to tell what the writer's purpose is. In this part of the lesson, students will revise vague writing to make it clear and precise—and as they do so, they will also work on making the purpose clear.

We suggest having students work independently on this portion of the lesson and allowing about 6–8 minutes for them to revise.

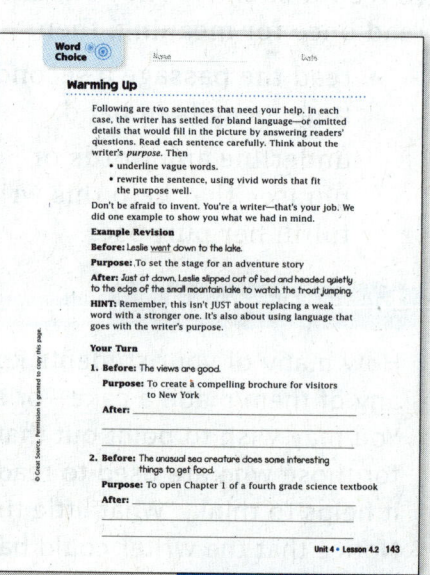

Student Traitbook p. 143

Share and Compare

Give writers time to share with partners or in writing circles. You may want volunteers to share with the whole class as well. Did your writers' revisions fit the purpose?

Here, just for the sake of comparison, are our revisions (yours do not need to match):

1. **Before:** The views are good.

   Purpose: To create a compelling brochure for visitors to New York.

   After: From the top of the Empire State Building, you'll see a matchless view of the whole city!

2. **Before:** The unusual sea creature does some interesting things to get food.

   Purpose: To open Chapter 1 of a fourth grade science textbook.

   After: The octopus, normally a shy creature, uses its powerful suction cups to pry open its favorite dinner: clams or crabs.

Ready, Set... Reach!

In this portion of the lesson, writers create an original piece to fulfill one of three purposes:

- To explain how to do something (like the cake recipe)
- To describe something (like the piece about the beach)
- To express personal feelings through poetry

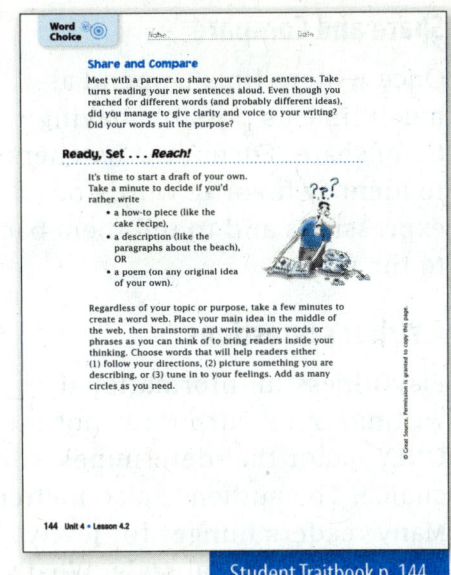

Student Traitbook p. 144

Coach's Corner

Note: If you are dividing this lesson into two parts, **Day 2 begins here.**

Allow about 20 minutes for this activity. Writers should spend

- about 5 minutes prewriting, using the word web in the *Student Traitbook*, and
- another 15 minutes writing, borrowing from the word web as they wish.

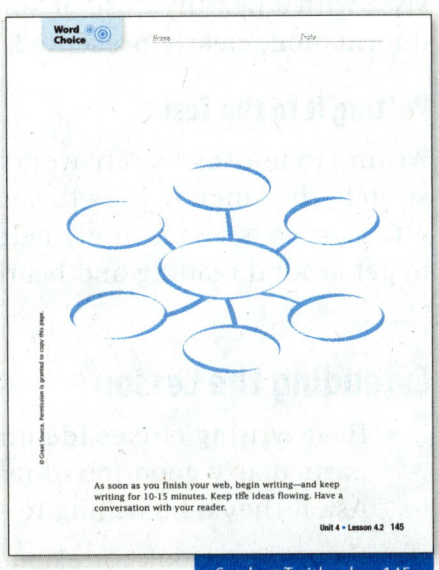

Student Traitbook p. 145

Coach's Corner

The word web is a beginning point—it is not meant to set parameters. Writers do not need to use all of the words from the web. Furthermore, writers should feel free to add new words or make any changes that occur to them as they write.

Bringing everyone in... **Differentiated Instruction**

For many writers, keeping the pencil (or keyboard) moving is the most difficult part of writing. Here are some things to suggest when the words do not seem to come: (1) close your eyes for a "thinking minute" to get a picture of what you're trying to explain or describe; (2) look back at your word web for ideas—and add to it if you wish; (3) take time to reread what you have written so far; and (4) think small—just try to add one line, not a whole book.

Word Choice

Practice Trait
Lesson 4.2

Share and Compare

Once writers finish, spend as much time as possible having them share. Encourage listeners to identify favorite words or expressions and to tell them back to the writer.

A Writer's Questions

Playfulness in informational writing? Sure! Purpose is not the ONLY factor that determines word choice. The audience also matters. Many readers hunger for levity or a conversational style. What's important is to accompany that style with a healthy dose of solid information, clearly presented.

Putting It to the Test

Writing to impress rarely works. Although we want writers to stretch, the language has to sound natural in order to work. A thesaurus is an infinitely helpful tool, but it is not a shortcut to get around reading and hearing language used well.

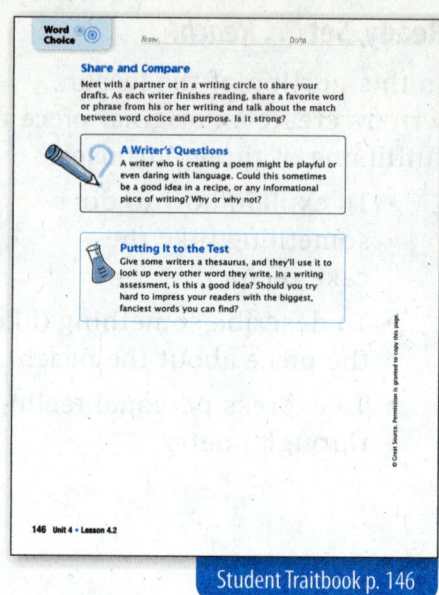

Student Traitbook p. 146

Extending the Lesson

- Have writing circles identify student writers who did a particularly good job of matching word choice and purpose. Ask if they'd be willing to share their writing with the class.
- Continue to look for examples of published writing in which the writer chooses words that help make the purpose clear. Create as diverse a collection as you can, from technical instructions to brochures, journalistic articles, novels, poems, recipes, and emails.
- Provide extra credit to any writer who revises even a very short published piece in a way that makes the purpose more clear.
- Do a recipe search on line. Which recipes offer the best insider tips for ensuring success?
- Create an online review of any cookbook or other book in which the writer does an especially good job of making the purpose clear. Discuss word choice in the review.

LESSON 4.3

The One-Two Revision Punch

Student Traitbook pages 147–152

Word Choice

Introduce Trait
Practice Trait
Lesson 4.1
Lesson 4.2
Lesson 4.3
Lesson 4.4
Conventions & Presentation
Apply Trait

We've all heard about the one-two punch in boxing. This is the same idea—but a slightly gentler version. The point of this lesson is that revision is never just one thing; it involves multiple tasks. Sometimes, taking things step by step makes the process more manageable—and yields better results.

Objectives

Students will
- understand that revision involves more than one step or task.
- identify clutter in a wordy piece.
- revise that piece by de-cluttering.
- revise a second piece with a one-two punch: de-cluttering, then adding detail.

Time Frame
Allow 50 minutes for this lesson. It can be broken into two parts.
- Part 1: Students look for clutter in a wordy writing example and revise to make it concise.
- Part 2: Students build on what they've learned, revising a second example to (1) eliminate clutter and (2) add vivid detail.

Unit 4 231

Word Choice

Practice Trait
Lesson 4.3

Coach's Corner

This is a good opportunity for you to share your own revision strategies. Are there any little tricks you have learned as a writer that might help your writers revise more efficiently? Don't be concerned about going beyond the scope of this lesson. We're focusing on two strategies, but the more your writers know about revision techniques, the stronger their revised drafts will be.

Setting Up the Lesson

This time, share the introduction to Lesson 4.3 *after* setting up the lesson.

Begin by brainstorming some of the things your writers do when they revise. Give them a minute or two to talk with partners or in writing circles and encourage them to make a short list of their own. Then, as they share, build a class list.

Your writers may mention any or all of the following:

- Reading aloud
- Leaving space for revising
- Discussing the text with another person
- Figuring out the main idea
- Getting rid of what isn't needed (de-cluttering)
- Adding details
- Writing a new lead
- Writing a new ending
- Changing order
- Writing with a stronger voice
- Fine tuning voice to fit purpose or audience
- Writing a new title

Keep this list posted where writers can refer to it. (You may even wish to add to it throughout the year.) Then let them know that for this lesson, you'll be focusing on just two strategies—a technique we're calling the "one-two revision punch."

NOW share the introduction to Lesson 4.3 to clarify.

Teaching the Lesson

The First Punch: De-clutter!

Review the directions to make sure they're clear. Then share the example titled "Good Shot!" aloud—or have a student read it (following some rehearsal). Students do not need to do any revising yet. However, they should

- look and listen for words or phrases that are repetitive or unnecessary.
- make any notes that will help them with the upcoming revision.

Coach's Corner

Keep in mind that this passage is quite long; you may want to have more than one reader present it.

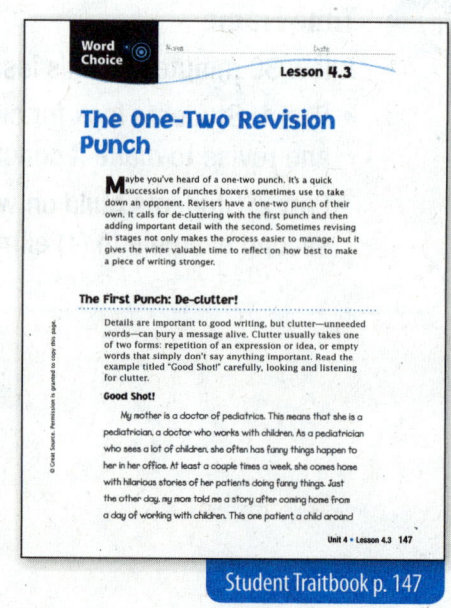

Student Traitbook p. 147

232 Unit 4

My Response

Give students time to look back at the passage once more and to fill in their personal response. When everyone has finished, discuss the piece as a class. Most should agree that it is "ridiculously wordy."

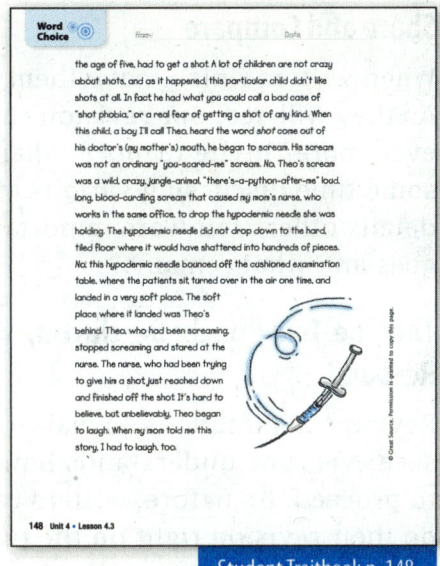

Student Traitbook p. 148

Coach's Corner

Have students guess the word count for "Good Shot!" Then, if you like, have them estimate what a good word count might be—once the piece is de-cluttered. Right now, it is 315 words long, excluding the title.

Partner Up to Pare Down

Review the directions to make sure everything is clear. Then have writers work with partners (or in writing circles, if you prefer) to de-clutter this piece, trimming it as much as they feel is necessary. Ask how many plan to cut just a little. How many plan to cut a modest amount—or really overhaul the piece? What is the shortest estimate?

Allow about 15 minutes for this revision. Remind writers to read their revised copy aloud to make sure it makes sense and has a smooth flow.

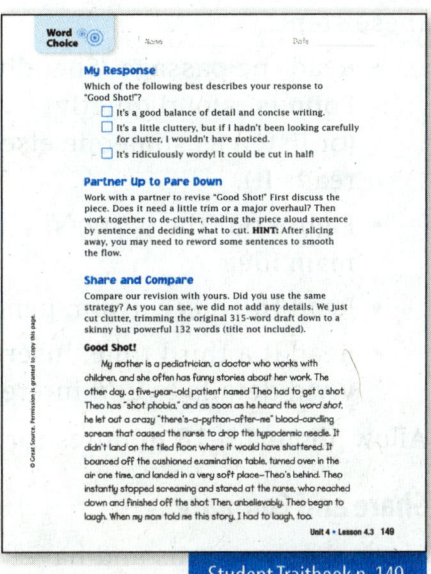

Student Traitbook p. 149

Coach's Corner

We included our revised version of "Good Shot!" in the *Student Traitbook* for easy comparison. Caution writers NOT to look at our revision until they have completed their own. Theirs may be more concise—and they may like it better. Looking at someone else's writing can influence a writer, and not always for the better.

Bringing everyone in . . . Differentiated Instruction

Some writers may want to revise simply by crossing out unneeded words. This is an important step in de-cluttering, but explain that by itself, it isn't enough. It is important to reread the copy to make sure that what's left makes sense and sounds right. Remind writers that they may need to reword some sentences to make their revision work. Also emphasize the importance of an individual approach. There are an infinite number of possible revisions.

Word Choice

Practice Trait
Lesson 4.3

Coach's Corner

Note: If you are dividing this lesson into two parts, **Day 2 begins here.**

Coach's Corner

As you know, this lesson focuses on two primary revision strategies: de-cluttering and adding detail. However, we have also incorporated other more subtle strategies that are important, and you may wish to point these out: double (or triple) spacing to leave room for revision, reading copy aloud, and figuring out the main message. These three strategies are critical to any good revision.

Coach's Corner

Some writers may be curious to know the word count for the original piece in order to make comparisons: it's 190.

Share and Compare

When writers finish, have them compare their revisions with ours. As they will see, our revision runs a lean 132 words. Did anyone cut even more? Invite teams to share their revisions aloud, and spend some time discussing various approaches: Did some teams delete details others felt were important? How do writers decide what goes and what remains?

The One-Two Punch: De-clutter, Re-build

Review the directions to make sure everyone understands how to proceed. As before, writers can do their revision right on the text. This time, encourage writers to work individually, following these steps:

- Read the passage "Shedding Pounds" aloud quietly (or listen as someone else reads it).
- Figure out the writer's main idea.
- Read the piece again, pencil in hand, deleting clutter.
- Read it a third time, inserting two or three (or more) vivid details to add interest and voice.

Allow about 15–18 minutes for this revision task.

Student Traitbook p. 150

Share and Compare

Share the directions and have writers meet with partners or in writing circles to share their revisions. They should

- make any additional revisions they wish at this time.
- list their revision strategies (as a team) in the space provided.

When they finish, invite volunteers to share their revisions aloud.

On the following page, for purposes of comparison, is our revised copy. It runs 84 words (excluding the title— which we changed, by the way).

Student Traitbook p. 151

Lifestyle Changes

Luckily, my parents are working to get fit—and changes in their lifestyle mean changes for me, too. For one thing, they're eating less junk food and more fruits and vegetables. That works for me. Unlike many teenagers, I actually *love* fruits and veggies. They're also exercising more, which includes walking, biking, running—even yoga. Fortunately, they still allow me to beat them at basketball at least once per week. I remind them that even though they always lose, they *do* get a workout!

Here's our list of revision strategies:

1. Read the copy once for meaning.
2. Figure out the main idea: the parents are getting fit.
3. Figure out the writer's perspective or attitude: he's happy about this.
4. Read again to delete unneeded copy.
5. Change wording to make copy flow smoothly—and give it more voice.
6. Change the title.
7. Read the revision aloud, checking meaning, fluency, and voice.

A Writer's Question

What's classified as "clutter" depends on the main idea. That's why figuring out the main idea is always an important part of any revision. Changing words and phrases has little impact without a strong skeletal structure (a clear message) to hang the revision on.

Coach's Corner

Though we provide our revision here for comparison purposes, this is an outstanding opportunity for you to model revision for your writers. Project the original and on the first go-round, de-clutter. Then go through the copy again, reading your revision aloud as you work and inserting details you think would be helpful.

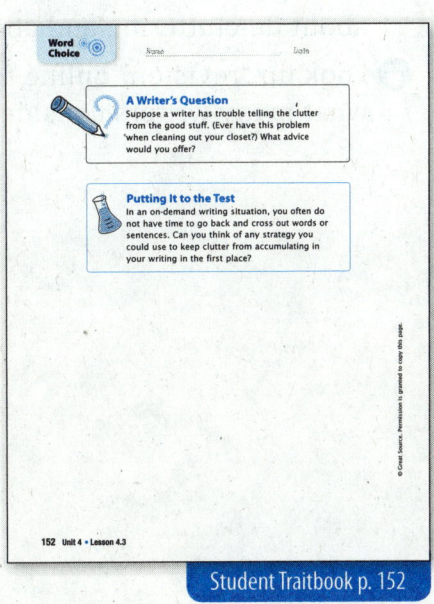

Student Traitbook p. 152

Unit 4   235

Word Choice
Practice Trait
Lesson 4.3

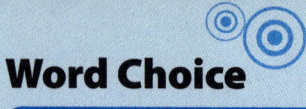

Putting It to the Test

A small amount of de-cluttering (crossing out words) is acceptable—even in a testing situation. But when time is limited, it's good to minimize the clutter in the first place. A good way to do this is to write the main message, in sentence form, on a piece of scratch paper and not wander from that message. Look at it now and then during the allotted writing time. Another helpful hint is to make a list of key points (essay) or events (story) you want to cover, then figure out—in advance—how much time you have for each one.

Extending the Lesson

- Talk about the advantages of revising in steps. Did it help some of your students to de-clutter first—then go back to add details? How many of them also noticed the inclusion of those subtler steps like reading aloud and identifying the main idea? How many also added the step of writing a new title?

- You can create a good de-cluttering lesson by starting with a passage you think is concise and well written. Enter this on the computer; then add your own clutter. Don't go crazy, but be sure you have at least two or three sentences that aren't needed. As a finishing touch, replace some clear, vivid language with vague words like *nice* or *good*. Remember to double space and leave BIG margins. After students finish revising, they can compare their work with the author's original. This leads to some productive discussions about clutter and revision!

- Keep your list of revision strategies going throughout the year. You may want one or two students to use what they know of Presentation to reformat your list so it's easy to read.

- Are your writers involved in any on-line discussion about good writing? If so, have them offer their own recommendations about de-cluttering and about revision in general.

- Look up "revision" online for a host of tips and lesson ideas on what many writers consider the heart and soul of good writing.

LESSON 4.4

Harness the Power of Verbs

Student Traitbook pages 153–157

Word Choice

Introduce Trait
Practice Trait
Lesson 4.1
Lesson 4.2
Lesson 4.3
Lesson 4.4
Conventions & Presentation
Apply Trait

Verbs are the engine of writing. They give writing energy, motion, and incredible visual power. Like all word choices a writer makes, though, verbs must reflect the intended meaning—and mood. It makes a big difference whether a character skips, dashes, creeps, or hobbles down the sidewalk, for example. In this lesson, students use their imaginations and their thesauruses to select the right verb for the moment.

Objectives

Students will
- recognize the power of verbs to energize writing.
- identify strong verbs in an example from literature.
- revise flat verbs to create vivid images.
- create and revise an original piece of writing that includes strong verbs.

Time Frame

Allow 50 minutes for this lesson. It can be broken into two parts.
- Part 1: Students identify verbs in one example and revise another example to strengthen the verbs.
- Part 2: Students create an original piece of writing featuring strong verbs.

Unit 4   237

Word Choice

Practice Trait
Lesson 4.4

Coach's Corner

Note: To set up this lesson, you will need an example of writing with strong verbs. It need not be long, but it should include at least three or four powerful verbs. You can share it by projecting it for the class to read or by making copies. The purpose will be to ensure that students know what a verb is and can easily recognize verbs in writing. Almost any good publication will work for this—but an especially good source is a sports column from your local newspaper or any book on sports.

Coach's Corner

It's important for students to understand that there is nothing wrong with these weak verbs per se. They're vital, in fact. We'd have one heck of a time writing without them. The problem arises when a writer relies exclusively on such verbs, never slipping in a word with more life or color. That tends to deflate the writing.

Setting Up the Lesson

Share the introduction to Lesson 4.4.

Have students write a personal definition of the word *verb* on a piece of scratch paper. Use their initial thinking to create a class definition. Look up the term in a dictionary or a writing handbook to see how close your definition comes. Then, have students—with partners or in writing circles—make a list of the **10 Weakest Verbs** they can think of. There is no right answer to this, of course, but verbs that are relatively low-energy include the following:

- is/are
- was/were
- have/has
- do/does
- go/goes
- went
- come/came

End this introduction by sharing the writing example you selected and having students look for both high and low energy verbs. What's the best verb choice in the passage? Is there one students think could have been stronger?

Bringing everyone in . . .   Differentiated Instruction

Often we assume that once students leave elementary school, they know precisely what verbs are and can recognize them at a glance. Actually, even some adult readers struggle with this definition. If some students have trouble identifying verbs, remind them to think of a verb as whatever someone (or something) IS or DOES. Strong verbs create a *moving picture* in the mind—and can be acted out. Look back at the introduction to this lesson. You might have student volunteers act out the various ways a character can move down the sidewalk. Let them add their own verbs to our list. See if other students can guess the verb being portrayed.

Teaching the Lesson

Sharing an Example: *Gulliver's Travels*

Share the directions to make sure the task is clear. Then have students read the example on their own, looking and listening for strong verbs. They should underline each one they find. Remind them to look for the high energy verbs—not *every* verb in the passage.

Share and Compare

Give students time to meet with partners or in writing circles to compare the verbs they underlined. Remind them to focus on those verbs they think are especially high energy. They should also ask themselves if they would replace any of the verbs in the passage with stronger options. Here are the verbs (in **bold**) we think are strongest:

- **bending** my eyes downward
- I **perceived** it
- I **roared** so loud
- **leaping** from my sides
- **struggling** to get loose
- **wrench** out the pegs

The One-Liner Warm-Up

Review the directions to be sure the task is clear. Have students work with partners or in writing circles to

- read the five sentences aloud, one at a time.
- discuss possible alternatives to each verb in **bold.**
- use a thesaurus to identify additional alternatives.
- revise each sentence, using favorite alternatives.

Allow about 10–12 minutes for this revision activity.

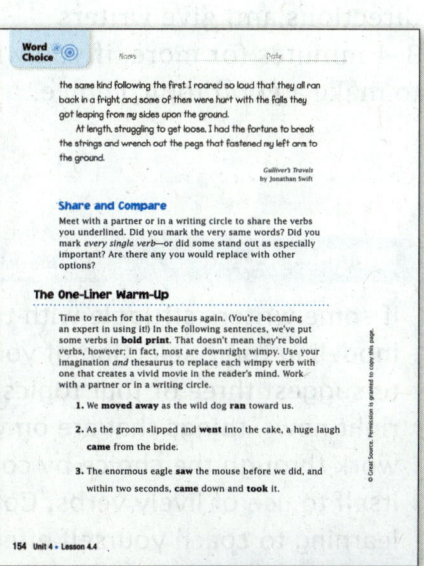

Student Traitbook p. 154

> **Coach's Corner**
>
> For this portion of the lesson, students will need access to a thesaurus. Partners or groups can share.

Unit 4   239

Word Choice

Practice Trait
Lesson 4.4

Coach's Corner

Consider making a class list of favorite alternate verbs—or have writers add favorites to their writing journals. Make sure writers understand that matching with another team is fine, but it's not the goal. The more different choices teams made, the more writing possibilities they will see.

Coach's Corner

Note: If you are dividing this lesson into two parts, **Day 2 begins here.**

Coach's Corner

Remind writers that any topic involving lots of action will make use of verbs easier. They should also choose something they like or feel strongly about. Our list is just meant to stimulate thinking, and they are not bound by it in any way.

Share and Compare

If students worked with partners, two teams can form a writing circle to share their revisions. If students worked in writing circles, they can share revisions with the whole class. Talk about verbs that work particularly well to create a strong image, influence mood, or add voice. Following are our suggested revisions—your students' versions need not match:

1. We **fled** as the wild dog **charged** us.
2. As the groom slipped and **plunged** into the cake, a huge laugh **exploded** from the bride.
3. The enormous eagle **spotted** the mouse before we did, and within two seconds, **swooped** down and **snatched** it.
4. The silent snake **slithered** through the grass, **sliding** alarmingly close to the campers' bare feet.
5. The thief **crept** away with his prize, **glancing** over his shoulder.

Paving the Way for Verbs

Remind writers of your previous discussion about strong verbs and their importance in creating vivid images, energy—and voice. Let writers know that today they will have a chance to draft an original piece using verbs to enliven the writing. This task begins with choosing a topic. Review the directions and give writers 3–4 minutes (or more, if you wish) to make a good topic choice.

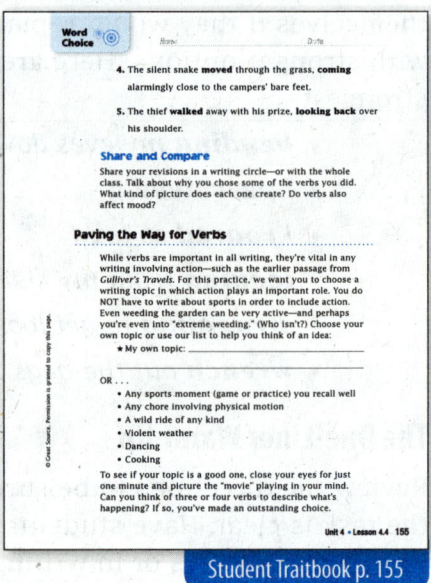
Student Traitbook p. 155

Bringing everyone in . . . Differentiated Instruction

If some writers struggle with topic selection, help them out by modeling topic selection of your own. One good way to do this is to suggest three or four topics you are thinking of writing about right now—things that are on your mind. Have writers help you work through the choice by considering which topic will best lend itself to use of lively verbs. Coaching others is a wonderful way of learning to coach yourself effectively.

Roughing It

Review the directions. Then give writers

- about 5 minutes to prewrite and plan.
- an additional 10 minutes to draft.

Each writer should transition from prewriting to drafting whenever he or she feels ready.

Revising with Verbs in Mind

To close this lesson, writers will do a short revision, focusing on strong verbs. Review the directions to make sure everything is clear. Then have writers

- read through their drafts.
- underline verbs.
- revise any that could be stronger.
- confer with partners or team members as necessary.

Share and Compare

Give writers time to share revisions with partners or in writing circles. As each writer shares, they should

- listen for favorite verbs.
- write just ONE on scratch paper or an index card, fold it, and give it to the writer.
- share favorites after everyone has read aloud.

A Writer's Questions

Many professional writers are careful not to overdo adjectives or adverbs, believing that precise nouns and strong verbs form the skeleton of strong writing. For some outstanding examples, check Laura Hillenbrand's historical narrative *Seabiscuit*. Passages that recount various races are notably free from modifiers—and the result is powerful.

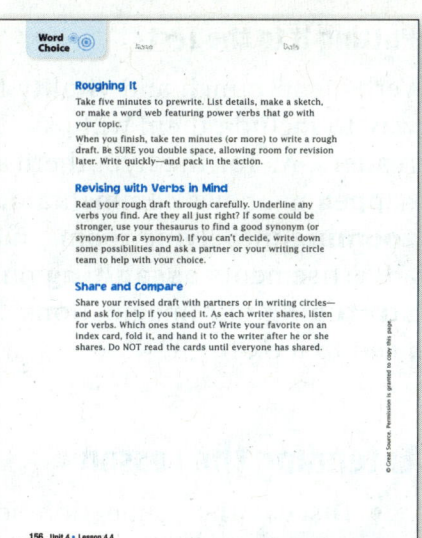

Student Traitbook p. 156

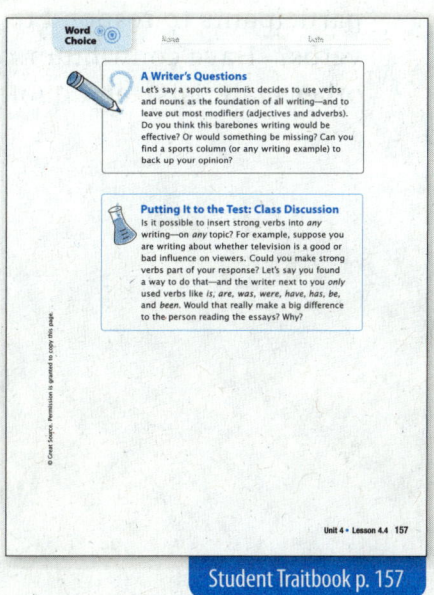

Student Traitbook p. 157

Coach's Corner

Remind writers to double space so they will have room to revise this draft—the second part of this lesson.

Coach's Corner

Writers do not need to revise *every* verb. That would be extraordinarily tedious—and not necessarily beneficial. It's important not to make the passage sound artificial and forced. A good—and efficient—approach is to identify from one to four verbs that would benefit from revision. Small changes can be powerful.

Coach's Corner

Throughout this program, we stress the value of abandoning writing for a day or two before attempting to revise. This time, writers are revising immediately after drafting. We have not changed our minds. The purpose of this focused revision activity is to help students see what a difference even a *small* change— replacing a handful of verbs—can make in a piece of writing.

Unit 4 241

Word Choice
Practice Trait
Lesson 4.4

Putting It to the Test

Verbs lend punch and vitality to *any* form of writing. Finding a way to include them will pay dividends because action wakes up readers. As for the hypothetical television prompt, consider what's happening: news commentators **seeking** details, sports events **zooming** into living rooms, meteorologists **pinpointing** storms, advertisements **assaulting** our ear drums, and documentaries **stretching** our imaginations. Action is everywhere. Writers just need to look for it.

Extending the Lesson

- Discuss the connection between strong verbs and Voice. As writers use verbs to strengthen Word Choice, are they, in fact, strengthening Voice as well? (Absolutely.)
- Review the Student Rubric for Word Choice. Does it sufficiently capture the strengths and problems covered in the four preceding lessons? If we left out something important, revise the rubric to make it more useful for you and your students.
- Look for any published piece—from a brochure at the dentist's office to the U.S. Constitution or Declaration of Independence—that makes good use of strong verbs. Have students continue this search for a time, and create a collection of the most diverse documents possible. That diversity is a testament to the importance of strong verbs.
- As a class, revise any piece in which verbs are not as strong as they should be. Read the before and after versions aloud and discuss the impact verbs make.
- Look up "verbs" online for many tips and activities.
- Continue your blog discussion on good writing by asking participants to respond to the question "How important are verbs?" Have contributors offer opinions, suggested books (or other materials), and quotations.

Without a verb, even if it's only suggested, there's nothing going on, just a lot of nouns standing around with their hands in their pockets.

—Patricia T. O'Conner
Woe Is I

Conventions and Presentation

Student Traitbook pages 158–168

Word Choice

- Introduce Trait
- **Practice Trait**
  - Lesson 4.1
  - Lesson 4.2
  - Lesson 4.3
  - Lesson 4.4
  - **Conventions & Presentation**
- Apply Trait

In this lesson, students explore two ways of connecting Word Choice with Conventions and Presentation. In the first part of the lesson (Level 1), students discuss homophones and use a list of common homophones to edit copy. In the second part of the lesson (Level 2), students review copy and layout for a menu—then design a menu of their own.

Objectives

Editing Level 1: Conventions
Students will

- understand what homophones are.
- identify homophones that give them particular trouble.
- use a list of common homophones to proofread and edit example sentences.

Editing Level 2: Presentation
Students will

- explore the importance of good Presentation in menu design.
- review and critique copy for a hypothetical restaurant's menu.
- draft a menu for a hypothetical restaurant of their own.

Time Frame

50 min.

This lesson has two parts. Allow a full class period for each.

- Part 1: Students review a list of homophones and use it in editing for correct spelling and meaning.
- Part 2: Students critique a restaurant menu and then design and write one of their own.

Unit 4   243

Conventions & Presentation

Practice Trait
Editing Level 1: Conventions

Coach's Corner

We suggest providing individual copies of the homophones list from this lesson so that students can slip them into their writing binders and refer to them often. Students should add other troublemakers to their personal lists as they identify them.

Coach's Corner

Working individually is important for this task because it is the only way to know for sure whether each student catches a particular error. Identifying homophones that cause a writer trouble is the first step in learning to use them correctly. Students should feel welcome to use dictionaries for this activity.

Editing Level 1: Conventions
The Troublemakers

Setting Up the Lesson

Editing Level 1 focuses on Conventions. In this part of the lesson, students will review a list of common homophones—words that are pronounced the same or nearly the same but have different spellings and meanings. Students will identify homophones that give them trouble and also edit copy to ensure the correct homophone is used for the intended meaning.

Begin with these steps:

- Share the introduction to this lesson.
- Have students identify as many of the incorrectly used homophones in the introduction as they can.
- Define the concept of *homophone* as a group and list a few with your students' help.
- Ask if any particular homophones give your students trouble—and mention any that are difficult for you.
- Discuss the fact that using homophones incorrectly can obscure meaning—this is why getting them right matters.
- Let students know that in this lesson they will be reviewing a list of common homophones and also editing copy in which some homophones are misused.

Student Traitbook p. 158

Teaching the Lesson

A Warm-Up

Go through the directions for this section together, taking time to discuss what spell checking programs on a computer can and cannot do. They are extraordinarily helpful, but they do not catch everything. For example, how many of the errors from this lesson's introduction did the authors' spell checking program catch? Have students make a guess. (Answer: Zero.)

Following this discussion, give students time to circle the correct homophone in each of the seven warm-up sentences. They should work individually on this activity.

Share and Compare

When students finish the warm-up sentences, have them compare their choices with those of a partner or circle team members. They should use a dictionary to settle disagreements. When they finish, have students coach you as you go through the sentences. Here, for easy reference, are the correct choices:

1. Chuck's broken ankle could **lessen** his chances of making the track team.
2. If the **flue** in the fireplace is blocked, smoke will back up and escape into the house.
3. As soon as he walked into his sister's room, Jorge sensed that his **presence** wasn't welcome.
4. When you quote someone's words, be sure to **cite** the source.
5. The doctor's **patience** was tested every time the twins came in for a check-up.
6. The **coarse** pepper left me sneezing violently.
7. I'm afraid I'm hooked on television **serials**.

Take time to explain any choice that gave students difficulty.

The Troublemaker List

In this part of the lesson, we offer a fairly extensive list of homophones for students to review. We suggest

- reading through the entire list quickly.
- having students mark any homophones that are troublesome to them personally.
- giving students a copy of this list to keep in a writing notebook.
- having them add to the list as other troublemakers pop up.

Allow about 10 minutes for this initial review, taking time to answer questions.

Student Traitbook p. 159

Student Traitbook p. 160

Coach's Corner

We chose some particularly challenging words for this warm-up, so writers should not feel bad if they did not get every one right. What is important is understanding what each word means and why it is the correct choice. You may also wish to point out that many errors with homophones occur not because the writer doesn't know the right word, but because the writer is working hastily.

Coach's Corner

Make sure students have access to dictionaries during this review. Even though you are answering questions, you want them to look up as many words as possible on their own.

Unit 4 245

Conventions & Presentation

Practice Trait
Editing Level 1: Conventions

The Top Six Troublemakers

Review the directions to be sure they are clear. Then give students a few minutes to identify their top six troublemakers. This is an individual choice, and each writer's list will probably be different.

Student Traitbook p. 161

Bringing everyone in . . . Differentiated Instruction

Some students may need a little additional help distinguishing between homophones that are puzzling to them. Obviously, this can become an enormous task if you try to tackle the whole list—so having students identify words that are special troublemakers makes it easier to begin making distinctions. Remind students that their personal list may change throughout the year. It will shrink as definitions and spellings become more clear—and may expand if new troublemakers are found.

Editing Strategies

Share the first set of directions. Then give students time to identify specific strategies they can use to make sure they are choosing the right homophone each time. Any reasonable answer to this is fine. Here are some possibilities:

1. Read the sentence aloud, focusing on the meaning.
2. Check a personal homophone list, if you have one—and read your own notes!
3. Check the definition in a dictionary.
4. Check with a friend.

After discussing potential strategies, review the second set of directions. Then give students about 10 minutes to identify and revise incorrectly used homophones in the five practice sentences. Students should

- read each sentence once for meaning, then again to look for errors.
- underline any word they think is wrong and correct it on the spot, or
- check it out using a dictionary.

Coach's Corner

There are a total of 17 homophone errors in the five sentences. Do not share this number right away, but after students have gone through the sentences one time, ask how many errors they have found. Then share the correct total and have them go back for one final look.

246 Unit 4

When students finish, go through the sentences one by one, having them coach you as you edit. Here, for easy reference, is a corrected copy with the edited words marked in **bold blue**:

1. I have to memorize all ten **verses** of this ancient poem, and it's a **real** pain.

2. From my room, I could **hear** my parents as they **discussed** whether or not I had worked hard enough to deserve a new tennis **racquet**.

3. If my brother **lends** his camera to his friend, it could come back with **some minor** damage.

4. I **heard** that the **principal** was going **to** honor a **pair** of students for **their** charity work.

5. For our research project, we have to correctly **cite** any Web **sites** we use—and that always **seems** to be hard **for** me.

Quiz Maker

Review the directions. Then give writers time to create a one-sentence quiz, using any set of homophones (whether from our list or another source). The sentence should be set up to offer choices with slash marks (/) between choices, just as in our warm-up sentences. Be sure that writers

- write just ONE sentence each.
- focus on homophones they feel might stump a classmate.
- know the correct answer so they can explain it.
- use a dictionary to check anything they're unsure about.

When writers finish trading, doing the quizzes, and discussing results, have volunteers share any examples that were particularly challenging or interesting.

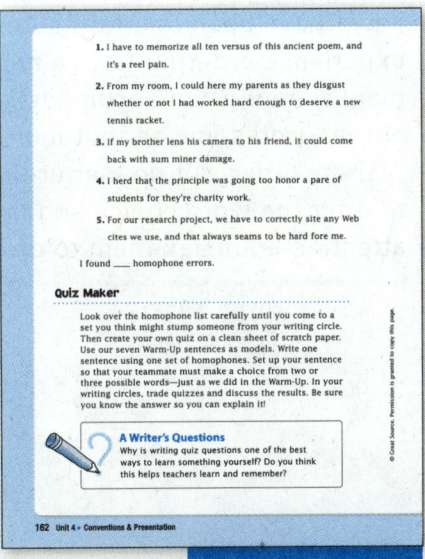

Student Traitbook p. 162

Coach's Corner

As all teachers know, being the test maker is one of the best ways to learn any subject. So even though you are only taking time for one sentence today, we recommend repeating this activity throughout the year, not just for homophones, but for any editing task that challenges your students.

Conventions & Presentation

Practice Trait
Editing Level 2: Presentation

Coach's Corner

Note that menus come in all sizes and shapes. As you build your collection, go for variety—everything from the half-page to-go menu to something more elegant. Look for variety in layout, fonts, colors, use of illustrations, and so on. And don't forget to include one or two you consider less effective—for whatever reason.

A Writer's Questions

Writing tests and quizzes is a helpful learning strategy for many reasons. Among other things, it requires the quiz maker to figure out what is most important—and also most challenging. In addition, it requires that person to know the answer or have a rationale for the "best" answer. If a quiz is really good (good questions, important questions), it should be just a little harder to make it than to take it.

Editing Level 2: Presentation
Today's Specials

Setting Up the Lesson

In this lesson, students have a chance to examine examples of restaurant menus and consider how Presentation and Word Choice work together to make the simple menu a masterpiece of persuasive writing.

It will be helpful if you can collect example menus for this purpose—and feel free to ask students to help you with this.

Bringing everyone in . . . *Differentiated Instruction*

Not all of your students may be experienced diners. Some may never have been to a formal restaurant. But most have some experience ordering from a menu of one kind or another. Not all menus are written documents. Some are blackboards with chalk entries, and some are outdoor marquees from which drive-through patrons order. But no matter the venue, restaurants rely on menus to offer the word choice and layout that will get customers' attention and coax them to order something.

Begin with these steps:

- Share the introduction to the lesson.
- Ask if students have a favorite restaurant—large or small.
- Does anyone have a favorite item to order? If so, can they recall how the restaurant describes that item?
- Does anyone—for whatever reason—recall a menu that impressed them? What about it caught their eye?
- Explain that this lesson is how Presentation and Word Choice work together to make menu items so appealing that patrons can't resist ordering them.

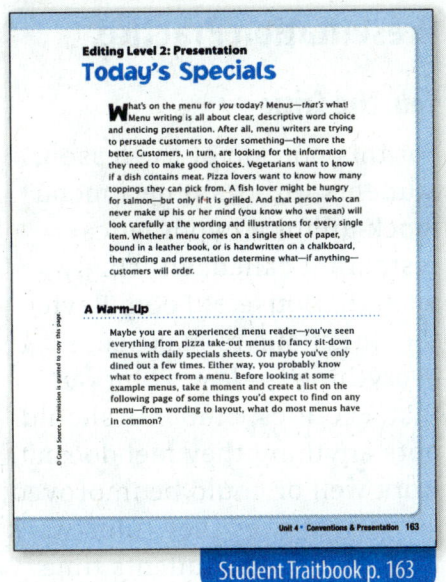

Student Traitbook p. 163

Teaching the Lesson

A Warm-Up

Share the directions and give students 2–3 minutes to brainstorm a list of features important to any menu. This is not a test, and students should feel free to think creatively—and to go beyond the six items we've made room for. It is fine for them to work with partners or in circles to do this.

Exploring . . . and Making Notes

Review the directions and share the example menus you and your students have collected together. Have students

- look for menus that seem especially appealing.
- keep their list of important features in mind—which menus have all six?
- make notes about effective wording, design, color, illustrations, and so on, in the space provided.

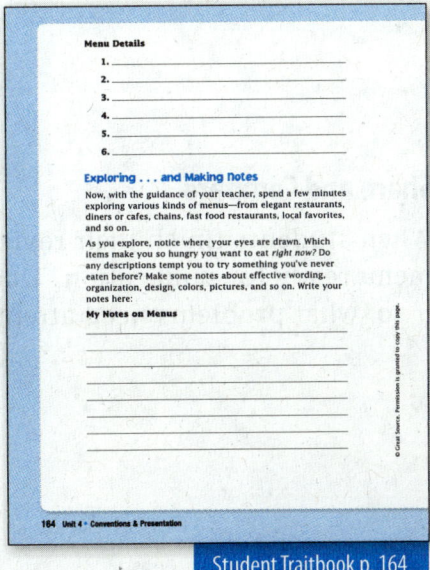

Student Traitbook p. 164

Coach's Corner

If you've assembled a truly diverse collection of menus, it may include examples that are less well done. That's good! It's extremely helpful to explore ineffective writing in order to know what doesn't work—and what to avoid in your own writing.

Conventions & Presentation

Practice Trait
Editing Level 2: Presentation

Presentation Practice

You, the Critic

For this portion of the lesson, students will examine a menu mock-up for a hypothetical restaurant called, enticingly enough, House of Food. Review the directions to make sure everything is clear. Point out that as critics, students should note anything they feel doesn't work well or could be improved, as well features they think work well. Then give students time to conduct their reviews, either working with partners or in writing circles. Encourage them to

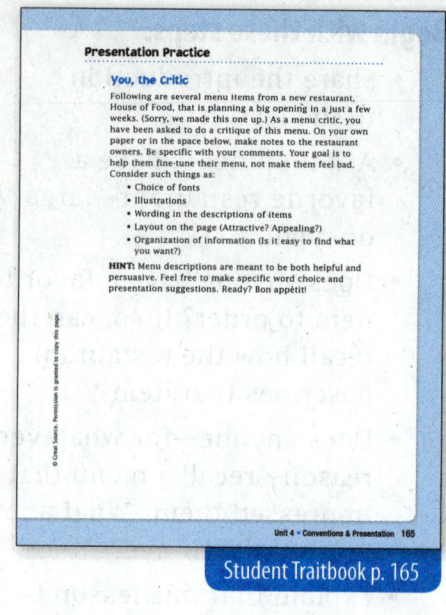

Student Traitbook p. 165

- look carefully at each section of the menu.
- consider all features identified earlier as important.
- make notes in the space provided or on their own paper.
- write as if their notes will be shared with the restaurant owners.

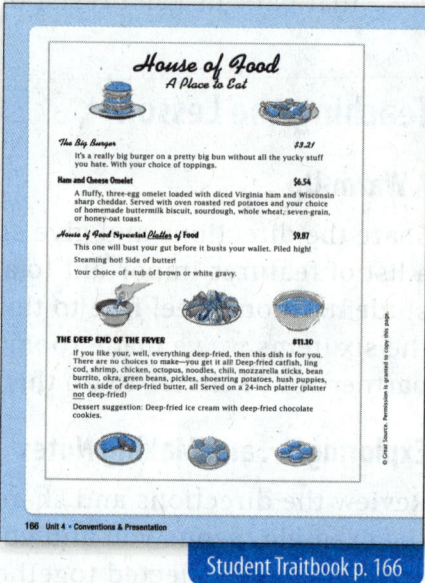

Student Traitbook p. 166

Coach's Corner

This lesson focuses on Presentation—but remember to emphasize the connection to Word Choice. The general layout and illustrations should complement the written copy, and they should work together in describing items in an alluring way.

Share and Compare

When students finish their reviews, discuss their responses. Is this menu ready for publication? Does it need revision or redesign? If so, what problems need attention before it goes to press?

A Writer's Questions

Most readers (and restaurant patrons) would likely agree that menu readers have certain questions about ingredients, preparation, portion size, and cost in mind when looking at a menu. They want these basic questions answered, but they don't necessarily want a bio of the chef or a step-by-step description of the preparation. Interesting though these details might be, they may not belong on the main part of a menu—though there could be space for such items on a back page.

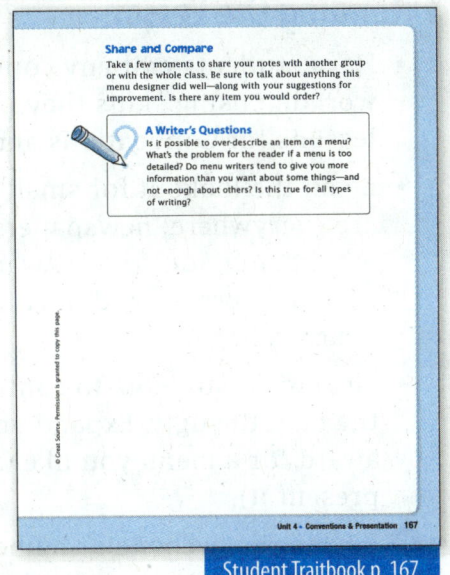

Student Traitbook p. 167

Presentation Matters

In this section of the lesson, students have an opportunity to use everything they have learned to create a menu for their own hypothetical restaurant.

Review the directions to make sure everything is clear. Then, have students work in writing circles to

- name the restaurant.
- create copy for five (or more) items.
- decide on a general format (single fold, double fold, full page, and so on).
- use Presentation and Word Choice to create a menu patrons would find irresistible.

Students can decide within each writing circle how they will divide up the work.

When students finish, share menus or display them so everyone can review the work of various groups. Be sure to comment on Word Choice or Presentation decisions that are particularly effective.

Student Traitbook p. 168

Coach's Corner

If students have computer access, they will likely find this activity considerably easier, especially since it will allow them to play with wording and arrangement of items on the page. This will also help the menu design go much faster—and will allow students to focus on such things as font selection and size.

Conventions & Presentation

Practice Trait
Editing Level 2: Presentation

I cannot teach in isolation and expect kids to apply it. I have to guide students by building an environment that supports writers in becoming their own critics, kids who look to punctuation and grammar to make their messages clear and interesting.

—Jeff Anderson
Mechanically Inclined

Extending the Lesson

- Have students edit any copy on which they are currently working, using skills they practiced in this and preceding lessons for Conventions and Presentation.

- Be on the lookout for small errors in published copy. They are everywhere: newspapers, journals, textbooks, novels, advertising, junk mail. Award extra credit to students who identify, correct, and post faulty copy. Create a bulletin board collage.

- Encourage students to continue looking at menus—the good, the bad, the ugly. Expand your collection—or make up an award for a menu you like (and if the restaurant is local, present it).

- Review any website or home page, applying the same criteria you identified for picking out successful menus. What more do you learn about little tricks that make presentation work?

- Check out online reviews of local restaurants. Do any mention discrepancies between the actual food and what the menu led them to believe they might receive? Obviously, a menu is important because without it, patrons cannot figure out what to order. But does a menu unintentionally offer other information about the restaurant or its owners and staff?

Notes

UNIT 4
Word Choice

Introduce Trait

Practice Trait

Apply Trait

Final Curtain Call 255
- Preview pages 255–263

Assessing and Revising Sample Papers 256
Sample Paper 15: *Invaders of Our Land*
 Score and Rationale
Sample Paper 16: *To the Bat House!*
 Score and Rationale
Revising Sample Paper 15: *Invaders of Our Land*

- Apply what students have learned by assessing Sample Papers 15 and 16
- Revise Sample Paper 15 for Word Choice

Revising and Editing a Personal Draft 261
- Have students revise their own writing for Ideas, Organization, Voice, Word Choice, and Conventions and Presentation
- Assess students' growth as writers

Parting Thoughts 263
- Conclude the trait of Word Choice

Final Curtain Call

It's time to give students a chance to apply what they have learned—and give you a chance to assess their growth as writers and revisers. Have students demonstrate their knowledge of Word Choice (as well as Ideas, Organization, Voice, and Conventions and Presentation) by following these steps:

1. **Apply knowledge of Word Choice by assessing and revising the writing of others.**

    Your students will read and assess Sample Papers 15 and 16. This time, they will work independently, applying what they have learned to

    - decide for themselves which piece is stronger.
    - score each sample paper, using the Student Rubric for Word Choice.
    - brainstorm ways of improving the weaker paper.
    - revise the weaker paper for Word Choice.

    Assessment Component: Base your assessment of growth on students' revision of Sample Paper 15: *Invaders of Our Land.* The revised version should achieve a final score of 4, 5, or 6 in Word Choice, as measured using the teacher rubric for that trait.

2. **Apply knowledge of Word Choice by assessing and revising personal writing.**

    Have students pull their rough drafts from their folders to revise and edit, applying everything they have learned from

    - reading and using student rubrics, checklists, and posters for Ideas, Organization, Voice, Word Choice, and Conventions and Presentation.
    - discussing and assessing the writing of others.
    - reading or hearing literature that exemplifies strengths in various traits.
    - completing lessons to build skills in five traits.
    - assessing and revising weaker writing samples.

    Assessment Component: Score each final draft and compare those final scores to the baseline scores you assigned earlier to writers' rough drafts. Do not base your assessment *exclusively* on the differences between these scores, however. Look carefully at the quality, nature, and extent of each writer's revision. What revision strategies did they apply? What risks did they take? Add additional points for good editing or creative presentation.

Coach's Corner

Remember to check out the Assessment Guidelines (in the back matter) for additional suggestions on effective ways to assess your student writers' performance and growth.

Coach's Corner

If a student's score on the final draft does not leap the river in a given trait, provide that student with an option to revise or edit further, focusing on problems that most need attention. In scoring Conventions and Presentation, look for conventions that support and enhance meaning and voice, and give credit for any design features that enhance readability or eye appeal.

Coach's Corner

As always, offer simple tips to make revision manageable. **Ideas:** Add important details. Make sure the message is clear. **Organization:** Make the lead and conclusion strong. Be sure the order is easy to follow. **Voice:** Write what you truly think, feel, or believe. **Word Choice:** Cut the clutter, strengthen verbs, make words precise enough to make a picture or movie in the reader's mind. **Conventions and Presentation:** Wait to edit until the draft feels finished. Read everything twice, silently and aloud, pencil in hand. Base layout on a model you find appealing.

Word Choice

- Introduce Trait
- Practice Trait
- **Apply Trait**
  - **Assessing and Revising Sample Papers**
  - Revising and Editing a Personal Draft

Assessing and Revising Sample Papers

Student Traitbook pages 169–172

Sample Paper 15: *Invaders of Our Land* and Sample Paper 16: *To the Bat House!*

1. Explain that this activity will give students a chance to see how they have grown as assessors and revisers with respect to Word Choice.
2. Refer each student to the Student Rubric for Word Choice.
3. Group students in writing circles and then refer them to Sample Papers 15 and 16.
4. Let students be a little more independent by
   - passing out both sample papers at once.
   - having them read the papers aloud to each other—in any order.
   - having them decide for themselves which paper is stronger in Word Choice. (Most teams should choose *To the Bat House*.)
   - scoring the two papers together, thereby using comparisons to help zero in on the best score for each.
5. As students score the two papers, they should think about the following

❓ Key Questions . . .

- *Are there striking words or phrases you would highlight?*
- *Does the writing make clear pictures in your mind?*
- *Are there words you'd like to remember—or use yourself?*
- *Do strong verbs create a sense of movement or energy?*
- *Does the writer's word choice contribute to the voice? If so, where?*
- *Are there sensory details? (Words that make you see, hear, smell, taste, or feel things clearly?) If not, should there be?*
- *Is the writing wordy? Would you cut anything?*
- *Are there overused words or expressions?*
- *Are any words used incorrectly?*
- *Is this writer writing to teach us—or to impress us?*
- *Are there places where you would say something differently? If so, where?*

Coach's Corner

Remember to vary the composition of writing circles from time to time—not for each activity, certainly, but often enough to let writers hear many perspectives and voices. Through this and other activities, give writing circles some freedom to manage their own scoring and revision practice.

Coach's Corner

The two sample papers selected for this activity are both informational. The writer of Sample Paper 16 knows his topic well, but he takes a somewhat playful approach. The writer of Sample Paper 15 has clearly done some research on starlings—but overwrites in a way that causes more confusion than clarity.

Coach's Corner

Remind students to mark text in a couple of ways—perhaps underlining or highlighting strong moments and putting a light question mark by any word or phrase they do not understand or think might be expressed in a better way.

256 Unit 4

6. When students are finished scoring, talk (as a class) about which paper is stronger in Word Choice and why. Have students identify strong features from *To the Bat House.* Which words or phrases stand out? Have students identify specific problems with *Invaders of Our Land.* What needs revision?

7. Compare students' scores with ours (see Scores and Rationales).

Score and Rationale for Sample Paper 15: *Invaders of Our Land*

Most readers agree that *Invaders of Our Land* **needs serious revision** in Word Choice. Though we can (usually) determine what this writer means to say, she is clearly writing more to impress than to enlighten—and may be a little heavy handed with the thesaurus. Some words are simply misused. *Predacious,* for example, usually refers to animals that hunt other animals—though it can be used to describe someone who attacks or steals from others. Similarly, *voracious* means ravenous or insatiable—not huge or overwhelming, as suggested here. We can translate: *. . . some ambitious scholar who read Shakespeare voraciously got the atrocious idea to import to America all of the birds mentioned in Shakespeare's plays.* But the point is: Why should we have to? It takes real concentration to figure out the writer's main points: starlings were imported by a Shakespearean scholar, and it was a bad idea; they take over the nests of other birds and consume precious grains, devastating farmlands. On the positive side, there are a few well chosen verbs: *wreaked, taking over, consume.* They don't compensate for the lack of clarity, however. This paper would receive a **score of 3 in the trait of Word Choice.** (Some writers may see it as a **2**.)

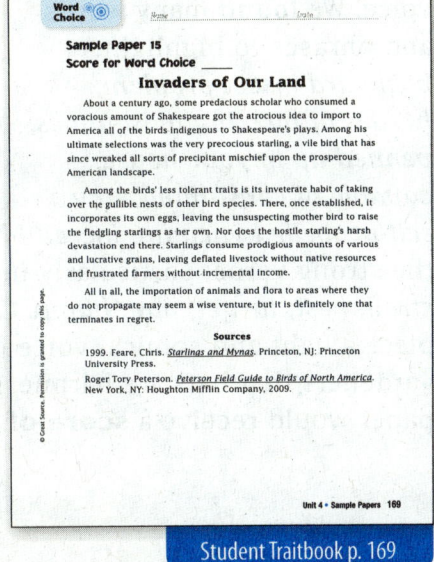

Student Traitbook p. 169

Coach's Corner

Did the writer of *Invaders of Our Land* use a thesaurus? Did she use it well—or overdo it? Encourage students to have a dictionary handy as they score this piece, to look up words they do not know, and to ask whether or not the writer has expressed each idea in the best way possible.

Coach's Corner

The writer's tendency to reach for the thesaurus makes *Invaders of Our Land* sound better than it really is. Only when we take it apart and look carefully at word meanings, do we realize that words that might be impressive in a list do not work in this piece because they are not used appropriately. It's how words are used in context that counts.

Word Choice

Apply Trait
Assessing and Revising Sample Papers

Coach's Corner

Notice that the writers of both Sample Paper 15 and Sample Paper 16 cite sources used in their research. In both cases, the source lists have conventional problems. As part of a separate lesson, you might have students look for and correct errors, using whatever writing handbook is approved for your classroom.

Score and Rationale for Sample Paper 16: *To the Bat House!*

Most readers agree that this paper is **strong** in Word Choice. In contrast to the writer of Sample Paper 15, this writer has a comfortable, natural style, consistently reaching for words that make meaning clear. He has a strong vocabulary, but he never uses words just to impress readers. Instead, he uses language that enhances both meaning and voice. We found many words and phrases to highlight: *backyard insect problem; hordes of buzzing mosquitoes; penned up in your house; capable of consuming; tiny, self-propelled vacuum; incredibly precise*—and many more. Notice the strong verbs, particularly in the fourth paragraph: *dive bomb, stroll, nest, target, nail, bump.* Carefully chosen words give this piece a light and comical voice just right for reassuring nervous gardeners that bats are harmless and helpful—to humans. This paper would receive a **score of 6 in the trait of Word Choice.**

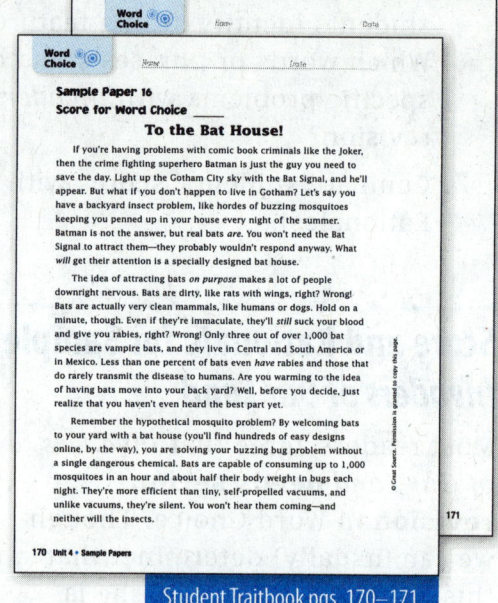

Student Traitbook pgs. 170–171

Revising Sample Paper 15: *Invaders of Our Land*

Have students revise the paper with the lower score in Word Choice: *Invaders of Our Land.* Their goal is to raise the score from a 3 to a 4 or higher. This challenge tests their knowledge of Word Choice, as well as their creativity in solving a challenging writer's problem—overwriting. (This is a very different task from the one they faced in revising the vague and general Sample Paper 14: *Most Embarrassing Moment.*)

Follow these steps:

1. Remind each student to refer to the Revising Checklist for Word Choice or the Student Rubric for Word Choice—their choice—as they work.

2. Have students (without looking at any guide) brainstorm some important features of strong Word Choice—in their own words. Their list might include any of the following:

   - *Strong verbs*
   - *Colorful, striking words and phrases you might highlight*
   - *Language that makes a picture in your mind*
   - *Lack of repetition*
   - *No vague language*—nice, good, great, special, awesome, and so on
   - *Word choice that creates voice*
   - *Sensory language to help you see, hear, smell, taste, feel the writer's experience*
   - *Words used correctly*
   - *New words or terms explained clearly*

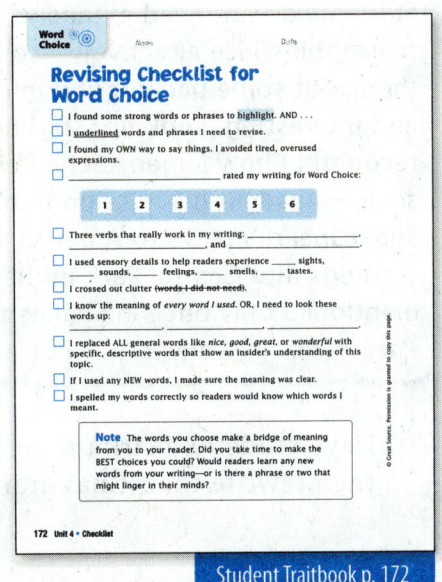

Student Traitbook p. 172

3. Have students look carefully at Sample Paper 15: *Invaders of Our Land.* Remind them that any helpful revisions are welcome, but their primary focus for this lesson should be on Word Choice. Students should work individually, but may do their planning with partners or in a writing circle, helping each other figure out word meanings.

4. Remind students that it is all right to change the wording or restructure sentences, add or delete details, add a new title—*anything at all.* They are in charge!

Coach's Corner

The biggest task for this revision will be to determine the meaning of various words this writer has chosen in order to decide whether or not they are used correctly. Students will need dictionaries and may wish to divide up the task of looking up words they don't know.

Word Choice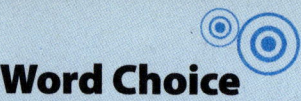

Apply Trait
Assessing and Revising Sample Papers

Coach's Corner

Here's a helpful tip as students work on their individual revisions: Have them imagine that they are translating this essay, sentence by sentence—making meaning clear for readers. Once they've done this, they can go back, read aloud, and smooth out the sentence flow.

Coach's Corner

Students know by now how valuable it is to have an intended purpose and audience. For example, this essay might be part of a biology textbook explaining the perils of bringing non-native plants or animals into an area. Or, it might make an interesting sidebar on a playbill for *King Henry IV, Part 1*.

5. Give students time to collaborate *in planning their revision*. Here are some suggestions:
   - Read the piece aloud, line by line.
   - Underline each word they do not know—and look it up.
   - Make notes about word meanings in the margin.
   - Figure out what, specifically, the writer means to say.

Bringing everyone in . . .   Differentiated Instruction

Students do not need extensive knowledge of starlings to revise this piece effectively—so long as the main idea is clear to them. But some background information could be both helpful and interesting. Look up "starlings" online for a host of articles recounting how Eugene Schieffelin, a member of New York society, made it his mission to bring various birds mentioned in Shakespeare's plays to America and released an estimated 100 starlings into Central Park in the spring of 1890. The starling is mentioned only once in Shakespeare's plays: in *King Henry IV, Part 1*, Act 1, scene 3.

6. Have students mark up the rough copy any way they wish—then rewrite their final draft by hand or word processing.

Assessment

Assess this activity by (1) scoring the final draft for Word Choice (using the teacher rubric for that trait) and (2) looking at the creativity and overall extent of the revision. Look for

- a final score of 4 or better in Word Choice.
- words that convey a clear message and help readers understand why the starling turned out to be such a pest.
- words used correctly.
- strong verbs, sensory details, or vivid descriptions.
- language that contributes to voice.
- absence of vague expressions or over-written passages.

Revising and Editing a Personal Draft

Applying Knowledge of Word Choice by Revising Personal Writing

The revision your students just completed on Sample Paper 15: *Invaders of Our Land* provides a good warm-up for revising their own writing effectively. Everything in this unit has been directed toward this goal: helping writers become strong, independent revisers of their own work.

1. Ask students to recall the personal writing they created after the Literature Connection (*The True Confessions of Charlotte Doyle* by Avi). This should still be in rough draft form in their folders.

2. Have them remove that writing from their folders and assess it for Ideas, Organization, Voice, Word Choice, and Conventions and Presentation, using the student rubrics for those traits. As they assess, students should ask themselves these

❓ Key Questions...
- Does this paper leap the river in each trait?
- What are its strengths? How can I expand on those?
- What problems do I see (or hear) that I need to work on?
- What notes can I write on my draft to help me remember what to do?

Bringing everyone in... | Differentiated Instruction

Writers have studied five traits now, so the revision possibilities are plentiful—and some writers may not be ready to take on *everything*. More challenged writers might focus on problems that stand out: need for a clearer message, better lead, vivid description, strong verbs, and so on. Stronger writers should be encouraged to do *more than one* revision. They might begin with a focus on message and organization, but revise a second time to fine tune voice and word choice. Push strong writers to review their work more than once, as professionals do.

Word Choice

- Introduce Trait
- Practice Trait
- **Apply Trait**
  - Assessing and Revising Sample Papers
  - Revising and Editing a Personal Draft

Coach's Corner
It's the "internal rubric" that drives a writer's own writing. You want your writers to look at their work and say, "I like the sound of that," or "I can say that a better way."

Coach's Corner
As always, students do NOT need to score their writing. In place of scoring, have them create a revision plan—which might take the form of notes written on the rough draft or a brief to-do list.

Coach's Corner
Writers should—by this point—have the option to work with partners or within writing circles at any point in the writing process, deciding for themselves how confident they feel about planning their own revision or if they need coaching.

Word Choice

Apply Trait
Revising and Editing a Personal Draft

3. Based on their own revision plan and priorities, students should revise their writing, marking up their rough drafts any way they wish—or revising on the computer. Their goal should be to make the final draft leap the river (scores of 4, 5, or 6) in *all five traits:* Ideas, Organization, Voice, Word Choice, and Conventions and Presentation.

4. Final drafts may be copied onto new paper—or entered into the computer.

5. **Rough drafts and final drafts should be stapled together** so that you can easily make comparisons and track the planning and flow of their revision.

Assessment

Assess this activity by (1) scoring the final draft for Word Choice—as well as for Ideas, Organization, and Conventions and Presentation (using the teacher rubrics for those traits) and (2) looking at the creativity and overall extent of the revision. Look for:

- Clear main idea
- Details that expand or enrich that idea
- Strong focus on the message
- Inviting lead
- Effective transitions
- Easy-to-follow design
- Conclusion that wraps up the story or essay
- Read-aloud moments of voice
- Engagement with the topic
- Voice that suits the genre
- Strong verbs and other striking words or phrases
- Precise terminology
- Vivid description or use of sensory language (as appropriate)
- Creative and appropriate title
- Strong conventions
- Presentation that makes information accessible or gives the piece eye appeal

Bringing everyone in . . . Differentiated Instruction

By now, your students have some experience with Presentation, but they may still need guidance about your expectations. Will you look for a cover? Dedication page? List of sources? Do you have guidelines about font selection or size? Placement of titles or subtitles? Offer some suggestions and keep in mind that Presentation can be highly challenging without computer access.

Parting Thoughts

It's vital to have a clear message in mind before deciding which words will best get that message across. Doing things the other way around is like shopping for ingredients without knowing what's for dinner. When a writer has something definite to say, he or she knows, at once, when the words are just right and when they're a bad fit. The "right" word isn't *necessarily* one from the word list of the week—or even one from the thesaurus (handy as that tool may be). It's just as often an everyday word, used in an unexpected or delightful way that reveals the writer's voice. It's the word that lights a spark in the reader's mind and makes that reader say, "Oh, I get what you mean" or "I can just *see* it." Words used to razzle-dazzle readers create roadblocks. They say, in effect, "Keep out. This is *my* message, and you probably wouldn't understand it anyway." Words chosen carefully, on the other hand, invite readers "inside," like a door swinging open to reveal a warm hearth. We're not born knowing these magical words. We have to hunt for them in the literature we love. But gradually, through reading, once-distant words become old friends, the ones we reach for naturally and share with our readers—who are always out there, listening.

Good writing is writing that works. It makes sense. It's both comfy and elegant. It says just enough and no more. It has manners, not mannerisms. Good writing has all the right words—and not too many of them—in all the right places.

—Patricia T. O'Conner
Words Fail Me

Vicki & Jeff

UNIT 5
Sentence Fluency

Overview

Fluent writing is immediately recognizable. It's rhythmic—sometimes musical. We hear it in the lyrical prose or poetry that speaks to us and in the songs we cannot get out of our heads. Good writers, like composers, play with language, listening for the right beat and meaningful word combinations. They make reading feel easy and natural. We encourage young writers to stretch and compress sentences, to experiment with patterns, to use literary mentors as guides in crafting **Sentence Fluency,** and above all, to trust their ears to tell them what works.

In this unit, you will be helping students to

- combine sentences to **create a smoother flow.**
- **vary sentence length and structure** to make text interesting.
- **use** transitional words **in moderation.**
- **combine multiple strategies** to make writing fluent.

TRAIT DEFINITION

Sentence Fluency is the rhythm and flow of language—how it plays to the ear. Fluent passages are marked by strong cadence, variety in sentence structure, purposeful repetition, and effective transitions that connect ideas. Fluent texts are free of unintentional repetition, persistent choppy sentences, and tangled structures that require rereading. Preventing such problems takes a good ear, developed by reading and hearing extraordinary literature. Fluency defies rules. Fragments, for example, can be disruptive—or remarkably effective. That's why, as writers compose, we want them to read aloud, experiment, and listen for the right sound—like a lyricist at the piano.

Vicki & Jeff

Unit at a Glance

Introduce Trait

Discussing Sample Papers 268

Making the Literature Connection 274

Writing a Personal Draft 277

Practice Trait

Lesson 5.1: Keeping It Rolling 282

Lesson 5.2: Tuning in to Variety 290

Lesson 5.3: Avoiding Transition Overload! 297

Lesson 5.4: Putting It All Together 303

Conventions and Presentation 308

Apply Trait

Assessing and Revising Sample Papers..................... 324

Revising and Editing a Personal Draft 329

Unit 5   265

UNIT 5
Sentence Fluency

Introduce Trait

	The Opening Act 267	• Preview pages 267–278
15 min.	**Discussing Sample Papers**............268	• Introduce trait language and rubric
	Sample Paper 17: *This Won't Hurt a Bit* Score and Rationale	• Analyze weak and strong writing
15 min.	Sample Paper 18: *Teaching Dad to Ski* Score and Rationale	
50 min.	**Making the Literature Connection** 274	• Model the trait of Sentence Fluency in literature: "The Gift of the Magi" • Connect reading and writing
50 min.	**Writing a Personal Draft**..................277	• Coach students in creating a piece of personal writing • Assess students' drafts to create benchmark scores

Practice Trait

Apply Trait

266 Unit 5

The Opening Act

Introduce the trait of Sentence Fluency by first discussing the concept: the rhythm and flow of language and how writing plays to the ear—especially when read aloud. Let students see and hear this trait in action, first in two writing samples, and then in a piece of literature, "The Gift of the Magi" by O. Henry. This classic story of love and sacrifice is beautifully told in sentences that invite expressive oral reading. Following **Making the Literature Connection,** students will have a chance to create an original piece of writing on a topic of their choice. They will revise and edit this piece down the road, using what they have learned about all six traits.

1. **Discuss and assess the sample papers.** Expand students' understanding of Sentence Fluency by discussing two sample papers: *This Won't Hurt a Bit* (in which varied sentences invite expressive oral reading) and *Teaching Dad to Ski* (in which choppy, repetitive sentences make reading feel like stop and go driving through heavy traffic).

   Encourage student writers to talk, to read the samples aloud to each other, to highlight sentence beginnings, and to refer often to their student rubrics. By this time, your students know to

   - scan strong samples for sentence patterns or strategies they might imitate.
   - notice problems in weaker samples—and think about how they might revise.

2. **Connect the trait to literature.** Continue your conversation by letting students hear the strong word choice in selected passages from our featured text for the unit, "The Gift of the Magi" by O. Henry. Use this or any text strong in Sentence Fluency. Remember to allow a full class period (or more) for the literature lesson. We recommend sharing several examples and also having students help identify passages they would like to share aloud with the class.

3. **Complete a personal draft.** Following the literature connection, have students write a personal draft on any topic of their choice. The writing may be inspired by "The Gift of the Magi," but it does not have to be. Writers should put that writing into folders for a time in order to create the mental distance needed to revise effectively. They will revise and edit the piece at the close of the unit, using skills gained through the five lessons that follow. Your assessment of the rough and final drafts, and comparison of the two, will give you one important measure of your writers' growth through this unit.

Coach's Corner

In discussing or scoring writing samples for this unit, remind students to read aloud—even if you have already read a piece first. Also remind students to consider how Sentence Fluency influences Voice.

Coach's Corner

As always, writers may return to their writing at any time. Some may need several hours or more to complete the writing, especially if it involves research. Some writing may be done in class and some at home. Be sure, however, to schedule time for revising—at least for planning revision—toward the close of the unit.

Sentence Fluency

- Introduce Trait
  - **Discussing Sample Papers**
  - Making the Literature Connection
  - Writing a Personal Draft
- Practice Trait
- Apply Trait

Coach's Corner

The link between the traits of Sentence Fluency and Voice is very strong. Remind students of this as they read aloud. When the fluency in a piece is very strong, it is easier to read with the expression and inflection necessary to bring out the voice of the piece.

Discussing Sample Papers

Student Traitbook pages 174–175, 220

Student Rubric for Sentence Fluency

Prior to presenting the two introductory sample papers to students, practice each aloud to yourself so you can read it with expression and bring out whatever fluency is present. It is important that writers assess with their ears as well as their eyes—especially for this trait. We provide questions to ask with respect to each paper, but please add your own to our list.

1. Quickly review the Student Rubric for Sentence Fluency. As always
   - a score of 6 indicates **strength**—but NOT perfection.
   - a score of 1 indicates a **beginning level** of performance—first thoughts.
   - the "river" divides writing in which strengths outweigh problems from writing in which problems outweigh strengths.

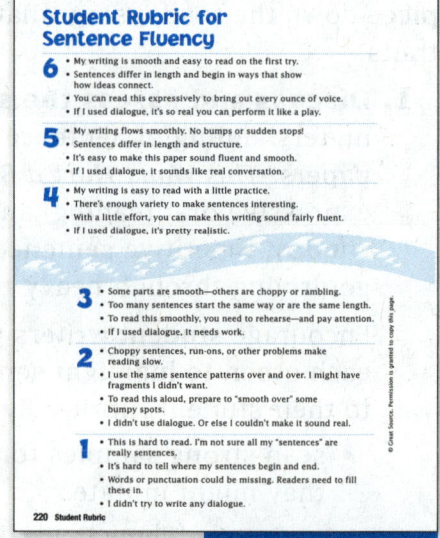

Student Traitbook p. 220

2. Respond to any questions.
3. Explain that for this lesson, students will rate two pieces of writing: *This Won't Hurt a Bit* and *Teaching Dad to Ski.* They will work with partners or in writing circles to discuss and score each paper, then defend their scores, using the language of the rubric.

Bringing everyone in . . .   **Differentiated Instruction**

Students within writing circles can take turns reading aloud—and decide for themselves who will read each passage. Encourage them to take turns, though. That way, each student can assess the trait of Sentence Fluency from two important perspectives: *How does the text sound as I listen to someone else read? And how easy is it for me, as a reader, to read aloud with expression and voice?* Both questions are important in measuring Sentence Fluency.

Sample Paper 17: *This Won't Hurt a Bit*

1. Read (or have a student read) *This Won't Hurt a Bit* aloud. As you read, tell students to think about these

   ❓ **Key Questions . . .**

   - *Do you like the sound of this paper? Does it flow smoothly?*
   - *Is the piece easy to read aloud—even on the first try?*
   - *Are there both long and short sentences—or are they all about the same length?*
   - *Do sentences begin in different ways—or, if there is repetition, is it effective?*
   - *Are there choppy parts—or places where you need to reread?*
   - *Should some short sentences be combined? Should some overly long sentences be divided?*
   - *Does smooth sentence flow contribute to the voice of the piece?*

2. Have students mark up the sample paper by highlighting sentence beginnings (the first three to four words). They might also put a check mark in the margin next to any sentence or group of sentences that seem to call for revision.

3. Have students score the paper, 1 through 6, using the Student Rubric for Sentence Fluency.

4. After scoring, have students discuss their scores and reasons with partners or in their writing circles.

5. When they finish, vote as a class (with a show of hands or by moving to corners) and tally scores. Tell students to
   - think about the key questions listed under Step 1 above.
   - state whether or not they think this paper leaps the river in Sentence Fluency.
   - defend their scores using the Student Rubric for Sentence Fluency.

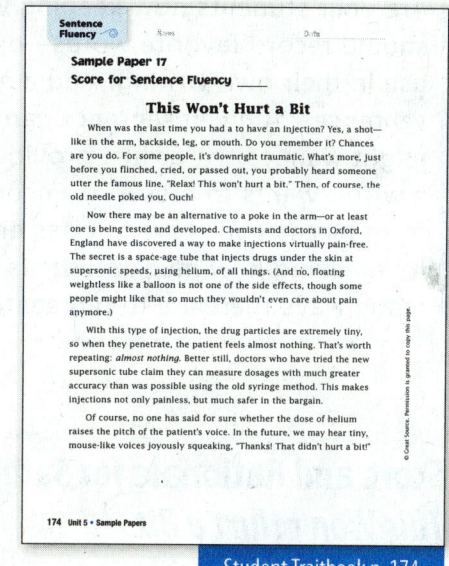

Student Traitbook p. 174

Coach's Corner

This Won't Hurt a Bit is an informational essay. Its purpose is to educate readers about a new form of medical injections and to make them curious to do a little research on their own. A good informational essay makes a clear point and offers an example or two as backup. Readers, in turn, feel they've learned—or gained a new perspective—about the topic. Does this essay succeed in doing those things?

Coach's Corner

Writers sometimes think that because variety is a plus, every single sentence must begin differently. Obsessing over variety can, however, lead to some awkward structures. The goal is to make the writing sound natural, not forced. More than one sentence can begin the same way without diminishing the fluency of a piece. What's more, occasional purposeful rhythm works: *I came, I saw, I revised.*

Sentence Fluency
Introduce Trait
Discussing Sample Papers

Bringing everyone in... Differentiated Instruction

Are your students now keeping writing journals? If so, they should record favorite words—ones they want to remember and use in their own writing. Add a new section: favorite read-aloud sentences. A given sentence can suggest a pattern that a writer might want to try, or just provide a good-read aloud moment that a writer wants to preserve. Encourage students to pull sentences from pieces you share in class or literature they read on their own. It's amazing how much students learn from simply recognizing how many ways there are to put sentences together.

Coach's Corner

For fun, try a little experiment. Beginning with the second paragraph, revise every sentence so it begins with "A new kind of injection" or "This new kind of injection." Read it aloud—you don't need to write anything out. The resulting monotony will help students appreciate even more the wonderful variety of Sample Paper 17. The ear loves surprise.

Score and Rationale for Sample Paper 17: *This Won't Hurt a Bit*

Most readers agree that this paper is **strong** in the trait of Sentence Fluency. Variety abounds. Sentences range from 4 to 29 words long and begin in a wide range of ways. We have statements, questions—even an exclamation: *Ouch!* What really matters, though, is that the overall sound is natural and expressive. The text simply floats from one sentence to the next, thanks to carefully crafted connections: *What's more, For some people, Then of course, Now there may be, The secret is,* and so on. This way of linking sentences guides us easily through the discussion. Moreover, the piece is very readable, even without practice. This paper would get a **score of 6 in the trait of Sentence Fluency**.

Sample Paper 18: *Teaching Dad to Ski*

1. Answer any new questions students may have about the Student Rubric for Sentence Fluency.

2. Consider switching partners or regrouping writing circles so students hear new voices and perspectives.

3. Read *Teaching Dad to Ski* aloud or have students read it aloud in their writing circles. As they do so, remind them to think about these

    ### ❓ Key Questions . . .

    - *Do you like the sound of this paper? Does it flow smoothly?*
    - *Is the piece easy to read aloud—even on the first try? Do you get the urge to revise some parts?*
    - *Are there both long and short sentences—or are they all about the same?*
    - *Do sentences begin in different ways—or, if there is repetition, is it effective?*
    - *Should some short, choppy sentences be combined? Should some overly long sentences be divided?*
    - *Does smooth sentence flow contribute to the voice in this piece?*

4. As before, have students underline or highlight sentence beginnings to look for repetition—or variety. Have them also put a check in the margin by each sentence or group of sentences that calls for revision.

5. Have students score the paper, 1 through 6, referring to the Student Rubric for Sentence Fluency.

6. Have students discuss their scores with partners or in writing circles.

7. When they finish, vote as a class (with a show of hands or by moving to corners) and tally scores. Tell students to

    - think about the key questions listed under Step 3 above.
    - state whether or not they think this paper leaps the river in Sentence Fluency.
    - defend their scores using the Student Rubric for Sentence Fluency.

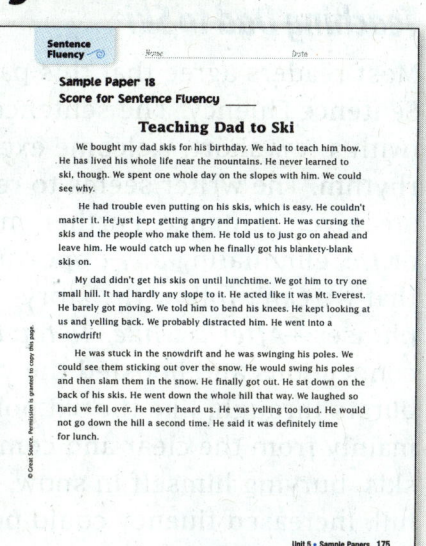

Student Traitbook p. 175

Coach's Corner

Teaching Dad to Ski is a personal narrative. The purpose of such writing is to tell a story. A good story sets the stage, recounts events building to a high point, then quickly winds down, usually offering insight about something learned or discovered. Did this writer achieve those goals?

Coach's Corner

If you can display or project these questions, you won't need to interrupt your students' discussions by asking them aloud. Students don't have to answer *every* question, worksheet style. These are simply reminders of things to look for.

Sentence Fluency

Introduce Trait
Discussing Sample Papers

Coach's Corner

Students may notice that all the sentences in Sample Paper 18 are grammatically correct. But Sentence Fluency is more than correctness. It's the rhythm and flow of individual sentences—as well as paragraphs. The good news is that a little sentence combining and a few new beginnings will dramatically increase the fluency of this piece.

Coach's Corner

As you score and discuss other writing examples, students may notice strengths or problems in Sentence Fluency that are not reflected in the rubric. Encourage them to note these—right on the rubric itself—and at some point, revise or expand the rubric so that it reflects your students' own thoughts and discoveries.

Score and Rationale for Sample Paper 18: *Teaching Dad to Ski*

Most readers agree that this paper **needs significant revision** in Sentence Fluency. The sentences are virtually all the same length (with a few short, welcome exceptions), creating a monotonous rhythm. The writer seems to resist putting more than one idea in any given sentence. Further, most sentences begin with either *We* or *He,* eliminating any opportunity for clear connections. It isn't that we can't follow the story—it's pretty simple. But connecting phrases—*After a while, To top it off,* etc.—would have crystallized connections and boosted the voice. Ironically, some voice still bursts through, like the ski poles from the snow bank. It comes mainly from the clear and comical images of Dad, fumbling with skis, burying himself in snow, and then sitting down to take the hill. Increased fluency could pop this voice right off the chart—the potential is there. Thanks to the relentless sameness in sentence length and structure, this piece would receive a **score of 3 in the trait of Sentence Fluency.**

Creating a Baseline Assessment

Have students revise Sample Paper 18: *Teaching Dad to Ski* (the weaker of the two introductory papers) working individually. Assess the *revised* drafts (using the Teacher Rubric for Sentence Fluency) to provide baseline scores reflecting students' revision skills for this trait. Record those scores. At the close of the unit, following direct instruction in Sentence Fluency, you can compare these early revisions to the revisions your students do on their own writing and on Sample Paper 19: *Chocolate and the Witch's Curse.* This comparison will tell you how much students have grown as revisers with respect to the trait of Sentence Fluency. (Below, **Extending the Lesson** provides suggestions on setting up this revision activity.)

Extending the Lesson

- Talk about other strengths in *This Won't Hurt a Bit*. What are some of the many ways this writer finds to begin sentences? (You might make a list.) How much influence does the fluency of this piece have on the voice?

- Have students become "sentence stalkers," like author/teacher Jeff Anderson, quoted in the margins of this section. Tell students to look for fluent, read-aloud samples in advertisements, book jackets, blogs, drama, novels, poetry—and their own work.

- Encourage students to read aloud everything they write and to experiment with writing sentences in various ways, searching for the combination that works.

- As a class or in teams, devise a plan for revising *Teaching Dad to Ski*. Students can work together to plan, but they should draft their own revisions. Since no research of special information is required, most should complete this task within 20 to 25 minutes. They can work on a printout of the paper itself, or rewrite on scratch paper. If time permits, you can enter the copy into the computer so that students can do many revisions. Suggest these strategies: (1) read aloud as you work, (2) combine some short sentences to make a longer, smoother one, and (3) rewrite some sentences to begin in different ways—avoiding, as much as possible, the overused beginnings *He* and *We*.

Coach's Corner

Whenever possible, have students revise on the computer. The reason is simple: It's faster. Faster does NOT just mean getting done sooner. It means having time to try multiple options. Few writers craft a truly fluent sentence on the first try. Having a chance to try and try again is key. Most students won't do this if they have to hand write. Can we blame them?

Bringing everyone in . . .   Differentiated Instruction

For English language learners, writing a sentence that makes sense in a new language can be a challenge. Now we are asking them to reconfigure sentences to change the sound! You can do things to make this easier. First, read aloud from a fluent, highly varied piece—right before the writer tries to revise. Second, record a wide range of sentence beginnings, so writers can see and hear possibilities. Third, suggest some sentence beginnings to try. For example, look at sentences 2 and 3 from Sample Paper 18. Suggest combining those sentences, beginning with the word *Though*. Suggest combining sentences 4 and 5, beginning with the word *After*, and so on. Be patient. Remember, the goal is not to read perfect text but to cultivate confident writers so they gain the courage to try something different.

- Create before-and-after audio recordings of *Teaching Dad to Ski*. Listen to both and imagine someone listening to them while driving—or just relaxing. Do you hear a dramatic difference?

- Search "writing with fluency" online for a host of articles, tips, and activities.

- Start a blog discussion about fluent writing. What secrets have your writers uncovered so far? What are some things never to do? What are the very best things to read for models of fluent writing?

- Listen to any book (or other work) on CD. Do you like the sound of it? If so, was variety part of the appeal? Could you hear a connection between fluency and voice?

I am a self-professed sentence stalker. I am always on the lookout for great mentor texts . . . I also constantly look for well-written student sentences . . . From posting a student's sentence on the door as a Sentence of the Week to using a piece of student writing as an example rather than an error, sentence stalking goes a long way toward building goodwill in any classroom.

—Jeff Anderson
Mechanically Inclined

Sentence Fluency

Introduce Trait
Discussing Sample Papers
Making the Literature Connection
Writing a Personal Draft
Practice Trait
Apply Trait

Coach's Corner
To teach Sentence Fluency, look for any text with a natural, musical rhythm and easy-to-read sentences of varying length and structure. Don't forget examples of good dialogue, effective repetition, or creative use of fragments. Read the whole text or any passage that shows how the trait of Fluency enhances meaning and Voice.

Coach's Corner
"The Gift of the Magi" is a classic holiday story that has been enjoyed by countless people for generations. Look it up online to find numerous study guides, summaries, discussion questions, and other instructional aids.

Making the Literature Connection

 **"The Gift of the Magi" by O. Henry**

Sentence Fluency creates an engaging and interesting journey for readers, enhancing the message much the way a movie soundtrack enhances our enjoyment of a film. One of the best ways to teach Sentence Fluency is by reading aloud. In so doing, we let students hear how fluency creates rhythm and meaning in the hands of a skilled writer. For this lesson, we have chosen O. Henry's classic short story "The Gift of the Magi." Though the word choice in this poignant tale echoes an earlier time, its fluency is timeless and lyrical, offering numerous read-aloud opportunities.

Sharing the Text

1. Show students the book and share the title and author. Let them know it was originally published in a New York City newspaper in 1905. O. Henry is the pen name of William Sydney Porter. Ask if any of your students are familiar with the story or with O. Henry's other stories, including "The Furnished Room," "The Last Leaf," "The Ransom of Red Chief."

2. Preview the book's main idea: The Youngs, James and Della, are a young married couple struggling to make ends meet. At Christmas time, they each make a great personal sacrifice in order to give the other a meaningful gift. This is a tale that has been told and retold in many forms, in many cultures, and holds themes of love and sacrifice common to stories new and old.

3. Ask your students if they are familiar with stories that are told to teach a lesson or moral. Is this one of the main reasons for storytelling?

4. Talk about the practice of gift giving. The characters in this story give gifts to celebrate a holiday—and out of love for each other. On what other occasions and for what reasons do people share gifts?

5. Let your students know you are going to read the whole story. It might be helpful if each student has a copy of it. The narrator speaks directly to the reader, asking us to take a close look at this young couple. Have students notice how Della's actions are described in great detail while the actions of her husband are not revealed until the end. (The reader is kept in suspense about the gift he plans to give her.) Talk about how this suspense gives the story an unexpected twist—one that is both painful and heartwarming.

6. With your students' help, recount the sacrifice of each character. What seems to motivate them?

7. Discuss the character's actions. Are they foolish?

> **Bringing everyone in . . .**   **Differentiated Instruction**
>
> We have chosen a short story that is from the turn of the twentieth century. The structure and rhythm of the sentences, along with the language, reflect this time period. They also exemplify the importance of varying sentence lengths and beginnings. To make the piece more accessible to students, consider—after reading it once—performing a portion of it as a play.

8. Have students identify moments in which they feel the trait of Sentence Fluency (especially variety in sentence length) is particularly strong.

Other Books You'll Love

Throughout this program, we rotate recommendations by genre:

- **Classic**—both traditional and contemporary
- **Poetry**—an individual poem or collection
- **Nonfiction**—picture book or longer text
- **Fiction**—picture book or longer text

Please keep in mind that your *own* favorite books are almost certain to include clear, smooth, rhythmic sentences. And don't forget to pull other examples from business writing, poetry, and the world of journalism. The following are some selections to explore.

Sentence Fluency

Introduce Trait
Making the Literature Connection

1. **Poetry:** "When I Heard the Learn'd Astronomer" by Walt Whitman

   First published in 1865, this poem speaks to the notion that while book learning and lectures have their place, a person should get out and experience the world first hand for the full perspective. This non-rhyming poem shows how purposeful repetition (first four lines begin *"When I ..."*) can create a rhythm for readers and helps them feel the impact of the writer's big idea.

2. **Nonfiction:** *Paths to Peace: People Who Changed the World* by Jane Breskin Zalben

   Sixteen men and women from different countries and times are profiled in two- to three-paragraph biographies focusing on courage and commitment. The book models focused, fluent informational writing. Art, quotations, glossary, further readings, resources, and index beautifully complement the content. Mahatma Gandhi, Mother Teresa, Cesar Chavez, the Dalai Lama, and Aung San Suu Kyi are among the people included.

3. **Fiction:** *After Tupac & D Foster* by Jacqueline Woodson

   Some students may be familiar with this author's work—*Feathers, Locomotion, Hush,* and *Miracle's Boys.* This Newbery Honor Book is about friendship, family, the power of music, and growing up in Queens, New York. The music of Tupac Shakur and his life-and-death struggles are interwoven throughout this story of three girls trying to find their "Big Purpose." Numerous passages model various hallmarks of fluency: varied sentence length and structure, purposeful run-ons or rhythmic repetition, and effective dialogue.

Writing a Personal Draft

Sentence Fluency

Introduce Trait
Discussing Sample Papers
Making the Literature Connection
Writing a Personal Draft
Practice Trait
Apply Trait

1. Let students know that they will now have a chance to create a personal piece of writing on a topic of their choice. Give them a few minutes to confer with a partner about possible writing topics. They can check their writing journals or consider a topic suggested by "The Gift of the Magi," such as:

   - An original story involving sacrifice and selflessness (narrative fiction)
   - The joy of giving someone the perfect gift (poetry, expository, narrative)
   - An object that has great value to you (poetry, narrative, descriptive)
   - Working for something important (narrative, expository, poetry)
   - Comparing hard times today to hard times at the turn of the century (narrative, expository, poetry)
   - The concept of sacrifice (expository, narrative, persuasive)
   - A historical report on the Magi, the Queen of Sheba, or King Solomon (informational, persuasive, expository)
   - What it means to be rich or poor (narrative, expository, poetry)
   - An essay exploring whether characters Jim and Della Young are rich or poor (expository, poetry)
   - Report on the real geography and time period of "Gift of the Magi"—New York City, 1905 (informational, expository, poetry)
   - Bio of O. Henry (informational)
   - Review of the story "Gift of the Magi" or one of O. Henry's other short stories (response to literature, persuasive)

Coach's Corner

Some writers may wish to incorporate technology into their writing. If possible, allow them to consider using it in this assignment. Audio, video, or PowerPoint can greatly enrich any presentation.

Bringing everyone in... Differentiated Instruction

"The Gift of the Magi" has been adapted for theater in several venues. Your students may enjoy adapting a portion of the story as a theater production—and performing it. Encourage them to write their own dialogue, using O. Henry's story as a basis for this, holding true to the story line while giving the piece a contemporary flavor. Students in a writing circle might work on this together.

Sentence Fluency

Introduce Trait
Writing a Personal Draft

Coach's Corner

Prewriting depends somewhat on genre. An informational piece usually requires the writer to gather facts and other details—which may be recorded on a list or on note cards. A poem, by contrast, might begin with a sketch or word web. As students think how to prewrite, ask, "How do you envision this piece? Is it a story? Is it a script for a television documentary? Is it a poem, a chapter in a textbook—or a picture book?" It makes a big difference.

Coach's Corner

Many students are likely unfinished. Consider devoting another class period to drafting—or as an alternative, allow about 10 minutes of planning time so students can coach one another on how best to finish their work outside of class. It's important for writers to collaborate in early stages of the writing process—not just after drafts are finalized. Writers respond to writing in much more meaningful ways when they have had a chance to be part of the planning and conceptualizing.

Write what makes you happy.

—O. Henry

2. Give students 5 to 8 minutes to discuss topics. This kick-off conversation encourages writers to try a topic or genre they might not think of on their own.

3. Record some writing ideas for whole-class reference and offer individual coaching as needed. Remind writers that they may choose any topic that suits them—whether inspired by "The Gift of the Magi" or not.

4. Allow about 5 to 10 minutes for sketching, making a web, writing a list of questions or details, and so on.

5. Provide students with as much time as possible to begin a draft. We recommend about 30 minutes (in addition to prewriting time), but please use your own judgment based on your curriculum and time available. This time may need to span more than one class period.

6. Remind students to double or triple space and allow ample room for revision.

7. When writing time is close to finished, suggest that writers confer with partners and/or write themselves a brief note about what to work on next.

8. This writing should now be placed in their writing folders. At the close of the unit, they will have time to look at this piece again and to revise it before it is assessed.

Notes

UNIT 5
Sentence Fluency

Introduce Trait

Practice Trait

Shifting the Spotlight..........................281	• Preview pages 281–320
Lesson 5.1...282 Keeping It Rolling	• Explore sentence combining • Analyze and revising choppy writing
Lesson 5.2...290 Tuning in to Variety	• Revise to create variety • Write an original piece with variety
Lesson 5.3...297 Avoiding Transition Overload!	• Identify transition overload • Revise to eliminate overload
Lesson 5.4...303 Putting It All Together	• Practice coaching skills • Use various strategies to create fluent writing
Conventions and Presentation.........308 Rev-edit-ising, Anyone? Concrete Poetry	• Combine revising and editing • Explore and write concrete poems

(Each lesson: 50 min.)

Apply Trait

Shifting the Spotlight

Your students have now assessed two sample papers for Sentence Fluency: *This Won't Hurt a Bit* and *Teaching Dad to Ski*. They have also seen and heard Sentence Fluency in action through your sharing of the short story "The Gift of the Magi" by O. Henry.

It is time to shift the spotlight, giving students a chance to practice specific skills they can use in revising and editing their writing. Several important features of Sentence Fluency are covered in the focused lessons that follow. Once students have completed all focused lessons, they will apply what they have learned by (1) revising *someone else's* writing and (2) revising and editing their own writing. Follow these steps:

1. **Complete Lessons 5.1 through 5.4.** Allow one or two days for each lesson. Through these lessons, students will learn strategies for
   - combining sentences.
   - varying sentence length and structure.
   - using transitional words in moderation.
   - combining multiple strategies to make writing fluent.

2. **Link Sentence Fluency to Conventions and Presentation.** Allow a full class period for each level. Students will learn that the trait of Conventions and Presentation supports strong Sentence Fluency through thoughtful combination of revision and editing strategies (Level 1: Conventions) and design of concrete poetry (Level 2: Presentation).

Encourage writers to continue *thinking like readers.* Have them look at the Sentence Fluency poster in the *Student Traitbook,* considering each thing the writer does (left column) and filling in the impact on the reader (*So the READER . . .*). After you have discussed all four elements, display the actual poster, comparing students' responses to ours. Throughout the year, have students use sentence strips to add their own ideas to this poster.

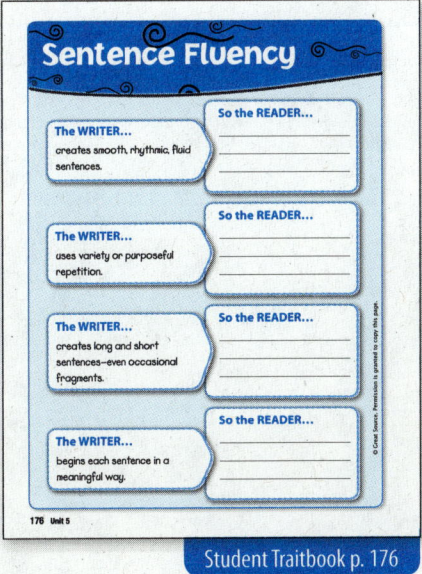

Student Traitbook p. 176

Sentence Fluency

Introduce Trait
Practice Trait
- Lesson 5.1
- Lesson 5.2
- Lesson 5.3
- Lesson 5.4
- Conventions & Presentation

Apply Trait

LESSON 5.1

Keeping It Rolling

Student Traitbook pages 177–182

Reading a long sequence of choppy sentences can feel like playing bumper cars. Stop, go, stop, go. Even bumper car fans can only take so much pounding and jostling—and readers feel much the same. Appealing text has a natural flow that makes reading easy, allowing readers to focus on the message. Reading aloud is a good way to ensure that a text is free of sudden stops and starts.

Objectives

Students will
- recognize the impact of choppy sentences on fluency.
- analyze and revise a passage for fluency.
- analyze and revise a second passage.

Time Frame (50 min.)

Allow 50 minutes for this lesson. We suggest dividing it into two parts.
- **Part 1:** Students analyze one passage for fluency and revise it, using any strategies they wish.
- **Part 2:** Students practice sentence combining and use that strategy to combine a second passage.

282 Unit 5

Setting Up the Lesson

Have students review the introduction to Unit 5 (*Student Traitbook,* page 173). Then, share the introductory paragraph of Lesson 5.1 (*Student Traitbook,* page 177).

The purpose of this lesson is to help students begin distinguishing between fluent and non-fluent writing—focusing particularly on the problem of short, choppy sentences.

Begin by sharing the example(s) you have chosen to open the lesson. Explain that you want students to use their ears—not their eyes—to judge the fluency. They should listen carefully to each passage you share, thinking about how it sounds. Is it appealing? Do any of them wish they'd written it? Would they like to hear more? If they agree that your samples are fluent, have them describe what they hear. What specific features make this writing work? Make a list.

For the second part of this warm-up, have students meet in writing circles to share the examples they identified themselves. Suggest that each writer take just 2 to 3 minutes to share one or two brief examples, inviting others to comment on what they hear and discussing why some passages are especially fluent. Share the strongest examples with the class as a whole and expand your list of qualities that contribute to fluency.

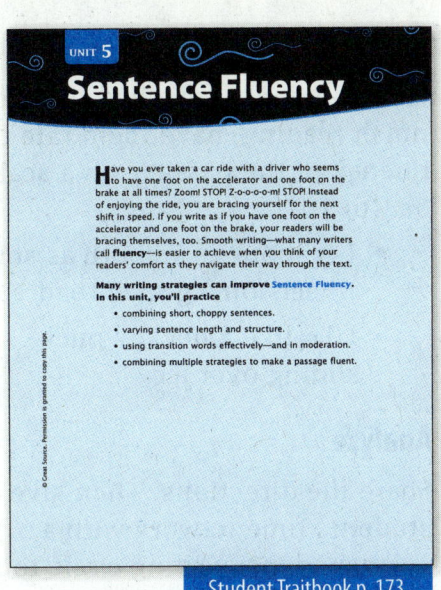

Student Traitbook p. 173

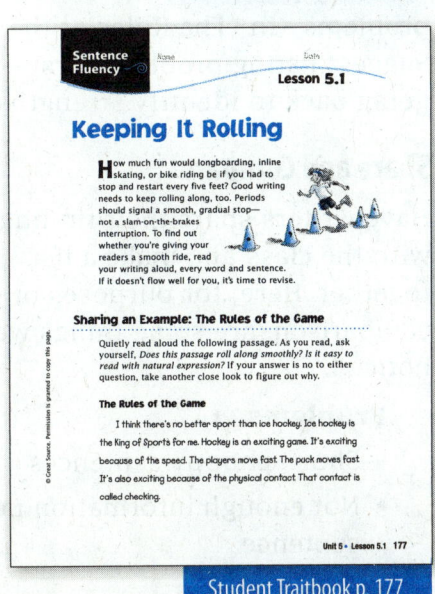

Student Traitbook p. 177

Teaching the Lesson

Sharing an Example: "The Rules of the Game"

Review the directions to be sure everyone understands the task. Then give students time to read "The Rules of the Game"—quietly, to themselves. As they read, they should ask themselves whether the passage is easy to read and moves along smoothly and naturally. If it doesn't, have them try to pinpoint why.

Coach's Corner

To kick off this lesson, each student will need a self-selected sample of fluent writing. They should make choices on their own from books you have in the classroom, books in the media center, or any writing at home—books, advertisements, newspapers, poems, musical lyrics, etc. Each sample can be as short as three or four sentences. Have students read aloud their selections in advance to practice sharing. **Note:** You will also need at least one example to share—you might share more.

Coach's Corner

We recommend that you do NOT read this example to students since your reading style will influence the fluency your students hear. You want them to form their own impressions.

Unit 5 283

Sentence Fluency

Practice Trait
Lesson 5.1

Coach's Corner
You may wish to sketch out a 10-point scale and record students' ratings in order to give the class a visual picture of how everyone voted. Most should rate it toward the lower end of the scale. We would give it a 4.

Coach's Corner
Students who gave this piece a low rating may wonder whether there could be strengths. Yes—almost every piece of writing has redeeming features, and this is a good time to point that out.

Respond

When students have had time to finish reading, have them rate the fluency of the passage on a scale of 1 to 10.

- 1 = about as smooth as square wheels on a gravel road
- 10 = like a hockey puck sliding over ice

Analyze

Share the directions. Then give students time to work with a partner or in a writing circle to identify specific strengths—or problems—in "The Rules of the Game." Suggest listing problems first—then going back to identify strengths.

Share and Compare

Have writers share their findings with the class and make a list together. Here, for purposes of comparison, are some things we noticed.

Problems
- Short, choppy sentences
- Not enough information per sentence
- Repetition
- Similar sentence beginnings
- Text that's hard to read with expression
- Sentences that aren't needed
- No transitions to connect ideas

Strengths
- Clear sentences that make sense
- Complete sentences
- Correct grammar

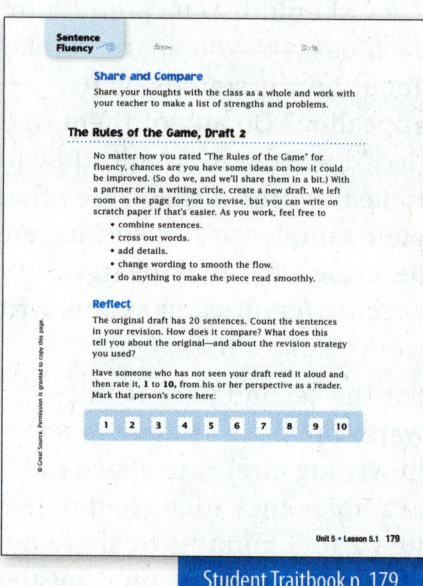

Student Traitbook p. 178

Student Traitbook p. 179

"The Rules of the Game," Draft 2

Review the directions. Then give writers time to work with a partner or in a writing circle to revise "The Rules of the Game." Writers should

- read the passage once more aloud, softly.
- review the notes from their analysis, focusing on the problems.
- revise *part by part*—combining sentences or using other strategies.
- revise on scratch paper or right on the original draft—their choice.

> **Bringing everyone in . . .** **Differentiated Instruction**
>
> Writers who try to revise *sentence by sentence* (versus part by part) will have a much harder time. That's because the main problem with this piece is choppy sentences that contain tiny bits of information. Reading a few sentences at a time and thinking about what this writer is trying to say will yield much better results. Remind writers that any good revision begins with figuring out the message.

Reflect

Review the directions. Then give writers time to count the number of sentences in their revisions—and compare that number to the **20 sentences** in the original. They should rate their revisions, using the same 1 to 10 scale they used for the original.

When they finish reflecting, tally scores for the revisions—and invite volunteers to share. Did many writers have

- a longer revision (more sentences)? This usually indicates addition of detail.
- a shorter revision (fewer sentences)? This usually indicates sentence combining.

Our **8-sentence revision,** for purposes of comparison, is on the next page. We combined many sentences and deleted some. We also changed the wording in spots, but added no new detail.

Unit 5 285

Sentence Fluency

Practice Trait
Lesson 5.1

The Rules of the Game

Ice hockey is the King of Sports. The sheer speed—of both the players and the puck—makes it incredibly exciting. Checking, the physical contact between players, adds to that excitement.

Referees go right out on the ice to enforce rules. Players who break rules may have to sit in the penalty box for two minutes or more—giving the other team an "extra player" advantage, called a "power play." Understandably, power plays often lead to goals.

Because of the drama, hockey is especially fun to watch live. When you know the rules, it's even better.

Coach's Corner

Note: If you are dividing this lesson into two parts, **Day 2 begins here.**

Coach's Corner

Draw your students' attention to the underlined parts of each original sentence. Those are the details that wind up, all together, in one combined sentence. This underlining strategy makes combining much, much easier.

Combining Sentences = Combining Ideas

Remind students of the keys to Sentence Fluency that they uncovered in the first part of this lesson. Then let them know that this portion of the lesson takes a close-up look at one strategy they've likely used already: sentence combining.

Review the directions. Give writers time to study the example on sentence combining. When they finish, have them tell you, *without looking,* the basics of sentence combining. They should mention these things:

1. The number of sentences decreases.
2. The number of words decreases.
3. The combined sentence contains several ideas instead of just one.

Student Traitbook p. 180

A Combination Warm-Up

Review the directions to be sure they are clear. Have students work individually, following these steps:

1. Read the four "starter sentences" about deer.
2. Underline details that could be combined in one final sentence.
3. Write a final sentence incorporating all underlined details.

When writers finish, record some of the results. Likely writers will see several ways of combining these ideas. Here, for purposes of comparison, are the original sentences with details underlined—and our resulting combined sentence.

> Deer pose problems for gardeners.
> + They pose a problem because they eat plants.
> + Deer will eat almost any kind of plant.
> + Deer are extremely hard to discourage.
> ___
> = Deer pose problems for gardeners because they will eat almost any kind of plant and are extremely hard to discourage.

Coach's Corner

Be sure to have students do a quick word count. Our example went from 4 sentences to 1, and from 27 words to 20.

Get This Writing Rolling!

Review the directions and let students know that they will be doing a little more extensive sentence combining. This time, they will work on a whole passage, not just four sentences. They will also work individually, rather than with partners or teams.

Give them 15 to 20 minutes to

- read the passage called "May Flower Service Project."
- think about which groups of sentences might be combined.
- underline details that could be combined within a new sentence.
- revise, using sentence combining as the main strategy, though it doesn't need to be the only one.

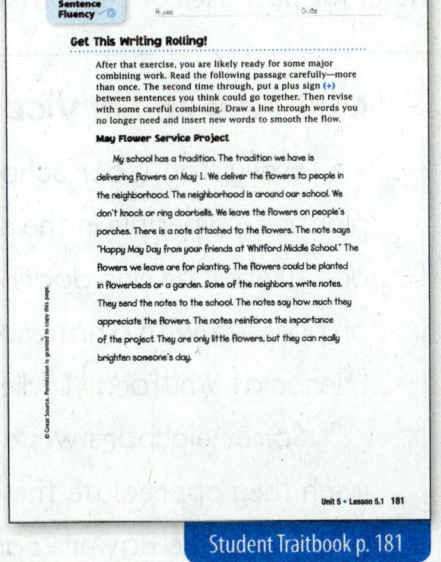

Student Traitbook p. 181

Coach's Corner

Students may work right on the text—we left room for that. Remind them that they can combine any number of sentences, not just 4. They might choose to combine 2, 3, 4—or more.

Unit 5   287

Sentence Fluency

Practice Trait
Lesson 5.1

Bringing everyone in... Differentiated Instruction

As much as possible, you want students to work independently on this task so that everyone has a chance to practice this skill. But if you have students for whom writing sentences in English is challenging, consider having them work with partners—or in a small writing circle with you as their guide. That way, you can take that first step of identifying which sentences could go together—and guide them to underline the key details that could all go into one final sentence.

Coach's Corner

If some of your students did a particularly skillful job of combining, consider having them model their strategies. They should begin with the unmarked original and talk their way through the revision (including underlining key details) so that others can follow their thinking and see how they made choices.

Share and Compare

When students finish, have them meet with partners or in writing circles to share their revisions and talk about the number of sentences they wound up with. Who had the fewest?

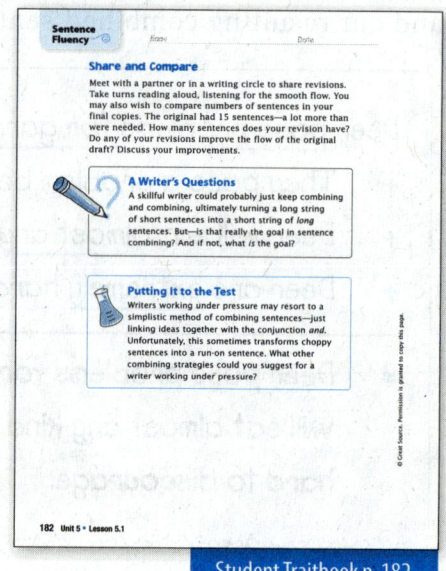
Student Traitbook p. 182

Here, for purposes of comparison, is our 5-sentence revision.

May Flower Service Project

Every May 1, our school delivers flowers, suitable for planting, to people in the surrounding neighborhood. We don't knock or ring doorbells. We just leave the flowers on porches with a note saying, "Happy May Day from your friends at Whitford Middle School."

Some neighbors write back to us, saying say how much they appreciate the flowers. Their notes are proof that even little flowers can really brighten someone's day.

As I write this chapter ... I hear every cadence, listen to every pause, and check every beat. I'm hoping that if you enjoy the rhythm of my words, you might be inclined to like my content as well.

—Mem Fox
Radical Reflections

A Writer's Questions

Writers can overcombine. (What if we had turned the passage on May Day into one humongous sentence?) The idea is to have a sentence carry a comfortable load of ideas. To achieve a good balance, imagine eating a glorious salad with a wonderful array of ingredients. You want to mingle flavors, but you don't want too much on your fork at any one time.

Putting It to the Test

The word *and* should send up a little red flag. It's a perfectly good word, one we all use—but too many *and*'s spoil the writing. Resist the temptation to use this linking word too much. Instead, consider opening a few sentences with fitting transitional words and phrases (i.e., *Because, Since, Finally, On the other hand, Meanwhile*, etc.) that show how two ideas connect. These words magically reduce the number of short, choppy sentences—and no *and*'s needed.

Extending the Lesson

- Continue to practice sentence combining. Write four or more starter sentences for students to combine. When they get fairly proficient, have them be the quiz makers for each other, with each writing circle creating starter sentences for another to work on.
- Give students time to do some further literary exploration, looking for particularly fluent passages to read aloud. Make reading aloud a daily practice, with different readers each time.
- Keep a running list of different ways writers begin sentences. Once your students notice and record these, they will be more daring in their own writing—and choppy sentences will be far less frequent.
- Search "sentence combining" online for a myriad of tips and practice activities.

Sentence Fluency

Introduce Trait

Practice Trait
- Lesson 5.1
- **Lesson 5.2**
- Lesson 5.3
- Lesson 5.4
- Conventions & Presentation

Apply Trait

LESSON 5.2

Tuning in to Variety

Student Traitbook pages 183–189

Repetition in writing can sometimes be a valuable strategy, driving home the writer's point: I need to write. I love to write. I live to write. *But most of the time, readers crave variety—in both sentence length and structure. New beginnings and a mix of long, medium, and short sentences are very pleasing to the ear, and keep readers tuned in, anticipating the writer's next move.*

Objectives

Students will
- recognize the value of variety in writing.
- consider two ways of achieving variety: sentence beginnings and sentence lengths.
- analyze two passages and revise one to make it more fluent.
- create an original fluent passage based on a topic of choice.

Time Frame

Allow 50 minutes for this lesson. We suggest dividing it into two parts.
- **Part 1:** Students analyze two passages for fluency and revise one to make it stronger.
- **Part 2:** Students choose a personal topic and create an original, fluent passage.

Setting Up the Lesson

Read the introductory paragraph of Lesson 5.2. Start this lesson by discussing the concept of variety. What are some everyday situations in which people appreciate variety? Give students one example of your own to kick off the discussion. Then make a class list—and talk about why variety is important in life. Your students may mention any or all of the following contexts in which variety is important.

- Television or other entertainment
- School classes or lessons
- Clothing
- Other products people buy
- Food/meals
- Weather
- Conversations with friends
- Activities—such as sports

For the second part of this introduction, emphasize the importance of variety in writing. Readers appreciate this, too! Talk about the value of the short sentence. What can a short sentence do that a long sentence cannot?

- Short sentences make reading easier.
- They are ideal for technical or any complex information where the reader needs to focus on one detail at a time.
- They give writing punch.
- They wake readers up.

On the other hand, what can long sentences accomplish that short sentences cannot?

- Long sentences can show connections between ideas.
- They can create complex, detailed images.
- They can create a musical, flowing sound, as in song lyrics.

Bringing everyone in... | Differentiated Instruction

Sentence length is relative. If you have students who are struggling to write sentences in English, remind them that *any* variety is welcome. If most sentences are 4 or 5 words long, having even one sentence of 10 to 12 words creates a dynamic difference. Further, sameness in length often springs from sameness in beginnings. Varying sentence beginnings almost *always* results in some variety in length because it disrupts the pattern.

Coach's Corner

If time permits, you may wish to have students look through a variety of written materials, including newspaper articles, children's picture books, textbooks, handbooks, technical manuals, and online song lyrics to see how long the sentences are—and how they are used. Where do they find the shortest sentence? The longest?

Sentence Fluency

Practice Trait
Lesson 5.2

Teaching the Lesson

Sharing an Example: *The Time Machine*

Review the directions to be sure the task is clear. Then have students

- read the passage from *The Time Machine* to themselves—aloud, but softly.
- think about the sentence fluency as they read.
- go back once more, noticing sentence beginnings and lengths.

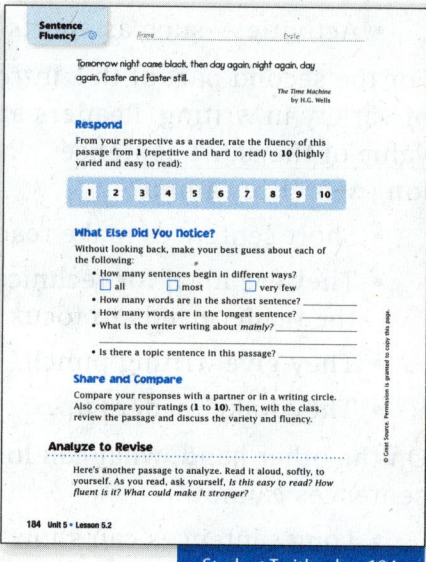

Student Traitbook p. 183

Respond

Give students a moment to record their responses as readers, rating the passage from 1 to 10.

- 1 = repetitive and hard to read
- 10 = highly varied and easy to read

As soon as students have finished marking their ratings, go on to the next activity.

Student Traitbook p. 184

What Else Did You Notice?

Review the directions. Be sure students understand that they should fill out their responses based on their impressions WITHOUT looking back at the Wells passage.

Once students finish, have them

- compare their responses with those of a partner.
- look back at the Wells passage to determine how accurate their responses were.
- share their thoughts in a whole-class discussion.

Here, for easy reference, are some facts about the passage:

- About half of the 11 sentences begin in different ways.
- The shortest sentence is 4 words long.
- The longest is 23 words long.

Coach's Corner

It is important for students to read this passage to themselves so that they form their own individual impressions about fluency—which may or may not agree with their partner's impressions.

Coach's Corner

Do NOT take time to discuss their responses just yet. You'll return to them in a moment, following the next activity.

Coach's Corner

This passage is from the classic science fiction novel *The Time Machine* by H.G. Wells. Originally published in 1895, it was the inspiration for several feature films, TV shows, comic books, and many popular sci-fi novels.

Coach's Corner

Not all paragraphs contain topic sentences by any means. Paragraphs serve many purposes. They introduce ideas, serve as transitions, present dialogue, describe a setting, or set off a single dramatic statement, which is what these paragraphs clearly do.

292 Unit 5

- Wells is writing about a first attempt at time travel.
- There is no clear-cut topic sentence. Rather, each sentence builds on the sensational detail and momentum of the sentence before it, propelling the entire passage forward to unleash a single dramatic event—successful time travel.

Analyze to Revise

Review the directions to be sure the task is clear—it is basically the same task students just completed, only this time (1) the passage is very different and (2) students will use their analysis as a basis for revision. Give students 2 to 3 minutes to read "Prisoner of the Food Channel" individually, focusing on the trait of Sentence Fluency.

Respond

When everyone has finished reading "Prisoner of the Food Channel," give students a minute to rate the passage on the 1 to 10 scale—but do not discuss their ratings yet. Move on to the next activity.

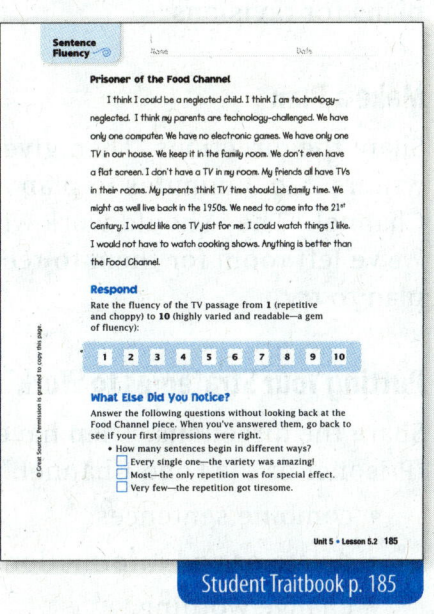

Student Traitbook p. 185

What Else Did You Notice?

As before, have students fill in their impressions without looking back at the passage. Then have them

- compare responses with a partner or in writing circle.
- check their responses against the actual passage.
- discuss results as a class, comparing "Prisoner of the Food Channel" with the passage from *The Time Machine.*

Here, for easy reference, are some facts about the passage:

- The 17 sentences begin in only a few ways. Most start with *I think, My,* or *We.*
- The shortest sentence is 5 words long.
- The longest is 9 words long (so contrast is minimal).
- The writer is *mainly* writing about living in a technology challenged family.
- We identified this as the topic sentence: *I think my parents are technology challenged.* (However, there are other possibilities, especially since the second half of the paper focuses mainly on how much the writer wants his own TV.)

Coach's Corner
The main reason to identify the topic sentence in this passage is to help writers figure out the main message. Without knowing the writer's point, it is much harder to revise.

Unit 5 293

Sentence Fluency

Practice Trait
Lesson 5.2

Share and Compare

Have students compare their responses. Encourage them to use what they know about the trait of Sentence Fluency to identify and discuss specific weaknesses in this piece. After their discussion, students should have a better understanding of what's needed to improve the piece and a few ideas they can apply as they make their plans for revisions.

Student Traitbook p. 186

Make a Plan

Share the directions. Then give writers 2 to 3 minutes to plan a revision of "Prisoner of the Food Channel." They should work with partners or in writing circles. We've left room for them to record three or four strategies they plan to try.

Putting Your Strategies to Work

Share the directions. Then have writers work together to revise "Prisoner of the Food Channel." They should feel free to

- combine sentences.
- delete or add information.
- change wording.
- make any other changes they wish.

Share and Compare

Have volunteers share their revisions by reading them aloud and talking about the strategies they used. What was the most popular strategy? Did any team try something no one else thought of?

Student Traitbook p. 187

294 Unit 5

Writing with Fluency

This section is divided into two parts. In the first part, students decide on a topic they know well and can easily write about at length. In the second part, students do a quick prewriting exercise before they create their first drafts.

Choosing a Topic

Remind students of your previous discussion on Sentence Fluency and the work they just completed in revising "Prisoner of the Food Channel." Let them know that today they'll have a chance to create a fluent passage of their own—one that will, we hope, have sentence variety similar to that in the passage from *The Time Machine*.

Review the directions for this part of the lesson to be sure students are clear. Then give them 5 minutes to choose a topic. We have provided a list of possibilities, but encourage students to choose any topic that interests them. They can also write in any prose form, such as the following:

- Story
- Description
- Personal essay
- Persuasive paragraph
- How-to piece

Student Traitbook p. 188

Planning and Drafting

Review the directions. Then give students about 20 minutes to plan and write, working independently. Remind them to

- keep pencils moving as much as possible.
- go for variety in sentences.
- be daring—try some sentence beginnings they have not tried before.

Coach's Corner

Note: If you are dividing this lesson into two parts, **Day 2 begins here.**

Coach's Corner

We suggest avoiding poetry for this particular lesson only because poems are often not written in sentences, and the purpose of this practice is to create sentence variety.

Coach's Corner

Do you keep a list of transitional words and phrases posted in your classroom? If so, you may wish to draw students' attention to that list as they consider new and different ways to begin sentences.

Coach's Corner

If time permits, have them go back and quietly read aloud what they have written. This is the time to change one more sentence beginning, combine two sentences—or divide one long sentence into two. Small revisions make big differences.

Unit 5 295

Sentence Fluency
Practice Trait
Lesson 5.2

Share and Compare

Give students time to share their writing with partners or in writing circles. Encourage listeners to comment on the amount of variety they hear.

A Writer's Questions

Have students look back at their revisions of "Prisoner of the Food Channel." Chances are that in improving the fluency of the piece, they also improved the voice—and perhaps other traits as well. It's all but impossible to revise for just one trait. Even tiny revisions influence writing in more than one way.

Student Traitbook p. 189

Putting It to the Test

A little trick experienced writers use is to skim back over the paper occasionally (as they write), reading just the first three or four words. This lets the writer know at once if he or she is falling into a pattern—or including plenty of variety. It's also important to use those transitional words and phrases to show how ideas connect. Writers who go for message first, thinking how ideas connect, almost never have a problem with repetition.

Extending the Lesson

- It's difficult to build fluency in one draft—or even one revision. Put one revised version of "Prisoner of the Food Channel" on the computer, and have students revise it one more time. Even five more minutes of work will make a huge difference. They can also do this with their own writing.
- Do you have a student writer or team who did a particularly stellar job of revising "Prisoner of the Food Channel"? If so, have them project the original electronically and present their revision strategies to the class, talking as they show their thinking behind their revision.
- Blog discussion: Among famous writers (or your students' favorites), who's writing has the most sentence fluency?
- Search "sentence variety" online for a vast array of tips, practice activities, and instructions for editing.

If you've been told that short sentences are always better than long ones, forget it. It's better to mix them up, because writing that has too many short, choppy sentences is just as tedious as writing that has too many long ones.

—Patricia T. O'Conner
Words Fail Me

LESSON 5.3

Avoiding Transition Overload!

Student Traitbook pages 190–194

Sentence Fluency

Introduce Trait
Practice Trait
Lesson 5.1
Lesson 5.2
Lesson 5.3
Lesson 5.4
Conventions & Presentation
Apply Trait

Transitions are ever so handy for clarifying connections between ideas. They can indicate time, place, cause and effect, contrast, order—even set up examples. But too many transitions (or the wrong transitions) can make readers a little cuckoo. This lesson is about not overdoing a good thing.

Objectives

Students will
- recognize that transitions, while important, should be used in moderation.
- identify "transition overload" in a passage from literature.
- analyze and revise a second passage to eliminate overdone transitions.
- create an original piece that uses transitions in moderation.

Time Frame

Allow 50 minutes for this lesson. We suggest dividing it into two parts.
- **Part 1:** Students analyze two passages and revise one to eliminate transition overload.
- **Part 2:** Students write an original piece using transitions in moderation.

Unit 5 297

Sentence Fluency
Practice Trait
Lesson 5.3

Coach's Corner
In conjunction with Lesson 2.3 (Unit 2, Lesson 3, Organization), your students may have slipped a list of transitional words into their writing notebooks—or you may have posted such a list in your classroom. That list will be extremely helpful for this lesson.

Coach's Corner
Students may wonder why, after studying transitions in conjunction with Organization, they are now revisiting these little "bridge" words as they study Sentence Fluency. The answer is simple: the two traits are closely connected. Sentence Fluency is definitely about sound and rhythm, and in this way, it supports the trait of Voice. But it's also about the logical flow of ideas, the trail of the writer's thinking. That's Organization. Transitions do double duty, supporting both the traits of Organization and Fluency.

Coach's Corner
The original version of this passage is from *"The Monkey's Paw"* by W.W. Jacobs.

Setting Up the Lesson

Share the introductory paragraph of Lesson 5.3. It may be a while since your writers studied transitions. (See Lesson 2.3.) Use this set-up time to review the concept of *transition,* and to help students recall some sample transitions and their function in sentences. We suggest four steps:

1. Begin by having writers define the word *transition*—just jotting down their definitions on scratch paper, then sharing them aloud. They may mention one of the following.
   A transition is
   - a link between ideas.
   - a connection between thoughts, sentences, or paragraphs.
   - a bridge that shows how the writer gets from one idea to another.

2. See how many transitional words or phrases your students can recall in just 1 to 2 minutes without looking at any list or other reference. Have partners or writing circle teams write quickly—then share what they remembered from their own reading and writing experiences.

3. Refer them to any transition list you may use in your classroom—whether a printed list in writing notebooks or a posted list.

4. Finally, ask them to think about how often good writers use transitions: In every sentence? Every other sentence? Once a month? What's a good balance?

Let writers know that in this lesson, they will practice using transitions judiciously—too many can make readers feel as if they cannot build the connections fast enough!

Teaching the Lesson

Sharing an Example: "The Monkey's Paw"

Review the directions. Then read the revised sample from "The Monkey's Paw" aloud—or have a student read it. As others listen, have them

- listen carefully for transitional words and phrases.
- underline those transitions they think *we added*—the ones the author *did not* put in.

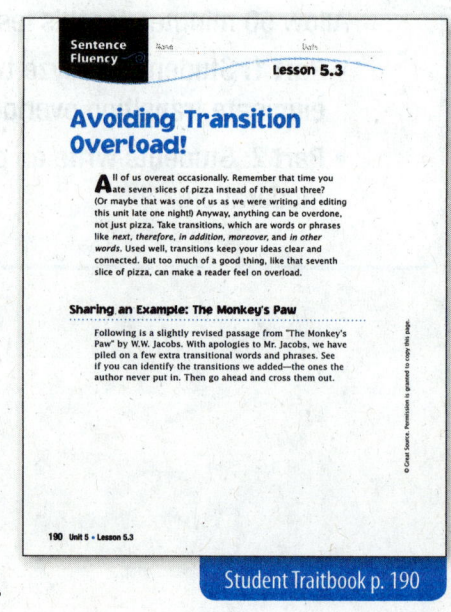
Student Traitbook p. 190

298 Unit 5

Your Response

When students have finished underlining superfluous transitions, have them indicate their responses to the passage by checking one of the three options. Most should agree that transition overload was weighing down the writing.

Listen and Reflect

Share the directions. Then read the passage below from "The Monkey's Paw" aloud as students follow along on page 191. This is the original text, which is free of overdone transitions. Read slowly so that students can follow along with their marked up copies, noticing whether they correctly identified all the extras, which they should have underscored.

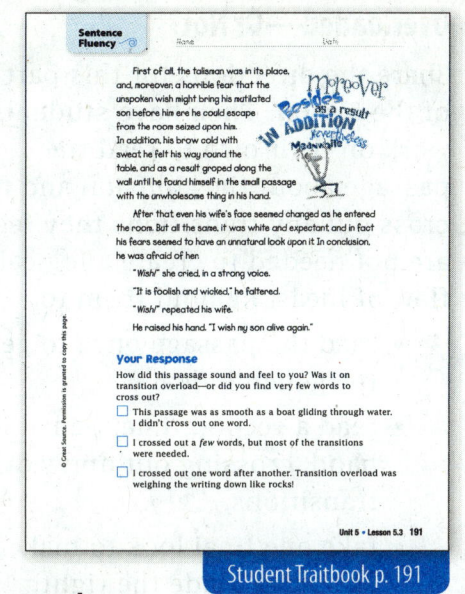

Student Traitbook p. 191

> The talisman was in its place, and, a horrible fear that the unspoken wish might bring his mutilated son before him ere he could escape from the room seized upon him. His brow cold with sweat, he felt his way round the table, and groped along the wall until he found himself in the small passage with the unwholesome thing in his hand.
>
> Even his wife's face seemed changed as he entered the room. It was white and expectant, and his fears seemed to have an unnatural look upon it. He was afraid of her.
>
> "Wish!" she cried, in a strong voice.
>
> "It is foolish and wicked," he faltered.
>
> "Wish!" repeated his wife.
>
> He raised his hand. "I wish my son alive again."

Sentence Fluency

Practice Trait
Lesson 5.3

Coach's Corner

This passage is overrun with transitions. But do not tell students that right away. Let them work on their own for a time, making their own decisions. When they feel almost done, suggest that if they have not crossed out at least eight transitions, they might want to take one more look.

Overloaded—Or Not?

Share the directions for this part of the lesson. Then have students work on their own to read the passage about the collision and to cross out any transitions they feel are not needed to create a logical flow of ideas. Remind them to

- read the passage once to get the general idea.
- read a second time, pencil in hand, crossing out unneeded transitions.
- take one final look to make sure they made the right decision.

Allow 6 to 8 minutes for this revision. Writers who finish faster than this should coach any classmates who are having difficulty.

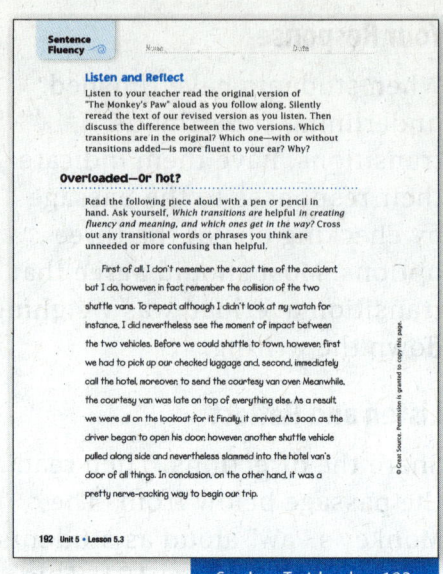
Student Traitbook p. 192

Bringing everyone in... Differentiated Instruction

It may seem confusing to some students that they were recently learning how to put transitions IN, and now they are learning how to take them OUT. Remind them that Sentence Fluency is all about balance—as are so many things in writing. A few transitions—like a few chocolate chip cookies—are terrific. Too many can make it hard to face that next cookie.

Coach's Corner

Note: If you are dividing this lesson into two parts, **Day 2 begins here.**

Share and Compare

Give students time to share their revisions with partners or in writing circles. In sharing, suggest that they read aloud the revised version (sans transitions) to see how it sounds.

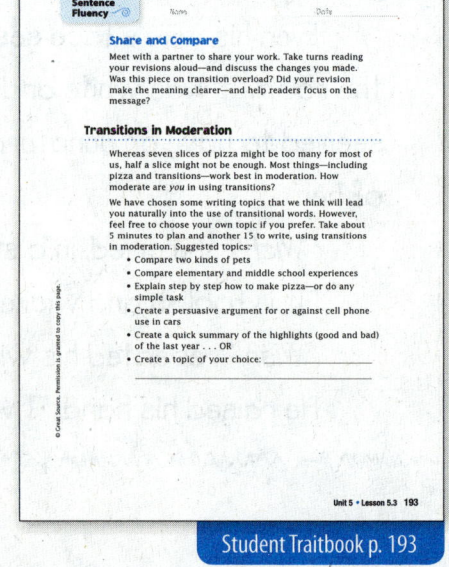
Student Traitbook p. 193

300 Unit 5

Feel free to share our revision (which follows), but wait until students have shared theirs. Remember that theirs does not need to match ours. We were ruthless!

> ~~First of all,~~ I don't remember the exact time of the accident, but I do, ~~however, in fact,~~ remember the collision of the two shuttle vans. ~~To repeat,~~ Although I didn't look at my watch ~~for instance,~~ I did ~~nevertheless~~ see the moment of impact between the two vehicles. Before we could shuttle to town, ~~however, first~~ we had to pick up our checked luggage and, ~~second, immediately~~ call the hotel, ~~moreover,~~ to send the courtesy van over. ~~Meanwhile,~~ The courtesy van was late ~~on top of everything else,~~ and as a result, we were all on the lookout for it. Finally, it arrived. As soon as the driver began to open his door, however, another shuttle vehicle pulled along side and ~~nevertheless~~ slammed into the hotel van's door. ~~Of all things. In conclusion,~~ I must say, ~~on the other hand,~~ it was a pretty nerve-wracking way to begin our trip.

Coach's Corner

Notice that we have listed topics that naturally lend themselves to use of transitions—to compare, explain step by step, draw contrasts, and so forth. In choosing a topic, whether from our list or not, guide students toward a topic and form that makes use of transitions easy.

Transitions in Moderation

Remind students of the discussions you have had through the first part of this lesson about using transitions in balance: enough to make connections, not so many you have transition overload.

Then review the directions for this portion of the lesson, and give writers about

- 5 minutes to choose a topic (from our list or their own).
- 5 minutes to prewrite and plan.
- 15 minutes (or more) to write.

Share and Compare

When students have had time to wrap up their passages, have them share their writing with partners or in writing circles. Based on the feedback they receive, encourage them to make any light revisions.

Sentence Fluency
Practice Trait
Lesson 5.3

A Writer's Questions

As always, reading aloud is the secret. If a transition sounds optional, it probably is. Try reading the text without it. Does everything make sense? Would it make sense to someone reading this passage for the first time? If so, it can go. With transitions, it's wise to "go light."

Putting It to the Test

The thing about testing situations—which isn't true in most other contexts—is that readers are almost always rushed and stressed. They need to read quickly, and they may be tired. In that situation, transitions can be extremely helpful. They prevent misunderstanding and help tired readers follow the writer's train of thought . . . *First, Next, Finally, A month later, To our surprise*, etc.

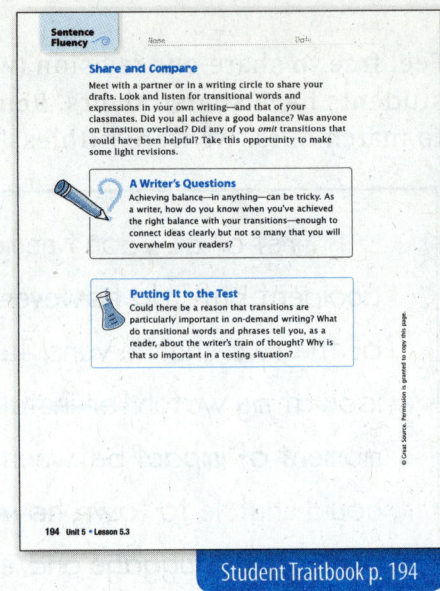

Student Traitbook p. 194

Extending the Lesson

- Have students look carefully at any piece of their own writing. Have they used transitions with care—enough to connect ideas but not so many that they cause confusion?

- Continue to collect sentences or longer passages in which transitions clearly show connections between ideas. Look especially for transitional phrases that may not appear on your class list—yet. Also keep in mind that transitions do not always occur in the form of a word or phrase. Sometimes they are whole sentences or paragraphs.

- Search "transition" online for a host of examples and activities to expand understanding of this important bridge.

- In a documentary film, each scene serves the purpose of a paragraph or chapter within the larger presentation. As a class, view all or part of any good documentary film and discuss the visual ways that writers create transitions. As you do so, talk about why transitions are important. We know they provide bridges from thought to thought. Do they serve any other purpose—especially in films?

LESSON 5.4

Putting It All Together

Student Traitbook pages 195–199

Sentence Fluency

Introduce Trait
Practice Trait
Lesson 5.1
Lesson 5.2
Lesson 5.3
Lesson 5.4
Conventions & Presentation
Apply Trait

Practicing individual skills and identifying strong literary passages to imitate is important in becoming a strong writer. But to really revise effectively, writers need to put everything they know together, drawing on multiple skills. They need an internal rubric to help them identify problems—and a repertoire of revision strategies to solve them.

Objectives

Students will

- coach you, their teacher, in creating and revising your own rough draft.
- write an original rough draft of their own.
- practice coaching skills as they listen to your draft—and share their own.
- revise their drafts for fluency, using all related skills they can pull together.

Time Frame

Allow 50 minutes for this lesson. We suggest dividing it into two parts.

- **Part 1:** Students assist you in identifying a topic, choose individual topics, and create an original draft.
- **Part 2:** Students share and reflect on their work, coach you and one another, and revise, pulling together all the skills they know for making sentence fluency strong.

Unit 5   303

Sentence Fluency

Practice Trait
Lesson 5.4

Coach's Corner
Of all the strategies we listed here, perhaps the most important are reading one's own writing aloud to hear how it sounds—and trying several variations of one sentence. Students who dare to experiment are usually rewarded with an upsurge in both traits of Sentence Fluency and Voice.

Coach's Corner
In this lesson, you will be writing along with your students. They will not actually see your writing (unless you want that to happen), but they will coach you in choosing a topic and will respond to your rough draft, setting you up to revise. The more open you can be to their suggestions, the stronger this lesson will be. Encourage them to offer you options so that you can choose a personally important topic—as you would wish them to do.

Coach's Corner
You should choose one of the suggested topics—or ask for additional suggestions. However, you do not necessarily have to share your choice with writers right away. If you prefer, keep that choice to yourself until you have finished your draft.

Setting Up the Lesson

Share the introductory paragraph of Lesson 5.4. Then brainstorm a list of skills your students have practiced during the preceding three lessons. Add (if you wish) any other skills students have used in revising for the trait of Sentence Fluency. Record their responses. As you do so, talk about which skills are especially helpful. Here are some possible answers:

- Reading text aloud to test the flow and rhythm
- Beginning sentences in different ways
- Using transitional phrases to begin sentences
- Using repetition for effect
- Varying sentence length
- Combining sentences
- Using transitions to link ideas
- Avoiding transition overload
- Writing sentences different ways to see what works best
- Imitating what skilled professional writers have done

Teaching the Lesson

Choosing a Good Topic
Part 1

Review the opening directions to make sure the general task is clear. Then share the directions for Part 1. Students should

- confer with a partner or members of a writing circle.
- think of just one or two suggestions for a topic they think YOU might enjoy writing about.
- take turns offering their suggestions as you record possibilities.

Student Traitbook p. 195

Bringing everyone in... | Differentiated Instruction

The underlying purpose of this lesson is to model various parts of writing process for students, beginning with topic selection. Each thing you do—including choosing a topic that works well for you, taking quiet time to draft, and later sharing your writing and receiving feedback gracefully—provides a model for your writers to follow. In this way, you show them writing process in action from topic choice through revision and sharing. Seeing you work can be immeasurably helpful to struggling writers.

Part 2

Review the opening directions for Part 2 so they are clear. Students should

- confer with a partner or members of a writing circle.
- think of a personal topic they would like to write about.
- choose a topic they know well.

Writing a Draft

Share the directions, emphasizing the importance of creating a double-spaced draft that will be easy to revise. Then give writers

- 5 minutes to prewrite and plan, using any strategy they like.
- 15 minutes to draft.

When students finish, have them tuck drafts away overnight (or until you finish this lesson) in a SAFE place where they are easy to find. Part 2 of this lesson will involve sharing and revising.

Sharing, Listening, Responding
Part 1

Share the directions for Part 1. Then share your draft aloud as students listen. Invite comments—and make some notes as they talk. You might conclude this portion of the lesson by indicating how you plan to begin your revision.

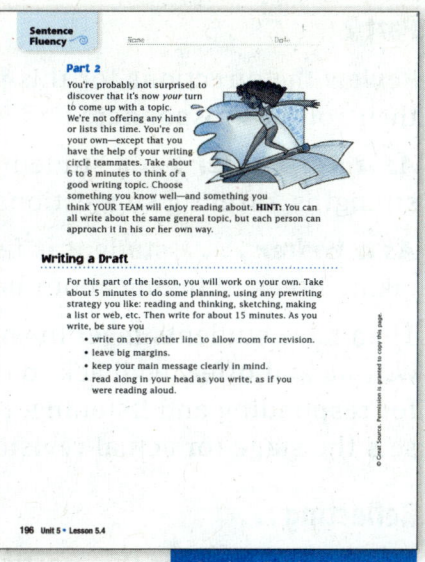

Student Traitbook p. 196

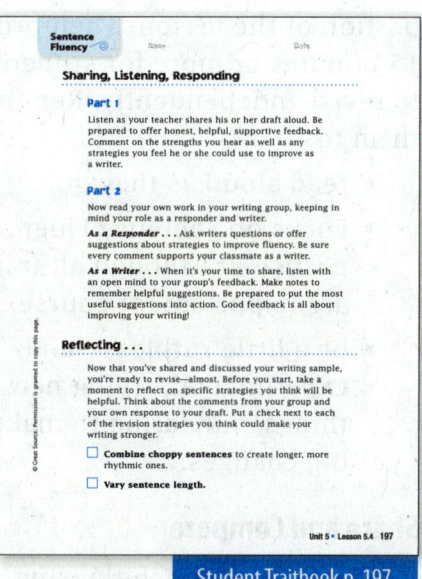

Student Traitbook p. 197

Coach's Corner

As students work, create your own rough draft, allowing room for revision of your own. Write quickly, not trying to make it too perfect. (You can then easily model revision later, if you wish.) This is also a good time to remind writers to keep the atmosphere reasonably quiet (workshop is seldom totally quiet) so that writers, including you, can concentrate and work quickly.

Coach's Corner

Note: If you are dividing this lesson into two parts, **Day 2 begins here.**

Coach's Corner

It's tempting as a teacher to lead the discussion, but for this portion of the lesson, try to keep your comments to a minimum. Encourage students to talk and to offer all the feedback possible. They may be timid about this at first because you are the writer. Your receptiveness to comments will encourage them to say more.

Bringing everyone in . . .   Differentiated Instruction

Students are often tempted to apologize for their work as they share. Don't do this when you share your work. If you do, you shift the focus from your writing to yourself—how shy you are, how fearful you are of not having your work received well, etc. Be bold. Just read—with confidence and an open mind. Later, remind your writers to do the same.

Unit 5   305

Sentence Fluency

Practice Trait
Lesson 5.4

Part 2

Review the directions for this portion of the lesson, focusing on their roles as responders and writers.

As a Responder . . . a student is asking questions, identifying strengths, offering suggestions, being supportive.

As a Writer . . . a student is listening, keeping an open mind, taking notes, thinking about how to revise.

Then have students meet in writing circles to share their own writing and offer feedback to others. Allow about 10 to 12 minutes for responding and listening, reminding writers that this sharing sets the stage for actual revision—coming up!

Reflecting . . .

Share directions for this portion of the lesson. Give students 2 to 3 minutes to reflect on the feedback they received and then to plan their revision. They should go through the checklist provided—but should also feel free to follow their own revision path, using ideas from our checklist or their own intuition about the writing.

. . . Then Revising

Review the directions for this portion of the lesson. Then provide 15 minutes or more for students to revise independently. Remind them to

- read aloud as they go.
- Focus on Sentence Fluency in particular—though all traits are important, of course.
- be a little ruthless—and experimental, trying new things and daring to make big changes.

Share and Compare

When students finish revising, wrap up by giving them time to share in writing circles. Remind them to

- read their revised drafts aloud
- encourage them to briefly discuss their revision strategies: *What did you do to improve the fluency of their piece?*

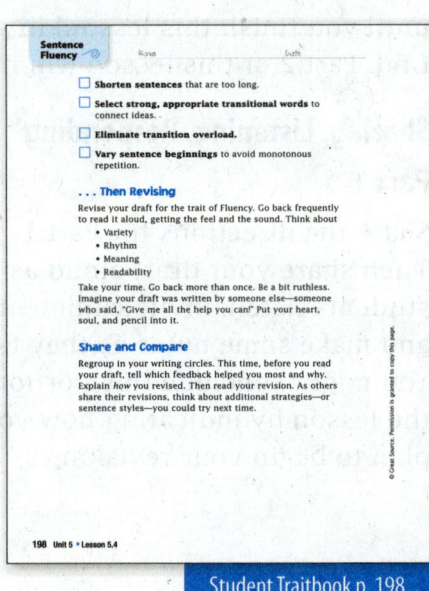

Student Traitbook p. 198

Coach's Corner

Also remind students that no one thinks of everything prior to writing. As professional writers write and read their work aloud, they continually think of new ideas and directions. Reflecting and revising work hand in hand—even for the pros!

Coach's Corner

If time permits, we recommend concluding this lesson by sharing your revision with the whole class. You could do this one of two ways: (1) Have a student read your original draft, then you can read your revision aloud for comparison. Or (2) project your original so students can see it clearly. Do your revision in front of them so they can see you work. When you finish, read the revision aloud. Discuss the specific strategies and suggestions that helped you.

A Writer's Questions

It is not the reviewer's job to plan the revision. It is the reviewer's job to share, clearly and honestly, his or her response to the writing. The writer must then decide which comments to heed most strongly. The draft always belongs to the writer.

Putting It to the Test

A rubric is a launching point for thinking about a trait—or about writing in general. An experienced writer and reader develops a rubric in his or her head and knows, upon reading, whether a piece of writing is working well or not. It's that personal rubric that forms the true basis for revision—and a good thing, too, since it's always with the writer.

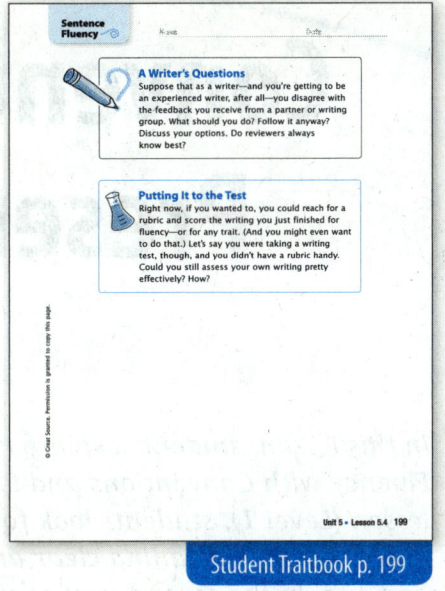

Student Traitbook p. 199

Extending the Lesson

- Continue to model revision. Keep it short, but do it often. Your writers will love watching you—and coaching you. And their coaching skills will grow as they do so. Remember that you do not always have to model the whole process, topic selection through revision. Any step you model gives your writers a visual picture of how process really works.

- Review the Student Rubric for Sentence Fluency. Does it sufficiently capture the strengths and problems your writers have now discovered for themselves? Chances are, they can think of a few revisions. Go for it!

- At every opportunity, encourage writers to share favorite passages aloud. Reading aloud, individually or through choral reading, deepens a reader's understanding of and sensitivity to the trait of Sentence Fluency. As much as any other single thing writers do, reading aloud prepares them to write with Fluency and Voice.

- Read aloud to your students—from the most fluent literature you can find. Many middle school students hear very little text shared aloud and thus lose the opportunity to hear great literature shared with inflection and voice. When you read aloud, you ARE presenting a lesson in the trait of Sentence Fluency—and in Voice, as well.

- Continue your blog discussion on good writing by creating your own online personal rubric or checklist for fluency. Invite others to contribute their ideas—students, teachers, editors, professional writers. You might be surprised by some of their comments!

Sentence Fluency

Introduce Trait

Practice Trait
- Lesson 5.1
- Lesson 5.2
- Lesson 5.3
- Lesson 5.4
- **Conventions & Presentation**

Apply Trait

Conventions and Presentation

Student Traitbook pages 200–209

In this lesson, students explore two ways of connecting Sentence Fluency with Conventions and Presentation. In the first part of the lesson (Level 1), students look for a wide range of errors, editing to make sentence meaning clear and to show where sentences begin and end. In the second part of the lesson (Level 2), students create and design a clear set of directions using a bulleted list to make those directions easy to follow.

Objectives

Editing Level 1: Conventions
Students will
- recognize differences between revision and editing—but also understand that they work together in improving writing.
- warm up by editing two short passages.
- shift into "overdrive," combining editing with revision.

Editing Level 2: Presentation
Students will
- explore the concept of concrete poetry.
- look at samples of concrete poems.
- complete one concrete poem as a warm-up.
- create an original concrete poem on a topic of choice.

Time Frame

This lesson has two parts. Allow a full class period for each part.
- **Part 1:** Students edit two short passages, then combine editing and revising skills to work on a longer passage.
- **Part 2:** Students review concrete poems and create an original concrete poem of their own.

308 Unit 5

Conventions & Presentation

Practice Trait
Editing Level 1: Conventions

Editing Level 1: Conventions
Rev-edit-ising, Anyone?

Setting Up the Lesson

In this part of the lesson, students have a chance to reflect on the processes of editing and revision, to consider how they work together, and to explore their personal writing process, asking which comes first for them: editing or revising?

Begin with these steps:

- Share the introductory paragraph of this lesson.
- Check to see that students have access to the resources you'd like them to use for this lesson: writing handbooks, dictionaries, and the Copyeditor's Poster, for example.
- Let students know that they will be working independently for much of this lesson but checking frequently with partners so there will be coaching support.
- Have students reflect on both editing and revising. How are they alike—and how are they different? Which task do students typically tackle first?

Student Traitbook p. 200

Coach's Corner

Encourage students to see revision as the making of big, sweeping changes—taking information out, adding information in, changing the order of details, or refining voice to better suit genre or audience. Editing involves making corrections in spelling, punctuation, grammar, or layout: packaging the material, in other words.

Bringing everyone in . . . | **Differentiated Instruction**

Students who are working at a beginning level or who are timid about making changes to writing may see editing as revising. This lesson can help them make a distinction. Correcting the tense or spelling of a word, using the correct preposition, or filling in missing periods, for example, is not revision. It's editing. *Revising* (re-visioning) truly means to see the message anew—to reshape a character, create a new setting, add a stronger argument, replace a lead or conclusion with something more insightful, and so on.

Unit 5   309

Conventions & Presentation

Practice Trait
Editing Level 1: Conventions

Teaching the Lesson

A Warm-Up

Go through the directions for this section together. Explain that the warm-up involves practice in editing two samples, both of which contain conventional errors.

Review the Editor's Checklist to be sure writers know the kinds of errors they are likely to spot.

> **Bringing everyone in . . .** **Differentiated Instruction**
>
> Have your students reflect seriously on why they missed the errors they did not catch. Was it hasty reading? Or, not taking time to (1) go through a piece a second time or (2) read aloud? If so, those are easy fixes. If there are rules they do not know or understand, make a list of the top three or four problems and then create short editing practice lessons that focus ONLY on those errors. Correcting one kind of error numerous times—as many as 20—is necessary for some students to internalize a rule.

Coach's Corner
Remind students that they do not need to add details, revise wording, or rework sentences. They ONLY need to make editorial corrections.

We recommend allowing 4 to 5 minutes to edit each sample, but adjust this time to suit your writers' needs.

Share and Compare

Have students compare their editing with that of a partner. Then ask them to coach you as you edit each sample, using the marks from the Copyeditor's Poster. For purposes of comparison, edited versions of each sample, with corrections in blue bold, are printed on the following page.

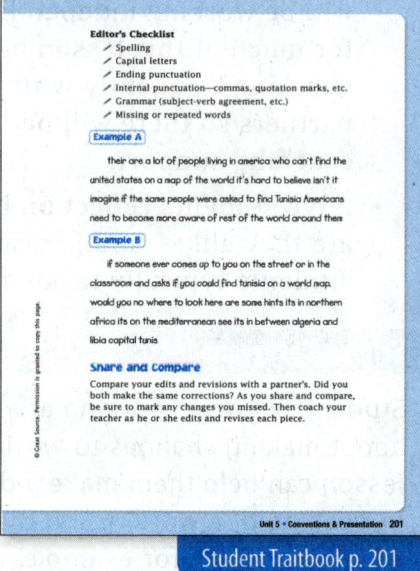

Student Traitbook p. 201

Example A

There are a lot of people living in America who can't find the United States on a map of the world. It's hard to believe, isn't it? Imagine if the same people were asked to find Tunisia! Americans need to become more aware of ~~rest of~~ the world around them.

Example B

If someone ever comes up to you on the street or in the classroom and asks if you could find Tunisia on a world map, would you know where to look? Here are some hints. It's in Northern Africa, it's on the Mediterranean Sea, it's in between Algeria and Libya, and its capital is Tunis.

Bringing everyone in . . .   **Differentiated Instruction**

Because Example B is a little more challenging than Example A, editors who struggle or just need more time might do only A, at your discretion. Similarly, those who find editing easy can coach others once they finish.

Coach's Corner

When writers believe they have caught all errors, share the actual number and ask them to take one more look. They should find 12 errors in Sample A and 24 in Sample B.

Conventions & Presentation

Practice Trait
Editing Level 1: Conventions

Shifting into Overdrive

In this portion of the lesson students combine editing with revision. Have them look for errors first if they are working on a computer. (This will clear some clutter.) We recommend revising first if they are going to add or delete information by hand.

Read the directions to be sure everyone understands the task. Then have students read the example once to get a sense of the message, a second time to revise (or edit), and a third time to edit (or revise).

Allow 12 to 15 minutes for this activity.

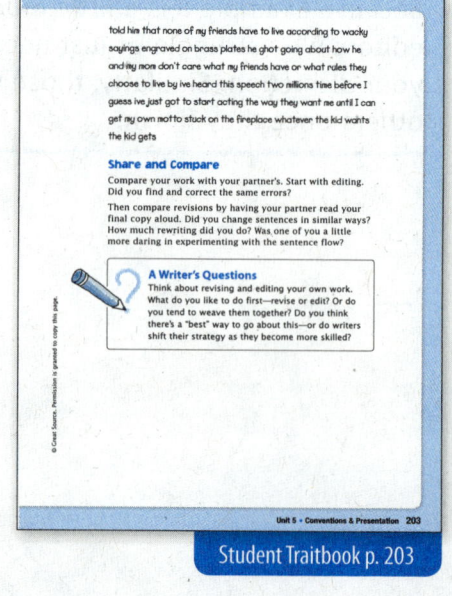

Student Traitbook p. 202

Bringing everyone in . . . Differentiated Instruction

Normally, writers revise *prior* to editing. The reason for this is simple. It's silly to worry about spelling and punctuation in a paragraph you might cut. On the other hand—as this practice shows—when a passage contains numerous errors, editing first can clear away conventional clutter, making it easier to focus on the message. This is an especially effective strategy when working on the computer.

Share and Compare

Give students time to compare how they edited and resived their work. When they are nearly finished, let them know there are 37 errors in all, and have them take one final look, making a count.

Student Traitbook p. 203

Then, model the editing of the text *as they coach you.* Following is a corrected copy, with changes highlighted in blue bold:

A New Motto

Whenever my parents think that **I'm** demanding something instead of asking politely, one of them always says, "You can't expect to **be** both grand and comfortable." **It's** this saying that we found engraved on **a** brass plate and stuck on the bricks just above the fireplace ~~in~~ in the house we moved into three year**s** ago. **I'm** not even sure what it means. **M**y dad tried to explain something about having to work **for** some of the extras in life. I **reminded** him that I'm only thirteen **and** adolescence is tough. I made a huge mistake. I told him that none of my friends have to live according to wacky sayings engraved on brass plates. **He got** going about how he and my mom don't care what my friends have or what rules they choose to live by. **I've** heard this speech two **million times** before. I guess **I've** just got to start acting the way they want me **to** until I can get my own motto stuck on the fireplace: **"W**hatever the kid wants the kid gets."

Coach's Corner

This is one error-packed piece! Finding 18 out of 37 errors (about half) is a *good* performance. Finding 25 is very good—and 30 or more is outstanding. Did any of your editors find all 37? Would you have found them all?

Conventions & Presentation

Practice Trait
Editing Level 1: Conventions

We thought the primary (nonconventional) problem with the passage was **wordiness.** Here, for purposes of comparison, is our revised, condensed copy.

Coach's Corner
We separated our revision and editing for easier reference. Here is a revision of the corrected copy.

A New Motto

Whenever my parents think that I'm being too demanding, one of them says, "You can't expect to be both grand and comfortable." This saying was engraved on a brass plate above the fireplace when we moved into our house. I'm not sure what it means, but dad says it has something to do with having to work for the extras in life. I reminded him that I'm only thirteen and none of my friends have to live according to wacky sayings engraved on brass plates. He went on for hours about not caring what rules my friends live by—a speech I've heard many times. I guess I'll have to start acting the way they want me to until I can get my own motto stuck on the fireplace: "Whatever the kid wants the kid gets."

A Writer's Questions

Most writers revise and then edit. This is efficient because it saves a writer from having to edit anything that's eventually deleted. However, when the number of conventional errors is high, it can make sense to edit first. So the answer depends on the writer and on the condition of the draft.

We revel in the craft of making the larger changes in the text—revising—and at the precise, line-by-line, word-by-word refining of the text—editing. Here our skills have a clear task: make it true, make it clear, make it graceful.

—Donald M. Murray
Shoptalk: Learning to Write with Writers

Editing Level 2: Presentation
Concrete Poetry

Setting Up the Lesson

In this lesson, students have a chance to explore concrete poetry, warm up for some writing by finishing one concrete poem, and then create one of their own.

It will be helpful if you can collect samples of concrete poetry for this lesson. Explore your own media center or any local library. Here are three suggested titles your students will enjoy:

- *A Poke in the I* by Paul B. Janeczko
- *Blue Lipstick: Concrete Poems* by John Grandits
- *Technically, It's Not My Fault: Concrete Poems* by John Grandits

Begin by

- sharing the introductory paragraph to the lesson, page 204 of the Student Traitbook.
- asking how many of your students like poetry. Do they like to read it? Write it? Memorize or quote it? Do they have a favorite form, poet, or poem?
- asking if anyone has had a bad experience with poetry. If so, what?
- asking how many students have heard of *concrete poetry* or know what it is.

Bringing everyone in . . . Differentiated Instruction

Not all of your students will know what concrete poetry is. Explain that it is sometimes called "shape poetry" because the shape or arrangement of the poem on the page is actually part of the message—as if the poem were a piece of sculpture. This is poetry at its most playful. Reading and writing concrete poetry invites imagination.

Explain that in this lesson, they'll have a chance to explore this type of poetry—and also write some of their own. No rhyming is required—though it's certainly allowed!

Conventions & Presentation

Practice Trait
Editing Level 2: Presentation

Coach's Corner

For a text that helps students explore a wide range of poetic forms, see also *A Kick in the Head: An Everyday Guide to Poetic Forms* by Paul B. Janeczko.

Conventions & Presentation

Practice Trait
Editing Level 2: Presentation

Coach's Corner

If you have a document projector, this can make sharing easy. However, because of the nature of concrete poetry, spontaneous reading can be a challenge! Be sure you preview any poems you plan to share to make reading aloud easier.

Teaching the Lesson

A Warm-Up

Review the directions for the first part of the warm-up. Then share any books or individual poems you have gathered.

For the second part of this Warm-Up, share the directions. Then have students meet in writing circles to review the three examples of concrete poems from the Student Traitbook:

- Poem 1: "Make it Go Away!"
- Poem 2: "Make a Wish"
- Poem 3: "Child's Play"

When everyone is done (or has gone as far as time permits), discuss the results:

- Did students have a favorite poem of the three? Which one—and why?
- Why does each sample fit the concrete poem genre?
- What do we learn about concrete poems (and the writing of them) from these examples?

Student Traitbook p. 204

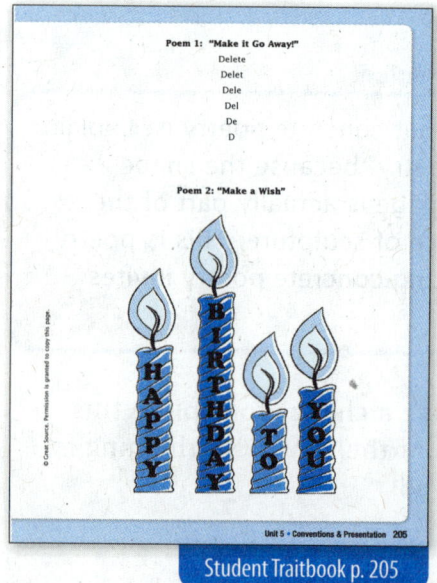
Student Traitbook p. 205

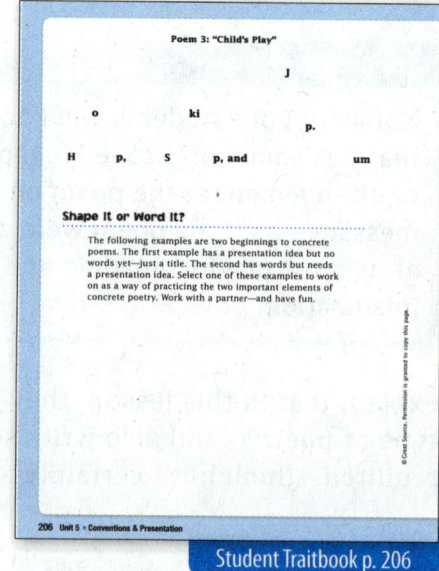
Student Traitbook p. 206

Shape It or Word It?

For this portion of the lesson, students will choose an unfinished concrete poem to complete. The examples are different and require different tasks:

Choice 1: "No Boots in the House!"

Here, students have the outline of a boot, but there are as yet no words to the poem.

Choice 2: Untitled (so far)

Here, students have words but no concrete shape.

Student Traitbook p. 207

Have students work individually or with partners for this activity. They should

- choose one poem or the other to finish.
- discuss the main message of the poem before completing it: What do they want to say to readers?
- take about 10 minutes to finish the poem.

Share and Compare

Have students share their poems in writing circles and talk about the various approaches they took. Ideally each poem will look (or sound) a little different from others. Did most students choose one form over another?

A Writer's Questions

Many young writers who have not enjoyed poetry previously find themselves drawn to concrete poetry. It is less formal than some forms and allows artistic expression. Do any of your students share those feelings? Do you?

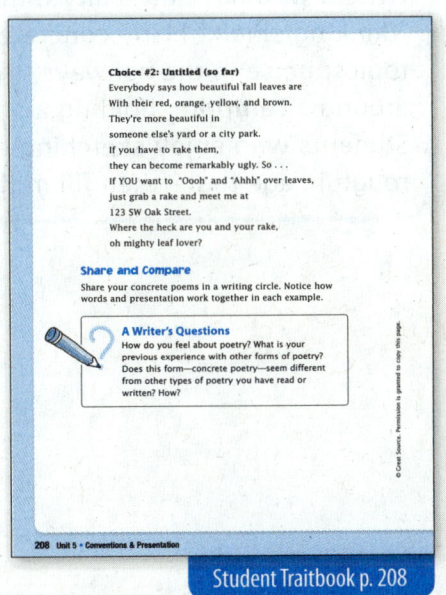

Student Traitbook p. 208

Coach's Corner

Writers who pick Choice #2 (on raking) should feel free to change the wording if they wish. It is also fine to shorten the poem to fit the concrete image they pick.

Unit 5 317

Conventions & Presentation

Practice Trait
Editing Level 2: Presentation

Coach's Corner

Because of the nature of concrete poetry, it can be very challenging for anyone but a design professional to create it on the computer. So students will be working by hand. You may wish to remind them of the importance of making individual letters large and legible enough to be read easily by others.

Presentation Matters

In this portion of the lesson, students have an opportunity to create a concrete poem of their own based on any topic. This time they will create words and design shapes.

Begin by reviewing the directions to see if they have any questions. Make sure students have

- writing and art supplies needed to create poems.
- appropriate paper for final drafts.
- samples to look at to inspire ideas.

Allow 15 to 20 minutes or more for writers to work. When they finish, give them time to share their poems in writing circles or with the whole class.

Student Traitbook p. 209

Bringing everyone in . . . | Differentiated Instruction

Writers who have difficulty thinking of a topic might begin by "thinking small." Many concrete poems are written about tiny topics: noise in the hallways, the smell of dinner cooking, sitting around a campfire, holding a small child's hand, or a bad hair day. Students who enjoy sketching may find it's easier to begin with a rough image first—then fill in the words.

Extending the Lesson

- Have students edit any copy on which they are currently working, using skills they practiced in this and preceding lessons for Conventions and Presentation.
- Continue to be on the lookout for small errors in published copy. Offer credit to writers who identify, correct, and post faulty copy. Expand your display.
- Find a way to display the poems writers created in this lesson—in the classroom, hallway, or display case.
- Write an online review of any of the books you used as examples for this lesson.
- Start a blog discussion on the value of concrete poetry. Could it transform the way some people think about poetry?

Concrete poetry is the yoga of words. Like feeling your breath and your bones, you begin to notice what words and sentences actually look like. (Chris Raschka, author and illustrator)

—Paul Janeczko
A Poke in the I

Conventions & Presentation

Practice Trait
Parting Thoughts

Parting Thoughts on Conventions and Presentation

The trait of Conventions and Presentation supports *every* other trait—helping the writer clarify the message, order information in an easy to follow sequence and design, accent voice, ensure that words are spelled and used correctly, and create readable sentences that flow smoothly from one to the other. Conventions and Presentation "packages" writing to make the message at the core accessible, appealing, and as error-free as possible.

When we teach Conventions and Presentation apart from message, we lose our chance to show the interplay between this trait and all others—to show how good paragraphing or a bulleted list or effective use of headings can make a discussion easy to follow, or to show how voice is influenced by color, design, illustrations, font choice—even use of italics.

In many ways, the trait of Conventions and Presentation is changing more (and faster) than any other. Daily—almost hourly—we discover new ways of using technology to create messages that reach an ever-growing audience of readers and viewers in continually evolving forms. Editing is not just about spelling and punctuation these days, important as those things are. It's about speed, impact, storage and retrieval, the synergy between content and format, sight and sound—and much more. Twenty-first century communicators must spell and punctuate correctly—and also ensure that the message is presented in a way that makes people look, understand, and remember. No wonder all traits depend on the one that defines the writer's final draft more than any other.

Vicki & Jeff

UNIT 5
Sentence Fluency

Introduce Trait

Practice Trait

Apply Trait

Final Curtain Call 323
- Preview pages 323–332

50 min. **Assessing and Revising Sample Papers** 324
- Apply what students have learned by assessing Sample Papers 19 and 20
- Revise Sample Paper 19 for Sentence Fluency

Sample Paper 19: *Chocolate and the Witch's Curse*
Score and Rationale

Sample Paper 20: *Spiders*
Score and Rationale

Revising Sample Paper 19: *Chocolate and the Witch's Curse*

50 min. **Revising and Editing a Personal Draft** 329
- Have students revise their own writing for Ideas, Organization, Voice, Word Choice, Sentence Fluency, and Conventions and Presentation
- Assess students' growth as writers

Parting Thoughts 331
- Conclude the trait of Sentence Fluency

Final Curtain Call

It's time to give students a chance to apply what they have learned—and give you a chance to assess their growth as writers and revisers. Have students demonstrate their knowledge of Sentence Fluency (as well as all other traits) by following these steps:

1. **Apply knowledge of Sentence Fluency by assessing and revising the writing of others.**

   Your writers will read and assess Sample Papers 19 and 20. This time, they will work independently, applying what they have learned to
   - decide for themselves which piece is stronger.
   - score each sample, using the student rubric for Sentence Fluency.
   - brainstorm ways of improving the weaker paper.
   - revise the weaker paper for one trait: Sentence Fluency.

   Assessment Component: Base your assessment of growth on students' revision of Paper 19, *Chocolate and the Witch's Curse.* The revised version should advance at least one point on the rubric, achieving a final score of 4, 5, or 6. Assess each student's final draft of *Chocolate and the Witch's Curse,* using the teacher rubric for Sentence Fluency.

2. **Apply knowledge of Sentence Fluency by assessing and revising their own personal writing.**

   Have writers pull their original drafts from their folders to revise and edit, applying everything they have learned from
   - reading and using student rubrics, checklists, and posters for all traits.
   - discussing and assessing the writing of others.
   - reading or hearing literature that exemplifies strengths in various traits.
   - completing lessons to build skills in all six traits.
   - assessing and revising weaker samples.

   Assessment Component: Score each final draft and compare these final drafts with the rough drafts you assessed earlier. Consider changes in scores—but look beyond them, too. Also consider the quality, nature, and extent of each writer's revision. Did they zero in on what needed attention—and did they come up with creative ways to make the writing stronger? Add points for good editing or creative presentation.

Coach's Corner

Remember to check out the Assessment Guidelines for additional suggestions on effective ways to assess your student writers' performance and growth.

Coach's Corner

Offer tips to make revision manageable. **Ideas:** Add important details. Make sure the message is clear. **Organization:** Make the lead and conclusion strong. Be sure the order is easy to follow. **Voice:** Write what you truly think, feel, or believe. **Word Choice:** Cut the clutter, strengthen verbs, make words precise enough to make a picture in the reader's mind. **Sentence Fluency:** Read everything aloud. Begin sentences in varied and meaningful ways that connect thoughts. **Conventions:** Wait to edit until the draft feels finished. Read everything twice, silently and aloud, pencil in hand. **Presentation:** Use a model you like as a guide.

Sentence Fluency

- Introduce Trait
- Practice Trait
- **Apply Trait**
  - **Assessing and Revising Sample Papers**
  - Revising and Editing a Personal Draft

Assessing and Revising Sample Papers

Student Traitbook pages 210–213

Sample Paper 19: *Chocolate and the Witch's Curse* and Sample Paper 20: *Spiders*

1. Explain that this activity will give students a chance to see how they have grown as assessors and revisers with respect to Sentence Fluency—and all other traits.

2. Refer each student to the Student Rubric for Sentence Fluency.

3. Group students in writing circles and then refer them to Sample Papers 19 and 20.

4. Let students manage their own assessment process by
   - passing out both papers at once.
   - having students read the papers aloud to each other—in any order.
   - having them decide for themselves which paper is stronger in Sentence Fluency.
   - scoring the two papers together, thereby using comparisons to help zero in on the best score for each.

5. As students score the two papers, they should think about the following

   ### ❓ Key Questions . . .
   - *Do you like the overall sound and rhythm? Is it more musical—or mechanical?*
   - *Is the piece easy to read aloud—even on the first try?*
   - *Is it easy to listen to as well?*
   - *Are there both long and short sentences—a good mix of the two?*
   - *Do sentences begin in different ways—or are first words often repeated?*

Coach's Corner

Remember that you (and your students) can decide which approach to revision you like best: simply mark up rough copy, write a new draft on paper, or enter the rough draft on the computer and make all changes electronically. Choose the method your students would normally use in revising their own writing.

Coach's Corner

Both Papers 19 and 20 are informational essays, based on research—and both have good information to offer. However, one is easier to read—or listen to—than the other. Remind students that having information isn't always enough. It's important to hold readers' attention long enough for them to take in the information.

- *Does the writer use transitional words and phrases, so one thought seems to flow right out of the next?*
- *Should some short sentences be combined? Or overly long sentences broken apart?*
- *Does the piece have a natural, conversational sound?*

6. After students finish scoring, discuss the two papers as a class. Which one is stronger—and what specific strengths do they notice? What specific problems call for revision in the weaker piece?

7. Compare students' scores with ours. (See Scores and Rationales.)

Score and Rationale for Sample Paper 19: *Chocolate and the Witch's Curse*

Most readers agree that *Chocolate and the Witch's Curse* **needs significant revision** in Sentence Fluency. The writer has good points to make, and we can follow what he is saying. However, the sentences are extremely long and convoluted with far too many individual ideas crammed into each one. It is very hard to read this piece with inflection and voice because the writer never pauses for breath—and it's hard to tell what to emphasize. Words like *and, so, which,* and *that* are overused, creating unnecessary links. To make things worse, there is no relief from long sentences until the very last sentence of the piece—and by then, readers are tired. Sentences, although grammatical, are wordy and repeatedly demand rereading in order to keep thoughts from unraveling. On the positive side, sentence beginnings are somewhat varied. Simply splitting long sentences into manageable parts will improve the rhythm and clarity of a potentially good paper. This piece would receive a **3 in the trait of Sentence Fluency.**

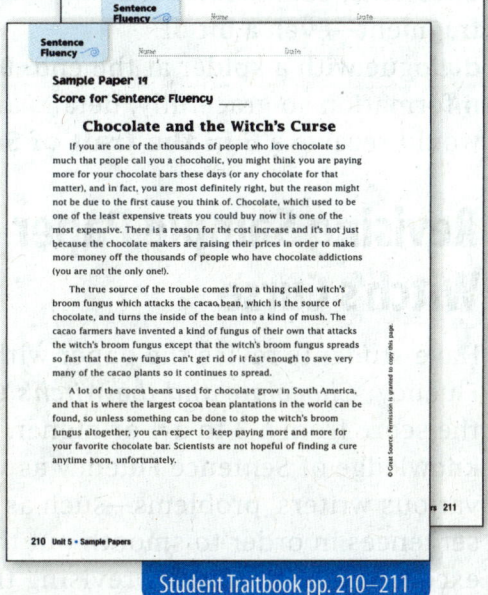
Student Traitbook pp. 210–211

> **Coach's Corner**
> Remind writers to mark up these papers as they discuss and score them—underlining first words or making marginal notes to indicate sentences that are choppy, overly long, unclear, etc.

Unit 5 325

Sentence Fluency

Apply Trait
Assessing and Revising Sample Papers

Coach's Corner

Note that both papers have source lists—and both lists contain conventional errors. As an extension of this lesson, you may wish to have your writers edit one or more entries from these lists, using whatever writing handbook is approved for use in your classroom.

Score and Rationale for Sample Paper 20: *Spiders*

Most readers agree that this paper is strong in **Sentence Fluency.** Sentences are written to be read aloud. They're varied, expressive, and filled with voice. Notice the purposeful sentence beginnings: *Remember . . . Well, Muffet wasn't the only one . . . The average human . . . Our first instinct . . .* and so on. Sentence length is also varied, and the writer uses a mix of statements, questions, commands, one fragment—even a bit of dialogue with a spider at the end. Because sentences carry information so gracefully, details are easy to remember. This paper would receive a **6 in the trait of Sentence Fluency.**

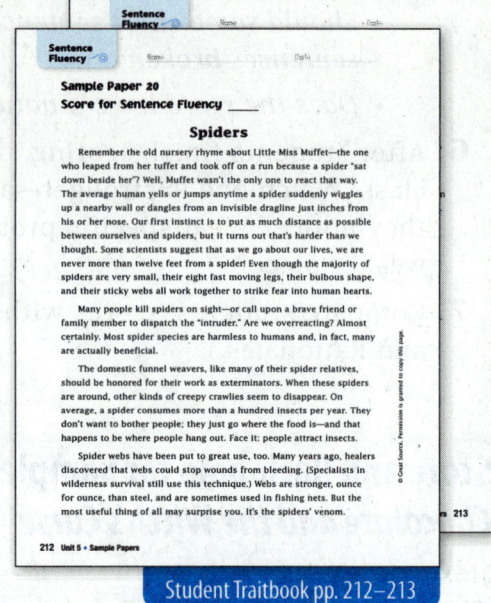
Student Traitbook pp. 212–213

Revising Sample Paper 19: Chocolate and the Witch's Curse

Have students revise the paper with the lower score in Sentence Fluency: *Chocolate and the Witch's Curse.* Their goal is to raise the score from a 3 to a 4 or higher. This challenge tests their knowledge of Sentence Fluency as well as their creativity in solving various writers' problems—such as how to deconstruct long gangly sentences in order to smooth out the informational flow. It is also excellent preparation for revising their own writing.

326 Unit 5

Follow these steps:

1. Remind each student to refer to the Revising Checklist for Sentence Fluency or the Student Rubric for Sentence Fluency—their choice—as they work.

2. Have students (without looking at any guide) brainstorm some important features of strong Sentence Fluency—in their own words. Their list might include any of the following.

   - *This piece is easy to read—silently or aloud.*
   - *The flow of words sound smooth and musical.*
   - *Sentences begin in different ways.*
   - *Sentence beginnings connect thoughts, sentence to sentence.*
   - *Sentences differ in length and structure.*
   - *The story or discussion is easy to follow.*
   - *If the writer uses fragments, they work.*
   - *The writer avoids run-ons—except to create a special effect (stream of consciousness).*

3. Tell students to look even more closely at Paper 19, *Chocolate and the Witch's Curse*. Remind them that all helpful revisions are welcome, but their primary focus for this lesson should be on Sentence Fluency. They may work in writing circles to brainstorm and plan but should do their actual revisions individually.

4. Remind students that it is all right to restructure sentences, delete or change words, add a new title—*anything at all*. They are in charge!

5. Give students time to collaborate *in planning their revision*. They should work together to identify the main problem (or problems) with sentence fluency—and also identify basic strategies for eliminating those problems.

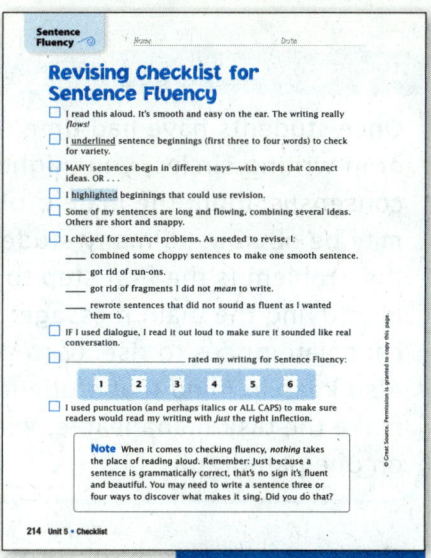

Student Traitbook p. 214

Coach's Corner

We've occasionally referred to the "internal rubric" that drives a writer's own writing. That remains important here. Rubrics or checklists written on paper serve primarily as reminders, and they should always be subject to revision by writers who use them.

Coach's Corner

As always, audience and purpose matter—so set writers up with a reason to revise and a group of readers (or listeners) to reach. Here's one suggestion: They might imagine that the writer is creating copy for a local news broadcast on the increasing price of chocolate. The story will be read aloud on the evening news and should run about 30 seconds. The audience is the general public.

Coach's Corner

Writers may need to try writing a sentence several ways to get the logic and rhythm right. This is tedious by hand—but quick and easy on the computer. Students who can revise electronically will usually do more—and also be more experimental.

Sentence Fluency

Apply Trait
Assessing and Revising Sample Papers

Bringing everyone in . . . | **Differentiated Instruction**

Once students have had time to discuss the piece with partners or in writing circles, you might see if your students can reach a consensus about the main problem (long, wordy sentences). This may be obvious to many students—but perhaps not to all. Knowing the problem is the first step toward good revision. Next step? Identifying the main message: A little known fungus is causing chocolate prices to rise. (Can your students identify this message?) Also keep in mind that students who struggle can work in teams to make the task manageable, with each person on the team taking on one paragraph.

6. Have students mark up the rough draft with cross-outs, inserts, arrows, or new punctuation. Final copy may be handwritten or word processed, and should be attached to the rough before it is handed in. Note: It is also fine to rewrite the piece—and the new draft can be shorter.

Assessment

Assess this activity by (1) scoring the final draft for Sentence Fluency (using the teacher rubric for that trait) and (2) looking at the creativity and overall extent of the revision. Look for

- a final score of 4 or better in Sentence Fluency.
- overall readability—a smooth, rhythmic flow.
- variety in sentence lengths, beginnings, or structure.
- logic—a sentence-to-sentence connection that creates a sense of "wholeness."
- absence of awkward construction or unintentional fragments and run-ons.

Coach's Corner

As an alternative to having students hand in papers, consider having students present their final drafts orally. Listen—and let your ears assess the extent of improvement. Have the rough copy (original Paper 19) in front of you as you listen. A moderate improvement should be enough to score a 4. A dramatic improvement scores a 5 or 6. And don't be surprised if revisions are significantly shorter than the original! Remember—it's clarity, not length, that counts.

Revising and Editing a Personal Draft

Applying Knowledge of Sentence Fluency by Revising Personal Writing

The revision your students just completed on Paper 19, *Chocolate and the Witch's Curse* provides a good warm-up for revising their own writing effectively. Everything in the unit has been directed toward this goal: helping writers become strong, independent revisers of their own work. Follow these steps:

1. Ask students to recall the personal writing they created after **Making the Literature Connection** ("The Gift of the Magi" by O. Henry). This should still be in rough draft form in their folders.

2. Have them remove that writing from their folders and assess it for all six traits, using the appropriate student rubrics as a guide. They do not need to score papers but simply use the rubrics as reminders of what to look for as they ask themselves these

   ? Key Questions . . .
   - Does this paper leap the river in each trait?
   - What are the main strengths—and can I add to them?
   - What problems do I need to work on?
   - What notes can I write on my draft to help me remember what to do?

Bringing everyone in . . . Differentiated Instruction

Remind your challenged writers to take it a step at a time and to focus on what most needs work—with one exception. It always, *always* helps to identify the main message first. That helps everything else fall into place. Stronger writers should be encouraged to do *more than one* revision. This is much easier if they are working on the computer. And here's a tip: Waiting a day or two between revision drafts will make a dramatic difference. No writer sees or hears everything with one reading. Model this with a sample paragraph of your own.

Sentence Fluency

Introduce Trait
Practice Trait
Apply Trait
Assessing and Revising Sample Papers
Revising and Editing a Personal Draft

Revision—look at that word: re-seeing—is a simple matter of putting in, taking out, reordering until the written line drawn, erased and redrawn, allows you to see what you are writing and what it means.

—Donald M. Murray
Shoptalk

Coach's Corner

As your students should be realizing, assessment is not always about scores. The kind of assessment a writer does in preparation for revision simply calls for identifying strengths and problems—and also asking, "What's my purpose? Who's my audience?"

Unit 5   329

Sentence Fluency

Apply Trait
Revising and Editing a Personal Draft

Coach's Corner

As before, give students the option to work with partners or within writing circles at any point in the writing process. They can decide for themselves what they can handle independently and which steps require some support or feedback from a partner or group.

3. Based on their own revision plan and priorities, students should revise their writing, marking up rough drafts any way they wish—or revising on the computer. Their goal should be to make the final draft leap the river (scores of 4, 5, or 6) in *all six traits*.

4. Final drafts may be copied onto new paper—or entered into the computer.

5. Rough drafts and final drafts should be stapled together so that you can easily make comparisons and track the planning and flow of their revision.

Assessment

Assess this activity by scoring the final draft for all traits. Look beyond scores, though, to the creativity and overall extent of the revision. Here's a quick checklist of things to watch for:

- Clear main idea
- Details that expand or enrich that idea
- Strong focus on the message
- Inviting lead
- Effective transitions
- Easy-to-follow design
- Conclusion that wraps up the story or essay
- Read-aloud moments of voice
- Engagement with the topic
- Voice that suits the genre
- Strong verbs and other striking words or phrases
- Precise terminology
- Vivid description or use of sensory language (as appropriate)
- Varied sentences
- General readability and smooth flow (plays well to the ear)
- Creative and appropriate title
- Strong conventions
- Presentation that makes information accessible or gives the piece eye appeal

Bringing everyone in . . . Differentiated Instruction

Use this or any checklist with flexibility, focusing on items most appropriate for the writer's chosen topic and genre.

Parting Thoughts

The art of crafting good sentences is vital to effective writing because sentences are the building blocks of meaning. A good sentence makes sense, rolls easily off the tongue, and—perhaps most important of all—fits logically and gracefully into the context of all surrounding sentences. A sentence almost never stands alone but works in harmony with what precedes or follows. That's why fragments work. Sometimes. As with many traits, reading aloud is the ultimate test. Our ears tell us more about writing than our eyes alone ever could. Continue to have your students read everything they write aloud—and read aloud from the best writers you and they can find.

Students have now completed five units of instruction on the six traits, and they have had a chance to revise and edit their own and others' writing for all traits. They should now have a big picture view of the traits, recognizing that they are interdependent. We suggest these next steps:

1. Continue to use **trait language** in conferences and any time writers share during workshop.

2. Keep **trait posters** up throughout the year to support students' growing understanding of what makes good writing work—remembering to add to the posters or revise the wording to reflect your own thinking.

3. Look and listen for various strengths in your discussions of **good literature.** Master writers can teach us all a thousand ways to begin or end sentences—and how to connect one thought to another both logically and gracefully.

4. Encourage students to reflect on their journeys as writers, using trait language to help express how they have grown or changed. Those reflections—together with additional samples of writing—can go into their **portfolios.**

5. As the need arises, weave additional **focused lessons** on various traits into writing workshops. Your students know all the traits now, so it is fine to jump around.

6. Review the sections titled **Extending the Lesson** for additional ideas on expanding students' skills.

7. Explore **additional genres.** What have your writers NOT tried? Poetry? Drama? Memoir? Journalism? Encourage them to branch out and to combine multiple genres within a given piece. Also encourage them (as technology permits) to include audio and video to enhance their work.

8. Continue to provide students practice in **assessing writing,** focusing on many kinds of examples, not just student work. Ask them to assess textbooks, news copy, film scripts, copy for museum exhibits, or anything else you (or they) can think of. Every type of writing they *assess* they will be better equipped to *write, revise,* or *format.*

9. **Share writing online.** Join a virtual writing group (Google Docs for free information on uploading, storing, or sharing writing) or consider blogging (Blogger or Wordpress for free personal publishing platforms).

10. Looking for a challenge? Bring everything together in **a final project,** in which writers work in teams to plan and coordinate the design and production of any publication, from a poem to a film. They choose topic, genre, and design, and delegate work within the group.

Vicki & Jeff

Appendices

Teacher Rubrics 334

Publishing House 340

Assessment Guidelines: How Well Do My
Students Write? 345

Enriching the Writing Process
with the Six Traits 351

Teacher Rubric for Ideas

6
- Main message or story is clear and compelling. It holds a reader's attention.
- Writer seems to have an in-depth understanding of the topic.
- Details are selectively chosen, making the writing memorable.
- Topic is narrowed to make the message focused and manageable.

5
- Paper makes sense from beginning to end. It is clear, never confusing.
- Writer knows enough about the topic to write expansively and convincingly.
- Writing contains many interesting details.
- Topic is narrowed so the main message stands out clearly.

4
- Reader can identify the main idea, even if it isn't stated directly.
- Writer has *some* knowledge of the topic; more would enrich the discussion or story.
- Enough unusual or intriguing details grab the reader's attention.
- Topic may be too broad; the writing loses focus now and then.

3
- Reader can guess what the main idea is.
- Writer *sometimes* sounds knowledgeable and sometimes searches for things to say.
- Details tend to be general, repetitive, or common knowledge.
- Topic is too broad to cover well.

2
- Main message is unclear. What is the writer trying to say?
- Writer repeats or rambles. He or she needs more information to draw from.
- Details are sketchy. The paper does not give much information.
- Topic may shift—or just be hard to pin down.

1
- Writer is still searching for a main idea or story to tell.
- Writing may be a list or first thoughts.
- There are no real *details* because there is no central idea to develop—yet.
- Writer hasn't chosen a topic yet.

Teacher Rubric for Conventions & Presentation

6
- There are no errors that catch the reader's eye.
- Writer's use of conventions enhances meaning and voice.
- The text appears to be publication-ready.
- Presentation has eye appeal and makes information accessible.

5
- Writing contains only minor errors easily overlooked with a quick reading.
- Writer often uses conventions to support meaning and voice.
- With quick touch-ups, this piece will be ready to publish.
- Presentation is a good match for the writer's message and purpose.

4
- Errors are noticeable but not serious enough to be distracting.
- Conventions are strong enough to support general readability.
- Light but careful editing is needed prior to publication.
- Presentation is acceptable. It works with the writer's message.

3
- Errors are noticeable and somewhat distracting.
- Errors at times affect readability or make the reader pause.
- Thorough editing is needed before publication.
- Writer needs more attention to presentation.

2
- Numerous errors make the text difficult to read in parts.
- Reader must do some mental editing to read through the errors.
- Line-by-line editing is required before publication.
- Writer has not given much if any attention to presentation.

1
- Serious, frequent errors make processing the text slow and challenging.
- Many parts require decoding.
- Extensive editing is required before publication.
- Editing is the first priority. Then the writer can think about presentation.

Teacher Rubric for Organization

6
- Everything connects to one clear MAIN message or story line.
- The writing is easy to follow, even with a quick reading—and may hold some surprises.
- The lead is striking and pulls readers right in.
- The conclusion is original—and leaves readers thinking.

5
- The writer never veers from the main message or story line.
- The writer's "trail of thought" is easy to follow, beginning to end.
- The lead is appealing and gets readers hooked.
- The conclusion wraps things up in a satisfying way.

4
- The writer may wander—but readers can usually see some connections.
- A reader can follow the discussion or story—especially with attentive reading.
- The lead sets the stage for the story or discussion.
- The ending brings things to closure.

3
- Readers sometimes have to work a bit to follow the trail of thinking.
- Or else, the writing may be *too* predictable, leaving readers wishing for surprises!
- The lead is familiar. It could use some sparks of excitement.
- The conclusion needs to wake readers up, surprise them, or make them think.

2
- The writing jumps from topic to topic.
- Some details could be moved around, while others seem interruptive.
- The lead is missing—or needs revision.
- The conclusion is missing—or needs revision.

1
- The writer has made a start—a list or first thoughts.
- Things don't go together yet; they don't add up to a cohesive "whole."
- There is no real lead. The piece just starts.
- There is no real ending. The piece just stops.

Teacher Rubric for Voice

- The voice is unique—it's definitely THIS writer and no other.
- Many readers would enjoy sharing this piece aloud.
- The writing is passionate, compelling, individual, and energetic.
- The voice fits the purpose perfectly and consistently reaches out to readers.

- This writing is individual and distinctive.
- A reader would likely share this piece aloud.
- The writer's enthusiasm for the topic is evident.
- The voice is well suited to the audience and purpose.

- This voice stands out from any others.
- There are some good moments to share.
- Passion, energy, and confidence emerge now and again.
- The voice is acceptable for the audience and purpose.

- This is a functional, sincere voice—even if not distinctive.
- Though the piece is not yet ready to share, minor revision could change that.
- Moments of energy are intermixed with more encyclopedic writing.
- This may not be the right voice for the purpose or audience.

- This voice does not stand out.
- The piece is not ready to share aloud—yet.
- The writing suggests some indifference to the topic.
- The voice may be wrong for the purpose or audience.

- This voice is difficult to hear, hard to describe.
- There is not a reason to share it aloud.
- No energy or excitement comes through.
- The voice is almost silent—it's as if the writer is not "at home."

Teacher Rubric for Word Choice

6
- Words are striking, original, precise—often memorable.
- Powerful verbs create energy, movement, and vivid imagery.
- Sensory details enhance meaning and enrich the reading experience.
- The writing is concise; every word counts.

5
- The writing is clear and often original.
- Strong verbs enhance imagery and energize the writing.
- Sensory language adds important detail at the right moments.
- The writing is concise. Words are well chosen and work to create meaning.

4
- The writing is clear and correct. More nuance or precision would help.
- The writer uses a strong verb or two—but *may* rely heavily on modifiers.
- Sensory language is used *as appropriate*—and not overdone.
- Wordy or repetitive moments never distort or overpower the message.

3
- Words are too general or used incorrectly.
- Strong verbs are rare. Adjectives and adverbs *may* be overused.
- Sensory language is minimal—OR there may be *sensory overload!*
- Wordiness, repetition, or over-writing are distracting.

2
- Words are frequently misused or vague.
- Verbs are mainly *is, are, was, were,* etc. Even modifiers are minimal.
- Sensory language is limited or missing.
- The writing is wordy, unclear, or too skimpy to say much.

1
- Word choice feels random or strained.
- The writer struggles to express ideas.
- It's hard to picture anything.
- The message is unclear.

Teacher Rubric for Sentence Fluency

6
- The writing is smooth, natural, and easy to read on the first try.
- Almost every sentence begins differently—*unless* repetition is used for effect.
- The piece invites expressive oral reading that brings out the voice.
- The writing has an effective, appealing cadence.

5
- The writing is smooth and easy to read.
- Many sentences begin differently.
- It's easy to make this piece sound smooth.
- The overall sound is natural and conversational.

4
- The writing reads like a good first draft.
- There is some sentence variety.
- With rehearsal, you can make this writing sound smooth.
- Strengths outweigh problems.

3
- Some parts are easy to read—others require rereading.
- Variety is limited.
- There may be a share-aloud passage.
- Choppy sentences, run-ons, or awkward moments are noticeable.

2
- The reader must frequently reread to get the meaning.
- Sentences are repetitive—or may not always be sentences.
- Reading aloud takes spontaneous revising (e.g., filling in missing words).
- Choppiness, run-ons, or awkward moments are frequent.

1
- Reading this text is a challenge.
- The writer doesn't write in sentences—or it's hard to tell where they begin and end.
- Choppiness, run-ons, or awkward moments block the message.
- This text is not ready to be shared aloud.

Publishing House

Welcome!

. . . to an exciting two-week wrap-up project that pulls together everything your writers have learned by studying and practicing

- writing process,
- cooperative coaching and planning,
- six-trait assessment,
- trait-based writing and revision,
- topic selection,
- and time management.

We are calling it *Publishing House* because writers will form their own small-group "publishing houses" to identify an idea they think is worthy of publication. Then they will see their project all the way through the publishing process. As "publishers," they will

- choose a topic to explore and present.
- choose a genre through which to do this.
- create an appropriate and effective format and design.
- target a specific audience.
- identify and delegate writing tasks within their group.
- produce and present the final publication.

A 10-Step Journey

We suggest about two weeks for the full project, given the time required for each of ten steps. Students will do much of their work in class, but some things (research and some writing or illustrating) will need to be done on their own time.

As you go through this journey together, record any personal planning notes in the blue space in the margins. But think of yourself as a consultant and advisor—not the editor in chief! As much as possible, encourage students to use what they have learned to make their own decisions and to manage their production time.

> **Coach's Corner**
>
> The whole purpose of this final project is to give writers freedom to make their own decisions. As a teacher, you will oversee the production schedule, reminding groups of various decisions they need to make at points along the way. Students, however, will be responsible for putting together their own vision and seeing it through from conception to final design.

Step 1: Forming "Publishing House" Writing Circles
(5 minutes)

Group students into writing circles: small groups of 4 or so. Let them know that each group will act as its own Publishing House—hence the project title. That means envisioning a publication, choosing a topic and genre, identifying an audience, and seeing a publication through from initial planning to final design.

Step 2: Creating a Vision
(20 minutes)

Within groups, have writers discuss their publication vision. They should decide upon

- a topic to explore and present.
- an audience (your class, the general public, adults, people their own age, young children, consumers, lovers of math or science, Shakespeare buffs, etc.).
- a central message they'd like to deliver to the intended audience.
- a genre that will best showcase that message (children's book, drama, poem, research report, handbook, documentary film, PowerPoint, etc.).

Coach's Corner
Some groups may know almost at once what topic they wish to pursue—and what genre appeals to them. Those who do not might look for ideas in their own writing notebooks or literature they love. Encourage writers to choose a topic and genre that holds high interest for them. All options are open.

Step 3: Assigning First Tasks
(20 minutes)

Based on their initial vision, have students list all the production tasks they can think of. Offer guidance at this step to make sure they haven't forgotten something important. They can (1) work together on selected tasks and/or (2) delegate tasks such as the following.

- Sketch out (or describe) what the final product might look like
- Create a list of questions to answer or an outline of subtopics to cover
- Research the topic on the Internet
- Conduct firsthand research (site visits or interviews)
- Explore literature for quotations or supportive details
- Write first drafts of various parts
- Coordinate any filming or photography
- Draw illustrations

Coach's Corner
Dividing up work within a group can lighten the load and make a project more fun. Caution writers to make sure the work is divided evenly, though, so everyone participates. It's helpful to designate one person as the managing editor. This person can oversee the group's work (as well as contributing) and will also set deadlines for various tasks.

Step 4: Hitting the Bricks!
(2 to 3 days outside class)

Writers will need a few days to carry out their initial tasks. During this time, you can check in to make sure everyone is finding the information they need, dealing with any technology required, and so forth. Remind writers to be flexible. If a plan is not working (e.g., they cannot fine enough information on the topic), it may be wise to redefine their task.

Step 5: Planning—and Finishing the Rough Draft
(30 minutes for planning, 2 to 3 days outside class to finish rough drafts)

Once writers have had a few days to collect information and begun putting their first ideas together, schedule a planning meeting, during which they can check their progress and plan next steps. At this point they should

- confirm their choices of topic and genre, OR
- make any necessary changes.

Then students should

- list what they've accomplished so far.
- list remaining tasks to be completed.
- hand out new assignments.
- set a deadline for finishing the draft, including design elements.

Step 6: Reviewing the Rough Draft
(30 minutes for review, 2 to 3 days outside class to complete revisions)

As soon as their rough copy is finished, have each Publishing House team schedule a time to review their initial draft (or product) as thoroughly as possible. Does it

- convey a clear message?
- speak to the intended audience?
- have any informational "holes"?

As a result of this review, the publishing team should plan their revision, again dividing tasks equally among members.

Step 7: Creating the Final Design
(30 minutes for planning, 1 to 2 days outside class to complete designs)

At this point, basic revision and editing should be completed. But the document or publication still needs to razzle-dazzle readers or viewers. That means ensuring final design or placement of any remaining items, such as

---

Coach's Corner

In some ways, this is the trickiest step in the project. Encourage writers to make an *honest* assessment of their progress and to take care in laying out ALL remaining steps—and distributing the work load.

Coach's Corner

Assigning tasks effectively is partly a matter of dividing work equally—but it's also about making good use of talent. Is one person a crackerjack editor? Is another creative with layout and design? Encourage teams to make the best possible use of members' skills.

Coach's Corner

The final design is complete only when the document or publication is ready to go public. That means it's fully ready for viewing by people outside the publication circle. Remember—critics can be cold!

- PowerPoint slides (if used).
- illustrations, photos, maps, and graphs (if used).
- a cover.
- any auxiliary pieces: table of contents, dedication page, source list, or author bios.

Step 8: Planning the Debut!
(30 minutes to plan, time required to present)

Every step within the Publishing House project leads up to this important moment: the unveiling, the presentation, the debut! Each publication team can decide how they want to go about this. Here are just a few possibilities. You may have others in mind.

- Reading or performing the project for your own class
- Reading or performing the project for the school (possibly including parents)
- Reading or performing the project for an appropriate outside audience
- Displaying the project in the classroom, hallway, or other school venue

Step 9: Creating and Receiving Reviews

First, *your* feedback . . . Likely, you will want to assess your writers' efforts on this major project. You can certainly use the traits to remind you of some important things to look for. But since you will also want to assess participation in the whole process, we're offering you an easy checklist to use or adapt. You can add to this checklist and decide how many points to give for each item.

- ✔ Clear vision: topic, genre, audience
- ✔ Effective assignment of tasks within the group
- ✔ Completion of initial draft
- ✔ Thorough plan for revision of the first draft
- ✔ Completion of revised and edited copy
- ✔ Completion of final design
- ✔ Presentation of publication to an audience
- ✔ Clear message
- ✔ Message and voice that speak to the intended audience
- ✔ Strong final editing: freedom from conventional errors
- ✔ Strong final design: good eye appeal, easy access to the message

Next, *your students'* feedback . . . Have writers identify, in terms of the traits, the strengths they feel are most outstanding in their own work.

> **Coach's Corner**
>
> Clearly the "best" presentation depends highly on topic, genre, and audience. For example, a play is best performed—not just put on display. A children's book might be shared with an age-appropriate audience who might be asked to provide feedback.

We recommend also having students offer feedback to every other Publishing House as they view their presentation. This might be as simple as a note on an index card, or you could ask them to respond to a specific question such as one of these.

1. What were the strengths of this presentation?
2. What did you learn about the topic—or about publishing?
3. Do you have an important question for the Publishing House members?

Step 10: Reflection

To bring this project to closure, we recommend having writers reflect on what they learned about their own special talents or about publication in general through this process. Is there anything they might do differently next time? What is most challenging or rewarding about seeing a product through to publication?

Assessment Guidelines: How Well Do My Students Write?
by Vicki Spandel

We know you want and *need* to know how well your students write, and with this new 2010 edition of *Write Traits,* you do not need to guess. Accurate, thorough, and appropriate assessment is built right into every grade level. Because our assessment is beautifully integrated within ongoing instruction, you'll find it easy to assess your student writers *as you teach.* Among other important features, our assessment approach is:

Directly connected to instruction. Our suggested writing assessments are based on everyday writing your students produce *as they learn,* not an isolated assessment divorced from your classroom instruction.

Based on more than one performance. Research tells us that good assessment does not rely upon a single performance. It is based upon a body of work, and our assessment plan is set up in just that way.

Relevant. The assessment you do will be based on writing activities you and your writers have a hand in designing, ensuring higher motivation with emphasis on the kinds of writing you and your class decide are important.

Ongoing. Students are assessed throughout the course of their instruction, helping them to identify strengths and target needs—right from the start.

Based on solid, proven criteria. The rubrics included in this program for assessing student writing performance are among the most widely used and tested available. They are based on the original six-trait rubrics developed by Oregon teachers in 1984, rubrics that have since been revised and used with hundreds of thousands of students at multiple grade levels throughout the world.

Valid. Our assessment is based on real-life writing tasks similar to those students are likely to encounter in a higher education or work environment: (1) assessing and revising writing created by others and (2) drafting, revising, editing, and designing original pieces of their own.

Instructional. Each assessment opportunity offers students a chance to learn more about writing even as they are being assessed.

Fair. Students are assessed only on what they have been taught. When they have studied Ideas, their writing will be assessed on that trait. Once they have studied Organization, their writing will be assessed on both traits, and so on.

Expansive. Over the course of each unit, students will have a chance to demonstrate performance on a wide range of writing skills, including

- conveying a strong central main idea.
- expanding that main idea through well-chosen details.
- staying focused on a main message.

- eliminating extraneous information (filler).
- capturing readers' attention with a strong lead.
- thoughtfully linking ideas through solid transitions.
- avoiding transition overload.
- wrapping up the writing with an appropriate ending.
- using a voice appropriate for the purpose and audience.
- enlivening writing with a voice that speaks to readers.
- clarifying meaning through precise words and phrases.
- relying on strong verbs to energize writing.
- using correct terminology.
- varying sentence length and structure.
- beginning sentences in purposeful ways.
- reading aloud to assess sentence clarity and fluency.
- using conventions correctly and creatively to support meaning and voice.
- using presentation to make the message appealing and accessible.

Overview

Though guidelines for assessing your students are provided throughout each lesson set, you may find it helpful to have an overview of how the whole assessment will look. It has several parts.

Part 1: Assessing and revising the work of others

The practice of assessing someone else's work, identifying problems, and revising to improve that writing provides an excellent foundation for revising one's own writing with insight and skill. Within each unit, students have two chances to assess, discuss, and revise relatively problematic writing—offering you two opportunities for assessment.

1. **Pre-instruction.** *Before* completing the focused lessons within each unit, students revise the weaker of two *introductory* writing samples. This activity allows you to see how skilled your students are at revision before they have any direct instruction in a given trait.

2. **Post-instruction.** *After* completing the focused lessons within the unit, students are asked to revise the weaker of two *concluding* samples. At this point, they can apply writing and revising skills they have gained through the lessons.

Comparing before and after samples provides an excellent indicator of how much students have learned through direct instruction. Revising someone else's work also provides students a valuable warm-up for revising their own original work.

Part 2: Creating and revising personal writing

Following the Literature Connection in each of the five units, students create a personal sample of writing. They are encouraged to choose their own original topics with coaching from you. (We suggest a wide range of possible topics and genres to consider.)

After writing, students put their rough drafts aside for a time. They will return to them after completing the five focused lessons within that unit. Each lesson presents valuable skills useful in planning, revising, and editing writing. When students have finished all five of the focused lessons, they pull their rough drafts out of the folders and revise and edit them, applying the various skills they have learned. Again, you will have two opportunities for assessment.

1. **Pre-instruction.** Students create their rough drafts *before* completing the focused lessons within the unit. Assessing these drafts gives you baseline scores you can later compare with the scores you assign to their final drafts.

2. **Post-instruction.** *After* completing the focused lessons within the unit, students revise their drafts using skills they've learned. Scoring these final drafts—as well as looking at the depth and scope of their revision—offers you a final assessment of each writer's growth.

Please note . . . Students produce a total of five original pieces of writing (one per unit) throughout this program. They produce the first piece as they study the trait of Ideas, the second as they study Organization, and so on. Each piece is revised and edited. This body of work, taken as a whole, provides an incredibly expansive and complete indicator of students' writing skills.

Part 3: Final Project—Publishing House

To bring all traits, all steps of writing process, and all related skills together, we offer an optional final project called Publishing House. Through this project, students work in small groups to plan and design a publication of their choice—any topic, any format, any genre. They not only do all planning and writing, but they coordinate production as well, taking responsibility for management and delegation of tasks. For a more complete description, see Publishing House in this appendix.

Tips for Assessing Well

Know the rubrics

Assess your students' writing using the six teacher trait rubrics that are part of this appendix. Be sure *you* are thoroughly familiar with these guides to scoring. You should feel comfortable assigning scores on all traits and describing traits in your own words. You may also wish to practice scoring before assigning scores that will become part of a student's grade. The text *Creating Writers* by Vicki Spandel (see Recommended Resources at the end of this section) provides numerous student samples for practice. Please note that all rubrics and scoring guides are forever evolving—and after working with ours for a time, you may wish to make additions that will truly make it your own.

Assess only writing that has gone through the whole process

Our lessons offer numerous short writing activities because we believe writers learn to write mainly by *doing* it—and doing it often. These "quick writes" are NOT meant to be assessed—except in the sense that writers themselves review, reflect, share, and seek feedback. But no scores are involved. As part of each unit, writers will, however, create one larger piece of writing. They select the topic themselves, prewrite, draft, and share their writing. At the end of the unit, they revise and edit, also adding any design features they wish. These five samples of writing (one per unit) provide a solid basis for assessment.

Encourage cooperative planning

Though students should do all actual revising independently, encourage them to work with partners or in writing circles (groups of 3 or 4) to plan their revision. Too often, students do not share writing or plan revision strategies until they are well into the process. As you will see in working through the lessons, we encourage extensive cooperative planning and discussion, pushing writers to strategize and coach one another from the planning stage right through editing.

Make students partners in assessment

Students should be partners in the assessment process, assessing their own writing (as well as that of others). Students should not assess their own work for the purpose of assigning a score or grade but for the purpose of identifying problems and planning revision.

Focus on growth and experimentation

Assess rough drafts *only* to get a baseline score. Base final assessments on the differences between rough and final drafts—as well as the score you assign the final draft. Also look for a willingness to take more risks, such as to revise a little more vigorously or to make bigger changes in the rough draft.

Focus on Conventions and Presentation lessons you've taught

Write Traits includes five lessons on Conventions and Presentation that emphasize ways in which this important trait links to *every other trait*. This helps you truly teach Conventions and Presentation in context. It is impossible, however, to cover all the issues related to this broad topic. We therefore suggest that when scoring for this trait, you focus on what is emphasized in our lessons together with other aspects of Conventions and Presentation that you have chosen to cover in your personal instruction. We also recommend choosing a good writing handbook as a final reference on such issues as punctuation, usage, and citations.

For Presentation, offer access to technology

Presentation—or the look and design of a document—is critical in newsletter copy, book covers, advertisements, or any publication that must capture a reader's attention *even before* the reader considers content. Much of the writing produced in school, by contrast, has few presentation issues beyond general neatness. If you wish to score Presentation as part of the larger Conventions and Presentation trait, be sure your students are creating documents and projects for which thoughtful, creative design is critical and achievable given the resources (particularly computer access) at hand. That way, you can fairly consider such issues as font choice, point size, layout on the page, incorporation of illustrations, and design of auxiliary features such as the cover, table of contents, source lists, and so on.

Consider the BIG PICTURE

Good assessment is about much more than scores. And since each classroom is a little different, consider how your students are spending their time. What information do you need to make a good judgment about their growth and performance as writers? Here are some examples of other things you *may* wish to assess. (You likely have personal additions to this list.)

- Participation in writing process (Do students prewrite/plan their work? Can they choose their own topics? Do they participate actively in peer response groups? Do they revise and edit? Do they write in multiple genres, for multiple purposes and diverse audiences?)

- Participation in reading process (Do students choose books for themselves? Do they share—in writing or orally—thoughts on what they have read? Do they complete assigned reading? Do they participate actively in discussions of literature? Can they choose and share passages to illustrate strengths in various traits?)

- Spelling skills

- Vocabulary growth

- Audiovisual literacy that allows incorporation of technology into the writing

- Additional writing activities outside the scope of *Write Traits*

Remember the value of observation

Assessment takes many forms, and it does not always involve testing or scoring. Observation, for example, plays a vital role. You may find you learn almost as much watching and listening to your students during an active discussion of a writing sample as you learn from looking at their actual revisions. As you listen, ask yourself questions like these.

- Do my students understand each trait? (For example, do students know that the trait of Ideas encompasses a main idea, clarity, focus, and details?)

- Do students recognize when a piece of writing is strong?

- Can they spot writing problems and plan appropriate revision?

- Can my students assess any kind of writing, not just student samples but newspaper or journal articles, advertisements, technical documents, and so on?

- Can they coach one another—or you (their teacher)?

- Can students describe each trait in their own words?

- Do students approach a writing conference with specific questions in mind or problems to resolve?

- Can students identify strong samples from literature they might emulate?

- Are students thinking like readers as they write? Can they anticipate the impact various writers' decisions will have upon a reader?

Consider portfolios

Anyone who has participated in a student conference knows the value of seeing actual samples of a writer's work. When these samples are collected over time, dated, and systematically organized, they offer a visual journey of performance that reflects where a student began, what he or she learned along the way, and where that student is right now on his or her way to becoming a strong writer. *Write Traits* supports portfolios beautifully because students are asked to write and to demonstrate revision skills at regular intervals. With each interval, students reach a new milestone of performance. Your students' portfolios might include any of the following.

- Samples of revised or edited writing (their own or from other writers)
- Original writing in multiple genres
- Collected quotations or select passages from favorite literature
- Personal goals
- Lists of future topics to explore
- Personal reflections on performance or growth as a writer

Recommended Resources on Sound Assessment Practice

Arter, Judith, and Jan Chappuis. 2007. *Creating and Recognizing Quality Rubrics.* New York, NY: Prentice-Hall.

Elbow, Peter. *Everyone Can Write.* 2000. New York, NY: Oxford University Press.

Graham, Steve, and Dolores Perin. 2007. *Writing Next: Effective Strategies to Improve Writing of Adolescents in Middle and High School.* Washington, D.C.: Alliance for Excellent Education.

Graves, Donald. *Testing Is Not Teaching.* 2002. Portsmouth, NH: Heinemann.

Kohn, Alfie. 1993. *Punished by Rewards.* New York, NY: Houghton Mifflin.

Kozol, Jonathan. 2007. *Letters to a Young Teacher.* New York, NY: Crown Publishers.

National Council of Teachers of English (NCTE) Task Force. April 2005. "The Impact of SAT and ACT Timed Writing Tests." Urbana, IL: NCTE.

National Writing Project and Carl Nagin. 2003. *Because Writing Matters: Improving Student Writing in Our Schools.* San Francisco, CA: Jossey-Bass.

Perlstein, Linda. 2007. *Tested: One American School Struggles to Make the Grade.* New York, NY: Holt.

Spandel, Vicki. 2009. *Creating Writers Through 6-Trait Writing Assessment and Instruction,* 5th edition. New York, NY: Pearson Education.

Spandel, Vicki. 2005. *The 9 Rights of Every Writer.* Portsmouth, NH: Heinemann.

Strickland, Kathleen and James Strickland. 1999. *Making Assessment Elementary.* Portsmouth, NH: Heinemann.

Wiggins, Grant, and Jay McTighe. 2005. *Understanding by Design, 2nd edition.* New York, NY: Prentice-Hall.

Enriching the Writing Process with the Six Traits

by Jeff Hicks

If writing were an act of fairytale magic or a matter of wishing, the word process would never apply to what people do when they write. All writers would have to do is wave their magic wands, rub their enchanted lamps to make their genies appear, or catch the one fish, from an ocean filled with fish, that grants wishes to the lucky person who hauls it in. I'd like a bestseller about a pig and a spider who live on a farm. Allakazam! Presto! Newbery Medal! Perhaps Roald Dahl was a fisherman and Beverly Cleary was a collector of antique lamps, right? Of course not!

Writers understand that writing is a process involving multiple steps and plenty of time. An understanding of the process of writing is an important foundation for all young writers. Once they have the process in place, students can grasp and use the six traits of writing to help them revise and assess their own work.

The Writing Process

The traditional view of the writing process is one that involves the following steps or stages:

- Prewriting
- Writing
- Revising
- Editing
- Publishing

1. Prewriting—This is the stage in which the writer finds a topic, narrows it, and maps out a plan. The writer usually isn't concerned with creating whole sentences or paragraphs at this point. Prewriting is done before the writer begins to write, and it is aimed at defining an idea and getting the writer's thoughts rolling.

2. Writing—In this stage, the writer's idea begins to come to life. Sentences and paragraphs begin to take shape. The writer may experiment with different leads. In this stage, writers need to know that they can change directions, cross out words or sentences, and draw arrows to link details that are out of sequence. The term *rough draft*, or *first draft*, refers to writing in motion, changing directions and gradually taking on a defining shape.

3. Revising—When writers revise, their topics and ideas come into focus. In this stage, writers do a great deal of math—adding or subtracting single words, phrases, or entire paragraphs. What to revise often becomes clearer to students if they have had some time away from their drafts. Putting a draft away, out of sight and mind for a few days or even more, may provide a sharper focus on weak areas. A writer might even ask, "Did I really write this?" The efforts made at revision will easily separate strong writing from weak writing.

4. Editing—This stage is all about making a piece of writing more accessible to readers. In this stage, writers fine-tune their work by focusing on correct punctuation, capitalization, grammar, usage, and paragraphing. Writers will want to be open to all the technological help (spell checker, for example) and human help they can find.

5. Publishing—Not every piece of writing reaches this stage. The term publishing refers to something more public than the kind of interactive sharing that should be happening at the previous stages. Writers should carefully select those pieces of writing that will be "published" in the classroom or put on display as finished work. For such writing, final editing and presentation are important. The text should be correct, and the writing should look appealing on the page and enticing to readers. The presentation, or format, should also assist readers in rapidly locating information they need.

Process in the Classroom

These steps are often presented in classrooms as being separate, mutually exclusive events. If I'm prewriting, I can't be revising. If I'm writing, I can't be editing. If I'm editing, I can't be revising or publishing. Mature writers know that while the process may proceed through the steps in linear fashion, it is far more likely that the various steps within the process will intertwine. Writing process doesn't seem so overwhelming if a young writer can gain this perspective.

I like to teach students several prewriting strategies—webbing, outlining, making word caches, drawing, and developing a list of questions—but I also like to show them through my own writing that prewriting and writing can occur simultaneously. Having students experience their teacher as a writer is the most powerful way to demonstrate the importance of each stage and how it connects with the others.

For instance, the best way for me to prewrite is to begin "writing." It is the act of writing that often gets my ideas flowing better than if I tried to make a web of the idea. I can show this to students by writing with them or asking them to coach me. Writing also allows me to demonstrate that I can revise at any time. I can cross out a sentence, change a word, draw an arrow to place a sentence in a different paragraph, add a few words, or move a whole paragraph. All of this can be done while I draft an idea. The option to revise at any time is very freeing. At the same time, I might even notice that I need to fix the spelling of a word or add a period—that's editing! And like revising, it can happen at any time. Of course, once I've revised a draft to the point where I'm happy with it, I'll show students the importance of going back for more thorough editing, taking time to read what I have written aloud, line by line.

Bringing in the Traits

Many young writers speak and act as if they have magical pens or pencils. These are the students who proclaim, "I'm done!" minutes after beginning, or the ones who say, "But I like it the way it is!" when faced with a teacher's suggestion to tell a bit more or to make a few changes. Other students frequently complain, "I don't have anything to write about."

Immersing these students in the writing process with a teacher who is also a writer is the clearest path to silencing these comments. Throw into this mix a strong understanding of the six traits of writing, and you are well on your way to creating passionate, self-assessing writers. Having a chance to assess the writing of others puts students in a place where they don't normally sit—the assessor's chair.

Suddenly, they are in charge. Their opinions are sought. It gives them confidence. The more they assess and discuss, the more they learn about what makes writing successful. It won't be long before those important lessons—what they have taught themselves about writing—find their way into both drafts and revisions.

Traits give both drafting and revision power. Try trait-based instruction. See for yourself.